Enduring Socialism

Enduring Socialism

Explorations of Revolution and Transformation,
Restoration and Continuation

Edited by

Harry G. West and Parvathi Raman

Berghahn Books
New York • Oxford

First published in 2009 by

Berghahn Books
www.berghahnbooks.com

© 2009, 2010 Harry G. West and Parvathi Raman
First paperback edition published in 2010

Library of Congress Cataloging-in-Publication Data
Enduring socialism : explorations of revolution and transformation,
restoration and continuation / edited by Harry G. West and Parvathi
Raman. -- 1st ed.
    p. cm.
Includes bibliographical references and index.
ISBN 978-1-84545-464-7 (hbk : alk. paper)
ISBN 978-1-84545-713-6 (pbk : alk. paper)
 1. Post-communism. 2. Socialism. 3. Communism. I. West, Harry G.
II. Raman, Parvathi.
 HX44.5.E63 2008
 335--dc22

                                                        2008032548

British Library Cataloguing in Publication Data
A catalogue record for this book is available
from the British Library.

Printed on acid-free paper.

ISBN 978-1-84545-464-7 (hardback) -- ISBN 978-1-84545-713-6 (paperback)

Contents

List of Contributors

Catherine Alexander is Reader in Anthropology, Goldsmiths, University of London.

Susan Bayly is Reader in Historical Anthropology, University of Cambridge.

John R. Campbell is Senior Lecturer in Anthropology of Development, SOAS, University of London.

Chris Hann is Director, Max Planck Institute for Social Anthropology, Halle.

Caroline Humphrey is Sigrid Rausing Professor of Collaborative Anthropology, University of Cambridge.

Jakob A. Klein is Lecturer in Social Anthropology, SOAS, University of London.

Kevin Latham is Senior Lecturer in Social Anthropology, SOAS, University of London.

Nicolette Makovicky is Junior Research Fellow in Social Science and the East European Member States of the European Union, Wolfson College, University of Oxford.

Parvathi Raman is Lecturer in Anthropology, SOAS, University of London.

Dennis Rodgers is Senior Research Fellow, Brooks World Poverty Institute, University of Manchester.

Harry G. West is Reader in Social Anthropology, SOAS, University of London.

Poetries of the Past in a Socialist World Remade

Parvathi Raman and Harry G. West

In *The Eighteenth Brumaire of Louis Bonaparte,* Karl Marx not only suggested that revolutions tended to 'conjure up the spirits of the past', but also expressed his hope and expectation that revolutionary socialism would not do so – not 'draw its poetry from the past', but instead, 'only from the future'. From the Soviet Union and Eastern Europe to China and Vietnam, from Ethiopia and Tanzania to Cuba and Nicaragua, the socialist revolutions of the twentieth century purportedly embraced Marx's mandate, endeavouring through varied means to thoroughly rewrite the landscapes upon which they occurred. Upon coming to power, socialist or communist regimes often sought completely to transform politics, abolishing multiparty regimes and electoral processes through which self-interested and divisive parties vied for political control, while conceiving of socialist 'new men' (in some cases, although not always, including women) as the locus of revolutionary political subjectivity and channelling political processes through ruling party institutions and hierarchies. Socialism similarly aspired utterly to transform economic relations through the abolition of various forms of private property and/or market exchange. In its most dramatic forms, such initiatives literally entailed the reconfiguration of urban and rural landscapes, including 'villagization' and the construction of communal infrastructures, and the razing of dispersed rural homesteads, urban 'slums', or 'unruly' marketplaces. In many revolutionary socialist contexts, the rituals of the ruling party – from party cell meetings to party congresses and rallies – were intended to supplant rituals of a religious nature, as devotion to ancestral spirits and deities gave way to investment in the common project of human progress. Allegiances to family, ethnicity and nation were to disappear entirely with the emergence of class-based consciousness and solidarity. In this brave new world, little of the old world was to be recognizable.

Curiously, at a time when socialism is said by most to have failed – in what has been defined by many as a 'post-socialist era' – those proclaiming socialism's end have inherited socialism's antipathy for the past (or, at least, the socialist past). The postsocialist doctrine of 'transition' – to a free market, to democracy, to a more 'open society' – has partaken of the same modernist self-assurance as did socialism in the middle decades of the twentieth century – an orientation that David Harvey warns has 'no respect even for its own past, let alone that of any pre-modern social order' (Harvey 1990: 112). Accordingly, with the dawn of postsocialism, reformers have, ironically, echoed socialist revolutionaries in asserting the erasure of socialism itself from the landscapes they have endeavoured to rewrite.

The fall of the Berlin Wall in 1989, which to most represented the collapse of socialism, was at once both keenly anticipated and surprising in its suddenness. According to Konrad Jarausch, 'only a few ... had noticed the rumblings of the communist earthquake, [and] historians were as confused as others about the sudden crumbling of the Soviet bloc' (Jarausch 2006: 59). Experienced as an epochal shift, the swift disintegration of Eastern European socialism was understood as the consequence of its inherent internal failures, combined with its inability to withstand the example of Western progress, which increasingly seemed to shape the desires of its citizens. The Soviet Union's last president, Boris Yeltsin, came to publicly embody the disintegration of the entire Soviet state, and an entire socialist project that could no longer be merely reformed. Indeed, attempts at reform were viewed by many as having opened the floodgates to collapse. Policy makers within socialist states and beyond suggested that the socialist misadventure now had to be subjected to a major economic and political intervention in order to address its terminal malaise. The cure was seen to lie in the dismantling of socialism itself – in the 'shift' to a market economy, the introduction of political pluralism, and the promotion of civil society, which was positioned in opposition to the 'totalitarian' state.[1]

To a significant degree, policy making in socialist states around the globe has, since the fall of the Berlin Wall, been informed by social scientists working in the field of 'Postsocialist Studies' who have sought to provide conceptual tools with which to understand a new global terrain. 'Post-socialism', for some, has come to mean the death of socialism and the triumph of capital (Derrida 1994), and has been dominated by the metaphor of 'transition'. Framed through Cold War discursive idioms, and reproducing its binary suppositions, commentators from both right and left have talked predominantly in the language of collapse, perceiving a 'transformational moment' which heralded either a triumphal 'end of history' (Fukuyama 1993), or the death of an experiment that was doomed to failure because of its inefficiency, repressive nature, and inability to be truly 'modern'. For much of the Western left, the Eastern European socialist 'experiment' was also viewed as a distortion, or even betrayal, of 'true' socialism' (Litziger 2002: 43). Expressing sentiments typical of analysis of that moment, Bruno Latour concluded that 1989–91 heralded 'the triumph of liberalism, of capitalism, of the Western democracies over the vain hopes of Marxism' (Latour 1993: 9), whilst for Manuel Castells, the inability of socialist society to transform itself into the 'information society' spelled its inevitable demise (Castells 1998). Indeed, technological stagnation became an increasingly common vindication for the redundancy of the socialist model.

Early postsocialist studies used the political instability and economic disintegration of Eastern Europe as an explanatory framework to predict or describe the crumbling of the so-called Soviet Empire in Africa, Latin America and Asia. Implicit in these studies was the idea that progression to democracy required a decisive break with the practices of the socialist state. The sudden collapse of the socialist world was thus commonly viewed through an entropic lens, where the measure of internal disorder and decay was not always outwardly visible, but the system was nevertheless rotting from within. By extension, this body of work also laid the foundation for fieldwork that sought to chart the success and failures of transition, asking what had gone wrong, and how it could be remedied.

Postsocialist 'transitology' is, of course, the legacy of a conceptual schema wherein socialism is seen as capitalism's opposite. The twentieth century has been retrospectively understood by many as a battlefield between the two ideological systems, each of which claimed to be the true bearer of the modernist project, even as they appeared diametrically opposed regarding how to achieve this end. Accordingly, 1917 is conceived of as a major watershed in world history – a moment when the world seemed to break in half – suggesting both an epochal transformation in linear time, and a rupture in the imagined space of homogenous capitalist expansion. The European periphery came to challenge the capitalist centre, and appealed to 'the people' by claiming that socialism was better equipped than capitalism to bring about the meaningful liberation of the masses, with economic justice and welfare provision for all. In doing so, it also presented a stark challenge to the capitalist premise that the political and the economic inhabited separate realms.

Although the Cold War did not officially begin until 1947, for the Western powers, the communist threat helped define both foreign and domestic policy from the start of the Russian Revolution. It was also inscribed in the popular imagination through cultural practices bound up with notions of a fight between 'good' and 'evil'. As early as 1918, Allied intervention in the Russian Civil War sought to physically contain the

Bolshevik threat, which was conceived of as a 'monster which seeks to devour civilised society' and 'destroy the free world'.[2] There was also the ideological peril to contend with – socialist ideals of utopian fulfillment which transgressed all attempts at territorial containment. In the period after the First World War, and particularly during the Great Depression, capitalism seemed badly wanting, and socialist rhetoric appealed to those seeking greater justice and equality. In the United States, an internal counteroffensive was launched against the 'enemy within'. The 'Red Scare' as it came to be known, targeted many of those who sought to exercise their democratic right precisely to challenge the system into being more democratic. During this time, the socialist foe was already growing into a phantasmagorical 'other', and haunting the ambitions of the capitalist powers. The perceived threat from socialism was also pivotal in propelling the United States into the role of 'defender of the free world'.

The Cold War rhetoric that developed from 1947, with the Truman Doctrine's declared intent to 'contain communism' (which was now spreading across the world), drew on this preexisting discursive terrain, expanding and entrenching the idea of an East-West divide, wherein freedom, democracy and individual liberty were at stake. As more nations were drawn into the orbit of the 'communist menace', the more naturalized the idea of a bifurcated world became, with capitalist and socialist political and moral economies positioned in stark opposition to one another.

The socialist world had of course also created its capitalist 'other', where the fight, seen in terms of class struggle, was nevertheless still fought in the name of 'freedom'. This socialist counternarrative stressed the importance of the international workers' movement and the battle for national self-determination in the struggle against imperialism and colonialism. Socialist discourse also acted as a critical intervention and commentary on the failures of capitalism. Whereas socialists accused their capitalist counterparts of greed, exploitation and injustice, capitalists rejoined with a diagnosis of economic stagnation, and totalitarian rule over societies that were caught in a 'time warp' (Horschelmann 2002: 55). The socialist project was declared 'Utopian' in its intent to standardize and perfect an imperfect and individualistic world, and was also accused of working against the very essence of human nature. Echoing the colonial vision of the 'white man's burden', the people of the socialist states, viewed as the victims of totalitarianism without agency or voice, were deemed suitable subjects for the project of liberal redemption through the implementation of capitalist political and economic models, which would allow them to catch up with a 'more enlightened west' (Litzinger 2002: 41). This view was given extra resonance by the assumption that socialism was a universally 'bad experience', and that those who had supported the system, or had an investment in its continuation, were either deluded, oppressed, or on the wrong side of the good/evil divide (Yurchak 2006: 4–5).

Notwithstanding the historical importance of such bipolar views on the world, actually existing socialism and actually existing capitalism were never so distinct, and never independent of one another. The twentieth century has, in fact, witnessed adaptive and hybrid forms of state building where 'pure' socialist or capitalist political economies simply have not existed. Instead we find assemblages drawn from a repertoire of overlapping cultural and political practices, where the forms of the past continued to shape the present. Economic and political models associated predominantly with capitalism or with socialism in fact bled into one another and irrevocably coloured one another's political geographies. In other words, despite the claims of twentieth-century socialism to have completely and irrevocably transformed economic, political, and cultural institutions and practices and to have produced 'new men', scrutiny reveals myriad ways in which preexisting institutions and practices were in fact woven into the very fabric of socialism.

Karl Marx may have expressed the hope and expectation that revolutionary socialism would draw its poetry 'only from the future', but he offered no detailed analysis of what socialist planning might look like, stating that he had little interest in putting together the 'cookbooks of the future'. Although twentieth-century revolutionaries set out to create 'brave new worlds', they inevitably had to build on the materials bequeathed to them by their predecessors. 'Future poetry' could only be realized via a more prosaic political, economic and social past, and, in the main, those involved in socialist construction were quickly made painfully aware of this fact. Moreover, the fundamental belief in an evolutionary pathway to socialist society, held by such influential theorists as Lenin and Mao, often provided ideological justification precisely for shaping the socialist future from the fabric of capitalism.[3]

Nowhere was this more apparent than in the Soviet Union after 1917. A closer examination of the birth of socialism in the USSR – a model that provided fundamental ideological and economic blueprints for revolutions across the world – reveals how the Bolsheviks themselves had to build on the legacies of Tsarist Russia, and to adapt practices associated with capitalist developmental models to their needs. Rather than eradicating 'bourgeois' politics and culture, the Bolsheviks sought to transform many aspects of them into vectors of socialist transformation (Verdery 1998: 291).

State building in the Soviet Union was predicated on a series of adaptive and experimental measures, and at no time was this more apparent than in the period known as the New Economic Policy (NEP), wherein capitalist and socialist forms coexisted in unstable combinations with older institutions, much like the revolutions that followed later in the twentieth century. When the Bolsheviks took state control in 1917 and prepared to implement their vision of socialism, Lenin was already aware that socialism had to be crafted out of the fabric of existing structures and institutions (Lenin 1957). The early years of the revolution consisted of a series of programmes and policies that attempted to overcome both inherited circumstances and contemporary political obstacles. The very first attempts at revolutionary change were built on the premise that capitalist forms could coexist with socialist initiatives, and the NEP was itself a conscious model of a mixed economy that it was hoped would help develop Russia's productive capacity. Market forces became the dominant feature of the political landscape, with the state becoming one competitor for business amongst many (Bandera 1963, 1970; Bean 1997).

In addition, the Communist Party in the Soviet Union looked to redefine a whole 'constellation of idioms' long associated with liberal capitalist politics, transforming their meanings into conduits of revolutionary change – as others would eventually do elsewhere (Hilton 2004). Socialists have generally not sought, or have been unable, to rid the world of 'bourgeois' concepts, but rather have had to reenvisage them as sites of struggle. Ideas of nationalism, citizenship, or indeed, the concept of democracy itself, have not been eradicated on socialist landscapes, but have instead been endowed with revolutionary intent.

NEP was not a mindless aping of capitalist developmental models. The Bolsheviks drew on preexisting Tsarist structures, sought advice from Western experts, and attempted to utilize the experience of its own small sector of capitalist enterprise, alongside measures that were conceived of as constitutive of socialist planning. NEP was an experimental and multifarious policy that was, above all, an act of translation for the Soviet context, where elements of past and present were reassembled to serve the needs of a reenvisioned future. What is more, the project met with some success. By 1925, the government had turned around a disastrous economic situation, and enjoyed some level of growth.

By 1927, of course, the political landscape was changing, and the party began discussing the possibility of implementing five-year plans. By the end of 1928, it was apparent that NEP had failed to deliver true economic recovery, and the tide turned to a model of centralized planning and state control. However, throughout the years of Stalin's rule over the Soviet Union, the command economy and a thriving informal sector – which had developed out of markets and networks in place during Imperial Russia and thrived under NEP (Ball 1987) – were entirely interdependent, and, far from disappearing, the market-driven exchange of goods and services continued to flourish in the Soviet Union, albeit underground.

NEP is most often described as the Soviet Union's failed experiment in market socialism, but its ideological and political traces can be excavated from a variety of global contexts throughout the twentieth century. Within the Soviet Union, reformers looked to the period as a model for a pluralistic economy at several points in history. NEP provided the ideological justification and precedent for a mixed economy. In the 1960s, Soviet economists tried to resuscitate the principles of NEP and state enterprises were given greater autonomy, with gross output targets replaced by the principles of profits and sales. Again, in the 1980s, Gorbachev made specific reference to NEP in his plans for Perestroika (Wallander 2002). In other Eastern European contexts, Yugoslavia developed a labour-managed market economy in 1949, where enterprises controlled by workers produced and exchanged goods (Bean 1997). In the 1960s and 1970s, this approach produced effective results in terms of economic growth. Hungary also established a market socialist model, and in the 1960s, its 'New Economic Mechanism' revived NEP precedents.

NEP also provided important examples for developing countries attempting to build socialism. In China in 1949, the principles of NEP were adapted to the Chinese context, and a mixed economy was promoted. In addition, much of the content of the programme of 'New Democracy' in the early years of the revolution was taken from political institutions and concepts formulated by the nationalist Sun Yat Sen, which were recast in the language of Chinese revolution (North 1951).

In the 1920s, Bukharin envisaged NEP and the *smychka*, the pivotal alliance between the peasantry and working class, as a wider model for developing nations, where the state would embark on a 'peaceful economic struggle with the private sector (Bean 1997: 3). This view was given added weight by the fact that, in 1920, at the Second Congress of the Communist International, many delegates considered that colonial countries would take longer to reach socialism, and had to proceed carefully through earlier stages, developing strategies that would enable them to overthrow their imperialist invaders, building an industrial base through class alliances under the control of the working class and the Communist Party. This stagist approach also provided ideological justification for a 'nationalist' phase in socialist revolution, and it was argued that, in the colonies, socialism could be built on the back of a national revolution. Thus, despite the fact that the nation state and nationalism have been conventionally understood as the most bourgeois of political forms, socialists reformulated their attitude to nationalist frameworks in the light of preexisting political geographies. Although early twentieth–century socialists wished to overcome the nationalist framework and create an international federation of socialist states, the failure of revolutions to spread throughout Europe, and the political form of anti-colonial struggles, called for a reformulation of socialist policy. A programme of national self-determination for the colonies not only suggested a moral agenda, but was also one that many socialists believed would be attractive to much of the world's population. It also seemingly had the capacity to fundamentally weaken imperialism and the capitalist powers. The nature of the relationship between nationalism and socialism dogged the communist movement throughout much of the twentieth century, and was never fully resolved, with theorists and policy makers zigzagging between ideas of united and popular fronts with national bourgeoisies. The evolutionary approach espoused by Lenin and others in the Second International suggested that the struggle for national democracy had the potential to feed into socialist revolution.

In practice, nationalism and socialism coexisted in the twentieth century. Nowhere did socialism overcome the form of the nation state. Ultimately, socialist revolutions were mediated through nation states, and in these contexts nationalist sentiment and revolutionary intent became inextricably linked. When Stalin decreed that the ideal of 'socialism in one country' was viable, the refashioning of socialism in nationalist form became ever more inevitable. Even in the Soviet Union forms of national identity continued unabated in multifarious ways, often becoming entangled with socialist identity. This was not always discouraged by the party. During the Second World War, Stalin built support amongst the Russian people by evoking the idea of the defense of the 'fatherland' (Buck Morss 2002: 7). This was possible because of the continued existence of Russian nationalism. In Cuba, the rallying cry 'fatherland or death' has long coexisted with the slogan 'socialism or death' and has been consistently used by Castro from the 1960s as a way of building solidarity amongst the Cuban people in their struggle against the 'Yankee'.

In addition to explicitly socialist states, the nonaligned movement – most significantly India in 1947 – also illustrates the adaptive and hybrid forms of state building that draw on both capitalist and socialist formations. India specifically set out to 'borrow' from both socialist and capitalist economic and political models and to combine these with indigenous institutions and cultural practices. Nehru sought to combine parliamentary democracy, socialist principles and centralized planning whilst trying to preserve idealized Indian traditions. The Nehruvian socialist model of state-guided national development drew inspiration from both the Soviet Union and Western forms of social democracy, whilst its agricultural programme took inspiration from the Chinese experience (Berger 2004: 14–15). The Bandung Conference in 1955 brought together anti-colonial leaders from around the world, and complex alliances were forged that undermined simplistic East/West divides while combinations of economic and social models attributed to both contexts took on their own specificity, in contexts ranging from Egypt to Indonesia (Abdulgani 1964).

In the 1960s and 1970s, as decolonization accelerated after the Second World War, a swathe of newly independent countries embarked on a socialist path with more radical zeal than their anti-colonial predecessors (Berger 2004: 21–22). At the meeting of the Tricontinental in Havana in January 1966, a revolutionary anti-imperialist agenda was put in place, as were alternative political geographies that cut across neat binary divisions. At this time, the lessons of NEP and the framework of nationalist politics once more gained wide purchase. In many instances, Soviet political economists developed new theoretical paradigms for 'developing countries' based on the experience of NEP. Throughout Africa, Asia and Latin America, the new socialist states attempted to craft political economies that were a combination of indigenous institutions, new socialist policies, and initiatives that would encourage the development of industrial and agricultural production with which to fuel the revolution. Here too, existing structures provided the raw materials for future society, and were once more reassembled in new combinations. In addition, many Pan-Africanist leaders sought to combine these forms whilst preserving idealized aspects of Africa's precolonial heritage. These socialist movements all took shape through national struggles and through the medium of the nation state. Postcolonial socialism and national self-determination became inextricably linked, and the concepts of state-guided industry and cooperative agriculture became synonymous with socialist practice (ibid: 23). But market mechanism were also in evidence at various times and places. In this period, the idea of revolutionary nationalism set out to construct collective nationalist sentiment out of the struggle against colonialism and foreign rule, and to harness this collective consciousness for the revolution.

As these various examples illustrate, it makes little sense to conceive of spaces as the bounded and uncontaminated containers of socialist or capitalist economies or polities, from which states deviate or transgress. By doing so, we inevitably 'reduce complexity to stereotypes'. Nor does the concept of stages, either capitalist or socialist, help frame the complex geographies of the contemporary world. Using NEP as a trope for wider economic, social and political cartographies helps perforate the imagined spaces of homogenous capitalist development, revealing fissures and complex trajectories that belie simple models of 'transition', whilst also complicating notions of 'before and after'.

This unsettling of conventional understandings of twentieth-century political economy suggests that ethnographic investigation of capitalism, including its most recent variant, neoliberalism, would expose equally complex developmental pathways, which undermine claims to universality, or indeed triumph. It also helps break down dichotomies that suggest easily located opposites of freedom and totalitarianism. For example, the market is often compared to the command economy in these terms. However, even under capitalism, markets most often are subject to some form of state control, and their mechanisms manipulated to produce hegemonic power relations between states. There is little that is 'free' about free trade in the contemporary global economy, as the control of borders, the imposition of tariffs, and price fixing mechanisms all help determine who can compete and who can win in a world marketplace. In addition, capitalist states have themselves taken recourse in command economies, not least in times of war, while capitalism's social democratic wing has borrowed heavily from the language, ideology and political practice of its estranged socialist cousins, devising its own five year-plans, welfare states and nationalized industries.

We have much to learn in this 'post-socialist moment' from a picture that shows us that socialism never obliterated its pasts, but instead carried within it much of what came before it. The idea of the 'post' is in many ways the bane of our times. Closer scrutiny, we argue, reveals postsocialism's ambivalence to the past, just as it does socialism's. To be sure, the trope of tradition's 'resurgence' – wherein reformers celebrate the restoration of spaces for the expression of dispositions and practices long repressed – has often figured prominently in the postsocialist narrative of triumph over socialism. Traditions 'revived' in the postsocialist era are, of course, as much the products of a present-day historical imaginary as of a past with which continuity is asserted. But this is not all that makes postsocialist neotraditions interesting. We suggest that, whereas postsocialist reformers may confess more openly than socialist revolutionaries the importance of that which came before, these reformers rarely admit the degree to which postsocialism harbours within itself elements of socialist origin, as well as the seeds of new forms of socialist practice.

Developments in Latin America over the last three decades are a good illustration of hybrid forms that have arisen in the wake of neoliberal reform, where even as democratic reform has taken hold increasing levels of poverty amongst new sectors of the population are evident. Born out of the policies of the Washington Consensus, neoliberal political reform has itself paved the way for the election of radical populist movements such as the one headed by Hugo Chavez in Venezuela, where the 'bending and moulding' of existing institutions lays the basis for programmes of social justice. Many fragments of the Latin American left, which were declared redundant after the fall of the Berlin Wall and the commencement of neoliberal reconstruction policies, have recombined through a highly heterogeneous set of political practices and new political alliances drawing on multiple sectors of society. Left politicians such as Morales in Bolivia have also reconceived their relationship to the state and to market forces, replacing strategic instrumentalism with a desire to recast these institutions as sites of struggle that can deliver national prosperity and independence from US domination. This new relationship has been combined with attempts to strengthen state structures in contexts where they are deemed a necessary prerequisite for the strengthening of the economy and the effective redistribution of wealth. From Mexico to Argentina, Brazil and Chile, the left is speaking to new political constituencies, drawing together not only the traditional left, but also newly impoverished sections of the middle classes, marginalized business interests, and the expanding numbers trapped in the informal sector. The 'newly discontent' are now mainly united through their opposition to neoliberalism, which has become a 'constitutive outside', but liberal democratic frameworks and market economics are being used to pursue social policies based on ideas of equality, and to expand programmes for health, education and democratic participation. Moreover, electoral campaigns themselves draw on marketing strategies and technological means – defining features of liberal democratic process – to persuade people of new anti-neoliberal perspectives. New circuits of trade generated by these left realignments have also provided sustenance for beleaguered socialist states such as Cuba, giving room for radical populist nationalism and socialism to converge, and for new languages of internationalism and solidarity to arise (Munck 2003; Panizza 2005; Bellamy Foster 2007).

In recent years, many analysts, including anthropologists, have attested to such global complexity and have challenged the idea of linear transition. A growing awareness of the contradictions and problems arising from marketization has led to an expanding volume of work that sets out to critique the very concept of transitology, highlighting both the inadequacies of the model, and the need for more nuanced accounts which do not view transformation as a one-way process of capitalist development. In *What Was Socialism? What Comes Next?* Katherine Verdery questioned not only simplistic models of transitology but also the inevitability of progression to a capitalist market economy in Eastern European states (Verdery 1996). Combining wider theoretical observations on the relationship between the command economy and the flourishing informal sector with acute ethnographic observation, Verdery highlighted key social elements that survived the collapse of the socialist system. Building on these insights, in *Uncertain Transition*, Verdery and Michael Buroway set out to chart the failures of capitalist reform through a collection of ethnographic essays that illustrate how markets do not always work to the benefit of the populace (Buroway and Verdery 1999).

This shift in perspective seemed ever more necessary as it became increasingly evident that the people of Eastern Europe were not simply falling at the feet of capitalism, in gratitude for being 'rescued'. By 1993, the reemergence of a constituency for the Communist Party in Russia, as well as the growth in popularity of Eastern European nationalist movements which were hostile to Western intervention, illustrated that many sectors of society in the former socialist states were not 'adjusting' to privatization and market liberalism. Some Soviet institutional forms persisted after the 'the fall', and continued to serve vital functions in the new economy, whilst the 'massive aid' promised to the Eastern bloc by Western governments often failed to materialize. This left many in the former Soviet Union with the feeling that a momentous change had not occurred, and that a number of policies had been foisted upon the Russian government, accelerating the deterioration of material and social conditions (Wallander 2002: 121–22). Yeltsin's attempts to hasten the process of liberalization, whilst abandoning social welfare programmes, was undertaken in the hope of enticing more financial support from Western donors, even as pictures of *babushkas*, reduced to begging and scouring rubbish bins for food, began to make an appearance in the Western media.

Anthropologists actively engaged with these new realities, carrying out micro-level analysis and, in the process, producing ethnographic interventions that attempted to add the texture of the everyday to the larger conceptual and discursive shifts implicit in the idea of 'Post-socialist Studies'. In texts such as Humphrey and Mandel's *Markets and Moralities*, emphasis was laid on tracing the complex character of transition to a capitalist economy and market ideology, where the focus moved to the fate of those once sustained by socialist institutions such as collective farms. This volume included an examination of the far-reaching consequences of the privatization of property (Humphrey and Mandel 2002). The contextual moralities of economic and social practice also came under scrutiny. Cultural trajectories established before the excavation of socialism were seen to have survived the socialist era, and were now evidently reformulated in the postsocialist present. The new position of factory workers, changing gender relations, and emerging patterns of consumption under economic liberalization were also revealed. Fieldwork, a practice that had been severely restricted under the socialist era, was stimulated by its very possibility and in some quarters became its own raison d'etre. In Berdahl, Bunzl and Lampland's *Altering States*, contributing authors abandoned any description of large-scale economic and political trajectories, and concentrated on micro-social processes that reveal not only the unpredictable directions taken by transition, but also question its very temporal siting. Instead, past and present practices were envisioned as interwoven phenomena, negotiated in multifarious ways (Berdahl, Bunzl and Lampland 2003).

These works helped unsettle dominant understandings of linear transition that underpinned much of Postsocialist Studies. Continuities across the fissure of collapse were revealed, as was an understanding of how 'the use of the socialist experience to understand the present presented state socialist forms and values as a ... resource ... [where] the lived past [served] as a resource for understanding the present and acting upon it' (Gilbert 2006: 16). These perspectives challenged the concept of socialism as an arcane experience from which one could learn to do better, where the socialist legacy shouldered all responsibility for the failures and complications of transition. Elsewhere, academics highlighted previous moments in time when socialists resorted to 'mimicking' capitalist economic methods as a survival strategy, illustrating that 'market socialism' is not a new phenomenon (Litzinger 2002: 34).

These studies have had some impact in the world beyond academia, where, for example, locally driven technologies, experiences and attachments to the past have been drawn on in an attempt to aid limited developmental goals. Recommendations for a shift to localized governance, which seeks to democratize practice through grassroots empowerment (Litzinger 2002: 48), and to mediate local and global political practice, has been presented as a form of critical developmental intervention, much as it was in the postcolony.

In other quarters, ethnographic specificity has been countered by a wider political and social vision. The work of Susan Buck Morss has shed light on the 'historical experiment of socialism (as) deeply rooted in the western modernizing tradition' (Buck Morss 2002), pointing to the symbiotic nature of the relationship between socialism and capitalism, and the profound effect this has had on their developmental trajectories. In a world dominated by the 'logic of unqualified difference', Buck Morss lays out alternative mappings of connectivity previously rendered invisible by an ideologically driven bipolar worldview.

However, many scholars of postsocialist transition, including some engaged in the critique of 'transitology', remain within its discursive terrain, even as they aspire to move the debate on to a more complex understanding of contemporary realities. The inability to move beyond the transitional model is betrayed by the very titles of many texts on postsocialism, and the term itself suffers from the same conceptual difficulties. Consequently, whatever its intentions, much of this critical intervention has remained firmly situated in a linear narrative of historical change, where charting issues such as the emergence of forms of civil society, privatization and new concepts of citizenship has been conceptually positioned within a modernist time frame that reaffirms the inevitability of the triumph of capital, even as it seeks to critique its more unjust practices. In addition, many of these studies also persist in describing a binary interchange between capitalism and socialism, albeit one repositioned within a dialectical model. Most often, the 'West' also continues to be viewed as the dominant half, acting upon the 'socialist other' and shaping its practices. On a wider scale, in the media and in public domains, conventional understandings of postsocialist transition remain largely unchallenged, and the difficulties inherent in 'modernizing' the spaces at the edge of Europe continue to be attributed not only to the long shadows of socialism, but to even older perceptions of Eastern European despotism and feudalism, which render true democracy an alien concept.

In this volume, we seek to build on the insights generated by this body of work, but also to move beyond them. We wish to reexamine the relationship between capitalism and socialism by going back to 'alternative beginnings'.[4] Both capitalism and socialism are underpinned by a model of linear development seeking to usher in an era of mass culture and politics, made possible by the 'material benefits of an urban industrialized society' (Buck Morss 2002: ix); both have created mass consumer societies and promoted the commodification of politics. By looking through a lens which locates both systems within a set of shared practices drawing on a mutual repertoire of social, economic and political idioms, with which they both have understood and acted upon the world, we seek to move beyond merely cataloguing similarity and difference, auditing change, or simply positing complexity as a counterweight to earlier models of understanding. In particular, we strive to disrupt certain categories that are traditionally allocated as defining features of either capitalism or socialism, where their utilization by the 'other side' is seen as symptomatic of a form of transgression, betrayal or inherent failure on that side's part. For example, command economies are seen as the hallmark of the socialist system, and market relations and private enterprise are viewed as core components of capitalism. We wish to suggest that, on closer examination, both capitalism and socialism have inhabited a complex, but mutual, discursive terrain, constituted through a series of unstable combinations of economic and social forms, which have continually sought to mediate the relationship between the state, the private sector and programmes of social justice. Moreover, the forms taken by socialist and capitalist societies have also differed over time and space, and in many contexts an informal sector has been vital to the functioning of the formalized economy. Despite the brave rhetorical claims of revolutionaries to have remade the world, now echoed by neoliberals in their desire to spread marketization and liberal democracy, both have had to draw on raw materials already in place. Historical and geographical excavation reveals economic and political practices that unsettle easy categorization of discrete socialist or capitalist political economies, or linear transitions within which the landscape is made afresh. Many traces of the past were visible in socialist geographies, and the traces of socialism are still to be found in the spaces now claimed by neoliberalism.

Against the historical backdrop of successive socialist and postsocialist claims to have completely remade society, the contributors to this volume explore complex and often paradoxical continuities between diverse 'postsocialist' presents and their corresponding socialist and presocialist pasts. Some of the chapters focus on ways in which – notwithstanding revolutionary socialist claims – presocialist economic, political and cultural forms in fact endured an era of socialism and have found new life in the 'postsocialist' present. Others centre on ways in which continuities with a presocialist past have been produced within the historical imaginary of 'postsocialism'. Still others take up the ways in which – notwithstanding the claims of neoliberal reformers – *socialist* economic, political and cultural forms have in fact endured in a purportedly postsocialist era. Several of the chapters in fact advance more than one of these arguments.

Together, the collected essays – drawn from papers presented during the winter and spring terms of 2005 in a weekly seminar convened in the Department of Anthropology and Sociology at the School of Oriental and African Studies (University of London) – lay foundations for historical, ethnographic and theoretical comparisons across boundaries that have heretofore generally divided scholars of socialism and postsocialism working in and on the former Soviet Union and Eastern Europe from colleagues examining similar issues in Asia, Africa and Latin America. What is more, where the 'collapse of socialism' in some parts of the world has defined an historical era of global dimensions, the volume in fact engages with the above themes not only in contexts once-but-no-longer defined as socialist, but also in those still labeled socialist (e.g., China and Vietnam), as well as in those never explicitly described as such (e.g., the United Kingdom).

In the first chapter of the volume, Harry West examines the 'revival' of 'traditional authority' in 'postsocialist' Mozambique. Neoliberal reformers espousing 'democratic decentralization' have celebrated recent legislation mandating rural government officials to work with 'Community Authorities', a category comprising chiefs and other influential local figures. Whereas the socialist FRELIMO government had rewritten local powerscapes by abolishing the chieftaincy after independence and establishing in its place a party-cell network reaching into every rural household, the investiture of 'Community Authorities' has been interpreted in more than one way. In the language of neoliberal reform, Community Authorities constitute essential components of an emergent postsocialist 'civil society'. Others have conceived of 'traditional authority' as a set of institutions rooted in the presocialist past that have endured socialist repression and reemerged in socialism's aftermath. West argues that 'Community Authority' is in fact a 'neotradition' – an invented tradition, referencing the past while serving the interests of its present-day inventors (including a no-longer-socialist FRELIMO government). West finds deep ironies in this neotraditional institution. In substantial ways, Community Authorities today look and act like the socialist party cadres they purportedly replace. Digging deeper, West suggests that party cadres of the socialist era in fact looked and acted much like the chiefs that they replaced. Notwithstanding this, today's Community Authorities differ greatly from their chiefly predecessors in crucial ways. The Mozambican case, West concludes, bears evidence not of socialism's historical superficiality in Mozambique, but rather of the way in which it drew profoundly on the presocialist world, as well as the way in which it substantially endures in the 'postsocialist' world.

Jakob Klein's contribution undertakes an examination of how present-day notions of 'traditional Chinese cuisine' constitute neotraditions of contemporary production that draw on both prerevolutionary and revolutionary pasts. Klein begins by reminding us that, while the ruling Communist Party would still categorize China as a socialist state, for most (whether foreign observers, or Chinese themselves) recent Chinese history is composed of three distinct periods: 'prerevolutionary', 'revolutionary' and 'reform'. The reform period, Klein suggests, has been marked by a 'booming nostalgia industry'. This nostalgia is of two sorts: the first, Klein reports, is a 'reaction against the virulent anti-traditionalism of the revolutionary era, in particular the Cultural Revolution', and references a prerevolutionary past during which such traditions supposedly prevailed; the second, Klein tells us, 'has been identified with perceptions of growing inequality, uncertainty, political immorality and a lack of accountability in the post-Mao era', and has given rise to an 'idealization of the revolutionary era itself'. Contradictory though they may be, both forms of nostalgia derive from perceptions of a world utterly transformed – perceptions that ignore or obscure vital connections across the boundaries between historical 'periods'. In bringing these connections to light, Klein interests himself in the nostalgia expressed by a growing Guangzhou middle class for 'antique style' foods, as well as in the restaurants and teahouses that have emerged, or been transformed, to meet their demands within the context of 'market socialism' – venues which served as sites for Klein's field research. Although the number of public eating establishments in Guangzhou declined precipitously during 'the Mao years' as revolutionaries cast restaurants and teahouses as sites of 'bourgeois consumerism' and sought to level differences in consumption through the establishment of communal dining halls, Klein shows how the revolution actually helped to *preserve* prerevolutionary tastes in crucial ways. Because 'good eating' was conceived of as a 'sign the socialist system was working', the communist regime in fact invested great energy in rendering Chinese cuisine more accessible to the masses. The revolutionary culinary project included state-sponsored publication of regional and national cookbooks, training of chefs and their deployment in state-owned restaurants, and the organization of food fairs – all of which Klein describes in detail. Through such initiatives, Klein argues, the communist regime not only *documented*, but also partially *invented*, the foods that Guangzhou residents now remember as 'traditional' (in this context, a term generally assumed to mean 'prerevolutionary'). Consequently, in consuming 'antique foods' today, Guangzhou residents simultaneously – if unwittingly – feed their appetites for a prerevolutionary, and a revolutionary, past.

In Chapter 3, Dennis Rodgers admits to having been drawn to conduct fieldwork in Nicaragua by his own nostalgia for the nation's recent socialist past. Challenging, as Klein does, strict historical periodization, Rodgers excavates the complex legacy of socialism in postsocialist Nicaragua, focusing on practices in which the socialist and, even, presocialist past in fact coexist with the postsocialist present in ironic or paradoxical form. Those with whom he worked spoke cynically of the 'Sandinista piñata' when describing how, upon leaving office in the aftermath of electoral defeat in 1990, leaders of the revolutionary party burst open and greedily carried off for themselves the limited wealth of the nation. Such blatant abuses of power were, to most, shockingly reminiscent of oligarchic privileges exercised under the Somoza regime, the moral critique of which had been fundamental to Sandinista ideology. Residents of the Managua neighbourhood in which Rodgers worked came to appreciate how certain local Sandinista leaders had opportunistically used the party to advance individual interests; this was made evident in the postsocialist period when some readily switched parties, or moved on to work for NGOs (nongovernmental organizations), in order to advance careers through which they might continue to 'make money on other people's backs'. To such figures, Rodgers contrasts 'Don Sergio', whose more genuine commitment to the welfare of his neighbours allowed him to transform himself from *barrio* leader under the Somoza regime to neighbourhood Sandanista Defence Committee chairman. With the fall of the Sandinistas, Don Sergio continued to assist *barrio* residents, albeit as facilitator for Alcoholics Anonymous (even as he scraped together enough to survive by harvesting empty beer bottles and collecting deposits on them). Rodgers' vignettes simultaneously illustrate how Nicaraguans draw on revolutionary and prerevolutionary social norms and institutions to navigate a postsocialist world defined by 'breakdown, fragmentation, apathy, disillusion, and social atomization', as well as the profound contradictions that animate such practices. Whereas the Sandinistas recreated the institution of *compadrazgo* – godparenthood – to consolidate revolutionary solidarity among 'comrades', for example, *barrio* residents today continue to demand 'social redistribution' in the form of patronage from ex-leader 'godfathers' now 'independently wealthy'. Meanwhile, youth gangs, who criminally prey on fellow citizens in other neighbourhoods but protect their own 'as family', claim to be the true heirs of Sandanismo. Although gang members' commitments to the *barrio* may be interpreted as the 'expression of desire for a certain sense of absent *"communitas"'*, Rodgers ultimately concludes that, in postsocialist Nicaragua, socialism lives in practices such as theirs as a 'dismal spectral afterimage'.

Although somewhat less desperately and somewhat more subtly than the Nicaraguans described by Rodgers, the Slovakians presented in Nicolette Makovicky's chapter also express disquiet about emergent socioeconomic relations in the postsocialist moment. Whereas reformers suggested that the economic opening of Slovakia would be defined not only by the inflow of Western goods and their enthusiastic consumption, but also by the emergence of Slovakian enterprises to competitively produce and provide similar goods, by Makovicky's account Slovakians have remained suspicious of both Western goods and domestic attempts to compete with them in the marketplace. Makovicky focuses on women who make bobbin lace in the town of Banská Bystrica and in the neighbouring villages of Španiá Dolina and Staré Hory. While many depend upon supplemental income generated from the production and sale of lace, most go to great lengths to downplay the commercial aspects of their lace making. Sales are described as the consequences of 'chance encounters' with tourists to whom lace making techniques are being demonstrated, or as the granting of a 'favour' to a friend, or a friend of a friend, who has seen a particular piece and expressed appreciation for it. The lace makers with whom Makovicky worked negotiated prices only with visible shame. The 'gift' of lace was often 'reciprocated' with the 'offer' of other material objects or specific services. When money was involved, many justified the sale of particular pieces by 'earmarking' funds earned for particular uses – generally the reproduction of the household – thereby 'redomesticating' their 'market' earnings and recasting market activities as serving to maintain household self-sufficiency. Makovicky traces such dispositions to the socialist period, in which productive work in the home was unfavourably compared to work in the state sphere, and in which the sale of such goods for personal gain was considered morally dubious. But Slovakian ambivalence to the marketplace runs even deeper than this, Makovicky suggests. Drawing on the work of economic anthropologists, she suggests that Slovakian socialism was but a particular form of a broader suspicion of the market – a moral economy with far greater claims to 'universality' than 'Western conceptions of the market'. Like Rodgers' informants in Chapter 3, Slovakians have socialized their economic exchanges in various historical contexts through kinship networks, 'real' or 'fictive', giving rise to or consolidating social relations. Under communism, they turned to networks of friends and family to navigate the state bureaucracy and to gain access to scarce resources. In the postsocialist period, they have used these same networks to mediate their experiences with the production and consumption of commodities, and to facilitate the making of money – an activity that, notwithstanding their discomfort, has become essential to their survival.

By contrast with Makovicky's Slovakian lace-makers, the Vietnamese international aid workers at the centre of Susan Bayly's accounts in Chapter 5 have more enthusiastically seized upon market opportunities, but they too have grounded their practices in discourses of deeper historical origin, as has the Vietnamese state itself. Bayly reminds us that, even before the advent of 'market socialism' in Vietnam, the socialist state – and, before it, the socialist insurgency – manifested a high degree of tolerance for the marketplace, whether domestic or international, so long as trade advanced socialist ideals. The slogan with regard to enemies was 'fight them and trade with them' while 'friendship' constituted the language of exchange with fellow socialist states. With the collapse of the Soviet Union and the liberalization of once socialist allies, sustaining access to trading partners has required renewed initiatives, however. Like Western nations seeking access to markets, the Vietnamese state has in recent years furnished technical assistance to willing recipients, but in so doing it has sought to differentiate its 'disinterested' aid from the more 'instrumental' assistance it suggests is provided by capitalist nations. To this end, the Vietnamese state has celebrated a long tradition of aid giving dating to the exchange of assistance within the 'socialist ecumene'. Technical specialists themselves have participated in the construction of this discourse of continuity, highlighting their own longstanding traditions of service to people in need while glossing over the material benefits they have garnered, in the reform era as in the past, through opportunities afforded by living and working abroad to participate in illicit, but lucrative, cross-border trade. Lingering beneath all of this, Bayly presciently points out, is a deep-rooted Vietnamese nationalist sentiment simultaneously working at individual and national levels. Being an 'aid-giver' – not merely a beneficiary of aid from more powerful states, but a force for the uplift of the less fortunate and a model for emulation – has served the Vietnamese state as a symbol of socialism's ongoing success. For aid workers themselves – generally descendants of the colonial-era francophone Vietnamese intelligentsia – it has constituted a means through which to actualize individual aspirations to 'modernity' that have only been partially realized – and sometimes been undermined – by the socialist project back home.

Catherine Alexander's chapter on waste in Almaty begins not with postsocialist pronouncements of positive transformation but, instead, with popular perceptions of an urban order coming undone. With Kazakh independence in 1991, the once celebrated garden city of the steppe – the product of a socialist architecture said to harmonize the natural and social environments – became clogged, by locals' accounts, with pollutants. New high-rise apartment blocks destroyed socialist-era aesthetics, while billboards blocked lines of sight and the flow of air currents. Alexander concludes, however, that these narratives of degeneration ultimately index historical processes of deeper roots, suggesting not that 'fings ain't wot they used to be, but that fings never had been what they used to be'. To be sure, neoliberal 'shock treatment' gave rise to unregulated development and new forms of excess and waste, as local authorities literally sold off portions of the city to emergent capitalist interests. Rural Kazakhs flocked to Almaty; these new residents, it was said, behaved as country folk in the city, polluting the urban environment by grilling meats on open flames and dropping rubbish in the streets. With the unravelling of the Soviet-built infrastructure, however, came revelations of socialism's sinister history – its own excesses and waste products – as well as of the continuing legacy of these in Almaty. Residents first got wind of the ways in which the state had prioritized industry (and the extraction of Kazakh resources) over social well-being during perestroika-era protests that revealed to them the existence of toxic wastes in the ground beneath them, in the air around them, and in the water they drank – protests whose repression revealed to them other Soviet excesses, namely, the willingness of the state to resort to violent force to preserve itself and its secrets. Thereafter, memories of violence were etched on the urban landscape, and public spaces like the main square fell into disuse. With independence, Almaty residents were left to encounter toxins in the Kazakh social body itself, as ethnic Russians and Germans once exiled to Kazakhstan as political prisoners – 'wastes' of the Soviet system – abandoned the city, leaving a *déraciné* Kazakh elite and rural newcomers to face the ways in which they had internalized decades of racism and cultural elitism. Both socialism and capitalism – indeed, all social systems - generate problematic forms of excess, Alexander concludes; what is more, these wastes linger on the landscape, as symbol and as substance, long after the systems that have generated them pass away.

John Campbell, too, focuses on a malaise of supposed postsocialist origin in his chapter on corruption in Dar es Salaam, Tanzania, and similarly suggests that the phenomenon is actually rooted in dynamics dating to the socialist-era. According to Campbell's detailed account, the socialist state's attempts to regulate access to essential goods and services – ranging from food and consumer goods to education, health care and affordable housing – overshot its ability to furnish these goods. Those who took it upon themselves to meet their own needs and/or to meet the needs of others through market initiatives gave rise to a vast informal economy and a repertoire of practices that underpins what is, by Campbell's definition, today called corruption. Campbell includes under this rubric: petty traders, who not only met the needs of their consumer-clients, but in so doing earned livelihoods in the absence of wage-employment opportunities; pirate transport operators, who similarly supported themselves while keeping the city of Dar es Salaam moving; property brokers, who matched the homeless with underutilized properties despite shortages of state-owned housing; 'fixers', who mediated between citizens and a cumbersome state bureaucracy, often brokering bribes; and vigilantes, who policed neglected communities and administered swift 'justice'. While much of this was formally condemned by party/state officials during the heyday of Tanzanian socialism, much of it was informally condoned. Campbell explains that through such practices, vital social needs were sometimes met, and the apparent failures of the state mitigated. The informal economy, by Campbell's account, was a 'moral economy' of dubious status, however. Pirate transport operators provided unsafe services, at high fees, and exploited their workforce, for example; vigilante justice often deteriorated into extortion. Corruption proliferated in the late socialist and postsocialist periods, becoming an intractable condition. Where previously the Tanzanian middle class – including doctors, teachers, civil servants, planners, accountants, tax collectors and police – perceived themselves to be corruption's 'victims', increasingly they became its agents. They found themselves tangled in webs that connected all the way to the top of the party/state hierarchy. In contrast with Ferguson and Gupta's (Ferguson and Gupta 2002) assertion that neoliberal reform has given rise to new forms of 'neo-liberal governmentality' wherein the state continues to govern only in league with transnational institutions and nongovernmental organizations, Campbell's evidence seems to suggest that, in Tanzania, *corruption* has become the prevailing mode of governmentality – i.e., that the ruling Chama Cha Mapinduzi (CCM) party effectively continues to govern through a network of pirates, fixers and vigilantes that it (informally) controls. The ironies in this run deep: the socialist CCM, which vociferously criticized such practices as being counter to socialism, not only created the conditions for their emergence and permitted them to continue for reasons of expediency, but now owes to them its ability to continue in power long after socialism's demise.

Kevin Latham's chapter on cynicism in 'postsocialist' China also focuses on a party still in power 'after socialism' despite widespread suspicion and resentment of corruption. In the aftermath of the failed policies of the Great Leap Forward and the Cultural Revolution, Latham reminds us, China analysts, not to mention the state itself, identified widespread cynicism as a potential threat to the regime. In the early 'reform period', cynicism was attributed not only to emergent (but not yet satisfied) consumerist desires, but also to resentment of entrenched political hierarchies and bureaucratic cronyism – phenomena traceable to the revolution and, even, to pre-revolutionary political culture. Latham also reminds us that events in 1989 in Tiananmen Square were more accurately described as a protest against the corruption of the ruling party than as a 'call for democracy'. More broadly, popular cynicism early in the reform era betrayed grave doubts regarding the ruling party's commitment to socialism and, just as importantly, its capacity to deliver on its promises of socialist modernity. Where the violence of Tiananmen drove cynicism back underground, though, 'market socialism' eventually provided increasing numbers of Chinese with modern amenities, ranging from luxury flats to cable and then satellite television, to landlines and then cell phones, to computers and then internet access, and to opportunities to meet foreigners and, for some, to travel abroad. In the midst of expanding consumer opportunities, doubts about the party's ability to deliver diminished. Doubts about the party's commitment to socialism were not so much alleviated as rendered irrelevant. By Latham's account, popular cynicism has now become so entrenched among Chinese that it has ceased to be a political threat: people can scarcely 'lose faith' in what they no longer 'believe'. But where China analysts no longer speak of cynicism, Latham suggests that cynicism remains essential to the maintenance of the ruling party. Where commentators previously measured cynicism as the disbelief of consumers in the media through which the messages of the Chinese state were disseminated, Latham shifts attention to the producers of such messages, namely journalists. In so doing, he argues for the importance of focusing not on beliefs but on concrete practices as expressions of cynicism. His chapter offers a detailed account of such practices as he travels with journalists who, as a matter of course, take their cues (and sometimes even their copy) from local state officials, 'playing a game' whose rules are known and accepted by all – a game that leads them to produce formulaic pieces that praise local government responses to any problems identified. Ironically, in the reform era, the state itself has embraced the cynicism of those who represent it to the nation in order to preserve its power long after all concerned have stopped 'believing' its messages.

By contrast with Latham's Chinese journalists, the Hungarian anthropologists at the centre of Chris Hann's chapter mostly ignored the mandate of the socialist state to serve as intellectual intermediaries. Twice over, in fact, these academics have endured attempts to remake their discipline: first at socialism's beginning, and then at its end. Hann argues that academia, like the world it purports to study, does not constitute a blank slate upon which reformers and revolutionaries may write what they wish. In Hungary, the discipline has long been defined by an emphasis on *néprajz*, the study of Hungarian folk (a nation building anthropology, by Stocking's definitions (Stocking 1982), rather than an empire-building anthropology as practised by Western European nations focused on the study of peoples in their colonies). Today the vast majority of Hungarian anthropologists remain *néprajzosok*, despite mounting calls by a number of young, generally English-speaking, Hungarian academics to transform and expand the discipline. Proponents of a more interdisciplinary, internationalist *'kulturális antropológia'* have attracted rapidly rising numbers of students in recent years. Nonetheless, *néprajzosok* have insured continuity in institutional profiles and research agendas, as well as in degree programmes and curricula. Hann suggests that the resilience of 'national ethnography' may be attributed to the continuing importance of legitimizing the Hungarian nation. Indeed, the 'backward-looking' focus of *néprajz* may serve as an antidote to the latent imperial threat of Western-led neoliberalization in the postsocialist era. In any case, this resilience has been made *possible* by the ironies of twentieth-century Hungarian history. Although the first socialist minister of education – himself an anthropologist – called for the discipline to embrace Marxism-Leninism, Hungarian *néprajzosok* generally concluded that the study of culture had little place within Marxism. They pursued diverse agendas: despite new Hungarian alliances with Third World countries, most continued to focus on Hungarian culture; a few attempted to work within a Marxist framework, but most studied topics of little relevance to Marxist debates. While most *néprajz* were members of the Communist Party, they generally only paid lip service to Marxism (in contrast to East Germany, for example, where the regime enforced ideological engagement among members of the discipline, giving rise to a Marxist ethnography). According to Hann, *néprajz* carried on as a 'living tradition, scarcely tainted by the minimal accommodations it had been obliged to make to socialist ideology'. (The fact that appointments were made on scientific merit rather than according to political allegiances made appointees secure in their posts well after the demise of the regime under which they were appointed.) Indeed, Hann suggests, *néprajz* thrived under socialism precisely *because* it identified with national culture rather than Marxism-Leninism. Thus, notwithstanding remarkable continuities in the structure of institutions and in the personnel inhabiting these institutions from the socialist period into the postsocialist, Hann concludes that Hungarian *néprajz* is as much, if not more, a case of national ethnography enduring socialism as it is a case of socialism enduring.

The actors at the centre of Caroline Humphrey's chapter on historical analogies in Russia have entered far more assertively into the game of discursive representation of power than Hann's Hungarian *néprajzosok* or Latham's Chinese journalists. They, in fact, have followed state actors in their attempts to give form to a bewildering present through connection with the past. In postsocialist Russia, Humphrey tells us, historical *analogy*, specifically analogy between contemporary and historical personalities, has replaced Marxism, meaning the analysis of historical *process*, in popular discourse. According to Humphrey, political leaders themselves use analogy to legitimate their policies. Russian President Vladimir Putin has been compared to Stolypin (prime minister under the last Tsar) and himself embraced the analogy for a time, making frequent reference to Stolypin in speeches. Like Stolypin, who was also head of the secret police, Putin has been a strong proponent of central power. The analogy also links these two men as advocates of agricultural modernization through privatization. This analogy, like other such historical representations, has become the stuff of great discussion and debate in postsocialist Russia. Analogies can be messy, Humphrey reminds us; where some seek to use them bluntly, others extend them and explore their inevitable ironies. Putin's critics, including rural Russians, have 'remembered' Stolypin as a pitiless agent of repression who violently put down peasant revolts and shipped people off to Siberia in railway cars (to this day, widely referred to as Stolypin's cars). By embracing the analogy in this way, critics of Putin's rural policies have cast him as the destroyer of a rural way of life they historically ground in the prerevolutionary Russian commune – the *mir* – whose members, by their depiction, shared the fruits of their labours along with their burdens and misfortunes. Stolypin saw the *mir* as an obstacle to modernization and fought to supplant it with a progressive class of private farmers. His initiatives were cut short by the First World War and the subsequent Russian Revolution. Ironically, Soviet-era agricultural collectivization more successfully displaced the *mir* than did Stolypin. With the end of the Soviet Union, then, came initiatives, first by Yeltsin and then by Putin, to break up collective farms and to foster commercial agriculture. These efforts have encountered much resistance, whether in the Duma, in the form of local governments subverting central policy, or in farmers themselves who have remained wary of going it alone. The gutted collectives that most farmers continue to cling to, however, no longer meet an array of economic and social needs. Not knowing what to make of what has become of the rural sector, Russians of all categories look to analogies to make sense of things, Humphrey tells us. Some of Putin's critics (those who vaguely celebrate 'socialism', not as the platform of any party to which they belong, but instead as a set of values that they celebrate and seek to preserve) thus suggest that the essence of the *mir* – by their reckoning a primordial, and somehow more genuine, form of 'socialism' – has, barely, survived collectivization (being incubated within the collective itself), while casting Putin, like Stolypin before him, as its mortal enemy. Such analogies can sometimes shape reality, Humphrey tells us, but she concerns herself far more with what they do to understandings of history and of socialism. Where advocates of postsocialist agricultural reform are likened to destroyers of the prerevolutionary *mir*, she suggests, socialism itself is no longer a theory of human progress or a process of dialectical transformation, but rather the embrace, in the here and now, of timeless essences, in this case the celebration of a specifically Russian institution – the *mir* – as the original, and somehow enduring, noncapitalist, morally superior form of existence.

The images of Che Guevara analyzed in the final chapter by Parvathi Raman are as contestable as the historical analogies studied by Humphrey. It was, after all, through dissemination of the photo of Guevara's corpse with severed hands, meant to portray his mortality, that Che achieved status as a martyr among many Latin Americans. Raman's chapter, however, is mainly concerned with another image, namely the 1960 photo taken by Albert Korda, known to most audiences in the form of a T-shirt silk screen. For the London youth appearing in Raman's ethnography who wear these shirts, Che references not only another historical context but also an entirely different semantic universe – one defined by the global ascendance of neoliberalism and its attendant claims that all desires can be satisfied through the unfettered flow worldwide of capital, goods and services. Of course, as Raman points out, the very desires neoliberal capitalism claims to meet through the market must remain unfulfilled for the market to continue to function. The restless insatiability of consumerism, however, not only perpetuates capitalism but also makes possible the emergence within the marketplace of things inimical to it, including anti-capitalist icons such as Che Guevara T-shirts. Despite the fact that it was, ironically, Korda's socialist-motivated refusal to take out copyright on his photo that made its commoditization possible, commentators, left and right, have suggested that the transformation of Che's image into commodity – indeed, fashion statement – tokens the final triumph of the market, and with it the end of revolutionary possibility. Such conclusions, however, are founded upon an assumption that this revolutionary symbol 'signifies nothing' today, even for those who wear it on their chests – an assumption Raman questioned in the conduct of interviews with young people in London who wore Che T-shirts. Che did signify something to these youth – indeed, his image was saturated with meaning – even if few spoke specifically of socialist revolution. To be sure, most found Che's youthful defiance 'cool'. Beyond this, everyone Raman interviewed knew who he was – defying commentators' suggestions to the contrary. Most, however, defined his 'struggle' rather unspecifically as one against political inauthenticity, corruption, oppression or injustice. When speaking more specifically, they sometimes invoked Che in their criticism of American imperialism and/or the US-led 'war on terror' – prescient associations, even if class war against capitalism is missing from the picture, considering that Che and the socialist revolutionaries with whom he fought were themselves cast as terrorists. Raman reminds us that British youths' readings of Che today must be situated within the world they know – a 'postpolitical' world of broken unions and middle-class values wherein the state brazenly ignores the views of those it purportedly represents and alternatives to capitalism are less conceivable to most than the end of the world itself. Like the Chinese middle-class consumers described in Latham's chapter, British youth are cynical, but by Raman's descriptions less 'satisfied'. The Che T-shirts they wore constituted 'internal critiques' of modern capitalist society launched from within the space of commodification itself. Through wearing such articles of clothing, Raman suggests, young people actually expressed a utopian imagination vis-à-vis the existing order of things, albeit one that situated transformative potential elsewhere through 'a desire for an alterity that interrogate[d] the self, ... contest[ed] the ego, and ... challenge[d] a partial truth ... being totalized'. For them, what existed in, and animated them within, the present was not a socialist past (cf. Rodgers, this volume; Humphrey, this volume); instead their expressions of discontent drew on deeper reserves of oppositional sentiment not necessarily associated with socialism (see also Makovicky, this volume). In a world without socialism, these young people nonetheless opposed much of what socialism had opposed. The image of Che Guevara etched on their bodies did not give socialism continuity in the present so much as give endurance to values and dispositions that have animated the socialist project in various times and places, betraying the possibility of socialism's future reconstitution.

Notes

1. Revealingly, these remedies echoed postcolonial developmental policy, but altogether ignored the problems that had come in the wake of such policies, as strategic planners continued to think in terms of developmental practices that would 'civilise the periphery'. See Litziger (2002: 45).
2. US Secretary of State Robert Lansing, quoted in Buck Morss (2002: 2).
3. In addition, aspects of the feudal past also proved to be resilient and often survived socialist reconstruction.
4. The idea of 'alternative beginnings' is taken from Walter Benjamin's writings on history.

References

Abdulgani, R. 1964. *Bandung Spirit: Moving on the Tide of History*. Prapantja.
Ball, A. 2007. *Russia's Last Capitalists: the Nepmen, 1921–1929*. University of California Press.
Bandera, V.N. 1963. 'The New Economic Policy as an Economic System', *Journal of Political Economy* 71 (3), 265–79.
Bandera, V.I. 1970. 'Market Orientation of State Enterprises during NEP', *Soviet Studies* 22 (1), July: 110–21.
Bean, J.J. 1997. 'Nikolai Bukharin and the New Economic Policy', *Independent Review* 2(1), summer: 79–98.
Bellamy Foster, J. 2007. 'The Latin American Revolt: an Introduction', *Monthly Review* July–August 2007: 1–7.
Berdahl, D., M. Bunzl and M. Lampland (eds). 2003. *Altering States: Ethnographies of Transition in Eastern Europe and the Former Soviet Union*. University of Michigan Press.
Berger, M.T. 2004. 'After the Third World? History, Destiny and the Fate of Third Worldism', *Third World Quarterly* 25(1): 9–39.
Buck Morss, S. 2002. *Dreamworld and Catsatrophe: The Passing of Mass Utopia in East and West*. MIT.
Buroway, M. and K. Verdery. 1999. *Uncertain Transition: Ethnographies of Change in the Postsocialist World*. Rowman and Littlefield.
Castells, M. 1998. *End of Millenium*. Blackwell.
Derrida, J. 1994. *Spectres of Marx: The State of Debt, the Work of Mourning, and the New International*. Routledge.
Ferguson, J. and A. Gupta. 2002. 'Spatializing States: Towards an Ethnography of Neoliberal Governmentality', *American Ethnologist* 29(4): 981–1002.
Fukuyama, F. 1993. *The End of History and the Last Man*. Penguin.
Gilbert, A. 2006. 'The Past in Parenthesis: (Non) Postsocialism in Post-war Bosnia-Herzegovina', *Anthropology Today* 22(4) August: 14–18.
Harvey, D. 1990. *The Condition of Postmodernity*. Cambridge: Blackwell.
Hilton, M.L. 2004. 'Retailing the Revolution: The State Department Store (GUM) and Soviet Society in the 1920s', *Journal of Social History* Summer: 939–64.
Horschelmann, K. 2002. 'History After the End: Post-Socialist Difference in a (Post)Modern World', *Transactions of the Institute of British Geographers* 27(1): 52–66.
Humphrey, C. and R. Mandel (eds). 2002. *Markets and Moralities: Ethnographies of Postsocialism*. Berg.
Jarausch, K.H. 2006. 'The Collapse of Communism and the Search for Master Narratives: Interpretive Implications of German Unification', *Telos* 59–75.
Latour, B. 1993. *We Have Never Been Modern*. Harvester Wheatsheaf.
Lenin, V.I. 1957. *The Development of Capitalism in Russia: The Process of the Formation of a Home Market for Large Scale Industry*. Lawrence and Wishart.
Litziger, R. 2002. 'Theorising Postsocialism: Reflections on the Politics of Marginality in Contemporary China', *The South Atlantic Quarterly* 101(1), Winter: 33–55.

Munck, R. 2003. 'Neoliberalism, Necessitarianism and Alternatives in Latin America: There Is no Alternative(TINA)?', *Third World Quarterly* 24(3): 495–511.

North, R.C. 1951. 'The NEP and the New Democracy', *Pacific Affairs* 24(1) March: 52–60.

Panizza, F. 2005. 'Unarmed Utopia Revisited: the Resurgence of Left of Centre Politics in Latin America', *Political Studies* 53: 716–34.

Verdery, K. 1996. *What Was Socialism? What Comes Next?* Princeton University Press.

Verdery, K. 1998. 'Transnationalism, Nationalism, Citizenship and Property: Eastern Europe since 1989', *American Ethnologist* 25(2) May: 291–306.

Yurchak, A. 2006. *Everything Was Forever, Until It Was No More: The Last Soviet Generation.* Princeton University Press.

Wallander, C.A. 2002. 'Lost and Found: Gorbachev's "New Thinking"', *The Washington Quarterly* Winter: 117–29.

CHAPTER 1

From Socialist Chiefs to Postsocialist Cadres: Neotraditional Authority in Neoliberal Mozambique

Harry G. West

In October of 1992, after sixteen years of brutal civil war in Mozambique, the ruling FRELIMO party and RENAMO insurgents signed a peace accord, laying the groundwork for elections to be staged in October of 1994. FRELIMO – the socialist revolutionary Front for the Liberation of Mozambique, which waged war between 1964 and 1974 to achieve independence from the Portuguese and to establish a postcolonial state – had acceded to IMF-sponsored structural adjustment in 1987, renounced its commitment to Marxism-Leninism in 1989, legalized opposition political parties in 1990, and redrafted the constitution to protect rights of religious and political expression in 1991. Its victory at the ballot box in 1994 was part and parcel of a second postcolonial revolution in Mozambique, this one neoliberal.

Mozambique's neoliberal revolution has been as profound an affair as the socialist revolution before it, even if its key battles have often been fought in foreign capitals, in the embassies of Maputo's Sommerschield district, and in the projects and workshops sponsored by UN agencies, the World Bank, and the legions of NGOs and PVOs working in the country (Hanlon 1991). By the late 1990s, reformers not only pronounced liberalization of the Mozambican economy and polity a success, they also suggested that Mozambique constituted a model for postsocialist transition and post-war reconstruction elsewhere in the post-Cold War world. Ironically, in so doing, they echoed socialist revolutionaries who had in previous decades asserted that Mozambique constituted a model for socialist modernization.

The neoliberal revolution has been most visible in Mozambique in the lively national assembly, in a vibrant independent media, in high rates of economic growth, in a sharp increase in air traffic (domestic and foreign), and in the appearance of upmarket resorts on the nation's stunning beaches. The revolution, however, has not been confined to the capital and other cities and towns, nor has it been limited to political and economic processes of national and international dimension. It has also been waged in thousands upon thousands of villages and settlements by reformers intent upon achieving 'rural development' where 'socialist modernization' failed. Debates about the causes of socialism's failure in Mozambique – its inherent collapse due to excessive centralization, commandism and bureaucratic incompetence versus its sabotage by external forces including South Africa and a RENAMO (Mozambican National Resistance) insurgency that, with South African support, destroyed the essential infrastructure of the socialist project – have given way to a dominant neoliberal discourse extolling the virtues of civil society and calling for its empowerment through varied forms of political and economic decentralization and democratization (Pitcher 2002). Indeed, through 'democratic decentralization', neoliberal reformers have sought to rewrite the political and economic landscape of rural Mozambique as completely as the socialist revolutionaries before them. As Domingos do Rosário Artur and Bernhard Weimer describe it, the objective of reform has been, at once, to move the nation 'from a commandist, centrally planned and largely, ineffective (war) economy to a more and more globally integrated free market economy', and 'from a one-party-regime of democratic centralism (with a hyper-centralized administration), to a formal multiparty democracy and the gradual introduction of a decentralized system of governance and administration' (Artur and Weimer 1998: 4).

In 1997, the Mozambican assembly passed a law establishing a framework for the creation of democratically elected local governments, but only in the nation's thirty-three largest towns and cities.[1] Democratic decentralization would take a different form in the nation's rural areas. After years of closed-door debate and equivocation, the Mozambican Council of Ministers issued a decree in June of 2000 preserving government's role in the appointment of district- and post-level administrators, but mandating these state officials to consult and cooperate with 'Community Authorities' (Buur and Kyed 2003). Included among those who might be 'recognized' as Community Authorities were FRELIMO party secretaries and members of their executive councils, 'traditional authorities', and 'other legitimate leaders' (including, presumably, influential religious leaders).

The inclusion of 'traditional authorities' within the category of potential Community Authorities was controversial but, as we shall see, was also the very essence of the Community Authorities Decree. During its guerrilla campaign against the Portuguese, FRELIMO had generally cast 'traditional authorities' as collaborators in the colonial exploitation of the Mozambican people (West and Kloeck-Jenson 1999: 456). The colonial administration had indeed used chiefs as tax collectors, labour recruiters and policing agents, rewarding them for their cooperation through commissions, and punishing them for noncompliance through beatings, deposition or exile. In its 'liberated zones' during the independence war, and elsewhere after independence, FRELIMO replaced the institutions of 'traditional authority' with party structures, staffed by loyal cadres.

The FRELIMO abolition of the chieftaincy met with mixed sentiments among rural Mozambicans in accordance with diverse local histories, differential social positions and perspectives, and ever-changing circumstances. During the civil war, RENAMO capitalized on rural ambivalence regarding this and other FRELIMO policies, in some cases finding ex-chiefs eager allies in their quest to capture and control rural areas (Geffray 1990),[2] and in some cases reproducing the institutions of 'traditional authority' in areas they already controlled through the nomination of a community member willing to serve the insurgency's interests and the bestowal upon that individual of the mantle of chief (Kyed forthcoming; Kyed and Buur 2006). Although in this way RENAMO sometimes mounted and sustained neotraditions of dubious local legitimacy, by the war's end 'traditional authorities' of one kind or another constituted the opposition party's most powerful constituency in the rural areas (West and Kloeck-Jenson 1999: 460, 467).

Denied power at the national and provincial levels by FRELIMO electoral victories in 1994 and, again, in 1999, RENAMO remained enthusiastic about the possibility of gaining power at local levels, envisioning the withdrawal of FRELIMO secretaries from those communities where 'traditional authority' was to be reestablished. RENAMO expectations and demands were underscored by international donors, who often conceived of 'traditional authority' as an African variant of civil society, the recognition of which would not only legalize forms of grass-roots governance long oppressed by the centralized hierarchy of FRELIMO socialism (Weimer 1996: 48–49; Artur and Weimer 1998: 23) but also serve in the contemporary moment as a means to empower local communities to solve their own problems with little or no cost to the downsized poststructural adjustment state (Alexander 1997: 3; West and Kloeck-Jenson 1999: 461; Buur and Kyed 2006).

Only after strategists within the FRELIMO party itself recognized the potential political gains – in fact, the urgent necessity – in separating 'traditional authorities' from RENAMO and, where possible, drawing them into cooperative relations with the ruling party, was the Community Authorities Decree issued, however (Artur and Weimer 1998: 6; Kyed forthcoming). By including FRELIMO secretaries and 'other legitimate leaders' along with 'traditional authorities' in the category of people eligible to be recognized as Community Authorities, and by leaving undefined the mechanism whereby the state was to determine and certify authorities 'recognized as such by their respective communities', the FRELIMO government granted local officials enormous leeway to steer the process in such a way as to support the ruling party agenda. In areas where FRELIMO enjoyed strong popular support – especially in the southern third of the country, or in the ex-'liberated zones' of the far north – FRELIMO party secretaries were generally (re)named Community Authorities. According to Lars Buur and Helene Maria Kyed, there were by April 2003 915 such appointments made throughout the country (Buur and Kyed 2006). By the same date, some 1,071 'traditional authorities' had been named as Community Authorities, often in areas where RENAMO enjoyed significant popular support (ibid.).[3]

Helene Maria Kyed provides a description of the process of recognition of Community Authorities based on fieldwork she conducted in Manica province:

> The implementation process began in 2001 with attempts to identify and then register 'true chiefs' ... This was followed later the same year by the convening of 'legitimisation meetings', where state officials consulted with communities verifying that the person whose name was inscribed in the *official register* was indeed considered legitimate by the community she or he represented. This process ended in 2002 with formal state-recognition ceremonies held by the district administrator. Here, a contract was signed between the registered chief and the state. The chief was bestowed with state regalia: the national flag, emblems of the republic and a sign reading *'autoridade comunitária'* – which bestowed upon him/her the title and status of 'community authority'. (Kyed forthcoming)

Through such acts, the landscape of authority in Mozambique has once again been dramatically rewritten. Unlike socialist revolutionaries before them, agents and advocates of this revolutionary intervention have readily admitted that the brave new world they conceive draws substantially from the past. Whereas RENAMO leaders – as well as many representatives of the donor community in Mozambique – trace a resuscitated 'traditional authority' to an historical past reaching up to the moment immediately prior to its suppression by the socialist state, researchers and policy makers in the Ministry of State Administration have painted a more imprecise picture of 'traditional authority' as a manifestation of 'customs and beliefs practiced from long ago' (African American Institute 1997: 14). Where the most obvious historical reference for 'traditional authorities' serving as administrative intermediaries in Mozambique would be colonial-era *'autoridades gentilicas'* – the three-tiered hierarchy of native authorities of which the *régulo* was the highest ranking – such references are, of course, generally muted in the present-day context of the celebration of 'traditional authority' as a form of African civil society.

Continuities between 'traditional authority', as instantiated under the rubric of Community Authority in the postsocialist era, and any historical predecessor are more tenuous than any of these parties admit. While in some locales FRELIMO socialism drove 'traditional authorities' underground, in others it drove them from their domains of authority altogether. Still other 'traditional authorities' were driven from their homes by the Mozambican civil war (Englund 2002; Kyed and Buur 2006; Kyed forthcoming). Some have since returned, and some have not. In any case, many died in the years between the ban and the 2000 decree, some leaving recognized successors and some not. In some instances, the very communities over which these authorities once presided have been radically reconfigured, whether by the socialist project of communal villagization or by flight during the civil war (Englund 2002; Kyed and Buur 2006). State officials seeking to identify and certify 'traditional authorities' are, consequently, as likely to touch off complex disputes between multiple claimants (Dinerman 2004: 27; Buur and Kyed 2006; Gonçalves 2006; Kyed and Buur 2006; Kyed forthcoming) as to find authorities 'recognized as such by their respective communities'.[4] State recognition of traditional authority in the neoliberal era has consequently been as much an exercise in the reinvention of tradition – even the invention of neotraditions – as in the revival of 'customs and beliefs practiced from long ago'.

While this point has been persuasively argued (West and Kloeck-Jenson 1999; Kyed forthcoming), it remains indisputable that essential forms of continuity do link presocialist and postsocialist forms of 'traditional authority' in Mozambique. Even where rural populations have been moved en masse into villages under the socialist-era villagization programme they have generally continued to conceive of themselves to some degree as members of distinctive kin groups. Notwithstanding disruptions, claimants to positions of 'traditional authority' today generally assert their legitimacy through lines of descent from presocialist office holders, and claim authority over fellow 'family' members, as in the past. Even the essential dynamics of legitimacy contests – commonplace in the precolonial era as well as the colonial – manifest some continuity with the presocialist past.

Simplistic portrayals of a 'revival' of 'traditional authority' conceal complexities that merit attention, however. In so far as the recognition of Community Authorities has constituted yet another iteration in an apparently never-ending process of the invention and reinvention of tradition – a process that simultaneously makes reference to the past while remaking the past in the present – the *presocialist past* has not been the *only* point of historical reference for those involved today in the (re)production of 'traditional authority' (or, the production of neotraditional authority). In substantial ways, the *socialist past* has also, paradoxically, served as a reference point for emergent forms of 'traditional authority' in the postsocialist period.

Community Authorities today in fact enact an authority much like that of the FRELIMO party cadres who supplanted 'traditional authorities' at the outset of the socialist era and whom, in some instances, they now replace in turn. To begin with, it falls upon Community Authorities – where appointed – to undertake many of the same tasks that FRELIMO secretaries and their executive councils (or 'dynamizing groups') undertook during the socialist period.[5] Included among these tasks are: the recruitment and organization of labour to build and maintain roadways, wells, dikes, drainage ditches, irrigation systems, cemeteries, health clinics, maternity wards, child nutrition centres, and schools; the recruitment and organization of community members to participate in vaccination and sanitation initiatives to prevent epidemics (including cholera, meningitis, diarrhoea, malaria, tuberculosis, and sexually transmitted diseases such as AIDS), and to build pit latrines; reporting to local administrators and the police of criminals and crimes (including the illegal exploitation, transport or sale of natural resources, and the existence of arms caches and land mines); contribution to community education in the management and sustainable use of natural resources (including the management of game, forest fires, firewood and charcoal); fostering agricultural production, the use of animal traction as a means of transportation (in coastal areas, the building and maintenance of boats), and the construction of local marketplaces and fairgrounds; encouraging parents to send their children to school; fostering school sports, games, and other character-building and educational recreational activities for children; preventing premature marriages; collaborating in the maintenance of peace and social harmony; cooperating with local tribunals in the resolution of small civil disputes (taking into account local customs and practices, within the limits of the law); organizing an annual census; organizing the collection of local taxes; and informing the community of ongoing government discussion and debates, and of the passage of new laws.[6]

Even a casual reading of this list of duties reveals its programmatic nature – one that not only contains myriad forms of social engineering closely associated with the project of socialist modernization (such as the construction of pit latrines, the use of animal traction, and the prevention of premature marriages), but also perpetuates the commandism of vanguard socialism.[7] Government documents laying the foundation for democratic decentralization through the recognition of Community Authorities refer to these institutions or figures as representatives of their respective communities, but make almost no mention of the ways in which community ideas and initiatives might figure in a new form of politics enacted through them (Kyed forthcoming). Conceived as such, Community Authorities, like party secretaries before them, serve as conduits for the transmission of information and/or directives from the state, rather than as means of expression or empowerment of 'their' communities (Buur and Kyed 2006; Gonçalves 2006; Kyed forthcoming). They constitute fingers that extend the reach of the state – still controlled by FRELIMO – into every village, every neighbourhood, indeed, every household (Kyed forthcoming), just as party structures (comprising village secretaries, neighbourhood secretaries and ten-house secretaries) did during the period of FRELIMO socialism.

To be sure, these newly recognized Community Authorities capture resources for the people they purportedly represent by securing state funding and/or attracting development projects to their villages or neighbourhoods. Where once the state controlled all such resources, in the neoliberal era local authorities may – indeed, must – cultivate direct linkages with international institutions, nongovernmental organizations, and sometimes even foreign investors, to achieve such ends. With much at stake, every lineage or household in the village seeks representation at the level of Community Authority; but this was also the case in the socialist period, when the potential benefits of having one's kinsman serve the party as secretary were considerable, and jockeying for such positions was consequently intense. In any case, like socialist party secretaries before them, today's Community Authorities broker powers external to the community rather than the power of the people they are said to 'represent' (Dinerman 2004: 145; Kyed and Buur 2006).

Where, in the wake of structural adjustment, the Mozambican state has steadily withdrawn from provision of social services to its rural citizenry, the Community Authorities Decree has effectively reestablished the state as a decisive player in local fields of power – one whose recognition vets the legitimacy of the 'traditional authorities' with whom the NGOs now providing such crucial goods and social services generally seek to collaborate. As Buur and Kyed demonstrate, where state recognition of local authorities is withheld, the flow of aid may in fact be jeopardized (Buur and Kyed 2006). From this resultant position of strength, state officials have manipulated the process whereby recognition is granted to Community Authorities so as to ensure that those 'recognized' are disposed to cooperate with the ruling party while those not so disposed remained unrecognized (just as the party orchestrated the 'election' of amenable village secretaries in the socialist period).

It must of course be remembered that FRELIMO's commitment to the recognition of Community Authorities derives from its objective to consolidate authority (and here the party's authority and the authority of the state are conflated, just as they were in the socialist era) in rural areas where, during the civil war and in its aftermath, an oppositional shadow state in the form of 'traditional authorities' allied to RENAMO coexisted with the official state headed by FRELIMO secretaries – a phenomenon referred to in the Mozambican context as 'double administration'.[8] Where RENAMO has enjoyed little support, the ruling party, as alluded to above, has merely (re)named local party cadres Community Authorities (Dinerman 2004: 144; West 2005: 220; Gonçalves 2006). Elsewhere, it has applied (often, but not always, subtle) force to achieve its ends. When Kyed asked officials involved in the process of recognizing Community Authorities in Sussendenga, 'What if a chief works for the opposition party?', or, 'What if a community authority is against the development programs of the government?', she was told that Community Authorities were the 'arm of the Government', that 'the activities of the Government cannot be prevented because of [oppositional] ideas', and that, while in principle, a Community Authority 'could be politically affiliated with the opposition', if such a figure worked to 'create impediments to development', 'then he [was] not a *régulo*' (Kyed forthcoming) (see also Gonçalves 2006). In short, 'traditional authorities' who support or are supported by RENAMO are rarely 'recognized' as legitimate claimants to posts as Community Authorities. Others have been recognized instead.[9] In the case of 'Struba', a chief-turned-Community Authority with whom Kyed worked, recognition necessarily coincided with a public shift of allegiance from RENAMO to FRELIMO. Privately, Struba frankly told Kyed: 'We can see that it is politics ... [FRELIMO] hope to gain the *régulo* to win the people, because the *régulo* can mobilize the people. We know that this is what it is about.'

By making 'traditional authorities' like Struba into Community Authorities, government officials have successfully established formal relationships with them through which they have been rendered more accountable, even dependent upon, the state. In the words of Buur and Kyed (Buur and Kyed 2006), 'Decree 15/2000 ... can be seen as an attempt to bring ... *de facto*, loosely organized forms of traditional authority and their subject populations under state control.' Closer scrutiny reveals that FRELIMO officials not only treat/use Community Authorities *like* party cadres but that they also often conceive of them *as* party cadres more literally. Salvador Cadete Forquilha (Forquilha 2005: 34) argues that, in presenting the Community Authorities Decree to residents of the northern province of Cabo Delgado in the context of a public meeting held in the village of Chai – the site of the inaugural battle in FRELIMO's armed struggle for independence – FRELIMO symbolically established a direct line of descent from the party's own revolutionary cadres to these new figures of authority. Kyed offers evidence of similar associations being forged where Community Authorities have not actually been former party cadres (as they have been in northern Cabo Delgado). A local administrator interviewed by Kyed in Manica told her: 'Today ... dynamising groups [the precursors to FRELIMO party secretaries and executive councils, and the name by which many rural Mozambicans still refer to FRELIMO party institutions] have been replaced by community and traditional leaders [Community Authorities]. They too dynamise the [policies] of the government at the local level and [spread] the politics of FRELIMO at the base ... The functions are the same, only the names and titles have changed ... '(Kyed forthcoming). Kyed even reports that 'recognized chiefs and sub-chiefs were viewed as instruments to facilitate FRELIMO allegiance (in RENAMO strongholds)' where, in the run-up to the 2004 elections, the ruling party 'obligated [chiefs] to have a picture of the FRELIMO presidential candidate, A[rmando] E. Guebuza, in a visible place in their homesteads', and 'actively used chiefs to mobilize the population for campaign meetings' (Kyed forthcoming). Through such means, then, the very figures meant to *replace party cadres* as grass-roots representatives of the people in the new multiparty democratic Mozambique have acted *as cadres*, albeit for a party to which many do not belong – a party whose ideology in the neoliberal era has been reduced to the reproduction of its own power.

Any attempt to explain such unexpected and ironic continuities in the structure and logics of authority from the socialist period to the postsocialist leads not only to the examination of deeper historical issues but also to the discovery of equally unexpected and ironic continuities in the structure and logics of authority from the presocialist period to the socialist. During the Mozambican war for independence, FRELIMO (as stated above) publicly cast 'traditional authorities' as collaborators with the colonial agenda, but on the ground, in the context of the insurgency, the revolutionary party generally sought to recruit the support of these figures in the anti-colonial campaign.[10] Where FRELIMO succeeded, 'traditional authorities' abandoned their settlements and moved their populations, en masse, into FRELIMO-held territories. Only after unsuccessful attempts to achieve this did FRELIMO target such authority figures for assassination.[11] The means by which 'traditional authorities' who collaborated with the Portuguese were killed reveals important dynamics defining the revolutionary (re)production of authority. To prevent such killings from fomenting division within the ranks of the insurgency, FRELIMO dispatched family members of the targeted individual to perform the deed lest such attacks be recast according to the logics of longer-standing enmities between families or lineages and sow division in the revolutionary ranks. Kinship networks were, in fact, the tenuous building blocks of the larger revolutionary national 'family'.[12] FRELIMO effectively used family networks to recruit members both before and during the independence war. In the FRELIMO-administered 'liberated zones', 'traditional authorities' were replaced by younger party cadres, but refugee families and lineages continued to live together. Although 'traditional authorities' were officially barred from holding leadership positions in wartime and postindependence political institutions, many (including ex-*régulos*) served on the councils that 'advised' the FRELIMO secretaries that governed these populations. In some cases, traditional authorities, or their delegates, were in fact appointed to positions as party secretaries (Alexander 1997: 12; Gonçalves 2006) – albeit in most instances not *as* chiefs but rather as people who had, through service, earned FRELIMO's trust (Dinerman 2004: 135);[13] even where 'traditional authorities' played no formal role, FRELIMO secretaries often solicited the opinions and/or assistance of such figures on matters pertaining to 'their' populations, whether during the war or after (Alexander 1997: 5; West and Kloeck-Jenson 1999: 481; Dinerman 2004: 135; Kyed and Buur 2006; Kyed forthcoming).[14] In any case, FRELIMO cadres often exercised authority over groups of the same dimensions as had kin-based authority figures before them. Whether in the environs of wartime bush-bases, or in the postindependence 'communal villages' that served as the backbone of FRELIMO's continuing socialist revolution in the countryside, prewar social geographies were reproduced, with residential proximity reflecting relations of kinship (West 2001).

'Traditional authority' infused the new FRELIMO hierarchy in other ways as well. Born of guerrilla insurgency, the FRELIMO administration was animated by the language of war; when not fighting the enemy, FRELIMO leaders mobilized people to *fight campaigns* against hunger, poverty, nudity, ignorance, superstition, sectarianism and corruption, to name but a few 'enemies' (Kyed forthcoming). As the independence war escalated and Portuguese counter-insurgency initiatives placed spies and saboteurs in the liberated zones, a revolutionary party that had initially focused attention on attracting popular support focused considerable attention on maintaining surveillance against 'enemies within' (West 2005: 148, 160-61, 176). At the same time, party institutions and practices became ever more hierarchical – ever less democratic. Although often associated with revolutionary party/state centralization, the militaristic culture of command (see also Buur and Kyed 2003: 7) – along with the ever-present threat of violence – that came to define FRELIMO in the context of anti-colonial insurgency and the subsequent defence of the socialist state was not altogether unfamiliar to rural Mozambicans. In its campaigns to build the socialist nationstate, FRELIMO increasingly partook of the tone and texture of authority as practiced by its predecessors, meaning not only Portuguese colonials (Alexander 1997: 2; Kyed forthcoming) but also the 'traditional authorities' that served them as administrative intermediaries (Kyed and Buur 2006).

Mozambican institutions of 'traditional authority' in fact have long and checkered histories (West and Kloeck-Jenson 1999: 473–79). The Portuguese conquest in most regions of the country was but the latest of multiple conquests through which local communities and their political institutions were violently shaped in the period prior to FRELIMO socialism. Predatory proto-states, slave dealers (along with regional chiefs seeking to satisfy their demands), and refugee warriors (such as the splinter groups produced by Shaka's consolidation of power to the south of Mozambique), all reshaped to their benefit the political hierarchies of those they subdued by violent force. In an atmosphere defined for centuries by life-and-death struggles between and among neighbouring peoples, political authorities sought to exercise dominion over others lest they be rendered subordinate to them. The cultivation of fear was an essential aspect of the reproduction of power (Alexander 1997: 11). In the Mueda plateau region, for example, leaders achieved status as such through manifesting qualities popularly regarded with deep ambivalence, including excessive pride and ambition, and the propensity to provoke one's rivals/enemies (West 1998, 2005). Although their authority was validated only by their abilities to create and sustain a mutually beneficial environment for the people in their charge, i.e., 'by feeding their people', those who rose to positions of authority reserved for themselves conspicuous privileges, including, for example, the right to consume the best of that which was brought into the settlement, whether from the hunt, from tending agricultural fields, or from trade at the coast. In other words, they ate first, and best, of all.

In the exercise of authority within the guerrilla command, and within the administrative postindependence socialist state, FRELIMO cadres – who had provoked the authority figures of the generation of their elders and realized their ambitions by subordinating these elders to the will of a people for whom they claimed to speak – acted much like powerful warlords of precolonial times.[15] In the wartime liberated zones, as well as in the agricultural cooperatives and on the collective farms that defined agriculture under the rubric of socialist modernization, these men spurred their people to put food on the collective plate while, at the same time, feeding them from it. They also helped themselves to choice cuts of meat, as had their forebears in power.[16] 'In the days of socialism, everything belonged to the people', I was once told, 'but there was always a place for the FRELIMO leader in the people's car!'

Where continuities exist in the form and function, as well as in the tone and texture, of authority not only from the socialist period to the postsocialist, but also from the presocialist period to the socialist, one might conclude that there is something of the dynamics and the tensions that define power in Mozambique that transcends historical periods as such. It would be errant, however, to conclude that *nothing* has changed in the exercise of power from the period before socialism, through socialism, to the period following it. The FRELIMO abolition of 'traditional authority' produced seismic upheavals in the identity of those exercising authority in rural Mozambique. FRELIMO authorities were not only younger and of mixed gender, but their capacities to govern were also measured by altogether different standards – including literacy and numeracy – than those of their elder predecessors (West 1998). While the settlements of their elders were writ small in the villages in which they governed, relations between the lineages and families gathered within these domains were dramatically changed as well; these 'backbones of socialist modernization' – or, according to their critics, 'rural slums' – afforded residents an array of novel political, economic and social opportunities, as well as presenting them with a host of novel problems (West 2001).

Whereas postsocialist reformers have in some cases explicitly celebrated the 'recognition' of Community Authorities as a *return to the past*, in substantial ways Decree 15/2000 similarly heralded a radically transformed future. State manipulation of the process of recognition of Community Authorities has, as we have seen, ensured that claimants to these new positions who support FRELIMO generally win out over claimants affiliated with RENAMO. The progressive elimination of parallel sets of claims to local authority has contributed substantially to dramatic shifts in the postwar balance of power between the nation's two major political parties in selected localities and, indeed, at the national level.

Notwithstanding changes wrought by successive socialist and neoliberal revolutions, paradoxical continuities also define these transformations in significant ways, however. As we have seen, during the independence war and in the postindependence years of socialist modernization, FRELIMO cadres acted in many ways *as chiefs* – albeit as *socialist chiefs*. Nominally class warriors, they remained beholden in essential ways to the logics and dynamics of kinship relations with and among their charges. Their propensities to command – backed by the threat of violence – were partly the stuff of revolutionary socialism, but also partly the stuff of a warlord tradition through which power had long been enacted in the region. Their legitimacy as leaders depended – as it did for 'traditional authorities' before them – on their abilities to ensure collective well-being even as they themselves lived well. Similarly, Community Authorities behave in the postsocialist era *as cadres* – albeit as *neoliberal cadres*. Nominally party neutral, their appointments are vetted by the ruling party. Purportedly grass-roots representatives of rural civil society, they represent a downsized state upon which they depend for recognition rather than representing their constituents. They serve the continuing developmental – and in some respects paternalistic – agendas of greater powers, disseminating directives and rationing out the limited largesse bestowed upon them by these powers.

The brave new world of neoliberal Mozambique is thus partly new and partly old. What is more, that within it which manifests continuity with the past constitutes a complex mix of a presocialist world that endured a decade and a half of socialism, and a socialist one that endures in the 'postsocialist' present. Indeed, such complexities bear evidence of the ways in which socialism partook of the world it encountered in Mozambique, as well as the ways in which neoliberalism, even today, partakes of Mozambican socialism.

Notes

1. See Law 2/97. A 1994 law (3/94) had established such mechanisms more universally, but was ruled unconstitutional and, thus, repealed in 1995 (Weimer 1996: 51).
2. Geffray's account must be read alongside others that paint rather different pictures. For example, Englund (Englund 2002: 72–78) tells of an ex-chief in Tete province who, after having 'invited' RENAMO into his area, fled upon experiencing RENAMO violence at first hand.
3. By this same date, no one belonging to the category of 'other legitimate leaders' had been recognized as a Community Authority anywhere in the country.
4. Kyed (Kyed forthcoming) reports that in no case she observed did more than 10 per cent of the population turn out for a ceremony recognizing a chief-turned-Community Authority.
5. In areas controlled by FRELIMO during the war for independence, secretaries were initially called 'chairmen'. In areas never liberated by FRELIMO during the independence war, FRELIMO established party 'dynamizing groups' before eventually setting up secretaries and executive councils; in many places, residents continued to refer to local party officials as 'dynamizing groups'.
6. Diploma Ministerial 107-A/2000.
7. As Kyed (Kyed forthcoming) points out, the list also echoes the tasks assigned to colonial-era native authorities in the late-colonial period when the Portuguese pursued a policy of 'community development' in order to contain anti-colonial sentiments.
8. For a nuanced ethnographic account of the experience of double administration, see Englund (2002: 137–59). See also Dinerman (2004: 142–44) and Forquilha (2005: 29-37).
9. See also Dinerman (2004: 156) for a case illustrating how RENAMO supporters were barred from becoming Community Authorities in Nampula.
10. For a detailed account, see West (1998, 2005).
11. For example, in the southern half of the Mueda plateau, where I have conducted extensive research on the history of the war, eight *régulos* went

over to FRELIMO and one was arrested by the Portuguese as a FRELIMO sympathizer; FRELIMO killed three, while two took refuge with the Portuguese and three more fled to Tanzania.

12. For a stimulating discussion of the importance of the idea of family to FRELIMO conceptions of the nation today, see Kyed and Buur (2006).
13. Cf. Englund (2002: 63–72), who offers an example (presumably not uncommon) of a chief's brother becoming a FRELIMO secretary not as the chief's appointee but instead as his rival.
14. Notwithstanding the abolition of 'traditional authority', some rural residents in fact continued to consult these familiar authority figures themselves, especially with regard to 'traditional matters' such as marriage and divorce, the distribution of land and the resolution of conflicts, and the staging of family rituals (West and Kloeck-Jenson 1999: 459). So long as such consultation remained discreet, it was often (although not always) tolerated by local party cadres.
15. Indeed, among the highest ranking of FRELIMO military commanders in the independence war were men who, as matrilineal nephews of the famed leaders of the Makonde resistance against the Portuguese (Malapende and Namashakole), proudly claimed this mantle.
16. Dinerman (2004: 131) reports that for a time Nampula residents conceived of labour on socialist-era collective fields as a form of tribute to which party leaders were entitled for having liberated the country; see also Alexander (1997: 11).

References

African American Institute. 1997. *Relatório sobre Círculos de Trabalho e Discussão.* Maputo: African American Institute.

Alexander, J. 1997. 'The Local State in Post-War Mozambique: Political Practice and Ideas about Authority', *African Affairs* 67(1): 1–26.

Artur, D.R. and B. Weimer. 1998. *Decentralization and Democratization in Post-War Mozambique: What Role for Traditional African Authority in Local Government Reform?* International Union of Anthropological and Ethnological Sciences, Williamsburg, Virginia, USA, 1998.

Buur, L. and H.M. Kyed. 2003. *Implementation of Decree 15/2000 in Mozambique: The Consequences of State Recognition of Traditional Authority in Sussundenga.* Copenhagen: Centre for Development Research.

———. 2006. 'Contested Sources of Authority: Re-Claiming State Sovereignty by Formalising Traditional Authority in Post-Conflict Mozambique', *Development and Change* 37(4): 847–69.

Dinerman, A. 2004. 'Processes of State Delegitimization in Post-Independence Rural Mozambique: The Case of Namapa District, Nampula Province', *Journal of Historical Sociology* 17(2/3): 123–84.

Englund, H. 2002. *From War to Peace on the Mozambique–Malawi Borderland.* Edinburgh: Edinburgh University Press for the International African Institute London.

Forquilha, S.C. 2005. *Des 'Autoridades Gentilicas' aux 'Autoridades Comunitarias': Les Trajectoires de la Chefferie Traditionnelle Face à l'Etat Moderne au Mozambique.* AEGIS 2005, SOAS, London.

Geffray, C. 1990. *La Cause des Armes au Mozambique: Anthropologie d'une Guerre Civile.* Paris: Karthala.

Gonçalves, E. 2006. 'Local Powers and Decentralisation: Recognition of Community Leaders in Mocumbi, Southern Mozambique', *Journal of Contemporary African Studies* 24(1): 29–52.

Hanlon, J. 1991. *Mozambique: Who Calls the Shots?* London: James Currey.

Kyed, H.M. forthcoming. 'Formalisation of Traditional Leaders in Post-War Mozambique: The Ambiguous Space between State and Non-State Domains', in A. Bellagamba and G. Klute (eds), *Beside the State: Emerging Forms of Power in Contemporary Africa.* Brill.

Kyed, H.M. and L. Buur. 2006. 'New Sites of Citizenship: Recognition of Traditional Authority and Group-Based Citizenship in Mozambique', *Journal of Southern African Studies* 32(3): 563–81.

Pitcher, M.A. 2002. *Transforming Mozambique: The Politics of Privatization, 1975–2000.* Cambridge: Cambridge University Press.

Stocking, G.Jr. 1982. 'Afterward: A View From The Centre', *Ethnos* 47: 72–86.

Weimer, B. 1996. 'Challenges for Democratization and Regional Development in Southern Africa: Focus on Mozambique', *Regional Development Dialogue* 17(2): 32–59.

West, H.G. 1998. '"This Neighbor is Not My Uncle!": Changing Relations of Power and Authority on the Mueda Plateau', *Journal of Southern African Studies* 24(1): 141–60.

———. 2001. 'Sorcery of Construction and Socialist Modernization: Ways of Understanding Power in Post-Colonial Mozambique', *American Ethnologist* 28(1): 119–50.

———. 2005. *Kupilikula: Governance and the Invisible Realm in Mozambique.* Chicago: University of Chicago Press.

West, H.G., and S. Kloeck-Jenson. 1999. 'Betwixt and Between: "Traditional Authority" and Democratic Decentralization in Post-War Mozambique', *African Affairs* 98(393): 455–84.

CHAPTER 2

'For Eating, It's Guangzhou': Regional Culinary Traditions and Chinese Socialism

Jakob A. Klein

Introduction

It is standard practice among Western observers to divide mainland China's recent history into three periods: 'presocialist' (or 'pre-communist', 'pre-revolutionary', sometimes 'traditional'), 'revolutionary' (or 'Maoist') and 'reform' (or 'post-Mao', increasingly 'postsocialist'). This is, in part, a convenient way of making complex historical processes more manageable by classifying them with the help of a limited number of key events – the communist victory of 1949, the announcement of economic reforms in 1978, and so forth. It is not easy to avoid this periodization when writing about contemporary Chinese society. Nor is it always desirable to do so; it would be absurd to argue, for example, that the communist victory of 1949 was not a momentous event and a condition for many subsequent changes. Moreover, the periodization is certainly useful for anthropologists interested in how people conceptualize their own histories: the tripartite classificatory scheme employed by Western academics and journalists corresponds closely to the tropes deployed by ordinary Chinese when narrativizing their past and its role in the present (Liu 2000). At the same time, these historical boundaries and periods are easily reified, obscuring not only shifts and ambiguities *within* the 'periods', but also the continuities and recurrences across the historical divides we have set up (cf. Cohen 1988). Indeed, this kind of reification plays an important role in the contemporary Chinese Party-State's self-legitimizing historical narrative. According to this narrative, the Party defines itself not only as the liberator from the evils of the pre-1949 'old society', but now also as the saviour of China from the mistakes committed by the 'ultra leftists' during the campaigns of the revolutionary years.[1] There appears, thus, to be a close relationship between the reification of historical periods and the teleological notion that China's (modern) history consists of a series of transitions from one stage to the next, and that she is also currently undergoing such a transition. This notion of 'transition', argues Latham, not only 'provides one of the key rhetorical mechanisms whereby the CCP sustains legitimacy' (Latham 2002: 231), but also characterizes much of the Western scholarship on contemporary China (ibid: 230).

In this chapter, I set out to blur the boundaries between 'presocialist', 'revolutionary' and 'reform-era' China and to complicate the teleological histories to which such reified categories often contribute. I do so by exploring the history of local cuisine and the catering trade, and the contemporary meanings of 'traditional food culture' (*chuantong yinshi wenhua*) in the southern city of Guangzhou (Canton), the provincial capital of Guangdong. Under the current drive to establish a 'socialist market economy' or 'socialism with Chinese characteristics', the celebration of 'Chinese tradition' (or at least those aspects of it not deemed to be 'superstitious') is one of the key devices used by the reformers to differentiate themselves from the iconoclastic revolutionary socialism of the 'Mao years' – not unlike those 'postsocialist' states, no longer ruled by parties calling themselves 'communist', where 'neoliberal reformers have often incorporated the trope of tradition's resurgence into narratives of triumph over socialism' (West, call for papers). In 'postsocialist' China, Guangzhounese/Cantonese and other local or regional cuisines are readily commodified and are promoted by government agencies, media, businesses and local writers as links to the glorious traditional past. In defining regional cuisines as aspects of 'traditional culture', these cuisines are clearly identified by these agents as products of the prerevolutionary period; while it is readily acknowledged that some traditions may change in line with current tastes and trends or that some 'traditional' food practices may have disappeared 'under Mao', what is obscured is the extent to which such 'traditional' culinary forms may have been shaped in *productive* ways by revolutionary socialism. This is similar to those Western scholarly accounts, which also situate 'traditional culture' firmly in the prerevolutionary past, either to be miraculously 'revived' after lying dormant during the revolution (Potter and Potter 1990) or else reinvented or 'recycled' to fit contemporary social needs (Siu 1989). In this paper, by contrast, I demonstrate that the revolutionary years were themselves productive of some of the cultural practices and forms that are identified as 'traditional culture' by contemporary Chinese in the People's Republic.

In rethinking the relationship between 'traditional' cuisine and Chinese socialism, my paper contributes along two main lines to this volume's ambition 'to explore the complex and often paradoxical continuities between diverse postsocialist presents and their corresponding socialist and presocialist pasts' (West, call for papers). Firstly, I take up West's argument that, despite revolutionary socialism's 'claims to have completely and irrevocably transformed [presocialist] economic, political and cultural institutions and practices ... in many instances such forms were woven into its very fabric' (ibid.). In China, I maintain, attempts to create a socialist food culture not only relied upon but even came to celebrate and solidify preexisting culinary practices and institutions. Indeed, while West emphasizes that revolutionary socialism often 'harboured' presocialist traditions, my suggestion here is that the revolutionary project in fact actively reworked or even produced 'traditional culture'. Secondly, in line with West's point that socialist forms 'have in fact endured in a purportedly postsocialist era' (ibid.), I argue that nostalgic imaginings and reinventions of 'traditional Guangzhou cuisine' in the reform era in fact have relied on revolutionary socialist reworkings of traditional food culture, and that this ambiguous ability of 'traditional Guangzhou cuisine' to invoke both socialist and presocialist pasts complicates the notion that nostalgic practices in contemporary China imply *either* a critique of the present condition *or* of the Maoist years, but that also they can imply both.

Culinary Nostalgia in Contemporary Guangzhou

My main research site during fieldwork in Guangzhou in 1999 and 2000 was a multi-storied combined teahouse-restaurant that I call the Glorious China.[2] Here I interacted with cooks, servers and other staff, managers and customers. State-owned and state-run since the 1950s, the Glorious China was originally founded in 1876. It was thus not only one of the oldest eating establishments remaining in the city, but also part of the dwindling state sector of the catering trade. It was, one might say, a 'survival' (cf. Feuchtwang 2002) of both the presocialist and the revolutionary socialist pasts.

During my time in Guangzhou I became increasingly aware of an enormous interest in the city's culinary past, among restaurateurs and cooks, in the media, and among 'ordinary residents'. One of the most conspicuous of the contemporary culinary practices which actively invoked the past was a nostalgia trend that had recently emerged on the city's restaurant scene. Across Guangzhou, a number of restaurants, teahouses and snack shops were busy redecorating their restaurants in what was referred to as the 'antique style' (*fanggu*), and labelling their dishes and snacks as 'traditional' or 'traditional Guangzhou style'. Food and eating were crucial elements in a large market that had emerged for all kinds of nostalgic goods and images. This commodified nostalgia centered on the notion of 'Old Guangzhou' (*Lao Guangzhou*), a term which covers the rapidly changing urban culture from the late nineteenth century through the 1940s and collapses it into a homogenized idea of 'pre-Liberation' or 'traditional' times. The booming nostalgia industry included the publication of a number of popular books celebrating the traditional foodways and other customs of the city and the region (e.g., Deng et al. 1997; Gong 1999; Huang ai dong-xi 1999; Ye 2000; Zhu 1999–2000), and also the highly publicized restorations of a number of late Qing and Republican-era trading streets, including their famous old teahouses (Liu 1999; Guangzhou Shi 2000: passim).

The Guangzhou City Government played an important role in this 'commodified nostalgia' (Robertson 1990; Graburn 1997). It invested tens of millions of yuan (millions of GBP) in the restoration projects, and high-ranking city officials often wrote prefaces or otherwise endorsed the nostalgic books on local customs. In addition to the potential income to be earned on such investments, the selective revival of the 'traditional culture' of 'Old Guangzhou' fitted into the state's self-glorifying historical narrative. In a localized variant of this narrative, promoting the commercial and outward-looking 'traditional culture' of Old Guangzhou supported claims by the political elites of Guangzhou to be returning the city to its true identity, which is represented in the nostalgia literature as being embedded in its historical role as a cosmopolitan centre of international trade (see Friedman 1994).

The commodified nostalgia for 'Old Guangzhou' had a sizable local market. Since the 1980s, several state-owned restaurants with histories dating back to before 1949 had been attracting daily busloads of mostly Cantonese-speaking tourists from Hong Kong and Macau (and in some cases had become, according to catering trade gossip, financially entirely dependent on these tourists). However, the 'antique style' restaurants of the late 1990s, which included both entirely new businesses, pre-1949 'historic' teahouses and restaurants that were refurbishing their dining halls and exteriors and rewriting their menus in a self-consciously neotraditional style, and also new subsidiaries or joint ventures of these older establishments, targeted not so much tourists as local consumers. Moreover, 'antique style' restaurants were appearing at most levels of the city's economically stratified catering industry, from street-side snack shops affordable to most budgets, to expensive restaurants that offered elaborate old-fashioned banquets to well-heeled businessmen and government cadres. Most, however, appeared to be targeting the city's growing middle class, not least middle-class families: these were restaurants, often situated in shopping areas or even inside shopping malls, that provided snacks and dishes at reasonable if not cheap prices by local standards, in settings that were designed not only to remind diners of 'Old Guangzhou', but also to meet growing demands for hygiene and efficient service.

The commodified nostalgia for 'Old Guangzhou' resonated with some of the sentiments expressed by several of my acquaintances in the city, and it might be suggested that restaurateurs and others were capitalizing on a preexisting nostalgic search for local tradition and identity. This search could be seen as a recent and local version of a nostalgia that has been widespread in China since the 1980s. In anthropologists' and other China scholars' accounts of nostalgia for the past in post-Mao China, two types are clearly distinguished. First, there is the nostalgia for the 'traditional culture' of 'pre-Liberation' China. This popular nostalgia for 'tradition' is often regarded by scholars as a reaction against the virulent anti-traditionalism of the revolutionary era, in particular the Cultural Revolution of the 1960s and early 1970s; it is seen as an attempt to restore senses of community or cultural identity in the aftermath of what is described as a 'traumatic' rupture with tradition during the Mao years (Yang 1996; Gillette 2000: 134–45). The second type of nostalgia has been described as an idealization of the revolutionary era itself, sometimes expressed in a renewed celebration of Chairman Mao (Barmé 1996). This nostalgia has been identified with perceptions of growing inequality, uncertainty, political immorality and a lack of accountability in the post-Mao years (Rofel 1999; Feuchtwang 2000, 2002; Yang 2003). Though both nostalgias are seen to have been commodified and thus to some degree blended in the marketplace (Wang 1996; Dutton 1998; Barmé 1999), they are nevertheless treated as having separate root causes – one in the aftermath of revolutionary zeal, the other in the demise of revolutionary ideals.

According to this logic one would understand the recent interest in traditional foodways in Guangzhou as a reaction against the revolutionary excesses of the socialist era. This was certainly present in the accounts I heard. Many people I spoke to stressed that Cantonese cuisine had indeed been 'revived' (huifu) since reforms began, and that this was made possible by the greater freedoms, living standards and material abundance of the last two decades. Often the Mao years were contrasted with the present using culinary metaphors based on the dualism in Chinese food between cooked grain staples (fan), on the one hand, and supplementary dishes of meat and vegetables, on the other (cai) (see Thompson 1994). People would say things like, 'Of course there was no food culture at that time – then we didn't even have enough staples to eat, how could we even think of supplementary dishes?' Yet many of the accounts I heard of 'traditional foods' complicate this story of the Mao years as the opposite of food culture or traditions, and the reform period as allowing for their revival. Let me cite an example from one of the many conversations I had in the Glorious China with 'Uncle Liu', who at the time was in his early seventies. Uncle Liu was a regular morning tea visitor at the teahouse, and was considered by his friends to be something of a food connoisseur. Talking about the 1950s, 1960s and 1970s, he told me:

> During this time, Guangzhou's restaurants 'lost the tradition' [*shichuan*]. When life got better in the 1980s, people thought that anything was good, though it was different for us old people who knew what things had tasted like before Liberation, and before the War of Resistance [against Japan, 1937–45]. The Glorious China still get some things right, like the steamed rice flour rolls [*changfen*], the steamed dumplings [*ganzheng shaomai*] and the beef balls [*niurouwan*], which are minced using two cleavers, not in a mincer. But mostly they have lost the tradition, too. Guangzhou used to have a famous congee, called the 'graduate's congee' [*jidizhou*] … It should have three ingredients: pork tripe [*zhufenchang*], pork liver [*zhugan*] and pork balls [*rouwan*]. Now it is chaotic [*luan*], they will put anything in it: beef slices [*niuroupian*], tripe and pork slices [*roupian*] instead of pork balls. Pork balls are much more civilized [*siwen*], they are like eating tiny dumplings [*shaomai*]. The same with 'riverboat congee' [*tingzaizhou*]. It used to be served off the boats in the canals. Before, it had seven [*sic!*] ingredients: jelly fish, roast duck, egg slivers, deep-fried noodles, fish slices, deep-fried peanuts, ground pepper, fresh coriander and spring onions. Now anything is just mixed together at will.

Uncle Liu was clearly scathing about the revolutionary decades. Yet in this account, it was not simply the case that traditional techniques had been lost during the Mao years, but also that they had not been properly restored during the consumerism of the post-Mao era. According to Uncle Liu, traditional tastes lost during the revolutionary years, far from being revived, had instead degenerated into 'chaotic congee' and 'uncivilized pork slices'. Correct methods had been substituted by a kind of gastronomic free-for-all. Nevertheless, Uncle Liu also implied that the break with the past was not complete – for him the most authentic traditional flavours were to be found in historic, state-run establishments like the Glorious China, although one had to know what to order and what to avoid. In the culinary chaos of the reform years, these older establishments provided at least a degree of order and certainty for self-styled 'Old Guangzhounese' like Uncle Liu. And he himself had morning tea and dimsum in the Glorious China several times a week.[3]

Like Uncle Liu's 'chaotic congee' and 'uncivilized pork slices' – phrases which I think he meant for me to understand as metaphors for wider social conditions – a number of people spoke about culinary confusion in the present in the same breath as social disorder and urban development, and contrasted it with a previous sense of order –not, however, necessarily the pre-Liberation 'order', but more often that of the revolutionary socialist decades. One elderly couple I was introduced to by Uncle Liu took me out for dimsum in the North Garden Restaurant, a large and beautiful establishment in the centre of town which dates back to the 1920s. They stressed that they preferred the older places, and claimed that things had been more straightforward in the 1970s. Then, they told me, each district had its representative restaurants. A person knew which teahouse to go to for which specialty, they pointed out. Now, they concluded, there were too many restaurants and styles and too much confusion – now, the city had grown beyond recognition.

Others I spoke with, especially people in their forties and fifties, focused on a changing moral order, contrasting the present with a time when every delicacy was a treat, when the availability of goods was uncertain and consumption was therefore more meaningful. In many ways this could be understood as part of what Judith Farquhar (2002) has identified as a widespread critique of the excessive nature of post-Mao consumerism, a critique that she argues is very much rooted in the frugal morality of the Mao years. One acquaintance of mine in his forties lamented that the quality of traditional snacks had been deteriorating in recent years. According to him this was because the skills were no longer being properly handed down from master to apprentice. Instead they were hiring in people from the outside. They could get away with this, he claimed, because people no longer cared, especially young people who had become too Westernized. People used to have a very strong 'brand consciousness' (*pinpai yishi*) when it came to eating. Everyone knew which shops or teahouses were the best at making a certain snack, and they were loyal to these places, he argued. I asked him when this brand consciousness was the strongest. He replied:

> When people were the poorest. Then, there were few opportunities to eat out, so everything was regarded more specially. Perhaps what is made now is better, but we have a special feeling for what was made then.

These accounts would suggest that the interest in traditional cuisine should be seen not only as a longing that emerged out of the Mao years, but also (and in some cases primarily) as a response – inflected by the experiences and morality of a more radically socialist time – to the rapid social changes that have been affecting Chinese cities since the early 1980s, including consumerism, globalization, rapid urban growth and rural-urban migration. Unlike some scholarly explanations of post-Mao nostalgia and neotraditionalism, which suggest a sharp division between the 'revolutionary period' and 'traditional culture', in the accounts I heard from people in Guangzhou 'traditional foods' did not stand in any simple opposition or contrast to the Mao years. In order to understand why this was the case, I suggest that it is not enough to interpret contemporary notions of 'traditional Cantonese foods' within the context of recent social changes – we must also take a closer look at the history of Cantonese cuisine itself.

Cantonese Cuisine and 'Old Guangzhou'

In late imperial times, the eating habits of different localities were written about, along with other customs, in the numerous local gazetteers (Cohen 1991: 121). However, only a few regions were recognized as having a distinctive cuisine in late imperial and even Republican (1912–49) times. These cuisines were identified above all by major cities of the region, and were associated not so much with everyday or rural foods but rather with the cooking styles of occupational cooks (Chang 1977: 14; Anderson 1988: 194; Wang 1993: 3). To some extent this is still the case. Although a number of local and subregional differences of 'Guangdong' or 'Cantonese cuisine' (*Yuecai, Guangdongcai*) are widely recognized, still in popular discourse in Guangzhou the cooking of the city, 'Guangzhou cuisine' (*Guangzhoucai*), often overlaps with or is taken to stand for the cuisine of the larger Pearl River Delta area, or even of the whole province of Guangdong, and sometimes also the cooking of Hong Kong and Cantonese speakers abroad and in neighbouring Guangxi. (The English term 'Cantonese cuisine' actually conveys some of this ambiguity quite nicely.) Furthermore, people I spoke to in the city recognized commercial cooking as playing a central role in defining 'their' cuisine: when asked to describe 'Guangzhou cuisine' people would invariably include teahouse fare such as dimsum and street foods like dog hotpot, and often would also mention the specialties of renowned establishments.

The identification of late Qing (1644–1911) and Republican-era Guangzhou with culinary achievements is in itself not simply an invention of postsocialist imaginations. Cantonese cuisine is now almost universally recognized among the 'great regional cuisines' of China, yet this recognition did not come until the Qing (Simoons 1991: 54–55) – and on some accounts not really until the end of that dynasty and during the subsequent Republican era (Gao and Gong 1999: 43). This reputation was encapsulated in the saying, 'For eating, it's Guangzhou' (*shi zai Guangzhou*) – part of a longer ditty on the attributes of famous Chinese cities that was popularized during Republican times (Gong 1999).

The emergence of great Cantonese restaurants and chefs and the eventual recognition of Guangzhou as a 'place for eating' were closely related to the city's role in international trade. Teahouses and restaurants first began to flourish in Guangzhou and the Pearl River Delta during the years of the 'Canton system' (1757–1842), during which time all of China's trade with the West was confined to Guangzhou (Ye 1992). Despite subsequently being overshadowed by Shanghai and Hong Kong, still Guangzhou remained an important and growing trading centre in the late nineteenth and early twentieth centuries, which together with Hong Kong linked the production of silks and other commodities in the towns and villages of southern China with markets in the West and Southeast Asia and north along the China coast (Faure 1989, 1996; Siu 1993: 25; Tsin 1999: 23). The catering trade developed in a context of growing prosperity – especially with the emergence of a large class of elite diners – but also because teahouses and restaurants were crucial to the city's trading economy. Among their other functions, these were sites where businessmen made contacts with business partners, wined and dined officials, conducted business negotiations, signed contracts and celebrated successful deals (Qiong'an 1948; cf. Shao 1998 and Skinner 1964).

At the risk of being guilty of the kind of essentializing implied in the notion of 'Old Guangzhou', let me make some general points about the teahouse and restaurant world of Republican Guangzhou. First, it was diverse and socially divided.[4] By mid-Republican times, a variety of eating places had emerged, offering different consumption styles and prices suited to different occasions and to different sections of the male population. Most restaurants or 'winehouses' (jiulou) catered to a relatively restricted segment of the population, providing set banquets, female entertainers and gambling facilities in secluded spaces for private parties of elite male diners (Wuxing Cihangzhi 1919: juan 4: 2–8; Gao and Gong 1999: 48; Gong 1999: 255). Indeed, many restaurants were indistinguishable from upmarket brothels (Ho 1993: 123–24). Teahouses (jiulou), in contrast to restaurants, served tea and snacks only and were often divided into three categories. 'Tearooms' (chashi) were small, elite institutions, serving freshly steamed dimsum and high-quality teas. The lowest class of teahouse, referred to in the 1930s as 'eight-penny shops' (baliguan) and catering to 'rickshaw pullers and other laborers' (Guangzhou Shizhengfu 1934: 251), merged with the city's numerous noodle stands and snack shops. In the middle was the multi-storied teahouse (chalou), the 'teahouse proper'. In contrast to the closed spaces of the restaurants, the multi-storied teahouses had common dining spaces and were affordable to most men in the city. However, the spaces were socially divided by storey, with the upper spaces in the teahouse serving the choicest teas and the daintiest snacks, and the ground floor serving cheap tea and simple snacks to laboring men (Huang 1936: 9–10; Blofeld 1985: 57–58). In the 1930s a growing number of combined teahouse-restaurants emerged, providing both banquets in secluded spaces and tea and snacks in open dining halls (Guangzhou Shizhengfu 1934: 250; Gao and Gong 1999: 49–53). These combined establishments proved extremely competitive, and became the norm by the late 1940s (Liao 1948: 49).

Second, competition was rife. Establishments competed with one another in terms of ambiance and facilities, in terms of the quality and variety of teas but above all in terms of foods. Competition reached almost unbelievable proportions. In the 1920s and 1930s, for example, a number of teahouses claimed to provide what they called 'weekly dimsum' (*xingqi meidian*), which involved offering at least twelve new varieties each week, six sweet and six savoury, and using different colours, shapes and sizes from the previous week's innovations (Gao and Gong 1999: 126–127).

Third, it was an outward-looking, 'globalized', commercial cuisine. Competing chefs were able to draw upon a large number of sources of inspiration and imported goods from both near and far. Guangzhou's role as a hub of international and intranational trade not only generated the economic prosperity and activities necessary to support a large catering industry but also helped to shape tastes in particular ways. Traders from the surrounding region set up snack shops in the city. Chefs in the grand teahouses often appropriated these regional snacks, and claimed to refine them in the process – serving them up in smaller portions, with more subtle flavours for their genteel customers (Gong 1999: 251–54). Cantonese sojourners in Shanghai, Southeast Asia and elsewhere arrived in Guangzhou with new ideas. The father of one of my cook-friends, for example, had worked as a chef in Hanoi for many years and introduced a number of Vietnamese specialties to the restaurant he opened in Guangzhou on his return in the 1940s. Hong Kong and Macau were also crucial as mediators of foreign influence, not least because from the 1920s many of the grandest Guangzhou establishments had begun to set up subsidiaries in these cities (Gao and Gong 1999: 45, 50). Chefs would often spend some time working in each city, picking up new ideas as they went along (Gao and Gong 1999: 50, 196–97). It is important to point out that even though Hong Kong had by Republican times become economically more powerful than Guangzhou, until the communist victory Guangzhou was still recognized in Hong Kong and Macau as being the foremost culinary centre in the region (Anonymous 1931; Faure 1996: 14; Tang 1999). In the 1920s and 1930s there were also a large number of Western-style restaurants in the city; dining on Western cuisine was all the rage among the elites and middle classes of the time (Ho 1991). After 1945 these were joined by a growing number of non-Cantonese regional Chinese restaurants, among which reports from the time single out the Sichuan-style restaurants as being the most popular (Cheng 1947: 73; Liao 1948: 49).

As Michael Tsin (2000) has discussed, Guangzhou experienced a massive spatial transformation during the early decades of the twentieth century. These changes included the emergence of new shopping areas, which eroded the earlier strict division between the walled, official city and the trading areas, primarily in the Western Suburb (Xiguan), located outside the walls (which came down around 1920). The new shopping areas boasted high-rise department stores and other 'modern' consumption venues, and a distinction was emerging between these 'modern' areas of the city and the more 'traditional' markets in Xiguan. Restaurants may have played a certain part in this division: not only did the department stores have Western-, Beijing- and Shanghai-style restaurants (advertisement in Wuxing Cihangshi 1919), but Cantonese restaurants attempting to attract people with new styles of signboards and novel installations like escalators tended to be located in the 'modern' shopping areas, while a number of establishments in Xiguan instead boasted of their long histories or were built in the style of classical Chinese gardens (advertisements in Liao 1948). Yet there is nothing in the sources I have seen from the Republican era or the 1950s which would suggest that the Cantonese food being served in these places was divided along similar lines, or indeed that any distinction was made at the time between 'traditional' and 'modern' or 'new-style' Cantonese cuisine. Such distinctions emerged, instead, as a consequence of the socialist project, to which I now turn.

Of Revolution and Restaurants

In rethinking the relationship between socialism and the material culture of food I do not want to suggest that Guangzhou's post-Liberation restaurant scene was remotely as lively as it had been in the 1920s and 1930s or in the late 1940s, or that 'traditional food culture' did not come under attack during the 'Mao' years. In 1948 there were an estimated 12,000 eating places (not including street stalls) (Qiong'an 1948: 24), in a city with a population of around one-and-a-half million people. By 1958, only 2,800 teahouses, restaurants, snack shops and sweet shops remained (Gao and Gong 1999: 60). And in 1972, there were a mere 512 operating public eating establishments (ibid.: 61), catering to a city of more than two million inhabitants.[5] Although efforts were made throughout the 1970s to increase the number of eating venues in Guangzhou, it was only in the 1980s that the industry regained anything like the kind of vibrancy it had enjoyed in the late 1940s.

The decline of the catering industry was evident not only in the dwindling number of establishments but also in the quality of their goods and services. State policies and economic conditions left relatively little space for teahouses and restaurants in 'socialist' Guangzhou. In the political economy of Chinese socialism, the cities were to produce industrial goods for the countryside, while the latter was to produce foodstuffs to support the urban workers (Whyte and Parish 1984). Trading cities like Guangzhou – often referred to as 'bourgeois cities of consumption' – were to be transformed into industrial centres through investments in heavy industry, with little investment going into infrastructure and retailing – including catering (Whyte and Parish 1984: 33–34; Schintz 1989: 314–16; Yusuf and Wu 1997: 113–14). The urban population was divided into work units, miniature societies which redistributed consumer goods and provided subsidized prepared food in canteens (Croll 1983: 231–34; Lü and Perry 1997). From the mid-1950s and into the 1980s there were frequent food shortages – most severe, of course, during the three-year nationwide famine that followed in the wake of the Great Leap Forward (1958–60), during which an estimated 30 million people lost their lives (Smil 2004: 72–92). Food rationing was the norm throughout this period, introduced not only as a response to shortages, but also as part of policies aimed at levelling differences in income and consumption and assuring basic nutrition for all city dwellers (Smil 1995: 280). Indeed, the production-led and increasingly collectivized and centrally planned economy was underpinned by a political morality that emphasized frugality, public service and a levelling of differences (Stockman 2000: 52–53). Consumption was to be restricted to necessities, and the consumption and leisure activities that were deemed acceptable were to be organized through the work units, ideally in collective forms that carried explicit political messages (Wang 1995).

The collectivization and politicization of consumption and leisure reached high points during the radical campaigns of the Great Leap Forward and the Cultural Revolution. At the start of the Great Leap Forward in 1958, 2.65 million communal dining halls were established in the new rural people's communes in an attempt to level differences in consumption and completely shift household preparation and eating to the collective (Chang and Wen 1997). The often free communal dining halls, argue Chang and Wen, 'encouraged and caused a tremendous wastage of food' (1997: 20). They rapidly exhausted local food stocks and 'severely damaged commune members' incentives to work' (ibid.: 21). Indeed, Chang and Wen maintain that the waste of food in the communal dining halls was a major cause of the Great Leap famine (Chang and Wen 1997), while Smil describes it as one of many contributing factors (Smil 2004: 85–86). Many of the radical policies of the failed Great Leap Forward were phased out in the early 1960s, and the remaining rural dining halls were abandoned by 1962 as the economic initiative of individual households was stressed in an attempt to improve production and distribution (Chang and Wen 1997: 7, 22). Communal dining halls were also set up in Guangzhou in the new urban people's communes. These urban communes were established in 1960 in a short-lived attempt to make the city self-sufficient in food, as the supply of agricultural goods from the countryside had become increasingly inadequate (Vogel 1980: 264–68).[6]

During the Cultural Revolution, beginning in 1966, teahouses and restaurants came under fierce attack as symbols of the 'old society' and 'bourgeois consumerism', and acquaintances in Guangzhou had numerous examples of the effects of these attacks. At the table service was abolished in all eating places. Under the slogan 'destroy the four olds' (old culture, old beliefs, old customs, old habits), red guards ravaged the teahouses' and restaurants' characteristic signboards with gold characters on black lacquer and destroyed the lavish décor and antique furniture that many of them still sported at that time. Several restaurants simply closed their doors, as a number of master chefs were criticized and abused and in many cases sent down to the countryside. Many chefs quit their jobs and not all returned after the end of the campaigns. The remaining establishments revolutionized their names and menus. Names at the time included 'Facing the Sun Teahouse' (*Xiang yang chalou*) – the 'sun' being Chairman Mao – 'The East is Rising Teahouse' (*Dong sheng chalou*) and 'The Present Exceeds the Past Restaurant' (*Jin sheng xi fandian*) – the latter, I was told, became something of a joke in the 1970s, since the Chinese characters could also be read the other way round: 'The Past Exceeds the Present'. A number of dishes and snacks were simply taken out of production, particularly festival foods, which were regarded as being 'wasteful' or 'feudal' in the context of the state's attempts to introduce a simplified, socialist ritual calendar (see Whyte and Parish 1984: 317–19).

All this begs the question: why did any teahouses and restaurants remain at all? By the 1970s, many of the remaining establishments had become supplements to the system of work units, as some work units did not have their own canteens and many could not provide housing near the workplace – people would often stop by the teahouse for a quick snack on their way to work. As 'supplementary canteens', teahouse opening hours were very limited and were meshed with the virtually uniform urban work schedule, allowing little time or space for leisurely interaction. In addition to these supplementary canteens, a number of upscale dining spaces, often hidden from public view in the back rooms or top floors in the city's restaurants and teahouses, were reserved for official banquets for high-level cadres and foreign delegations (see Hsu and Hsu 1977: 93). Despite the rhetoric of frugality and egalitarianism, political elites clearly enjoyed a level of food consumption denied to ordinary citizens (Davis 2000: 14).

Celebrating Cantonese Cuisine:
The Socialist Culinary Project

So far I have described the survival of some public culinary establishments as exceptions that did not quite fit into the ideals of Chinese socialism, as necessary supplements to the work unit canteens or as semi-secret concessions to the new system of political privileges. I would now like to complicate this picture and suggest that there were also productive attempts to transform Cantonese cuisine, rather than simply negative actions aimed at suppressing or destroying it.

The Maoist project has been described as a 'utopian' one that involved the constant deferral of needs and desires onto the future. The frugality and virulent anti-consumerism I described earlier were indicative of this emphasis on individual sacrifices in the present for future rewards for all. By contrast, the reforms have been seen as a shift to gratifying needs in the here and now (Croll 1994). The two may be seen as being linked, as post-Mao consumerism has for example been described as the fulfillment of Mao's hedonistic promises for the future (Ci 1994). But throughout the revolutionary period itself policies shifted and messages were mixed. During the Great Leap Forward it was announced that communism had already arrived, and millions of rural inhabitants were urged to eat as much as they could in the free communal dining halls. At other times, for example in the aftermath of the Great Leap famine, there was a willingness to liberalize marketing systems in order to improve the supply and circulation of agricultural products (Skinner 1985). There was a tension embedded in the revolutionary project, between frugality and sacrifice for the future on the one hand and immediate gratification on the other.

This tension was tied up in crucial ways to the legitimacy of the party itself. The Chinese revolution has been described as a 'hungry revolution' (Yue 1999). In Mao's writing and in the literature promoted by the party, the language of socialism was translated into a familiar language of food, drawing on the fear and experiences of hunger in particular among the rural population but also on millennia of Chinese political philosophy, in which the legitimacy of the ruler ultimately relied on his ability to 'nourish the people' (*yangmin*) (Solomon 1975: 33–53; Yue 1999: 150–83; cf. Knechtes 1986). This was not only about quantity, of being able to fill one's belly with grain staples. Rather, the surest sign that people were indeed being fed was their ability to eat a variety of tasty foods. Not being able to 'eat well' (Farquhar 2002) implied that staples were insufficient. Much revolutionary policy and rhetoric may, as mentioned earlier, have emphasized the importance of *fan* in comparison to the reform-era emphasis on *cai*, yet the two are complementary, not dichotomous. If the economy of socialist China was production-led, then consumption and distribution were still crucial to its political legitimacy. If luxury consumption was frowned upon, good eating was nevertheless a sure sign the socialist system was working. In this sense, the aesthetics of food could not simply be deleted from the socialist ethics of frugality (Yue 1999; Farquhar 2002).

Seen from this perspective it becomes less surprising that the commitment to 'nourishing the people' and the aversion to distinctions of taste were not only expressed through virulent anti-consumerism and extreme frugality. At certain times and in certain contexts during the revolutionary years, local and national culinary traditions were loudly celebrated and avidly researched. Instead of simply abolishing cooking and eating practices that were seen to have been monopolized by the elites, the emphasis was on 'massification' (*dazhonghua*). 'Massifying' (Cantonese) cuisine meant above all three things: the reformation (*gaige*) of restaurant cooking in line with socialist ethics; the division of delicacies more equally among the population; and the improvement of cooking practices in work unit canteens and homes. Arguably, one can speak of a socialist 'culinary project'. My discussion here of this project focuses on Guangzhou, yet it is important to bear in mind that it was paralleled in cities across China and was to some extent coordinated at the central level. This culinary project reached its high point during the mid-1950s, although traces can be found in the 1960s and 1970s and, as I will argue later, in the reform era itself. The massification of cuisine was pursued through the reorganization of restaurants, the arrangement of culinary expositions and the production of cookery books.

Rearranging Restaurants

The nationalization of the catering trade was a necessary condition underpinning the socialist culinary project. Nationalization was at first a gradual process. In the first few years after 1949, privately owned restaurants and teahouses were tolerated. Beginning in 1953, however, restaurateurs were coerced through various means into accepting joint ownership and management with the state. In 1956, this process was speeded up under the national slogan of 'socialist transformation', and during that year the majority of catering and other businesses in the city had accepted the new system of 'joint public-private management' (*gong-si heying*) (Vogel 1980: 156–73). In 1958, however, the state took over the entire ownership and management of these businesses. Virtually all of the city's restaurants, teahouses, snack shops and bakeries now came under the centralized authority of the Guangzhou Food and Drink Service Company (*Guangzhou Yinshi Fuwu Gongsi*), a municipal-level company which subsequently (in the early 1970s) was divided into district-level subunits.

Increasingly coordinated from above, restaurant facilities were rearranged in significant ways during the mid-1950s and early 1960s. Despite the overall decrease in the number of eating establishments, during this period many of the old teahouse-restaurants were expanded and several new ones were built. In fact, many of the most famous 'historical' establishments[7] in the 1990s had actually been insignificant in the Republican era. These included the Panxi Restaurant, a small establishment when it was founded in 1947, but following refurbishments allegedly China's largest 'garden-style' restaurant. The nearby Guangzhou Restaurant first opened in 1939 and had been a well-known elite restaurant in the 1940s. Its dining spaces were refurbished and considerably enlarged (Gao and Gong 1999: 198).

Not only the dining spaces but also the food was to be improved in these establishments. Famous chefs from restaurants around the city were allocated to certain prioritized establishments. For example, the famous dimsum master, Luo Kun, was allocated to the Panxi in 1960 to take charge of the dimsum section, and many of his former apprentices were still working there in the 1990s (Li 1996: 12–13). In the Guangzhou Restaurant, several famous chefs were hired in the 1950s. These included Wu Luan, who had been known as Guangzhou's 'shark's fin king' in the 1930s, and the head dimsum chef, Xuan Dongling, who had once been known as one of the 'four heavenly kings' of the teahouses of Guangzhou, Hong Kong and Macau. Xuan had actually settled in Hong Kong in the 1940s but returned to take over the Guangzhou's dimsum section in 1956. Xuan was also to preside over the new 'research centre' for cuisine that was being set up at the restaurant (Liu 1999: 25–29).

It is important to emphasize that although many of these 'improved' dining spaces – and in some cases entire restaurants – had, by the 1970s, been reserved for high-level cadres and foreign visitors, their original transformation in the 1950s was carried out under the slogan of 'massification'. Restaurants like the Guangzhou and the Panxi offered not only tea and snacks but also set meals and banquets at prices that were meant to be affordable to ordinary residents. Perhaps even more telling were the so-called 'mass' or 'communal' dining halls (*dazhonghua shitang* or *gonggong shitang*) that were being built in the city already several years *before* the Great Leap Forward. Beginning in 1954, a central public dining hall was established in each of what were then called the West, East, Central and North Districts of the city (Gao and Gong 1999: 60), and several smaller public dining halls were set up in the South District. According to elderly acquaintances in the Guangzhou catering trade, the idea behind these public dining halls was in some ways quite different from those experimented with during the Great Leap Forward, although at least the West District Dining Hall was in fact used as such a canteen in 1960. The idea, I was told, was to create the ultimate Cantonese restaurants by moving some of the best cooks from a number of the previously privately run restaurants into a single, joint–or state-run establishment. As with the Panxi and the Guangzhou, the food was meant to be affordable to ordinary residents who were to be able to enjoy the quintessence of Guangzhou cuisine – and what that quintessence was, was defined in part during the food exposition of 1956.

Displaying Cantonese Cuisine: The Food Fair of 1956

The 'Guangzhou City Exposition of Famous Dishes and Delicate Dimsum' (*Guangzhou Shi mingcai meidian zhanlanhui*) was held between 1 June and 1 July 1956. It received massive coverage in the local daily newspapers. Its timing was very significant, coinciding with the acceleration that year of the 'socialist transformation' of urban commerce and industry. It was a celebration of Cantonese cuisine, of the new culinary regime and of the still relatively new party-state behind it. It was also a display of the state's commitments to levelling gustatory distinctions by democratizing access to local delicacies. The Exposition announced socialism in a culinary language in which socialist ethics and the aesthetics of eating were complementary rather than opposed.

The Exposition centred on an exhibition hall in the ground floor of the Guangzhou Restaurant, where the exhibits were presided over by chefs and dimsum chefs from around the city. It also included six 'tasting shops' (*changshidian*), located in famous teahouses in the Central and West districts of the city. All members of the public were encouraged to visit the tasting stations and the exhibition hall. Tickets to the latter, though free of charge, were limited in number and had to be organized in advance. The events were to be interactive, and people were encouraged not only to 'look', but also to 'taste, criticize and instruct' (Anonymous 1956a).

During the month-long exhibition, a total of around 230,000 visits were made to the exhibition hall in the Guangzhou Restaurant and a further 480,000 visits were recorded at the tasting shops. In addition to these, delegations arrived from cities across Guangdong and China, and from several foreign countries. In conjunction with the Exposition, over a hundred meetings, lectures and classes on Cantonese cuisine were held for cooks working in Guangzhou's restaurants and canteens, and for visiting delegations (Dai 1956).

Knowledge about Cantonese restaurant cuisine was spread to the 'masses' through the exhibitions and also in a number of feature newspaper articles. For example, in an interview conducted at the exhibition with the renowned dimsum master, Lu Zhen, the reader is informed not only of the number of different dimsum currently available in Guangzhou – over 600 according to Lu – but also how these are categorized by cooks. Moreover, Lu gives detailed instructions on how to prepare one of his own specialties, 'egg-fried sticky rice wrap' (Lu 1956). Other articles, including a column entitled 'For eating, it's Guangzhou', provided histories and recipes of the specialities of famous chefs working in the city's restaurants and mass dining halls – quite revolutionary considering that prior to nationalization these recipes would have been cornerstones of the chefs' occupational capital.

The newspaper reports all emphasize that it was the people, and in particular occupational cooks, who were the true agents behind the development of Cantonese cuisine. By contrast, the influence of the elites of the 'old society' is downplayed. In a recipe for 'The Grand Historian's Frog' (*Taishi tianji*), the journalist writes that it was created in the Qing Dynasty in the private kitchen of a certain Jiang Xia, who 'crowned it with the title of his own office in order to display his understanding of the art of cooking, when in fact it was the creation of his household chef' (Yan Dui 1956).

The 1956 Exposition was meant to spread the word about Cantonese cuisine and improve cooking standards in restaurants, canteens and homes. It was also permeated with the ambition to define and quantify Cantonese cuisine and delineate its boundaries with other culinary styles. The main exhibition hall was named the 'Guangdong food hall', and included mostly Guangzhou delicacies, but also examples of Chaozhou style and East River cooking – the two other acknowledged schools in the province, here represented as 'sub-schools' of Cantonese cuisine. A smaller section, called the 'regional food hall', did not exhibit many items but did give visitors the opportunity to compare and contrast different schools. Journalists discussing the exhibitions compared what they described as the 'heavy', 'rich' and 'hearty' non-Cantonese Chinese food to the 'light', 'dainty' and 'refined' cuisine of Guangdong. They further established that the exhibits reflected the fact that Cantonese cuisine was 'equally appreciative of high and low' (Anonymous 1956b).

In total, over 600 dishes and 138 dimsum were put on display (Anonymous 1956a; Lu 1956). In conjunction with the Exposition a count was made of the number of different dishes and dimsum provided at that time by the city's catering industry: a total of 5,457 dishes and 825 dimsum were enumerated (Gao and Gong 1999: 6). One report from the exhibition tells us that a Guangdong recipe book was in the process of being compiled, and that the draft was already three inches thick (Anonymous 1956b).

Collecting Culinary Knowledge: The National Cookbook Projects

The text referred to in the report mentioned above was probably a draft version of the Guangdong sections of the *Cookbook of China's Famous Dishes* (Di'er 1959), a twelve-volume collection of regional recipes published between 1957 and 1965. This collection is, to my knowledge, China's first-ever expressly national cookbook. It is one of two national cookbook projects carried out during the revolutionary years. The second one, *The China Cookbook,* was also written in twelve volumes. It was begun in 1976 and completed in 1981. Both cookbooks explicitly attempt to inscribe the representative dishes of each of the nation's regional cuisines. The two volumes dedicated to Guangdong in the earlier project were published in 1959; the single Guangdong volume in *The China Cookbook* was published in 1976.

Recipes for both cookbooks were collected from urban restaurant chefs through the network of nationalized restaurants. In the Guangdong cookbooks, as in the 1956 Exposition, the emphasis is on Guangzhou-style dishes. Although there is some space for the categories of Chaozhou and East River (Hakka) cuisine –the two most widely recognized 'sub-cuisines' of the province apart from Guangzhou cuisine – yet, like the Guangzhou-style dishes, these are also represented by restaurants in the provincial capital. The cookbooks are also expressly written for members of the official catering trade and for other occupational cooks employed by work unit canteens. (The earlier *Cookbook of China's Famous Dishes* is a so-called *neibu* publication, i.e. for 'internal' circulation only.) Many of the recipes are house specialities of Guangzhou's teahouses and restaurants, most of which date back to the Republican years. Going one step further even than the Exposition and the newspaper articles, once jealously guarded recipes were now to be reproducible in innumerable canteens and restaurants. In theory, famous recipes were divorced from their inventors and the specific restaurants with which they were associated. Recipes and methods became widely shared among restaurants in the state catering trade – a cooperation that in fact had not entirely disappeared around 2000, even between establishments that were now alleged competitors. In practice, however, the alienation of recipes from their creators did not prevent distinctions being made by customers and caterers. Thus, although the recipe for the Glorious China's cold cut chicken (*baiqieji*), their 'house chicken' (*zhaopaiji*), had been brought in from another state-run restaurant (the Qingping) in the 1970s and was, according to cooks at the Glorious China, identical in terms of methods and ingredients to that served in several state-run establishments, still each establishment gave it a different name, and while the Qingping *was* still famous among Guangzhou diners in the late 1990s for its chicken, the Glorious China was not.

Although written for occupational cooks, as with the 1956 Exposition the cookbooks explicitly aimed at spreading the experience of Cantonese restaurant cuisine beyond the narrow confines of elite diners of the 'old society'. I quote from the preface of the 1976 cookbook:

> [I]n the evil old society, most exquisite delicacies were monopolized by the exploitative ruling classes. They were made in order to serve the corrupt life of pleasure led by the bureaucrats, compradors, landlords and capitalists. The great numbers of working people who had created these dishes, by contrast, were never able to enjoy them. (Zhongguo 1976: 2)

In addition to spreading cuisine to the masses, the cookbooks also aimed to 'reform' it according to socialist standards, by removing wasteful dishes and promoting instead the 'refinement of coarse ingredients' (*culiao jingzhi*), and by changing the names of dishes that had carried a sense of 'feudalism, capitalism and revisionism' (*feng-zi-xiu*) (Zhongguo 1976: 3). For example, 'The County Magistrate's Chicken' (*taiyeji*) had allegedly been created at the end of the Qing by a magistrate-turned-merchant. In the 1930s it became a famous dish at the Six Kingdoms' Restaurant (*Liuguo Fandian*). The name was now considered 'feudal' and was changed to 'Tea-fragrance chicken' (*chaxiangji*).

Although 'reformed' (*gaige*) and 'massified' (*dazhonghua*) for more frugal and allegedly more egalitarian socialist times, in terms of named dishes there was very little innovation in the Guangzhou volumes of the national cookbooks. The 1976 cookbook does include a few post-Liberation innovations, but as in the 1959 cookbook, the majority of recipes were of well-known specialities from famous Republican-era houses. In 1976, almost thirty years after the communist victory, Cantonese cuisine as it was represented in the national cookbook appeared virtually unchanged.

To the best of my knowledge, prior to the food exposition and cookbook projects of the revolutionary years no coordinated attempts had been made to quantify Cantonese cuisine or delineate its representative dishes. Regional cookbooks of any kind were rare in late imperial times, and the twenty-odd Republican-era cookbooks I have seen, published between the 1910s and the 1940s, were typically concerned with spreading 'modern' notions of hygiene and nutrition to the growing number of urban, middle-class housewives.[8] None was explicitly aimed at representing the cuisine of a region or the nation. The interest in inscribing and delimiting the boundaries of Cantonese restaurant cooking – which as I have suggested remains the core of both scholarly and popular Chinese concepts of cuisine – is staggering, not just in the context of socialist ethics of frugality but also when we consider the central state's deep hostility to expressions of 'localism' during the revolutionary years (Vogel 1980: 91–124, 211–16, 357–68).

Opportunities to savour first-rate cuisine in Guangzhou's famous houses were limited in the revolutionary years. Yet knowledge about professional cooking techniques and the specialities of local restaurants were spread to cooks in households and work unit canteens via the food exposition, newspaper articles and cookery books. Other Guangzhou residents accessed this knowledge through eating experiences at home, in work unit canteens, and in the teahouses and restaurants. Local and 'national' cuisines – once cleansed of their feudal and capitalist traits – clearly had a place in the new, socialist Chinese culture, even if that place was at times an uneasy one.

Yet despite claims of reforming Cantonese cuisine, cookbooks and restaurant and teahouse menus on the whole reproduced pre-Liberation flavours. There were a number of reasons for this. First, with no competition between the now centrally planned establishments, recurrent critiques of 'bourgeois consumerism', no large class of affluent diners able to demand novel tastes, and an unreliable access to raw materials there was little incentive or wherewithal to innovate.

Second, it had to do with the relative isolation of Guangzhou. In sharp contrast to Qing and Republican times, the new industrialized Guangzhou was no longer a major hub of domestic and international trade. Although links with the outside were never entirely severed, still the city became increasingly isolated from the outside world (Guldin 1992; Chan 1995: 48–49). This was exacerbated by China's strict household registration policies which made it difficult for Guangzhou residents to move elsewhere, and which divided the urban and rural populations, making it nearly impossible to migrate to the cites (e.g., Cheng and Selden 1994). This relative isolation was reflected in the make-up of Guangzhou's restaurant trade, which in contrast to the 1940s was now almost exclusively Cantonese. By the early 1980s there were only a handful of restaurants offering either non-Chinese foods or Chinese cuisine from outside the province. The strict demarcation of regional cuisines was thus reflected in the organization of urban space itself, a fact reflected in comments by informants, referred to above, to the effect that eating in the city had previously been a much more orderly affair.

Third, it was widely held among cooks and caterers that Guangzhou's restaurants were completely dominated by the old Republican-era masters and the disciples they trained in the 1950s and 1960s. It was really only in the mid-1980s that this began to change. Hong Kong chefs were brought into the new hotel restaurants and some of the state restaurants. They trained up a new generation of elite chefs in what became called 'Hong Kong style' or 'New school' Cantonese cuisine. The impact of Hong Kong on Guangzhou dining was to be massive throughout the 1980s and 1990s.

In the early 1980s, however, a small number of state-run teahouses, dining halls and snack shops had been serving up virtually identical dishes and snacks for thirty years. A limited number of cooking practices and specialities from the 1940s had become firmly established as typical Guangzhou-style Cantonese cuisine. And although countless traditions were seen to have been lost through lack of resources and political campaigns, by the early 1980s Guangzhou had preserved a number of practices and tastes that had changed quite dramatically in Hong Kong and elsewhere in the Cantonese-speaking world (Tam 1997; Cheung 2002).

The culinary project of the Maoist years, I argue, profoundly influenced the ways in which Cantonese cuisine has subsequently been conceptualized, practiced and deployed in post-Mao Guangzhou. To restaurant-goers in the 1980s and 1990s, cooking styles and menus of the Mao years appeared 'traditional' by contrast with the many novelties introduced during the reform years, particularly those from Hong Kong. Moreover, in contrast with the ever-changing menus and outside influences of the 1980s, the 'traditional delicacies' had become part of a common stock of knowledge shared by Guangzhou residents. Also, in contrast to the largely anonymous chefs in the new restaurants, 'old masters' like Luo Kun and Xuan Dongling were still household names in the late 1990s. And despite claims that we heard earlier from Uncle Liu and others concerning the culinary ignorance of the younger generation, I found that this kind of knowledge was to a surprising degree shared by people of different age groups. Friends of mine who had grown up in the city and were now in their mid-20s often had very specific ideas concerning the best old places to get specific traditional snacks. While they did not on the whole express the kind of nostalgia for a 'socialist morality' that I found among people of their parents' generation, many did lament the loss of what they termed 'traditional' delicacies of the city. Knowledge of the best old restaurants, teahouses and snack shops appeared to me at the time to distinguish native Guangzhounese from recent migrants and other outsiders more than it did generations.

Why did the relatively young – astute consumers of globalized fast food, regional Chinese delicacies and other novelties in the city – share this knowledge and these sentiments with their elders?[9] In the 1990s traditional tastes were still being carried forward through the post-Mao era in the state-run 'remnants' of the socialist culinary project, including the Glorious China. More importantly, in the 1980s the state-run catering trade could hardly be described as a 'survival of socialism' (Feuchtwang 2002). Then, the socialist culinary project was very much alive. True, the new private entrepreneurs were crucial to the reinvigoration of the city's catering industry, an industry that boomed in the 1980s and 1990s not only because of the rise of living standards and real incomes, but also because the socialist work unit was becoming gradually less central to urban life – work units were no longer obliged to provide collective forms of recreation, and a growing number of people were leaving the security of their work units (at first willingly, then in the 1990s increasingly because of layoffs), meeting in restaurants, teahouses and other consumption venues to create new social and business ties (Naughton 1997; Dutton 1998: 214–21; Davis 2000). By 1987 Guangzhou boasted nearly 8,000 registered venues, the majority of them run as individual or family businesses (Guangzhou Nianjian 1988: 250). Yet until the 1990s the state was reluctant to let the state restaurants go bankrupt and supported them through a variety of means, while at the same time promoting internal management reforms. According to official statistics, the state sector stood for 52.1 per cent of the catering industry's total turnover for 1989 (Guangzhou Nianjian 1990: 268).

In the 1980s the Guangzhou government still appeared to take very seriously its revolutionary commitments to levelling Cantonese cuisine by distributing delicacies to ordinary people. The continued economic significance of the state industry enabled the city and district governments to present their culinary institutions as the legitimate heirs and administrators of historical heritage of Cantonese cooking. Food fairs, cooking competitions and other culinary events were organized throughout the decade by the city and district governments. The tone was set in the 1983 city-wide food exposition. It was the first of its kind since the 1956 event and was closely modelled on the latter. The emphasis was once again on 'massification' and combining high, middle and low, as stressed by the erstwhile mayor of Guangzhou in his opening speech. Public participation, study and criticism were similarly crucial. This was to be about managing, carrying forward and improving the common culinary heritage. The greatest difference from 1956 was the stated goal of 'restoring Guangzhou's culinary reputation' – of reviving the saying, 'For eating, it's Guangzhou'. In this spirit, many so-called 'traditional' dishes and dimsum that had been lost during the Cultural Revolution were now being restored for the first time for the Exposition, subsequently to be reinstated onto regular menus. In addition, many hundreds of innovations were introduced. Out of this combination of dishes and dimsum labelled 'traditional' (*chuantong*) and 'newly created' (*chuangxin*) – categories that did not exist in descriptions of the 1956 Exposition – a 'menu for the 1980s', as it was put in one report, was to be created.[10]

The early reforms had not simply enabled the revival of Republican-era golden years, but the revival of a culinary project from the mid-1950s and early 1960s that had been suppressed during the Cultural Revolution. If the 1956 Exposition was a celebration of 'socialist transformation' then the 1983 event signified that the promises of socialism, though thwarted by the excesses of the Cultural Revolution, were now to be fulfilled, albeit by different means.

This was altogether different from the neotraditionalism and the commodified 'Old Guangzhou' nostalgia of the turn of the twenty-first century. By now the state restaurants had indeed become survivals. Most of the state restaurants that had thrived in the 1980s had either gone out of business, been contracted out to private entrepreneurs or been sold to private companies. Many grand old teahouses – which being important meeting places had tended to be situated at street junctions and other prominent sites – had been razed to the ground to make way for the building of roads, underground stations and other projects, and did not have the funds to set up business elsewhere. The (now annual) Guangzhou food exposition was no longer organized by the catering trade but by the city's tourist board and held at an outdoor sports stadium. Rather than seeking to educate the public, it was now almost entirely concerned with advertising and on-the-spot sales. One strategy that the remaining state-run restaurants were increasingly turning to, however, was catering to the nostalgia trend, by refurbishing their dining spaces and redoing their menus in a 'traditional style'. This was evident also in the 1999 food exposition, in which the state-run restaurants rented their own, traditionalized section called the 'Street for historic restaurants' (*Laozihao yi tiao jie*).

For many Guangzhounese, as I suggested earlier, these 'socialist survivals' enjoyed a degree of legitimacy to sell 'traditional' foods. The remaining state restaurants were widely seen to have a greater continuity with the past than their rivals, a perception that several managers were trying to use to their advantage. Nevertheless, most of the Guangzhou diners I knew were discerning eaters and ultimately judged an eating place on the taste, look and texture of the foods. Some managers in the state catering trade were aware of their customers' discriminating palates. For instance, one manager of a new state-owned snack shop which sold famous, traditional delicacies that were associated with several different historic teahouses (all of which had belonged to the same company until the late 1990s and were still loosely associated in 2000) insisted that each snack be prepared only by cooks who had worked in the establishment where the snack had first been created – people could tell the difference, he held, between 'famous snacks' (*ming xiaoshi*) that had been prepared according to the correct methods, and those that had not.

Conclusions

One effect of what I have described as the 'socialist culinary project' of the mid-1950s to the 1980s – the nationalization of the catering trade followed by the production of national and regional cookbooks, the rearrangement of urban restaurants and the organization of food expositions – was the mutual definition, 'creation' even, of a 'national' cuisine and the 'regional' cuisines of which it was comprised, similar to the process discussed by Appadurai (1988) in the context of cookbook writing in post-Independence India. Notions of both regional and 'pan-Chinese' (or at least 'Han') eating and cooking practices of course predated the socialist culinary project – a situation very different from Appadurai's account of pre-Independence India. Yet prior to the 1950s the distinguishing features of these cuisines were ill-defined and their boundaries were not policed by a centralized culinary authority, let alone mapped onto the cityscape of provincial capitals such as Guangzhou. The culinary project was clearly part of a wider attempt at 'nation building'.[11]

Nation building in post-Liberation China went well beyond the production of national symbols and identities; it cannot be separated from the more radical transformative ambitions of revolutionary socialism. Boris Groys (1992) has argued that Stalinism in the Soviet Union was a 'politico-aesthetic' project, which took over from the Russian avant-garde of the 1920s not only the notion that art should be committed to transforming the world, but also the idea that 'communism be built as a total work of art that would organize life itself according to a unitary plan' (1992: 23).[12] In China, too, revolutionary socialism was very much an aesthetic project, committed to remoulding every aspect of the daily lives of the people. The attempts to transform everyday cooking and eating habits – to level differences and restore delicacies to the working masses, to make public the secret practices of chefs, to map out a national geography of taste and enforce its boundaries, in short, to harmonize the chaotic culinary life of the 'old society' according to a unitary design – were all part of this politico-aesthetic project.

Nonetheless, the artistic directors of China's communism could not start entirely from scratch, but had to work with many preexisting (as well as imported) forms, materials, methods and symbols – even during the most radical phases of the Cultural Revolution (cf. Feuchtwang 2000). While cooks and diners in nearby Hong Kong and in the Cantonese diaspora, lacking a unitary plan (if surely not self-styled regulators of taste), continued to develop flavours and cooking styles by adopting 'outside' techniques and ingredients, Guangzhou's state-run caterers were left, for reasons discussed earlier, to rehash leftovers from the 1940s. The reforms of the 1980s that at first created unprecedented economic possibilities to realize the artistic designs of culinary socialism also – by opening up the catering trade to competition – proved its undoing. As the limited but more organized eating of the revolutionary socialist and early reform periods gave way to greater abundance, diversity and disorder, goods associated with the unified aesthetics and frugality of socialism acquired a degree of attraction as remnants of what now at times appeared to many to have been a more ordered mode of existence. This attraction is similar to that, discussed by Humphrey (1995), which many post-Soviet Muscovites continued to feel for state-produced goods, defined as 'ours' in opposition to 'foreign' goods. But in sharp contrast to the strong 'Soviet' (Humphrey 1995) or 'Russian' (Caldwell 2002) identity of 'our' goods in 1990s Moscow, the goods produced by the Guangzhou state catering trade had become intimately bound up with the construction of *local* tastes and identifications.[13]

Finally, it would be wrong to set up a simple opposition between 'traditional' cuisine and its nostalgic consumers on the one hand and new-style Cantonese cuisine with its novelty-seeking consumers on the other. On the contrary, many of the most nostalgic eaters I knew, including Uncle Liu, would go out of their way to try out a new style of cooking or a new restaurant. Nor do we have to think of either 'traditional' or 'new-style' cuisine as being more 'authentically' Cantonese than the other – my acquaintances in Guangzhou did not. Whereas Guangzhou's commercial cuisine of the Republican era had been competitive, cosmopolitan and innovative, the 'traditional' cuisine of the 1970s was centralized, closed and static. It had become fixed as a tradition and (at least subsequently) valued as such by many people in the city. Yet for many Guangzhounese I spoke to, including cooks and diners, it was the changeability, openness and competitiveness, and the ability to draw on new foodstuffs and new sources of inspiration, which characterized the spirit of Cantonese cooking. The same people who on some occasions would wax lyrical on the texture of the Glorious China's steamed rice flour rolls (*bula changfen*), rolled by hand in a cloth according to 'traditional methods' (*chuantong zuofa*) and stuffed with beef that had been minced 'using two cleavers, not in a mincer', would in other contexts make scathing remarks about the same state-owned restaurant's inability to keep up with the latest tastes. Both notions of what Cantonese cuisine in Guangzhou were or could be were part of the present, post-reform condition, yet neither version is really comprehensible without some sense of the complex twentieth-century history of that cuisine. Tracing this history requires that we rethink the relationship between the prerevolutionary, Maoist, and reform 'periods', and that we explore the complex ways in which revolutionary socialism continues to inform what is now locally understood as 'traditional culture'.

Acknowledgements

An earlier version of this paper was presented on 19 January 2005 at the Department of Anthropology Seminar, School of Oriental and African Studies, convened by Harry G. West on the theme of 'Enduring Socialism: Neoliberalism and Neotraditionalism in the Postsocialist Era'. I would like to thank all those at the seminar who commented on my paper. In the paper I draw heavily on my Ph.D. thesis (Klein 2004), and I would like to thank my supervisors, Kevin Latham and Stuart Thompson, and my examiners, Chris Pinney and Harriet Evans, for their many helpful suggestions.

Notes

1. Despite the widespread practice of dividing China's recent history into three discrete eras or periods, the precise dates of these eras may differ somewhat depending on the terms used, and also with different authors. Thus, for example, the 'reform' era is usually said to have begun with Deng Xiaoping's proclamation of economic reforms in 1978, while the 'post-Mao' years must, strictly speaking, begin with the Chairman's death in 1976. The 'revolutionary' or 'Maoist' years sometimes cover the entire period between the communist victory in 1949 to the beginning of reforms in 1978, while others use these terms to refer to the period between the acceleration of 'socialist transformation' in 1956 until the end of the Cultural Revolution in 1976 (sometimes earlier). In mainland China, the standard division is pre- and post-Liberation in 1949 and pre- and post- 'Reform and opening up' in 1978. Yet despite some differences in terms and usages, the tripartite structure is itself nearly universal, and is perhaps all the more powerful for the ambiguities of the terms, which allow users to collapse different times and events into homogeneous 'eras' or into markers of transition from one era to another.
2. This paper is based on ten months of ethnographic fieldwork and archival research between August 1999 and August 2000 on the restaurant and teahouse world of Guangzhou, and an additional five weeks of library work in Shanghai in 2001. Fieldwork was conducted in both Mandarin and Cantonese; in this paper I have transliterated all Chinese words in Mandarin. My research was partially supported by a Research Studentship from the Economic and Social Research Council (ESRC).
3. My point here is to highlight Liu's seamless and subtle shift from a critique of the Mao years to a critique of the present, all in the idiom of a 'loss of food traditions'. This rather literal reading of Uncle Liu's recollections of course downplays complex and important issues concerning the relationship between taste, memory and historical consciousness (Sutton 2001; Ben-Ze'ev 2004), which because of space constraints I am unable to expand on in this piece.
4. See Shao (1998) on social divisions in the teahouse world of late Qing and early Republican Nantong County, Jiangsu Province.
5. These figures are comparable to those for Beijing provided by Whyte and Parish (1984). In 1949, Beijing had fewer than two million inhabitants and over 10,000 eating places. By 1979 there were 656 restaurants for a population of nearly five million (ibid.: 98).
6. It is not entirely clear to me why and when the communal dining halls were abandoned in Guangzhou. Vogel writes: 'The end of urban communes was

never officially announced, but the mess halls faded away within months and the planting of crops gradually dropped off as the food shortage eased' (1980: 268).

7. Referred to as *laozihao*, literally 'old names in business', a term used throughout the Peoples Republic of China to denote existing businesses that have histories predating 1949.

8. Typical titles include *The Household Cookbook* (Li 1917), *Food and Health* (Zhang 1936) and *Useful Dietetics* (Gong and Zhou 1939).

9. This is not to suggest that their attitudes towards and knowledge of food did not in other ways distinguish them from their parents and grandparents – for a fascinating account of the 'generation gap at the table' in urban and rural Chinese contexts see Guo (2000).

10. My description of the 1983 exposition is based on the following reports: Anonymous (1983a, 1983b), Liang et al. (1983), Zhang and Situ (1983) and Zhong (1983).

11. As John Campbell pointed out in his comments on my seminar paper. For an interesting piece on nationbuilding and the policing of regional Chinese cuisines in a Singaporean context, see Chua and Rajah (2001).

12. Thanks to Chris Pinney for drawing my attention to the work of Groys.

13. According to Caldwell (2002) the discourse of 'our' foods in 1990s Moscow was bound up with Russian nationalism rather than with nostalgia for Soviet times per se. However, she also argues that the value attributed to 'our' (Russian) foods needs be understood against the background of the more homogeneous consumption of the Soviet era, when access to imported commodities was extremely limited. Patico (2003) argues that for people in late 1990s St Petersburg the attraction of 'our' foods over imports was not so much a matter of patriotism, but had above all to do with suspicions concerning the origins of these products and the routes they had taken to St Petersburg's markets. Not unlike my acquaintances in Guangzhou, for Patico's St Petersburg interlocutors order and reliability were often associated with foods that were produced by well-known, *local* businesses. Thanks to an anonymous reviewer for drawing my attention to these works.

References

Anderson, E.N. 1988. *The Food of China*. New Haven: Yale University Press.

Anonymous 1931. 'Shi zai Guangzhou. Si da jiulou' (For eating, it's Guangzhou. The four great restaurants), *Huaxing* (The China Star), 28 March.

———. 1956a. 'Guangzhou Shi mingcai meidian zhanlanhui qishi' (Announcement for Guangzhou City Exposition of Famous Dishes and Delicate Dimsum), *Nanfang ribao* (Southern Daily), 30 May.

———. 1956b. 'Fang mingchu, kan zhanlanhui, lüetan Guangzhoucai' (An interview with famous chefs, a visit to the exhibition, some words on Guangzhou cuisine), *Nanfang ribao* (Southern Daily), 3 June.

———. 1983a. 'Rang "shi zai Guangzhou" meiyu fayang guangda' (Enhance Guangzhou's culinary reputation), *Guangzhou ribao* (Guangzhou Daily), 23 October.

————. 1983b. *Guangzhou mingcai meidian pingbi zhanlan tekan* (Special Publication on the Guangzhou Famous Dishes and Delicate Dimsum Competition and Exhibition). Official brochure, October.

Appadurai, A. 1988. 'How to Make a National Cuisine: Cookbooks in Contemporary India', *Comparative Studies in Society and History* 30: 3–24.

Barmé, G. 1996. *Shades of Mao: The Posthumous Cult of the Great Leader.* Armonk, NY: M.E. Sharpe.

————. 1999. *In the Red: On Contemporary Chinese Culture.* New York: Columbia University Press.

Ben-Ze'ev, E. 2004. 'The Politics of Taste and Smell: Palestinian Rites of Return', in M.E. Lien and B. Nerlich (eds), *The Politics of Food.* Oxford: Berg.

Blofeld, J. 1985. *The Chinese Art of Tea.* London: George Allen & Unwin.

Caldwell, M.L. 2002. 'The Taste of Nationalism: Food Politics in Postsocialist Moscow', *Ethnos* 67 (3): 295–19.

Chan, M.K. 1995. 'All in the Family: the Hong Kong-Guangdong link in Historical Perspective', in R.Y.W. Kwok and A.Y. So (eds), *The Hong Kong–Guangdong Link: Partnership in Flux.* Armonk, NY: M.E. Sharpe.

Chang, Gene Hsin and Guanzhong James Wen. 1997. 'Communal Dining and the Chinese Famine of 1958–1961', *Economic Development and Cultural Change* 46(1): 1–34.

Chang, K.C. 1977. 'Introduction', in K.C. Chang (ed.), *Food in Chinese Culture: Anthropological and Historical Perspectives.* New Haven: Yale University Press.

Cheng, Tiejun and M. Selden. 1994. 'The Origins and Consequences of China's Hukou System', *The China Quarterly* 139: 644–88.

Cheng Zhizheng. 1947. 'Chi zai Guangzhou' (Eating in Guangzhou), *Lüxing zazhi* (The China Traveler) 21(7): 72–73.

Cheung, Sidney C.H. 2002. 'Food and Cuisine in a Changing Society: Hong Kong', in D.Y.H. Wu and Tan Chee-beng (eds), *The Globalization of Chinese Food.* Richmond, Surrey: Curzon.

Chua Beng Huat and A. Rajah. 2001. 'Hybridity, ethnicity and food in Singapore', in D.Y.H. Wu and Tan Chee-beng (eds), *Changing Chinese Foodways in Asia.* Richmond, Surrey: Curzon.

Ci, Jiwei. 1994. *Dialectic of the Chinese Revolution: From Utopianism to Hedonism.* Stanford: Stanford University Press.

Cohen, M.L. 1991. 'Being Chinese: the Peripheralization of Traditional Identity', *Daedalus* 120(2): 113–34.

Cohen, P.A. 1988. 'The Post-Mao Reforms in Historical Perspective', *The Journal of Asian Studies* 47(3): 518–40.

Croll, E. 1983. *The Family Rice Bowl: Food and the Domestic Economy in China.* London: Zed Press.

————. 1994. *From Heaven to Earth: Images and Experiences of Development in China.* London: Routledge.

Dai Zhen. 1956. 'Guangzhou Shi mingcai meidian zhanlanhui zuori bimu' (Guangzhou City Exposition of Famous Dishes and Delicate Dimsum concluded yesterday), *Guangzhou ribao* (Guangzhou Daily), 2 July.

Davis, D.S. 2000. 'Introduction: a Revolution in Consumption', in D.S. Davis (ed.), *The Consumer Revolution in Urban China.* Berkeley: University of California Press.

Deng Duanben et al. 1997. *Lingnan zhanggu* (Anecdotes from Lingnan), 2 vols. Guangzhou: Guangdong Lüyou Chubanshe.

Di'er Shangyebu Yinshiye Guanliju (ed.). 1959. *Zhongguo mingcaipu* (Cookbook of China's Famous Dishes), Vols. 4 and 5. Beijing: Beijing shipin gongye chubanshe.

Dutton, M. 1998. *Streetlife China*. Cambridge: Cambridge University Press.

Farquhar, J. 2002. *Appetites: Food and Sex in Postsocialist China*. Durham, NC: Duke University Press.

Faure, D. 1989. *The Rural Economy of Pre-Liberation China*. Hong Kong: Oxford University Press.

———. 1996. 'History and Culture', in B. Hook (ed.), *Guangdong: China's Promised Land*. Hong Kong: Oxford University Press.

Feuchtwang, S. 2000. 'Religion as Resistance', in E.J. Perry and M. Selden (eds), *Chinese Society: Change, Conflict and Resistance*. London and New York: Routledge, pp. 161–77.

———. 2002. 'Remnants of Revolution in China', in C.M. Hann (ed.), *Postsocialism: Ideals, Ideologies and Practices in Eurasia*. London: Routledge, pp. 196–13.

Friedman, E. 1994. 'Reconstructing China's National Identity: A Southern Alternative to Mao Era Anti-imperialism', *The Journal of Asian Studies* 53 (1): 67–91.

Gao Xuzheng and Gong Bohong. 1999. *Guangzhou meishi* (Guangzhou's Cuisine). Guangzhou: Guangdong Sheng ditu chubanshe.

Gillette, M.B. 2000. *Between Mecca and Beijing: Modernization and Consumption among Urban Chinese Muslims*. Stanford: Stanford University Press.

Gong Bohong. 1999. *Guangfu wenhua yuanliu* (Origins and Development of Cantonese Culture). Guangzhou: Guangdong gaodeng jiaoyu chubanshe.

Gong Lanzhen and Zhou Xuan. 1939. *Shiyong yinshixue* (Useful Dietetics). Changsha: Shangwu yinshuguan.

Graburn, N.H.H. 1997. 'Tourism and Cultural Development in East Asia and Oceania', in Shinji Yamashita et al. (eds), *Tourism and Cultural Development in Asia and Oceania*. Bangi: Penerbit Universiti Kebangsaan Malaysia.

Groys, B. 1992. *The Total Art of Stalinism: Avant-Garde, Aesthetic Dictatorship, and Beyond*, trans. Charles Rougle. Princeton: Princeton University Press.

Guangzhou Nianjian Bianzuan Weiyuanhui (ed.). 1988. *Guangzhou Nianjian* (Guangzhou Yearbook). Guangzhou: Guangzhou nianjian chubanshe.

———. (ed.). 1990. *Guangzhou Nianjian* (Guangzhou Yearbook). Guangzhou: Guangzhou nianjian chubanshe.

Guangzhou Shi Lishi Wenhua Mingcheng Baohu Weiyuanhui (ed.). 2000. *Guangzhou mingcheng cidian* (Dictionary of the Famous City of Guangzhou). Guangzhou: Guangdong lüyou chubanshe.

Guangzhou Shizhengfu. 1934. *Guangzhou zhinan* (Guangzhou Guide). Guangzhou: Guangzhou Shizhengfu.

Guldin, Gregory Eliyu. 1992. 'Urbanizing the Countryside: Guangzhou, Hong Kong, and the Pearl River Delta', in G.E. Guldin (ed.), *Urbanizing China*. Westport, CT.: Greenwood Press.

Guo Yuhua. 2000. 'Family Relations: the Generation Gap at the Table', in J. Jing (ed.), *Feeding China's Little Emperors: Food, Children, and Social Change*, Stanford: Stanford University Press, pp. 94–113.

74 | Jakob A. Klein

Ho, Virgil Kit-yiu. 1991. 'The Limits of Hatred: Popular Attitudes Towards the
West in Republican Canton', *East Asian History* 2: 87–104.
———. 1993. 'Selling Smiles in Canton: Prostitution in the Early Republic', *East
Asian History* 5: 101–32.
Hsu, Vera and Francis L.K. Hsu. 1977. 'Modern China: North', in K.C. Chang (ed.),
Food in Chinese Culture: Anthropological and Historical Perspectives. New Haven:
Yale University Press.
Huang ai dong-xi. 1999. *Lao Guangzhou: jisheng fanying* (Old Guangzhou: The
Sound of Clogs and the Shadow of Sails). Nanjing: Jiangsu meishu
chubanshe.
Huang Minghui. 1936. *Guangzhou ji Xianggang* (Guangzhou and Hong Kong).
Shanghai: Xin shengming shuju.
Humphrey, C. 1995. 'Creating a Culture of Disillusionment: Consumption in
Moscow, a Chronicle of Changing Times', in D. Miller (ed.), *Worlds Apart:
Modernity Through the Prism of the Local*. London: Routledge, pp. 43–68.
Klein, J.A. 2004. 'Reinventing the Traditional Guangzhou Teahouse: Caterers,
Customers and Cooks in Postsocialist Urban South China', unpublished
Ph.D. thesis, University of London.
Knechtes, D.R. 1986. 'A Literary Feast: Food in Early Chinese Literature', *Journal
of the American Oriental Society* 106(1): 49–63.
Latham, K. 2002. 'Rethinking Chinese Consumption: Social Palliatives and the
Rhetorics of Transition in Postsocialist China', in C.M. Hann (ed.),
Postsocialism: Ideals, Ideologies and Practices in Eurasia. London: Routledge, pp.
217–37.
Li Gong'er. 1917. *Jiating shipu* (The Household Cookbook). Shanghai: Zhonghua
shuju.
Li Xiusong. 1996. 'Xu' (Preface). In *Guangdong dianxin – Luo Kun dianxin zhuanji*
(Guangdong Dimsum: A Special Collection of Luo Kun's Dimsum), 2nd
edition, Guangzhou: Guangdong keji chubanshe.
Liang Li et al. 1983. 'Guangzhou mingcai meidian pingbi zhanlan kaimu' (The
Guangzhou Famous Dishes and Delicate Dimsum Competition and
Exposition Commences), *Guangzhou ribao* (Guangzhou Daily), 23 October.
Liao Shulun (ed.). 1948. *Guangzhou daguan* (Grand Spectacle of Guangzhou).
Guangzhou: Tiannan chubanshe.
Liu Dan. 1999. 'Xiguan fenqing jiri chongxian' (Xiguan atmosphere to return
within days). *Guangzhou ribao* (Guangzhou Daily), 27 September.
Liu Manqiu (ed.). 1999. *Guangzhou diyi jia: Guangzhou Jiujia jian dian liushi zhounian*
(The Foremost House in Guangzhou: The Sixtieth Anniversary of the
Establishment of the Guangzhou Restaurant). Guangzhou: Guangdong
gaodeng jiaoyu chubanshe.
Liu, Xin. 2000. *In One's Own Shadow: An Ethnographic Account of the Condition of
Post-Reform Rural China*. Berkeley: University of California Press.
Lu Huan. 1956. 'Ming dianxinshi tan dianxin' (Famous dimsum chef talks about
dimsum), *Guangzhou ribao* (Guangzhou Daily), 28 June.
Lü Xiaobo and E.J. Perry. 1997. 'Introduction: the Changing Chinese Workplace in
Historical and Comparative Perspective', in X. Lü and E.J. Perry (eds),
*Danwei: The Changing Chinese Workplace in Historical and Comparative
Perspective*. Armonk, NY: M.E. Sharpe.

Naughton, B. 1997. '*Danwei*: the Economic Foundations of a Unique Institution', in X. Lü and E.J. Perry (eds), *Danwei: The Changing Chinese Workplace in Historical and Comparative Perspective*. Armonk, NY: M.E. Sharpe.

Patico, J. 2003. 'Consuming the West but Becoming Third World: Food Imports and the Experience of Russianness', *Anthropology of East Europe Review* 21(1). http://condor.depaul.edu/~rrotenbe/aeer/aeer21_1.html. Accessed on 2 April 2007.

Potter, S.H. and J.M. Potter. 1990. *China's Peasants: The Anthropology of a Revolution*. Cambridge: Cambridge University Press.

Qiong'an. 1948. 'Guangzhou qingdiao' (The feel of Guangzhou) *Lüxing zazhi* (China Traveller) 22(8): 24–25.

Robertson, R. 1990. 'After Nostalgia? Wilful Nostalgia and the Phases of Globalisation', in B.S. Turner (ed.), *Theories of Modernity and Postmodernity*. London: SAGE.

Rofel, L. 1999. *Other Modernities: Gendered Yearnings in China after Socialism*. Berkeley: University of California Press.

Schintz, A. 1989. *Cities in China*. Berlin: Gebrüder Borntraeger.

Shao, Qin. 1998. 'Tempest over teapots: the vilification of teahouse culture in early Republican China', *The Journal of Asian Studies* 57(4): 1009–41.

Simoons, F.J. 1991. *Food in China: A Cultural and Historical Inquiry*. Boca Raton, FL: CRC Press.

Siu, H.F. 1989. 'Recycling Rituals: Politics and Popular Culture in Contemporary Rural China', in P. Link et al. (eds), *Unofficial China: Popular Culture and Thought in the People's Republic*. Boulder: Westview Press.

———. 1993. 'Cultural Identity and the Politics of Difference in South China', *Daedalus* 122(2): 19–43.

Skinner, G.W. 1964. 'Marketing and Social Structure in Rural China', part 1, *The Journal of Asian Studies* 24(1): 3–43.

———. 1985. 'Rural Marketing in China: Repression and Revival', *The China Quarterly* 103: 393–13.

Smil, V. 1995. 'Feeding China', *Current History* 94(593): 280–84.

———. 2004. *China's Past, China's Future: Energy, Food, Environment*. New York and London: RoutledgeCurzon.

Solomon, R.H., with T.W. Huey. 1975. *A Revolution Is Not a Dinner Party: A Feast of Images of the Maoist Transformation of China*. Garden City, NY: Anchor Press.

Stockman, N. 2000. *Understanding Chinese Society*. Cambridge: Polity Press.

Sutton, D.E. 2001. *Remembrance of Repasts: An Anthropology of Food and Memory*. Oxford: Berg.

Tam, S.M. 1997. 'Eating metropolitaneity: Hong Kong Identity in *yumcha*', *The Australian Journal of Anthropology* 8(3): 291–306.

Tang Zhengchang. 1999. 'Yuecai pian' (A note on Cantonese cuisine), in his *Zhongguo yinshi wenhua sanlun* (Essays on Chinese Culinary Culture). Tapei: Taiwan shangwu yinshuguan.

Thompson, S. 1994. 'Riz de Passage? Life Bytes and Alimentary Practices', *China Now* 149: 10–12.

Tsin, M. 1999. *Nation, Governance, and Modernity in China: Canton, 1900–1927*. Stanford: Stanford University Press.

————. 2000. 'Canton Remapped', in J.W. Esherick (ed.), *Remaking the Chinese City: Modernity and National Identity, 1900–1950*, Honolulu: University of Hawai'i Press.

Vogel, E.F. 1980. *Canton under Communism: Programs and Politics in a Provincial Capital, 1949–1968*, 2nd edn. Cambridge, MA: Harvard University Press.

Wang, Shaoguang. 1995. 'The Politics of Private Time: Changing Leisure Patterns in Urban China', in D.S. Davis et al. (eds), *Urban Spaces in Contemporary China: The Potential for Autonomy and Community in Post-Mao China*. Washington D C: Woodrow Wilson Press and Cambridge: Cambridge University Press.

Wang, Jing. 1996. *High Culture Fever: Politics, Aesthetics, and Ideology in Deng's China*. Berkeley: University of California Press.

Wang Xuetai. 1993. *Zhongguo yinshi wenhua* (China's Culinary Culture). Beijing: Zhonghua Shuju.

Whyte, M.K. and W. Parish. 1984. *Urban Life in Contemporary China*. Chicago: University of Chicago Press.

Wuxing Cihangshi. 1919. *Guangzhou zhinan* (Guangzhou Guide). Shanghai: Xinhua shuju.

Yan Dui. 1956. 'Shi zai Guangzhou' (For eating, it's Guangzhou), *Guangzhou ribao* (Guangzhou Daily), 19 June.

Yang, Guobin. 2003. 'China's *zhiqing* Generation: Nostalgia, Identity, and Cultural Resistance in the 1990s', *Modern China* 29(3): 267–96.

Yang, Mayfair (1996. 'Tradition, Travelling Anthropology and the Discourse of Modernity in China', in H.L. Moore (ed.), *The Future of Anthropological Knowledge*. London: Routledge.

Ye Chunsheng. 1992. 'Rong Zhong Xi yu yi lu, ji shi yi yu yi tang – Guangzhou chalou wenhua yanjiu' (Mixing Chinese and Western in one oven, combining food and art under one roof: a study of Guangzhou's teahouse culture), in Shanghai minjian wenyijia xiehui (ed.), *Zhongguo minjian wenhua* (Chinese Folk Culture), Vol. 8. Shanghai: Xuelin chubanshe.

————. 2000. *Guangfu minsu* (Cantonese Folk Customs). Guangzhou: Guangdong renmin chubanshe.

Yue, Gang. 1999. *The Mouth That Begs: Hunger, Cannibalism, and the Politics of Eating in Modern China*. Durham, NC: Duke University Press.

Yusuf, Shahid and Weiping Wu. 1997. *The Dynamics of Urban Growth in Three Chinese Cities*. Oxford: Oxford University Press.

Zhang Lin and Situ Yan. 1983. 'Guangzhou mingcai meidian pingbi zhanlan jieshu' (The Guangzhou Famous Dishes and Delicate Dimsum Competition and Exposition Is Over), *Guangzhou ribao* (Guangzhou Daily), 12 November.

Zhang Siting. 1936. *Yinshi yu jiankang* (Food and Health). Shanghai: Shangwu yinshuguan.

Zhong Huai. 1983. 'Mingcai meidian he dazhong xiaoshi yiqi chulong' (Famous dishes and delicate dimsum appear together with popular snacks), *Yangcheng wanbao* (Yangcheng Evening News), 22 October.

Zhongguo Caipu Bianxiezu (ed.). 1976. *Zhongguo caipu (Guangdong)* (The China Cookbook: Guangdong). S.l.: Zhongguo caizheng jingji chubanshe.

Zhu Xiaodan (gen. ed.). 1999–2000. *Ke'ai de Guangzhou congshu* (Beloved Guangzhou Series), six volumes. Guangzhou: Guangdong Sheng ditu chubanshe.

CHAPTER 3

Searching for the Time of Beautiful Madness: Of Ruins and Revolution in Post-Sandinista Nicaragua

Dennis Rodgers

Now as many times before, I am troubled by my own experience of my feelings, by my anguish simply to be feeling something, my disquiet simply at being here, my nostalgia for something never known.

(F. Pessoa, *The Book of Disquiet*, p. 5).

Introduction

I first travelled to Nicaragua in July 1996, as an anthropology graduate student searching for what the Uruguayan writer Eduardo Galeano has evocatively described as 'the time of beautiful madness' ('*el tiempo de hermosa locura*').[1] The celebrated Sandinista revolution that his expression refers to held sway in Nicaragua between 1979 and 1990, and had been an important contributing factor to the development of my political consciousness as a teenager. Although I was six years too late to experience at firsthand what seemed from afar to have been an exceptional moment of social effervescence and experimentation, unlike the 'revolutionary widows' that Galeano describes so well, moving from one Third World revolution to another, loving them tenderly as they unfold but leaving them when disenchantment sets in,[2] I was determined to uncover the legacy of this particular revolution that had so influenced me, and see at firsthand what changes it had wrought on Nicaraguan society. I consequently went to Nicaragua with a doctoral research project that aimed to investigate the means through which individuals and communities were creatively organizing themselves socially and culturally in order to cope with the economic crisis and insecurity that were widely reported to be characteristic of postrevolutionary Nicaragua at the time, hoping – on the basis of my personal political biases – to find that these would be founded on forms of solidarity and spontaneous cooperation deriving from the period of Sandinista revolutionary rule.

At one level, such expectations were also typical of a certain anthropological tradition, which as Chris Hann (1993: 3) points out has long fixated on collective forms of action and organization, something that is perhaps most obvious in the discipline's repeated attempts to document the communal property ownership structures of so-called 'primitive' societies. At the same time, though, they were by no means necessarily unreasonable expectations to have in view of the wider literature on urban poverty in Latin America, much of which focuses on the emergence of reciprocal forms of solidarity among impoverished individuals and communities (see for example Lomnitz 1977; Lloyd 1979; and González de la Rocha 1994). It quickly became apparent, however, that examples of such cooperative forms of collective organization were few and far between in postrevolutionary Nicaragua, and what I found instead were circumstances overwhelmingly characterized by breakdown, apathy, disillusion and social fragmentation. Deeply imbued with idealism as I was, my response to this 'appalling face of a glimpsed truth' closely echoed Kurtz's vision of human nature – 'The horror! The horror!' – in Joseph Conrad's famous novel *Heart of Darkness* (1990 [1902]: 64–65), which I happened to be reading at the time. Indeed, the conclusion of the doctoral dissertation I subsequently wrote ended on the last line of this same novel, offered as a dismal encapsulation of the postrevolutionary Nicaraguan social reality: 'The offing was barred by a black bank of clouds, and the tranquil waterway leading to the uttermost ends of the earth flowed somber under an overcast sky – seemed to lead into the heart of an immense darkness' (ibid: 72).[3]

Although by and large I still stand by this pessimistic vision of Nicaragua's predicament, both the increasing distance from my initial visit, as well as further experiences that I have acquired over the past decade, have led me to rethink some of the specifics of my interpretation.[4] In particular, a large part of my dissertation was devoted to exploring the disappearance of a sense of identification with revolutionary ideas and practices in the previously staunchly pro-Sandinista *barrio* Luis Fanor Hernández,[5] a poor urban neighbourhood in Managua, the capital city of Nicaragua. I'd concluded that 'Sandinismo is to all intents and practical purposes no more than a rapidly fading memory', but I have come to believe that this assessment needs to be nuanced. I hasten to add, however, in view of the November 2006 reelection of Daniel Ortega as

President of Nicaragua, that I do not think my analysis was wrong in terms of the demise of Sandinismo as a formal political project promising progressive social change. Considering the way the upper echelons of the Sandinista National Liberation Front (Frente Sandinista de Liberación Nacional, or FSLN) have venally integrated themselves into the elite oligarchy that has ruled postrevolutionary Nicaragua since 1990 (see Rocha 2002, 2004; Rodgers 2006b), Ortega's recent victory constitutes little more than a wry illustration of Karl Marx's famous aphorism that 'great historic facts and personages recur twice, ... once as tragedy, and again as farce' (Marx 2004 [1852]: 3). Seen in this light, there can be little doubt that Sandinismo as a political ideology is quite unequivocally 'dead', to borrow from Friedrich Nietzsche (1995 [1954]: 90).

When postrevolutionary Nicaragua is 'brush[ed] against the grain' (Benjamin 1992 [1968]: 248), however, from a perspective that looks beyond formal political praxis as the index for the revolutionary past's permeation of the present, a potentially much more meaningful Sandinista legacy arguably emerges. This is particularly the case when attention is focused on a range of manifestations of everyday contemporary Nicaraguan social life that constitute 'everyday site[s] where differing forms of historical consciousness ... commingle and interact' (Harootunian 2000: 105). These constitute particular forms of institutionalization of Sandinismo in the postrevolutionary context that allow us to grasp its legacy from a perspective that sees the past neither as a 'foreign country' (Hartley 1953: 17),[6] nor as something that 'survives' unchanged into the current epoch, but rather in terms of a 'history of the present', to borrow from Michel Foucault (1977: 31).[7] Such an approach highlights how the past can 'inhabit' the present in ways that challenge 'the received fixedness and inevitability of the present' (Barry, Osborne and Rose 1996: 5), and is a task for which social anthropology has 'a good record' according to Ernest Gellner (1993: xiv), because 'its practitioners are trained to distinguish between the manifest and the latent elements in social institutions. They possess a good technique for locating the latter, and a fine sense for both the interrelatedness of things and the tensions liable to arise between various strands in the life of any one society.'

This chapter begins by outlining key elements of the revolutionary and postrevolutionary periods, for purposes of contextualization, before presenting three loosely interconnected 'vignettes' that draw on research carried out in Nicaragua in 1996–97 and 2002–3. Each vignette depicts a contemporary discourse or practice associable with Sandinismo – albeit often rather tenuously or sometimes even contradictorily – that illustrates the way in which the revolutionary period can be said to have had an enduring legacy in the postrevolutionary era, although in many ways, as the last vignette explicitly emphasizes, what this ultimately highlights is the clear existence of a degree of institutional continuity within

Nicaraguan political culture. Taken together, however, the vignettes provide a sense of the 'uncanny topography' of this political culture that is always 'a precipitate of the past in the present' (Bear 2007: 347).

Sandinista Nicaragua: The Time of Beautiful Madness

As Roger Lancaster has succinctly summarized, 'the Sandinista revolution represented an authentically Nicaraguan attempt to transcend Nicaragua's long history of colonialism, exploitation, underdevelopment, and poverty' (Lancaster 1992: 3). It began in 1961 as a guerrilla insurgency against the Somoza dynastic dictatorship that had been ruling Nicaragua since 1934. Like so many such movements of this period, the FSLN aimed not just at 'national liberation' but also sought a more equitable distribution of wealth and power in society along broadly socialist lines. At the same time, unlike many such movements of the period, the Sandinistas were a highly syncretic group, and constituted a blend of diverse nationalist, Leninist, Guevarist and radical Christian influences, thereby giving them 'a unique revolutionary vision' (Walker 1985: 24). Sandinismo was not a coherent or dogmatic ideology as such, however, but more something of a way of life (see Lancaster 1988: 127–39), encompassing in particular 'new' Christianity's 'belief in the ultimate redemption of the poor and the oppressed' and the 'Marxist philosophical tradition cult of a new socialist man' (Hodges 1986: 288).

The self-avowed ultimate goal of the revolution was 'the total elimination of the exploitation of man by man' (Borge 1985: 38). A 'new Nicaraguan Man' was to be created, and people were to be 'empowered'. As Omar Cabezas, a prominent FSLN leader put it: 'We want[ed] the people to organize for what they want to do ... to work for the things they want. We [sought] to stimulate people to resolve their own problems. We [told] the people that they [could] transform their own reality if they organize[d]' (cited in Selbin 1993: 78). Although Sandinismo clearly stood for a radical social agenda, it did so while explicitly embracing respect for human rights, private property and popular power in a context of political pluralism and competitive elections. When an FSLN-led mass revolution finally overthrew the Somoza dictatorship in July 1979, a multiparty junta was constituted and it immediately began the drafting of a new electoral law, modelled on Western European practices. While all of the Somoza family's property was nationalized, private property was otherwise respected, and key economic portfolios were given to representatives of the private sector (Walker 1997: 9).

Galvanized by the Sandinista discourse, a majority of Nicaraguans mobilized en masse to participate in the post-insurgency reconstruction and development of their country, most dramatically perhaps in the context of the popular education and primary health care campaigns. The 1980 education 'crusade' reduced the national illiteracy rate from 52 per cent to 13 per cent in under a year (CIBC 1983 [1981]: 334–37), for example, while amongst the successes of the grass-roots health campaigns was the inoculation against polio of all children under the age of one in 1983 (Garfield and Williams 1989: 51–52). Other achievements of the new regime included the delivery of electricity and drinking water to a greater proportion of the population than ever before (Vargas 1993), and participatory 'mutual aid' low-income housing construction projects (Vance 1985 and Drewe 1986). Grass-roots organizational activity grew, including in particular the nationwide Comités de Defensa Sandinista (CDS – Sandinista Defence Committees), community action groups aimed at improving local living conditions that implemented wide-ranging local-level social and economic programmes such as the organization of community vigilance, health and vaccination campaigns, food distribution, and voluntary work brigades.

Some of the sweeping changes introduced by the new regime were very clumsily executed, including in particular forcing peasants to establish of cooperatives, introducing price controls on basic foodstuffs, and initially mistrusting and repressing indigenous groups on the country's Caribbean coast, all of which led to a significant degree of internal resistance to the revolution. Within two years the revolution, however, Sandinista Nicaragua faced an especially formidable external enemy in the form of the USA. President Ronald Reagan made his opposition to the Sandinistas clear even before taking office in January 1981, and, once in place, severed all aid programmes, pressured multilateral organizations and international banks to cease lending to Nicaragua, and cut off trade links to the extent of imposing a full embargo in 1985 (Bulmer-Thomas 1991). In November 1981, President Reagan authorized covert operations against Nicaragua, and the CIA began to organize several thousand members of Somoza's ex-National Guard who had escaped to Honduras in July 1979, and these became the nucleus of a counterrevolutionary military force known as *la Contra*,[8] which rapidly began to launch attacks into Nicaragua (Harrisson et al. 1988; Torres Rivas 1991).

Although never a military threat to the regime, the well-funded and trained Contras had a devastating effect on the economy, destroying and disrupting communication and economic infrastructure, and terrorizing and demoralizing the Nicaraguan population. As Lancaster has graphically illustrated, however, there was nevertheless generally a pervasive optimism and support for the revolution amongst most Nicaraguans in the early and mid-1980s (Lancaster 1988). In spite of the war, the first few years of revolutionary rule brought sweeping improvements to the lives of the majority. The 1984 elections saw the

FSLN and its presidential candidate, Daniel Ortega, win 67 per cent of the vote in elections that international observers – the USA excepted – as well as the six losing parties, considered to be 'transparent, free and fair' for the first time in Nicaraguan history (Walker 1997).

In many ways, though, this was the high point of Sandinista rule, as the latter half of the 1980s saw a gradual erosion of popular optimism and support for the revolution. Although the second half of the Sandinista period saw a number of significant social achievements, the war against the Contras and a profound economic crisis created a difficult situation for the revolutionary regime. Official government statistics suggest that the death toll of the Contra war stood at over 30,000, that is to say over 0.9 per cent of the population, or over 38 times the US death toll for the entire Vietnam war (Walker 2003: 56). Compulsory military conscription of youth over the age of sixteen introduced from 1983 onwards also proved extremely demoralizing, and led to widespread resentment and draft dodging. Economically, by 1988 inflation was running at a Latin American record rate of 33,547.6 per cent (Green 1995: 233). Unemployment and poverty rose fivefold between 1985 and 1991 (Arana 1997: 82), and real wages dropped to less than 10 per cent of their 1980 level (Conroy 1990: 17). Basic goods became scarce, malnutrition reappeared, and infant mortality began to rise. Not surprisingly, the Nicaraguan people's revolutionary enthusiasm faded, and on 25 February 1990, weary of war and economic crisis, the Nicaraguan people voted the FSLN and President Ortega out of office. With the threat of renewed Contra funding by the USA and an explicit promise from President Bush to renew commercial exchanges in the case of a FSLN defeat, the Unión Nacional Opositora (UNO – National Opposition Union) – an eclectic coalition of fourteen parties from the right, left and centre of the political spectrum – won 55 per cent of the vote, compared to 41 per cent for the FSLN.[9]

Postrevolutionary Nicaragua: Economic and Ontological Insecurity

Although 1990 is clearly a landmark date in Nicaraguan history, it by no means signaled the end of the country's 'continuous rite of blood' (Rushdie 1987: 18). Indeed, it instead arguably indicated the beginning of a new period of instability and uncertainty, as social conflicts have exploded during the subsequent decade and a half of non-Sandinista rule under Presidents Violeta Barrios de Chamorro (1990–96), Arnold Alemán Lacayo (1997–2001), and Enrique Bolaños Geyer (2002–06). Certainly, Katherine Isbester (1996: 455) contends that Nicaragua has been 'caught in a downward spiral into chaos', while Padre Arnaldo Zenteno, the Jesuit coordinator of the Managua Christian Base Communities, unambiguously identified 'violence', 'political confusion', 'hunger', and 'social breakdown' as the 'new leitmotivs' of post-Sandinista Nicaragua during the course of an interview in July 1996 (see also Lancaster 1992: 293–94; Galeano 1998: 322–24). To a certain extent, this dramatic predicament can be linked to the lingering legacy of revolutionary insurrection and civil war, but Nicaragua's situation is arguably largely the result of more contemporary factors, including a general debility of state institutions – principally due to the application of Washington Consensus prescriptions – corruption and political polarization, declining levels of international aid, the effects of a devastating hurricane in 1998, as well a profound economic crisis.

Indeed, in the latter respect, by almost any measure, Nicaragua is extremely poor. According to the Government of Nicaragua, the country is the second poorest in the Western hemisphere after Haiti on a purchasing power parity basis, and drops to poorest if per capita nominal GDP numbers are used (Government of Nicaragua 2001: 6). The United States Agency for International Development (USAID) suggests that 'approximately 70 per cent of the … population lives in extreme poverty (less than US$1 per day)' (USAID 2006: 124), while the country ranked 112th out of the 177 countries for which UNDP (United Nations Development Programme 2006: 285) calculates its Human Development Index (HDI) in 2006. The combined unemployment and underemployment rate is generally estimated to be 'around 60–65 percent' (USAID 2006, 124). Job creation is scarce in the context of local economic activity that is often illicit and exclusive (Rodgers 2007a), or else ill-adapted to a global political economy in relation to which the Nicaraguan economy is arguably caught in a structural vice of '(mal)development' (Robinson 1998). These macro trends were confirmed at a more micro-level perspective by a survey that I carried out in barrio Luis Fanor Hernández in November 1996, which tallied an open unemployment rate of over 45 per cent, with a further 25 per cent of the economically active population underemployed. There was little evidence of any local economic enterprise in the neighbourhood apart from theft and delinquency, and there were few opportunities outside the barrio for a labour force that tended to be highly unskilled. Most of those who worked did so in the informal sector, and the median monthly income was around 700 córdobas (about US$85 at the time), although many earned less.

Partly as a result of these desperate economic conditions, as well as the massive rise in crime and insecurity since 1990 (Rodgers 2006a), the erosion of the social fabric has reached such dramatic proportions in Nicaragua that it is no exaggeration to talk of society having undergone a veritable process of social fragmentation (see Rodgers 2007b). Certainly, 'each to their own' – *cada uno por su mismo* in the original Spanish – was a phrase repeatedly used by informants in barrio Luis Fanor Hernández, and there was little sign of any collective economic solidarity when I was there in either 1996–97 or 2002–03. Neighbours did not trust neighbours, refusing to share anything or oblige themselves, as Don Sergio dramatically described in an interview in 1997:

'Nobody does anything for anybody anymore, nobody cares if their neighbour is robbed, nobody does anything for the common good. There's a lack of trust, you don't know whether somebody will return you your favours, or whether they won't steal your belongings when your back is turned. Misery kills hope, I tell you! It's the law of the jungle here today... We're eating one another, as they say in the Bible...'

Although an emergent drugs trade created localized networks of capital accumulation that benefited a significant minority in a number of rural communities and urban neighbourhoods from the late 1990s onwards (Dennis 2003; Rodgers 2007a), for the vast majority the situation is stagnant, as Doña Yolanda made clear during an interview in 2002: 'Life is hard in Nicaragua, and you've just got to look out for yourself and try and survive by hook or by crook. It was the same five years ago; nothing has changed, except that we're now five years on, and the future didn't get any better ... '

The intense economic crisis and social atomization of the postrevolutionary period clearly contrast starkly with the past experiences of the pervasive solidarity and collective support that by all accounts existed through much of Nicaragua during the 1980s (Ekern 1987; Higgins and Coen 1992; Lancaster 1988, 1992), has have led to a profound and widespread sense of collective demoralization, as Doña Ursula explained in relation to barrio Luis Fanor Hernández in 1996:

'First the war and now the economic crisis have led to people becoming disillusioned and withdrawing from the community. Daniel [Ortega] lost to Violeta [Chamorro] here in 1990, like in the rest of the country, because people were tired of hardship, but Chamorro hasn't changed anything, things have only got worse – all there is, is more poverty, more violence, more unemployment, more insecurity than before ... We're in a critical situation, people are demoralized, and don't mobilize anymore, and so nothing will change ... *No hay remedio* [There's no solution] ... '

This sense of demoralization can also be linked to the existence of a generalized feeling of what one might call – reversing Anthony Giddens's (1991) classic formulation – 'ontological insecurity' in postrevolutionary Nicaragua, whereby the reference points of social agents are felt to be extremely uncertain, largely as a result of the country's highly surreal and fluctuating post-1990 political topography. Politicians and parties seem to split, reinvent themselves and seek new allies at a bewildering rate in contemporary Nicaragua, generally very blatantly, with little concern for ideology, and contradictorily. The FSLN, for example, is a case in point. Following its defeat in 1990, it attempted to rally supporters with a slogan of 'government from below' (*'gobierno desde abajo'*), but immediately undermined its possibilities for doing so by first negotiating with, and then supporting, the Chamorro government. It subsequently split in two in 1994, with most of the party's deputies joining a new 'renovating' Sandinista party, the Movimiento Renovador Sandinista (MRS – Renovating Sandinista Movement), which then lost heavily in the 1996 elections while the rump 'orthodox' FSLN led by Ortega regained the united FSLN's 1990 share of the vote, which it maintained through to the latest elections in November 2006, despite entering in 1999 into a formal 'pact' of co-governance with Alemán's right-wing Constitutionalist Liberal party (Partido Liberal Constitucionalista – PLC).[10]

Perhaps the most emblematic event that can be linked to the emergence of a sense of 'ontological insecurity' in postrevolutionary Nicaragua is what is widely referred to as the *'piñata'*, however. A *piñata* is a papier-mâché figure that is filled with sweets and is an obligatory feature of Nicaraguan parties, where it is struck with a stick until its contents spill out and a scramble ensues as everybody attempts to grab as many treats as possible. The expression is used to refer to the way the FSLN rather blatantly transferred large amounts of state property to the party leadership ranks during a two-month interregnum period after losing the elections in 1990. Corruption is of course by no means new to Nicaragua; Somoza was notorious for accumulating a personal wealth greater than the average GDP of the country, as well as directly owning over a quarter of the country, for example. Furthermore, people in Nicaragua talk not only of the 'Sandinista piñata', but also of the subsequent privatization-linked 'Conservative piñata' under the Chamorro government (1990–96), and the 'Liberal piñata' under Arnoldo Alemán's presidency, which saw large amounts of international aid siphoned off, particularly in the wake of international mobilization following Hurricane Mitch in 1998.[11] The FSLN leadership's actions were, however, viewed as particularly damning by rank-and-file Sandinistas, partly because most did not benefit materially from the piñata, but also because the party's political authority was based on an 'exemplary authority' linked to notions of sacrifice and egalitarianism, and 'to the extent that the [Sandinista] political elite was perceived as enjoying special privileges, its authority was undermined' (Lancaster 1992: 288–89).

Mutatis Mutandis: Excavating the Legacy of Sandinismo in Postrevolutionary Nicaragua

If Eduardo Galeano's expression 'the time of beautiful madness' is the best shorthand description of Sandinista Nicaragua, the most pithily appropriate depiction of postrevolutionary Nicaragua is perhaps Salman

Rushdie's (1981: 432) term 'sperectomy', which he uses to indicate a 'draining out of hope'. The obvious question that this raises is how anything of the utopian dreams of Sandinismo can remain in 'sperectomied' postrevolutionary Nicaragua. In this regard, a range of contemporary discourses and practices that I observed in barrio Luis Fanor Hernández in 1996–97 and 2002–3 can arguably be directly linked to the transformations wrought by the Sandinista revolution during the decade it held sway over Nicaraguan society, in ways that are less obvious than the forms of (party) political action typically focused upon by studies of the enduring legacies of revolutionary philosophies and practices in Latin America (see for example Selbin 1993). These more everyday manifestations of social life highlight how new discourses can be grafted onto old political practices, while new practices can become imbued with old meanings, and how individuals can oscillate between fluctuating forms of political cognition in order to remember the past and resolve the contradictions of the present. The following subsections attempt to delineate some of these processes, highlighting their contingent and often contradictory natures, as well as their historical roots and evolution through time. They should not necessarily be read as a seamless narrative, but rather as a series of loosely interlinked ethnographic vignettes that together provide a view of what arguably constitutes the continued but tenuous legacy of Sandinismo in postrevolutionary Nicaragua.

Corruption as Socialist Redistribution

The bitterness that many harboured against the Sandinista piñata emerged time and time again in the interviews that I carried out with inhabitants of barrio Luis Fanor Hernández – both Sandinistas and non-Sandinistas – during my stay in 1996–97. Perhaps most vociferous in her criticism was Doña Yolanda, the matriarch of the Gómez household with whom I stay during bouts of fieldwork, and who over the course of a series of interviews between July and October 1996 repeatedly criticized the FSLN hierarchy for having 'stolen the people's property', and provided me with details – both real and imagined – about what certain leaders had stolen, who was living in what expropriated house, and who owned what factory or business, and so on. At the same time, however, Doña Yolanda would simultaneously rather contradictorily also express a strong admiration – indeed almost a personal cult – for Ortega, and always concluded her interviews by informing me that she was going to vote Sandinista in the October elections, that she hoped they would win this time, and how things would be much better under Ortega than they had been under Chamorro. I always found this apparent incongruity difficult to understand, but as I went over my field notes in preparation for my return trip to Nicaragua in February 2002, one episode emerged that suddenly allowed me to see how Doña Yolanda's inconsistency was in fact perfectly reconcilable, and indeed perhaps necessary in order for her to make sense of the cognitive uncertainty of the postrevolutionary context, as she reframed the piñata in terms that assimilated it with a past Sandinista discourse of socialist redistribution.

We had been halfway through an interview one afternoon in early October 1996 when Doña Yolanda suddenly said to me, 'Dennis, since you have pen and paper with you, I want you to write a letter for me.'

'Certainly,' I replied. 'To whom are we writing?'

'We're going to write to the *Comandante* Daniel Ortega,' she answered. 'I need to ask him a favour.'

'You know Ortega?' I asked, somewhat ingenuously.

'A little, yes, I met him when I worked for Colonel Alvaro López. He was the officer in charge of Daniel's security, when he was the President. I was the Colonel's *empleada* [domestic worker] for seven years. Of course, Daniel probably won't remember me, but it doesn't matter, he was the Colonel's chief and he's also a friend of all the little people such as myself, so he has to help me.'

'Why don't you ask the Colonel to help you instead? He's sure to do so, no?'

'*¡Como no!* He helped me get Alberto out of prison when he was caught that time he got drunk and started shooting everybody. But the problem is that the Colonel himself is in prison right now – he was caught smuggling drugs from Corn Island to the mainland last year, and was sentenced to ten years in jail.'

'Aha – I can see how that makes things difficult! OK, a letter to Daniel it is, then. Nothing ventured, nothing gained, I suppose ...'

'Start with the date. We're the seventh, no? Now write: 'Dear *Comandante* Daniel Ortega ... Congratulations for your recent gains in the opinion polls. I am convinced that you will win the coming elections, and that in doing so, it will also be the triumph of all the Nicaraguan common people such as myself.' – How does that seem to you?'

'Good ...'

'OK, now write: 'I used to work for Colonel Alvaro López, when you were President. I was one of the employees who received you every 31st of December, New Year's Eve. I'm sorry to bother you, but I'm writing because I would like you to help me ... My father is seventy years old, and in ill health. He can't work anymore, but he has a car, and I would like you to help me obtain a taxi licence for it, so that I may drive it and earn money to support him.'

'Wait a minute, Doña Yolanda,' I interjected, 'you told me the other day that your father was long dead!'

'Yes, he is. The taxi licence is for Saturnino [Doña Yolanda's boyfriend], but Daniel doesn't have to know that. It sounds better if it's for my ailing father, don't you think?'

'Definitely, but what are you going to do if Daniel does answer your letter, or sends somebody to check your story? It wouldn't look good, would it?'

'*¡Ni mierda! ¡Me vale verga!* [No shit! I couldn't give a fuck!],' she exclaimed. 'The Sandinistas owe me. I was Sandinista right from the beginning, and I didn't even get half a córdoba as a result! The leaders all got their nice houses and acquired businesses when they left power, from the Piñata, so the least they can do now is give me a taxi licence! All the Transport Cooperatives are Sandinista, so all they have to do is ask and they'll give it to them. Saturnino can't afford to buy one, it costs like 4,000 córdobas, and in any case, those sons of whores wouldn't give him one if he could, because he isn't Sandinista! For fuck's sake! They can give *me* the licence, and *I'll* give it him! They owe me, you understand, and I couldn't care less what they think. We're the ones living in poverty, not them. We're the ones who are without work, without resources, not them. We're the ones who were affected by the war, by all the suffering, not them… They always talked about socialism; well then, it would be like socialist redistribution! They owe me, and I want them to give me what they owe me, so let's finish this fucking letter! Write: "My name is Doña Yolanda Aburto. My address is from where the Álvarez cinema used to be, 2 blocks towards the lake, half a block east, house number 14, Barrio Luis Fanor Hernández. I would be very grateful if you helped me, and hope to hear from you soon. From your friend who admires you and cares for you, yours sincerely," and now let me sign!'

Vigilant(e) Socialism

Doña Yolanda's reinterpretation of the notion of socialist redistribution was not the only example of the 'reinvention' of the meanings of Sandinismo in barrio Luis Fanor Hernández. A much more profound mutation could also be observed in what was arguably the most prominent social organization in the neighbourhood, namely the local youth gang, or *pandilla*. Youth gangs are one of the most visible features of the postrevolutionary Nicaraguan social panorama, roaming the streets of the country's cities, and robbing, beating and frequently killing as they engage in delinquency and gang warfare. I have described the dynamics of these gangs in detail elsewhere, highlighting a number of features that can be directly linked to the revolutionary era, including in particular certain gang behaviour patterns such as the barrio Luis Fanor Hernández pandilla's organization into 'companies' and 'commandoes' during gang warfare, which can be directly related to the experience of civil war in

Nicaragua during the 1980s, for example (Rodgers 2006a, 2007c). A much more direct link, however, can be made with Sandinismo in the form of the pandilleros' self-professed 'love' – literally, *'querer'* – for the barrio which they claimed motivated their engaging in semi-ritualized forms of gang warfare with other local gangs. These conflicts were underpinned by a range of prescribed rules, including a cardinal one that involved never attacking local barrio inhabitants but in fact doing everything possible to protect them instead, something gang members claimed derived directly from Sandinismo, of which they often said they were the 'last inheritors'.[12]

Certainly, all the barrio Luis Fanor Hernández pandilleros were discursively staunchly pro-*Sandinista*, and furthermore, many of the practices of pandilleros, both between themselves and with regards to their vigilante-style protection of the wider barrio community, can be conceived as reflecting a strong sense of solidarity and cooperation that is readily associable with Sandinismo. At the same time, however, this clear sense of political affiliation puzzled me, as it was obvious from conversations with the pandilleros that few of them had clear or precise memories of the Sandinista era. Most had been born after the revolution, or just before. Their enthusiasm was obviously for things they had heard about, rather than experienced, such as the literacy or primary health care campaigns of the early 1980s, as well as standing up to the USA and being 'strong', while their lived memories, more often than not very vague, were of the last years of Sandinismo, when the war and the economic crisis were at their peak. Furthermore, the independent development of the pandilleros' political consciousness had occurred in the politically confused context of 1990s Nicaragua, characterized by a generalized disillusionment with much of the revolutionary process in general and the Sandinista party in particular, not least due to the large discrepancy which existed between its rhetoric and its action.

There also existed a telling discrepancy between gang members' political rhetoric and the concrete reality of their political practices. Although the pandilleros all actively volunteered to help with Daniel Ortega's campaign for the October 1996 elections, putting up banners and distributing flyers in the barrio, for example, this support remained exclusively local in scope. None of the pandilleros volunteered to help outside the barrio, even when Ortega's campaign tour stopped at the nearby Roberto Huembes market, where they often spent much of their time. Moreover, nor did any of the pandilleros make any efforts to go to the FSLN's campaign closing rally in downtown Managua on 16 October 1996, despite it being widely publicized, and free buses being laid on by the FSLN in order to boost attendance. In many ways, it seemed as if the pandilleros' Sandinista sympathies were more a result of the historical associations of Sandinismo with the barrio – in-so-far as it had been a hotbed of anti-Somoza activity during the insurrection, as well as the pilot neighbourhood for the new revolutionary government's urban reconstruction plan in the early 1980s – rather than Sandinismo proper, and thus tied in with notions of barrio history.[13]

This was very clearly reflected in an episode that occurred one morning in early October 1996, when I chanced across a pandillero called Julio cleaning up a pre-1990 barrio graffito extolling the virtues of the Juventud Sandinista – 19 de Julio (or JS-19 – the Sandinista youth organization), over which a person or persons unknown had crudely painted in bright red – the colours of Arnoldo Alemán's Constitutionalist Liberal party – the night before. As Julio began to angrily berate the '*Somocista* sons of bitches' who had done this, I initially assumed that this was just one more exemplification of his overt Sandinista sympathies, but it quickly became apparent that he was less angry at this act of vandalism as an attack on Sandinismo than annoyed at what he perceived as the desecration of a historical material manifestation of *local* Sandinismo. 'Those *jodidos* [fuckers] don't respect anything in the barrio, Dennis,' he vociferated, 'nothing! OK, so they don't like the Sandinistas, that's how it is, but this is more than just a Sandinista *pinta* [graffiti], it's a part of the barrio history. *Our* history! It's something that belongs to the community, to all of us; it shows us who we are, where we come from, how the FSLN made us into a community. It shows what the barrio is, and people should therefore respect it, whatever their political opinions.'

It is especially significant that Julio saw the despoiled graffito as a symbol of 'community', and maintained that this was 'what the barrio is'. As I have described above, the barrio was patently not a 'community', but rather caught in a vice of breakdown and social fragmentation, and to this extent, the pandillero 'love' for the barrio can be conceived as an affinity with an ideal of what they felt the barrio should have been, which drew its inspiration from the Sandinista past, and indeed from what was arguably an idealized vision of the past, for although Sandinismo undoubtedly wrought profound changes in the barrio, whether these included making it a 'community' is debatable (see Rodgers 2000; and also Montoya 2007 for a similar experience elsewhere in Nicaragua). In many ways, though, it is less the reality of the image that was important, and more the contrast it obviously constituted in relation to the atomized conditions of social life in contemporary urban Nicaragua. The pandilleros' 'loving the barrio' in such circumstances can be interpreted as an expression of desire for an absent sense of '*communitas*' (Turner 1969) that, real or imagined, was thought to have existed during the Sandinista era.

'Honest Turncoat' vs. 'Dishonest Defector'

A similar search for community organization was also evident in my interactions with Don Sergio, an elderly neighbourhood inhabitant with whom I would go and chat, have a coffee, and share a few cigarettes in the Alcoholics Anonymous locale that he ran every Wednesday afternoon during my stay in 1996–97. Don Sergio would often begin our chats by telling me that he in fact found the whole idea of Alcoholics Anonymous rather preposterous, particularly as he made his living by collecting abandoned empty beer and rum bottles in barrio Luis Fanor Hernández in order to return them to corner stores and collect their deposit, and also because his weekly meetings to educate the neighbourhood drunks about the evils of alcohol rarely involved more than four or five people, at least three-quarters of whom were invariably in a drunken stupor. He would, however, justify his running the local chapter of the organization by saying that it reminded him – in an almost sympathetically magical manner, one might say – of when he had been one of the barrio leaders during the Sandinista period, running the neighbourhood Comité de Defensa Sandinista (CDS – Sandinista Defence Committee). This had especially involved mobilizing and educating people, and there were obvious parallels with his activities for Alcoholics Anonymous, even if he did not believe in their aims in the same way that he believed in Sandinismo, which he would often proclaim was 'in his blood'.

Certainly, Don Sergio repeatedly complained that political organization both in the barrio and in the country more generally had gone 'cold'. He blamed this on the economic situation, arguing that the dramatic impoverishment of the population and spiralling unemployment meant that people could no longer mobilize but had to devote their attention to seeking a means to survive. He would tell me how it had been much better under the Sandinistas, how nobody had starved because the government took care of everybody, and gave everybody who needed them special subsidized food rations. Indeed, during one of our discussions in the run-up to the October 1996 elections, he gleefully poked fun at a short-lived anti-Sandinista electoral advert run by the pro-Liberal Asociación de Confiscados 'Arges Sequeira Mangas' ('Arges Sequeira Mangas' Association of Confiscated Individuals – i.e. those who had had some property nationalized by the Sandinistas during the revolutionary period), which tried to persuade people not to vote for the Sandinista party by reminding them of the rationing that had been in operation in the late 1980s, enumerating what each household had been permitted to buy from state-subsidized shops:

> 'They've really screwed up with this advert, Dennis. I mean, how many of us can afford even half of the rations that we could buy in the 1980s? This has to be the stupidest way of trying to get people to believe that things will

be worse if Daniel [Ortega] gets back into power, people are now going to vote for us because they can see that if the Frente comes to power again at least nobody will starve like they do now.'

But while Sandinismo may well have been in Don Sergio's blood in view of his fiery pro-Sandinista rhetoric – which did not decline in intensity following the Sandinista party's electoral defeat in the October 1996 elections – from a more personal and practical point of view he arguably seemed to undergo what might be described as something of a 'blood-letting' after the elections. During an interview in April 1997, he told me:

'I did a lot for the revolution in this *barrio*. I helped mobilize people, and educated them about Sandinismo, about how it would change our lives for the better. I attended many FSLN workshops where they told us how to do this, how to make them understand what the revolution was about … I still have all the certificates I was awarded for my efforts … The revolution was something special, it worked, and I'm proud of all I did, of my involvement, but the question is what's left of it all now? The war and the crisis destroyed everything, and all that I have left to show for the revolution are these certificates … From the perspective of today, I'd have preferred that the FSLN had given me money for my labours instead, that at least would be useful to me in trying to survive … These certificates are worthless now; there won't be a second coming … *Esa época ya pasó* [that time has passed] …'

Don Sergio's changed perspective troubled me, because of all my informants he was the most steadfast in his commitment to Sandinismo, most optimistic about the future of its legacy in Nicaragua, and proudest of his revolutionary activities. If he was wavering, I thought, what chance was there for those who were already in a state of flux and confusion? I never resolved this quandary, and it contributed greatly to the extremely pessimistic outlook I gradually developed concerning Nicaragua and the legacy of the Sandinista revolution. It therefore came as something of a shock to find out in February 2002 that Don Sergio had not only been a barrio leader during the revolutionary period, but also under Somoza's dictatorship. Don Sergio having died two years previously at the ripe old age of eighty-one years, I made this discovery when sifting through the photographic archives of Don Baltasar, the barrio photographer. Don Baltasar had refused to talk to me in 1996–97, due my habit of taking photos of people and giving them away for free, something that was obviously bad for his business. However, I managed to befriend him during my visit in 2002 by offering to buy several hundred photographs from his archives, which went back to the mid-1960s. As we went through his stock of yellowed negatives and dusty old photographs, I came across a slightly stained, grainy black and white picture of a group of some thirty men, women and children lined up behind a banner proclaiming them to be the 'Comité Liberal Nacionalista Pro-René Castellón E., 1963, barrio Santa Esperanza'.

[© Don Baltasár. NB/This photograph has been modified to protect the anonymity of the neighbourhood.]

The Partido Liberal Nacionalista (PLN – Nationalist Liberal Party), which was banned after the revolution, had been Somoza's political party, with René Castellón a puppet figurehead in the early 1960s; and 'Santa Esperanza' had been the prerevolutionary name of barrio Luis Fanor Hernández. As I examined the photograph more closely, to see if I could identify anybody, I suddenly noticed a familiar figure, and asked Don Baltasar, 'That's not Don Sergio, is it?'

'Yes it is! He looks much younger than when you knew him, doesn't he?'

'But … but what is he doing in this photo? I mean, he was Sandinista, why is he with all these PLN people?'

'You mean you don't know? He was one of the major PLN organizers in the barrio before the revolution! If you ever wanted something from the government, or you had problems, you'd always go to him.'

'What? I can't believe it, this is … it doesn't make sense, he was perhaps the staunchest Sandinista I knew in the barrio …'

'Of course, he had to in order to continue to be a barrio *dirigente* [leader]. I mean, he knew how to get things done because he'd been doing it for so long, and so when he became a Sandinista after the revolution, well, nobody said anything. Don Sergio was always fair and always did his best for everybody, whether you were for Somoza or not, and everybody knew that he would continue the same way, so some of the *muchachos* [Sandinista guerrillas] vouched for him and that was that, he was elected to the CDS and things continued as before.'

'Just like that, then, it didn't bother anybody that he'd been connected to Somoza's regime?'

'No, Don Sergio was honest, he never snitched on anybody, and he didn't get rich from his activities, not like some of the other supposed Sandinistas on the CDS. You've heard about René Mendoza, no, the CDS treasurer who ran away to Miami with all the money collected for Hurricane Juana?'

'Yes, but I thought he was an isolated case.'

'Well, nobody else did anything like that, but plenty of others did all sorts of shit. Ligia Martínez, for example, she was one of the most vocal Sandinistas in the barrio, and had actively supported the muchachos during the insurrection and all that. She was also one of the first to be voted onto the CDS when it was formed, and stayed on it right up until the end of the 1980s, when it fell apart. The thing is that she was always trying to make people fall into her debt, doing favours for them but then saying that they owed her this or that, or had to support her when she did this or whatever. In that way, she was exactly like Mercedes Zúniga and Raquel Herrera, who were Somocista barrio dirigentes like Don Sergio before the revolution, except that Don Sergio was always honest with you, while they'd always try to put you in their debt and then make you do things for them, like go to a Somoza rally or clean and repair roads before a foreign dignitary visited Managua. After the Sandinista defeat, Ligia became like the Frente representative here in the barrio, promising all sorts of things and all, like organizing people to vote Sandinista. Although the Frente lost in 1996, she was elected as a Sandinista councillor to the district municipality, but straight after being elected, she went over to the Liberal party. The Frente expelled her, of course, but they couldn't get her off the council, so the Liberals controlled it.'

'Do you know why she switched party?'

'She says she did it because she knew that the Frente wouldn't win the next time and wanted to be with the winners because it's only with the winners that you can change things in the barrio. If she had been a bit more like Don Sergio, I might believe it, but I think that she did it for the money. She really played the Liberals over her switch, and she now owns like three houses in the barrio, two cars, and has several taxi licences that she rents out to people. Even when she was in the CDS there were rumours of her illegally keeping some of the state-subsidized food for herself, that kind of thing. After switching to the Liberals she didn't even pretend to want to help people, although she said it was because they wouldn't let her. Instead she just spent her time partying and drinking ...'

'Did she get reelected in 2000?'

'No, because not only did she get it wrong and the Liberals lost, but they also didn't let her run as one of their candidates.'

'So what is she doing now?'

'I don't know exactly, she's involved in some kind of organization, what do they call them ... an N-G-O, something to do with women, but knowing her it's probably just another scheme to make money on other people's backs ...'

Conclusion

The 'vignettes' that I have presented in this chapter clearly highlight the extreme fluidity of Nicaraguan politics before, during and after the revolution. Drawing on specific political practices, including the reinterpretation of revolutionary discourse by individuals and groups and the changeable nature of local political figures, I have explored the complex ways different political cultures are linked, focusing particularly on the contemporary legacy of Sandinismo, which in many cases was itself built on continuities from the past. In doing so, the ethnographic material presented highlights how past, present and future are intricately interlinked, and how these backward and forward linkages can account for an enduring resilience of a particular political culture, even if often rather tenuously and almost always somewhat contradictorily. In adopting this particular focus, I have explicitly placed myself within the tradition of Walter Benjamin's iconoclastic historiography. Benjamin considered that true 'historical understanding' could only be 'grasped' through 'the refuse of History' (1999a: 460–61), or, in other words, a focus on everyday social life and 'the tradition of the oppressed' rather than 'universal history' and the logic of hegemony (Benjamin 1992: 248, 254). He was positioning himself against what he called 'vulgar historical naturalism' (Benjamin 1999a: 461), and promoting an alternative approach to historical inquiry that went against linear constructions of experience driven by 'presumptions of continuity and the conviction ... that the present constitutes no problem other than supplying a platform from which the historian can look back on the past' (Harootunian 2000: 15).

Susan Buck-Morss (1989: 57) has suggested that this approach is perhaps best captured in 'the image of the ruin'. Ruins, according to Benjamin (1998: 177–78), were 'highly significant fragment[s]' that in 'the realm of things' were equivalent to 'allegories in the realm of thoughts'. Their allegorical significance derived from the fact that a ruin is 'at once shattered and preserved' (Benjamin 1999b: 329), and therefore bears 'the imprint of the progression of history' (Benjamin 1998: 180), yet at the same time provides 'evidence of counter lives' (Fritzsche 2004: 104), which means that it 'explodes the continuity of universalizing conceptions of history' (Hanssen 1998: 66). The ruin is something from the past, which exists as something different in the present, and will become something else in the future, while inherently embodying alternative potential trajectories. In other words, the contingent temporality of transience that imbues a ruin raises critical questions about 'the givenness of here and now, and the possibility of contrary movement in the flow of history' (Fritzsche 2001; see also Simmel 1959). As Peter Fritzsche (2004: 105) explains: 'The fragmentary nature of the ruin, the accidents and particularities of its broken profile, become the marks of its individuality and therefore autonomy ... Rather than signs of death and decay ... the fragments of the past [are] still partially alive. They possess a sort of half-life, the power to inspire and frighten.'

From this perspective, the significance of a ruin is not that it represents something from the past that casts a light on the present, nor that it is a remnant of the past that is reinterpreted by the present, but rather that it constitutes 'that wherein what has been comes together ... with the now' (Benajmin 1999a: 462), in a dialectical relationship that gives both past and present 'a meaning they did not have originally' (Buck-Morss 1989: 220). Even if this relationship is frequently extremely tenuous and often highly contradictory, as has been shown to be the case of the cultural practices that constitute the legacy of Sandinismo in postrevolutionary Nicaragua, the existence of fragile 'antinomies' and 'counter-working tendencies' is precisely what constitutes the dialectical connection between past and present as a meaningful 'historical frame' (Fritzsche 2004: 104), and allows us to understand 'the possibilities deposited from the past' (Harootunian 2000: 101). Sandinismo from this perspective is viewed less in terms of what it achieved during the 1980s and more through the lens of what these achievements have come to mean in the present, with the 'ruins' that I have 'excavated' a means through which to grasp and understand the legacy of Sandinismo as it is 'actualized in a different configuration' in the present (Harootunian 2000: 20). This is a legacy that can clearly be said to have endured, but has done so in a way that is not only unexpected but also tenuous, embodying the ambiguities of a Nicaraguan present that ultimately does not seem to imply any clear form of progress. At the same time, however, this ambiguity is perhaps also the best means through which to understand Nicaraguan Sandinismo, not only in the present, but also the past, and in particular the way in which, in the words of Sergio Ramírez (1999: 17), noted Nicaraguan author and Vice-president of Nicaragua between 1984 and 1990 (himself citing Charles Dickens' 1859 novel *A Tale of Two Cities*): 'It was the best of times, it was the worst of times, it was the age of wisdom, it was the age of foolishness, it was the epoch of belief, it was the epoch of incredulity, it was the season of Light, it was the season of Darkness, it was the spring of hope, it was the winter of despair.'

Acknowledgments

Early drafts of this paper were presented in seminars at the University of London School of Oriental and African Studies on 22 February 2005, and the University of Liverpool Institute of Latin American Studies on 2 November 2006. I thank participants at both seminars for their comments, including especially Linda Heiden and Harry West. I am also grateful to Laura Bear, Sharad Chari, Eduardo Galeano and Rachel Sieder for encouragement and inspiration, as well as most especially to the Brighton Syndicate for its uniquely constructive deconstruction of my text.

Notes

1. I have been unable to ascertain where Galeano first coined this phrase, but he confirms that he has used it on various occasions (personal communication, 18 February 2005).
2. See Rafael Varela and Eduardo Galeano (1989), 'Entrevista con Eduardo Galeano por Rafael Varela', available online at: http://www.2culturas.com/entrevistas/galeano/index.html (accessed 21 February 2005). The same phenomenon is referred to in a similarly evocative manner in Southern Africa as cases of 'red feet' (personal communication, Harry West, 26 July 2005).
3. See Rodgers (2000). My doctorate was based on one year of fieldwork carried out in Nicaragua between July 1996 and July 1997, ten months of which were spent in a poor neighbourhood in Managua, the capital city. I subsequently revisited this neighbourhood in February–March 2002 and in December 2002–January 2003.
4. I am by no means the only Nicaraguanist anthropologist to have written from a perspective of yearning for revolution and then searching for what was left – in this respect, see the work of Les Field (1999), Florence Babb (2001), and especially Rosario Montoya (2007).
5. This name, as well as those of all the individuals mentioned in this article, is a pseudonym.
6. See also Ingold (1996: 199–248).
7. I am 'borrowing' from rather than 'following' Foucault because my use of the notion of the 'history of the present' is somewhat different from his, which focuses on the way history 'can be written only on the basis of what [is] contemporaneous' (Foucault 1970: 208), while I am concerned with the intermingling of the past and the present.
8. From the Spanish word *'contrarevolución'* ('counterrevolution').
9. Also important in explaining the decline in support for the revolutionary process was that 'the Sandinista [leadership] fail[ed] to guard against bureaucratism and its ensuing privileges, thus driving a wedge between themselves and their supporters … [I]n the context of a revolution whose ethos was aggressively egalitarian, and against the backdrop of dire hardship for the masses, this failure contributed to the failure of Sandinismo as a political project' (Lancaster 1992: 10). Active popular participation declined,

also as a result of accentuated 'verticalist management' by the FSLN, which was mainly a function of the war, as Dora María Téllez, a senior FSLN leader, explained: 'every war, just, unjust, more just, or less just, all presuppose a single command, vertical action, and absolute authority. All wars. There has never been a war that did not presuppose this. ... What philosophy strengthens that idea? The philosophy of command. The philosophy of the defense mission. ... It is objective. Like it or not. It is produced as a natural and also necessary phenomenon in organizing for defense. The authoritarian mentality is strengthened. And that is when the problem begins. ... That is where we made mistakes' (cited in Hoyt 1997: 51–52).

10. A more superficial example of the FSLN's rather surreal mutability was evident during the 2006 election campaign, when the party's traditional '*rojinegro*' ('red and black') flag was replaced by pink banners sporting yellow hearts (this also occurred in 2001), and revolutionary songs gave way to a Spanish version of John Lennon's 'Give peace a chance'.

11. No monetary estimations exist of either the Sandinista or Chamorro piñatas, but Arnoldo Alemán is thought to have personally siphoned off an estimated US$100 million during his five years as president (Transparency International 2004: 13).

12. A parallel can thus conceivably be made with the 'love' that Ernesto 'Che' Guevara saw as the mark of 'the true revolutionary' (Guevara, 1969: 398). He was of course referring to an abstract 'love of the people', while the pandilleros were motivated by a more narrow form of affection grounded at the local barrio level, but the analogy is nevertheless intriguing, particularly considering the strong associations between Sandinismo and the 'Cult of Che' (see Lancaster 1988: 132, 185).

13. This idea is implicitly further supported by the fact that not all Managuan pandillas are pro-Sandinista. The increased political polarization that followed the 1990 elections led to a spatial reorganization of the city's population. New barrios emerged and coalesced, some pro-Sandinista and others pro-Contra – the post-electoral return migration of refugees also greatly contributed to the formation of the latter – and the pandilleros in barrio Enrique Bermúdez (who was the commander of the Contra Northern Military Front during the war in the 1980s) are in no way sympathetic to Sandinismo, for example. Instead, this particular gang's solidary ways are grounded in identification with the historical experiences of the barrio Enrique Bermúdez population's opposition to the Sandinista regime, just as the barrio Luis Fanor Hernández pandilleros can be said to be discursively pro-Sandinista as a result of the neighbourhood's historical association with Sandinismo.

References

Arana, M. 1997. 'General Economic Policy', in T.W. Walker (ed.), *Nicaragua Without Illusions: Regime Transition and Structural Adjustment in the 1990s*. Wilmington: Scholarly Resources Inc.

Babb, F.E. (2001). *After Revolution: Mapping Gender and Cultural Politics in Neoliberal Nicaragua.* Austin: University of Texas Press.

Barry, A., T. Osborne and N. Rose. 1996. 'Introduction', in A. Barry, T. Osborne and N. Rose (eds), *Foucault and Political Reason: Liberalism, Neo-Liberalism and Rationalities of Government.* Chicago: University of Chicago Press.

Bear, L. 2007. *Lines of the Nation: Indian Railway Workers, Bureaucracy, and the Intimate Historical Self.* New York: Columbia University Press.

Benjamin, W. 1992 [1968]. 'Theses on the Philosophy of History', in W. Benjamin, *Illuminations*, translated by H. Zohn and edited by H. Arendt. London: Fontana Press.

———. 1998. *The Origin of German Tragic Drama.* London: Verso.

———. 1999a. 'On the Theory of Knowledge, Theory of Progress', in *The Arcades Project.* Cambridge, MA: The Belknapp Press at Harvard University Press.

———. 1999b. 'J [Baudelaire]', in *The Arcades Project.* Cambridge, MA: The Belknapp Press at Harvard University Press.

Borge, T. 1985. 'This is a Revolution of the Working People', in B. Marcus (ed.), *Nicaragua: The Sandinista People's Revolution –Speeches by Sandinista Leaders.* New York: Pathfinder Press.

Buck-Morss, S. 1989. *The Dialectics of Seeing: Walter Benjamin and the Arcades Project.* Cambridge, MA: MIT Press.

Bulmer-Thomas, V. 1991. 'Nicaragua since 1930', in L. Bethell (ed.), *Central America Since Independence.* Cambridge: Cambridge University Press.

CIBC (Council on Interracial Books for Children). 1983 [1981]. 'Education for Change: A Report on the Nicaraguan Literacy Crusade', in P. Rosset and J. Vandermeer (eds), *The Nicaragua Reader: Documents of a Revolution under Fire.* New York: Grove Press.

Conrad, J. 1990 [1902]. *Heart of Darkness.* Mineola: Dover Publications.

Conroy, M.E. 1990. 'The Political Economy of the 1990 Nicaraguan Elections', *International Journal of Political Economy* 20(3): 5–33.

Dennis, P.A. 2003. 'Cocaine in Miskitu Villages', *Ethnology* XLII(2): 161–72.

Drewe, P. 1986. 'Integrated Upgrading of Marginal Areas in Managua', *Cities* 3(4): 333–49.

Ekern, S. 1987. *Street Power: Culture and Politics in a Nicaraguan Neighbourhood.* Bergen Studies in Social Anthropology No. 40. Bergen: Department of Social Anthropology, University of Bergen.

Field, L. 1999. *The Grimace of Macho Ratón: Artisans, Identity and Nation in Late Twentieth Century Western Nicaragua.* Durham: Duke University Press.

Foucault, M. 1970. *The Order of Things: An Archaeology of Human Sciences.* New York: Pantheon.

———. 1977. *Discipline and Punish: The Birth of the Prison.* New York: Vintage.

Fritzsche, P. 2001. 'Specters of History: On Nostalgia, Exile, and Modernity', *The American Historical Review* 106(5), available online at: http://www.historycooperative.org/journals/ahr/106.5/ah0501001587.html (accessed 28 January 2007).

———. 2004. *Stranded in the Present: Modern Time and the Melancholy of History.* Cambridge: Harvard University Press.

Galeano. E. 1998. *Patas Arriba: La Escuela del Mundo al Revés.* Madrid: Siglo XXI.

Garfield, R. and G. Williams. 1989. *Health and Revolution: The Nicaraguan Experience*. Oxford: Oxfam.

Gellner, E. 1993. 'Foreword', in C.M. Hann (ed.), *Socialism: Ideals, Ideologies, and Local Practice*. ASA Monograph 31, London: Routledge.

Giddens, A. 1991. *Modernity and Self Identity*. Oxford: Polity.

González de la Rocha, M. 1994. *The Resources of Poverty: Women and Survival in a Mexican City*. Oxford: Blackwell.

Government of Nicaragua. 2001. *A Strengthened Growth and Poverty Reduction Strategy*. World Bank, Washington, DC, available online at: http://www.imf.org/external/np/prsp/2001/nic/01/073101.pdf (accessed 28 January 2007).

Green, D. 1995. *Silent Revolution: The Rise of Market Economics in Latin America*. London: Cassell & Latin America Bureau (LAB).

Guevara, E. 1969. *Venceremos: The Speeches and Writings of Che Guevara*, edited by J. Gerassi. New York: Simon and Schuster.

Hann, C.M. 1993. 'Introduction: Socialism and Social Anthropology', in C.M. Hann (ed.), *Socialism: Ideals, Ideologies, and Local Practice*, ASA Monograph 31. London: Routledge.

Hanssen, B. 1998. *Walter Benjamin's Other History: Of Stones, Animals, Human Beings, and Angels*. Berkeley: University of California Press.

Harootunian, H. 2000. *History's Disquiet: Modernity, Cultural Practice, and the Question of Everyday Life*. New York: Columbia University Press.

Harrisson, P., with J.P. Lagnaux and C. Mehrmann. 1988. *Etats-Unis contra Nicaragua*. Geneva: Centre Europe-Tiers Monde (CETIM).

Hartley, L.P. 1953. *The Go-Between*. London: Hamish Hamilton.

Higgins, M.J., and T.L. Coen. 1992. *¡Óigame! ¡Óigame! Struggle and Social Change in a Nicaraguan Urban Community*. Boulder: Westview Press.

Hodges, D.C. 1986. *Intellectual Foundations of the Nicaraguan Revolution*. Austin: University of Texas Press.

Hoyt, K. 1997. *The Many Faces of Sandinista Democracy*. Athens: Ohio University Press.

Ingold, T. (ed.) 1996. '1992 Debate: The Past is a Foreign Country'. *Key Debates in Anthropology*. London: Routledge.

Isbester, K. 1996. 'Understanding State Disintegration: The case of Nicaragua'. *The Journal of Social, Political and Economic Studies* 21(4): 455–76.

Lancaster, R.N. 1988. *Thanks to God and the Revolution: Popular Religion and Class Consciousness in the New Nicaragua*. New York: Columbia University Press.

————. 1992. *Life is Hard: Machismo, Danger, and the Intimacy of Power in Nicaragua*. Berkeley: University of California Press.

Lloyd, P. 1979. *Slums of Hope?: Shanty Towns of the Third World*. Manchester: Manchester University Press.

Lomnitz, L.A. 1977. *Networks and Marginality: Life in a Mexican Shantytown*. New York: Academic Press.

Marx, K. 2004 [1852]. *The Eighteenth Brumaire of Louis Napoleon*. Whitefish: Kessinger Publishing.

Montoya, R. 2007. 'Socialist Scenarios, Power, and State Formation in Sandinista Nicaragua', *American Ethnologist* 34(1): 71–90.

Nietzsche, F. 1995 [1954]. *Thus Spoke Zarathustra*. New York: Cambridge University Press.

Pessoa, F. 1991. *The Book of Disquiet*. London: Serpent's Tail.

Ramírez, S. 1999. *Adiós Muchachos: Una Memoria de la Revolución Sandinista*. Mexico City: Aguilar.

Robinson, W.I. 1998. '(Mal)development in Central America: Globalization and Social Change', *Development and Change* 29(3): 467–97.

Rocha, J.L. 2002. 'Microsalarios y megasalarios: Megadesigualdad y microdesarrollo', *Envío* No. 240 (March), available online at: http://www.envio.org.ni/articulo/1131 (accessed 27 January 2007).

———. 2004. 'Hacia dónde ha transitado el FSLN?', *Envío* No. 268 (July), available online at: http://www.envio.org.ni/articulo/2168 (accessed 27 January 2007).

Rodgers, D. 2000. Living in the Shadow of Death: Violence, Pandillas, and Social Disintegration in *Contemporary Urban Nicaragua*, unpublished Ph.D. dissertation, Department of Social Anthropology, University of Cambridge, UK.

———. 2006a. 'Living in the Shadow of Death: Gangs, Violence, and Social Order in Urban Nicaragua, 1996–2002', *Journal of Latin American Studies* 38(2): 267–92.

———. 2006b. 'The State as a Gang: Conceptualising the Governmentality of Violence in Contemporary Nicaragua', *Critique of Anthropology* 26(3): 315–30.

———. 2007a. 'Managua', in K. Koonings and D. Kruijt (eds.), *Fractured Cities: Social Exclusion, Urban Violence and Contested Spaces in Latin America*. London: Zed.

———. 2007b. 'Each to Their Own: Ethnographic Notes on the Economic Organization of Poor Households in Urban Nicaragua', *Journal of Development Studies* 43(3): 391–419.

———. 2007c. 'When Vigilantes Turn Bad: Gangs, Violence, and Social Change in Urban Nicaragua', in D. Pratten and A. Sen (eds.), *Global Vigilantes: Anthropology, Violence, and Community in the Contemporary World*. New York: Columbia University Press.

Rushdie, S. 1981. *Midnight's Children*. London: Picador.

———. 1987. *The Jaguar Smile: A Nicaraguan Journey*. New York: Penguin.

Selbin, E. 1993 *Modern Latin American Revolutions*. Boulder: Westview Press.

Simmel, G. 1959. 'The ruin', in K.H. Wolff (ed.), *Georg Simmel 1858–1918: A Collection of Essays, with Translations and a Bibliography*. Columbus: Ohio State University Press.

Torres Rivas, E. 1991. 'Crisis and conflict, 1930 to the present', in L. Bethell (ed), *Central America since Independence*. Cambridge: Cambridge University Press.

Transparency International. 2004. *Global Corruption Report 2004*. London: Pluto Press and Transparency International.

Turner, V. 1969. *The Ritual Process: Structure and Anti-Structure*. Chicago: Aldine.

United Nations Development Programme (UNDP). 2006. *Human Development Report 2006 – Beyond Scarcity: Power, Poverty, and the Global Water Crisis*. New York: Oxford University Press.

United States of Agency for International Development (USAID). 2006. *Central America and Mexico Gang Assessment*. report prepared for the USAID Bureau for Latin American and Caribbean Affairs Office for Regional Sustainable Development, April.

Vance, I. 1985. 'More than bricks and mortar: women's participation in self-help housing in Managua, Nicaragua', in C. Moser and L. Peake (eds), *Women, Human Settlements and Housing*. London: Tavistock Publications.

Vargas, O.R. 1993. *Entre el Laberinto y la Esperanza: Nicaragua 1990–1994*. Managua: Ediciones Nicarao.

Walker, T.W. (ed). 1985. *Nicaragua: The First Five Years*. New York: Praeger.

———. 1997. 'Introduction: Historical setting and important issues', in T.W. Walker (ed.), *Nicaragua without Illusions: Regime Transition and Structural Adjustment in the 1990s*. Wilmington: Scholarly Resources Inc.

———. 2003. *Nicaragua: Living in the Shadow of the Eagle*. 4th edition. Boulder: Westview.

CHAPTER 4

The Object of Morality: Rethinking Informal Networks in Central Europe

Nicolette Makovicky

Walking through the small mountain village of Špania Dolina, Central Slovakia, on warm summer days, I often found elderly lace makers sitting on their verandas or in their front gardens on low stools, their pillows placed in front of them. As we chatted, I could see how they kept a sharp eye out for all movements – other villagers walking to and from the village store, hikers on their way up the mountain, the cars of cottagers maneuvering their way through the narrow streets – and often had juicy gossip to share about those who happened to come by. Their position, however, was also a form of advertisement: they had lace for sale and were waiting for potential clients to show up. Despite the picturesque effect, craftswomen themselves described this practice to me as vulgar and 'indecent'. In Špania Dolina, the commercial activities of others were the subject of much gossip, criticism and condemnation. Beneath the tranquil, picture-postcard surface of this village, I discovered that relations within the community were far from harmonious.

Tracing the production, trade and consumption of handmade bobbin lace made in the provincial town of Banská Bystrica and in two nearby villages, Špania Dolina and Staré Hory, this paper examines the moral conundrums of lace making as small-scale entrepreneurial activity amongst a group of craftswomen for whom commercial activities caused profound discomfort. The technique of bobbin lace making arrived in this area with German, Bohemian and Croatian immigrants, particularly miners, in the sixteenth century (Marková 1962). Lace was made by the wives and children of immigrant miners to supplement the families' incomes, eventually developing into a cottage industry. Yet, despite having been produced as a commodity in the local area for centuries, fieldwork conducted in 2003–2004 showed that lace makers had grave misgivings about their own commercial activities. Whether club members or villagers, craftswomen maintained that they rarely sold their wares, and made lace for gifting or 'for the drawer' – meaning their production had no recipient. A stigma was attached to commercial activities and this stigma compelled lace makers to employ socially and geographically extended networks of personal contacts in order to secure an income, creating a divide between their role as producer and as an actor in the market. As it turned out, however, lace artifacts played an additional role in the construction of these 'economies of favours' (Ledeneva 1998) in that they figured as popular gifts for network contacts.

It is by virtue of these networking practices that lace in Slovakia has a 'social life' (Appadurai 1986). The nature of this social life, however, reveals how in everyday life craftswomen must negotiate between the workings of the market economy to which they are bound as producers and consumers, and the obligations of a moral economy to which they belong by virtue of kin and social relations. Previous anthropological studies of the relation between material culture, morality and praxis in postsocialist society have tended to deal with issues of consumption (e.g. Veenis 1999; Féhervȧry 2002). This study questions this prevailing tendency to regard the study of consumption as the primary access to the experience of postsocialist populations (e.g. Patico and Caldwell 2002). An examination of domestic production in contemporary consumer society, this research sheds light on the continuing importance of the household for the creation of social and material value. As I show in the following, two forms of economic thinking and practice associated with domestic production, namely 'community economy' (Gudeman 1996) and 'house economy' (Gudeman and Rivera 1990), have endured and adapted to the political and economic changes of the socialist and postsocialist period. These form normative frameworks for the creation of moral and social value amongst lace makers in urban and rural Central Slovakia, promoting ideals, practices and identities which at times are at odds with the entrepreneurialism fostered by market activities.

In this case, it is the use of networks and networking practices by lace makers that holds the key to unraveling the complex interplay between enduring normative values, forms of economic practice and long-term political and economic change. The reconfiguration of socialism's networks in postsocialist society has received considerable attention from scholars (e.g. Grabher and Stark 1997; Ledeneva 2000, 2001; Seabright 2000; Segbers 2001). Although they document a surprising range of variations in practice across Central and Eastern Europe, these studies show a growing tendency for networking practices to be employed in the service of business and entrepreneurial activities. While this is the case amongst the lace makers I studied, older forms of informal exchange known during the socialist period – such as the presentation of gifts to low-ranking officials and doctors – persist, and all are described using the language of social intimacy (that is, as 'favours' and 'mutual help'). Taking a material culture approach, this study examines the workings of these practices by examining the significance of the lace artifacts exchanged as 'gifts of appreciation'. The meaning of such transactions, I argue, is created within the frame of certain moral aesthetic conventions that establish a connection between beauty and normative behaviour. Indeed, I start by showing how lace makers are able to speak about the socially and morally contentious issue of commercial activities by recasting issues of ethics into matters of aesthetic judgement.

Lace or String? The Moral Aesthetics of Commercial Production

Lace makers in Špania Dolina were particularly interested in how much lace was being sold in the house of Ana Paličková and her family, where I became an apprentice lace maker in the summer of 2003. Dagmar, Ana Paličková's daughter-in-law, mounted the raw lace on cloth for most of the surrounding lace makers in the upper end of the village. These craftswomen delivered the lace together with a length of cloth onto which Dagmar sewed the lace for a nominal price using her sewing machine.[1] Thus, there was a constant circulation of lace made by village lace makers in and out of the house and each piece was evaluated and commented on by Dagmar and Ana. Inspecting the work of others, they evaluated not only the choice and range of pattern but the quality of the execution. These inspections and conversations with other lace makers made it clear to me that not all lace makers and their products were conceived of as equal within the village community.

At the top of the village hierarchy were the 'true' lace makers, women who, like Ana Paličková, were born in the village and had made lace all their lives. While many gave up lace making as their only means of income and took other paid work once they had children, this did not disqualify them as 'true' lace makers. This is seen in the case of Mária Červená, a 'true' lace maker from the village:

> As there were a lot of us, we had to work [as children]. When I got married, also after that I worked and then I cooked in the kindergarten for thirteen years. Even then I was registered in 'Kroj',[2] after that my mother had to [do the] work for me. (Mária Červená, Špania Dolina)

The 'true' lace makers were contrasted with the growing group of lace makers who learned the art of making lace in their late fifties or in their sixties and produce it to supplement their income, commonly retirement benefits. These were considered distinctly 'false' and their products were considered substandard. In an outburst of agitation Pany Paličková once told me that what they make 'isn't lace, it is strings' (*to nie je čipka, to je šipagát!*).

Milada Pomarančová, living several houses further towards the central square of the village, was considered a 'false' lace maker by the Palička family. Milada was very business minded, eager to promote her products and was rumoured to sell most in the village. I was told by Dagmar that Milada only learned how to make lace in her later years and that she had done 'all sorts of things', such as working in the village store and helping out in the village pub. Her work was presented as substandard: it did not have the desired stiffness. While there was some discussion of whether this was because she used cheap nonlinen thread, it was presented to me as a sign of her 'inauthenticity'.

Milada Pomarančová herself, however, told me that she learned how to make lace as a child and had helped supplement the family income while attending school. Throughout the interview she did not hide her eagerness to sell, but projected it as resulting from the authenticity of her work:

> I am always getting letters, because many people know me as a lace maker. From America too. Now Polish TV came when the Pope was here in [Banska] Bystrica. Well, they came here first of all for the lace. And I asked 'what did you come for?' And they said for our Holy Father and for lace and please make some lace. And they filmed me. They were interested in it, because they make lace in Poland too … People are interested, because it is handicraft. When they see those bobbins, well that alone says something. (Milada Pomarančová, Špania Dolina)

Whether Milada did indeed learn to make lace as a child is less interesting than the fact that it is assumed that the somewhat dubious quality of her lace was inextricably connected to her commercialism. The authenticity of a lace maker in the eyes of others, then, relied less on whether they were born in the village or whether lace making had been a constant in their adult life, than on their apparent disinterestedness in craft activity as a means for additional income. Disapproval was expressed through degradation of their skill by applying negative aesthetic judgements on their particular execution and stylistics: their lace was described as 'too dense' or 'too wide-meshed', 'nothing special' and 'repetitious' (meaning that the lace maker made only very simple, quick patterns), or 'like a rag' (meaning the lace was loose and lacked stiffness). The critique of lace made by craftswomen such as Milada Pomarančová, in other words, was that of a faulty or incomplete transformation of the materials ('flimsiness'), as seen most evidently in Ana Paličková's assertion that the lace made by 'false' craftswomen was nothing more than 'strings'.

In short, lace makers in ·pania Dolina were open to the criticism of their colleagues and others in the community by virtue of their commercial activities, despite the fact that lace makers considered their craft practice paid work and some even exhibited them publicly outside their homes in fine weather. Yet, for the majority of the craftswomen in Špania Dolina and beyond extra income was universally wanted and quite often also needed. Often, it was precisely the income gained from craftwork that was their gateway to participation in consumer society. Many lived off old-age pensions that had been reduced to covering only basic expenses by high inflation and rising prices. Others, though employed, had homes to refurbish and children that had to be put through university:

> I admit, it is for commercial sale … it isn't for me, or for my household or for someone … because I have to sell it. I have to support myself somehow … and I have a 21-year-old son, I was alone with him, from his young years I was alone with him, so I couldn't give him much … I still need to take care of him. He decided to go to university in Bratislava, so … until he finishes his studies … I simply have to consider things in a way … because I have to earn a livelihood. (Hana Majerová, Banská Bystrica)

While making lace was one of many ways of getting a second income in contemporary Central Slovakia, lace had already been produced as a commodity in the local area for centuries. As mentioned earlier, the technique of bobbin lace making arrived to this area with immigrants in the sixteenth century (Marková 1962), and lace made by the wives and children of immigrant miners eventually developed into a cottage industry. Before the Second World War, unmarried young women from these villages would buy up lace from family members and fellow villagers and travel within the Slovak territories and beyond to Hungary, Romania, Croatia and Slovenia to sell their wares. My informants were extremely proud of their mothers' and grandmothers' travels selling lace: in the village of Staré Hory I was repeatedly treated to the story of how village women surprised German and Romanian soldiers quartered there during the Second World War with their ability to speak their language.

Considering the historical practice of trading lace in these villages, and the pride with which lace makers today recall it, the shame with which commercial dealings were associated by craftswomen today appears somewhat surprising. Studies of postsocialist trading have shown a continual association of trading activities with moral ambiguity prevalent during socialist times (Humphrey and Mandel (eds) 2002; Kaneff 2002). In the light of the fact that the majority of my respondents were middle-aged or elderly, most of them had spent the majority of their education and working life in socialist institutions.[3] During socialism the value of work was seen as lying in the meaningful participation in state production (Pine 1998). Consequently, socialist ethics deemed exchange for profit as 'speculation', an activity serving only the individual interest of the trader without contributing to the wider good of society through production. 'Speculation' therefore not only sat uncomfortably with socialist work ethics, but ultimately the egalitarian ideology of socialist progress through communal labour. Thus, while it was not illegal to sell a product of one's own making during socialism, this sort of activity toyed with the boundaries of the acceptable.

Speaking to both lace makers and lace consumers of the older generation, I ascertained that public sale of lace gradually declined throughout the 1950s. Women continued to sell lace, but conducted these sales within the confines of their home – a practice that is standard today. It seems, then, that the early socialist period did indeed signal a (temporary) end to the petty trade of lace in the public sphere. It is worth noting, however, that it was the commercial practice, rather than the mode of production, which was discouraged by the socialist authorities. Thus, the domestic production of lace (and other goods) continued throughout the socialist period.[4] In fact, lace makers and other crafts(wo)men were organized in the government organizations such as the Centre for Folk Art Production (Ústredie ľudovej umeleckej výroby – ÚĽUV), established in 1954, and in other craft collectives. Orders and sales were centrally controlled by these organizations along the guidelines of the planned economy. In this way, lace makers could be ideologically construed as participating in state production even as they worked at home.

Thus, while attitudes to commercial activity have fluctuated over time, the mode of production has remained unchanged. Indeed, the very persistence of the connection between the production of lace, the domestic sphere and craftwork as the means to a supplementary cash income may hold the key to understanding the anti-market sentiments. As shown by Bloch and Parry (1989; also Gudeman and Rivera 1990), Marx's writings form part of a larger philosophical tradition stretching from Aristotle, which emphasizes value as created through production, self-sufficiency and the condemnation of exchange for profit. Negative moral evaluations of engagement in market exchange has been well documented in studies of societies outside the postsocialist world (for example Taussig 1980; Schneider 1989; Graeber 2004). Thus, rather than viewing the shame and moral ambiguity lace makers associate with commercial sales as a persistence of 'socialist values' amongst an older generation,[5] I suggest that the moral conundrums of sales should be examined in relation to the economic and social role they play in the lives of craftswomen.

In the case of Špania Dolina, the smallness of the village community (with a population of barely 200), as well as the relative fame of the local lace within the region, undoubtedly contributed to a competitive atmosphere amongst local craftswomen. Indeed, both clients and income gained from lace making were considered a limited good:

> When they sell lace down there [on the village square], I can't sell this. *But you do better work than them?* Yes, that's true. And they sell! I didn't sell anything this year. One little square. *Wouldn't the others take it down for you and sell it? And then give you the money?* Maybe they would. *You haven't asked?* No. (Mária Červená, Špania Dolina)

In addition, lace makers were drawing on local craft knowledge and local designs that were held collectively and passed on from generation to generation in order to produce and sell their lace. As a commons, craft knowledge formed part of a 'community economy' (Gudeman 1996), in which the drive to sustain a way of living was seen as paramount to individual acquisition and wealth. This meant not only that lace makers in Špania Dolina made every effort to keep technical knowledge and designs out of reach of craftswomen from outside the community, but that the efforts of individual lace makers within the village to gain an income from their craftwork was in constant tension with an underlying sense of communality. Lace makers who appeared very commercially successful were seen as a threat to the prosperity of the community as a whole.

Market activity, then, was seen as having the potential to disrupt local social relations by urging the individual to maximize their gain, ultimately at the detriment of others. Consequently, the most pressing concern for lace makers was how to balance their wish to gain income against the possibilities of appearing to engage in morally questionable commercial practices. As I show in the next section, this is largely done through maintaining an apparently disinterested attitude to sales.

Lady Luck and the Creation of Needs

In the urban setting of Banská Bystrica, where there are more possibilities for sale by placement of wares in shops or hotels, regular fairs and exhibitions, the potential tension between lace makers is far more diffuse than in Špania Dolina. Yet, here too, sale is viewed with discomfort among the lace makers, whether they were members of lace-making clubs or worked independently. When asked about their commercial activities, lace makers were eager to project their craftwork as a labour of love. Like their colleagues in Špania Dolina, lace makers in Banská Bystrica down played the importance of their sales and dismissed the suggestion that they were the result of a concerted effort on their part. Often they presented a sale as a fluke, the result of being in the right place at the right time:

And you sell it sometimes?
It has happened to me that I have sold a few, but it was like this, I was sitting in the museum and demonstrating lace making and some French people came along. Or in the Kulturny Dom a lady came [up to me] and said her daughter worked in England and lived with someone and she wanted some sort of present for them … (Zuzana Antonová, Banská Bystrica)

Another way to achieve the appropriate air of disinterestedness was to delegate commercial transactions to a friend or relative. These people usually work voluntarily to facilitate orders and relay payments for finished pieces, receiving no dividends themselves. In ·pania Dolina, Ana Paličková left the sale of lace to her daughter-in-law Dagmar. In fact, she literally hid in her room when customers showed up at the door. Mária Cervená handed her products over to her son, who sold them to a long-term contact in the capital, Bratislava.
   A relation or friend may thus take on the responsibility for handling the majority of product sales, but these individuals often make use of their own social and professional relations, and their relations of their contacts, in order to place lace artifacts in commercial outlets:

How many pieces did you send to Bratislava?
Seven pieces.
Seven pieces and they've already been sold?
They were sold within the week. They phoned up my mother to say that it was sold already.
Do they want more?
Yes, they do.
So you are really doing through your mother?
Yes, through her colleague who makes some embroidered tablecloths – she arranged it. (Jaroslava Genderová, Banská Bystrica)

In her work on the personal exchange relations in Soviet and postsocialist Russia, commonly known as *blat*, Alena Ledeneva has described such exchanges as a 'distinct form of non-monetary exchange, a kind of barter based on personal relationship' (Ledeneva 1998: 34). Ledeneva emphasizes that blat relationships are based not only on social relations, but more importantly on the individual's professional life, which allows access to resources, skills or information valuable to others. Similarly, men and women in Central Slovakia were more likely to seek help with practical or financial matters within their wider social circle, before contacting professionals or unfamiliar practitioners. Consequently, I found that the social milieu of any given lace maker was best understood as a personal social network, or 'ego-based network', in the language of network analysis.[6] These networks were characterized by a high degree of multiplex ties, that is, lace makers had several different kinds of relationship with their network alters. Thus, a lace maker's network was not simply a list of kin, friends and acquaintances with whom he or she had relations, but also a social resource which could be used to access information, labour and goods. It was these networks that were employed in order to facilitate sales and orders of lace – save those that were made to tourists who came to Staré Hory and Špania Dolina and bought on the spot. In this way, commercial ventures were established and strengthened by chains of personal acquaintance, and, as we saw in the quote above, the actions of contacts were articulated in terms of 'favours' and 'helping out' amongst friends and family.

The reluctance of lace makers to represent themselves in commercial dealings and their use of intermediaries thus results in the snowballing of contacts as one person makes use of another's network and incorporates it into his or her own field of action. Consequently, lace artifacts and money may move between several intermediaries who may be only casually acquainted with the producer or not familiar with her at all. Ledeneva has described the use of intermediaries in Russian blat as a method of covering up the reciprocal nature of blat relations, delaying repayment of favours, or negotiating requests one was embarrassed about or incapable of asking for directly. However, in this case intermediaries were not primarily used to make a favour appear to be a singular, exceptional event, or because the order of lace was embarrassing. Rather, they worked in reverse: by dispersing and displacing dealings temporally and geographically through the use of contacts in their own and others' personal networks, the lace maker did not have to pursue clients. Rather, the clients appeared to be drawn to her. Networking, then, solved lace makers' problems in maintaining the appearance of being relatively uninterested in commercial sales, while at the same time allowing them to benefit financially from their work. In other words, it transformed the sale of lace from a question of earning extra income, to the satisfaction of the needs of others.

The way in which this discourse of needs is applied to the ordering of lace is probably best illustrated by the following story. This was recounted to me by an informant who did not make lace herself, but had an elderly neighbour lace maker originally from the lace making village of Staré Hory:

> ... because she would make things and always say it was a present. And I felt sorry, because she lived off her pension. So I always told her, that I had showed my colleague something and that she would like one too. Or that it is her birthday and she'll be fifty or thirty or whatever. So she made it and named a price, but it was always ridiculous prices. But I kept it every time. She would have made it for me anyway, but only as a present. (Ana Hrinová, Banská Bystrica)

In this case, Ana invented not only a fictional receiver, but lied about the motivation for the purchase, claiming it was a gift when it was not. She constructed these small lies to legitimize not only the lace maker's income, but also her own consumption.

Pulling on network contacts, however, was key not only to the commercial practice of craftswomen, but, as the quote above suggests, to their consumption practices as well. When I asked my informants how they disposed of the income they gained from craft activity, most of them put added emphasis on the fact that the money was not used on 'frivolous expenditures', such as cosmetics or entertainment:

> *And that which you earn, do you save it for something?*
> No, save ... well, to tell the truth, what I earned I bought this apartment for. And then I had a son who was unemployed for two years. He was unemployed and had three sons. So I helped. When I earned two thousand, I gave him a thousand. When I earned a thousand I gave him five hundred ... So this is what my money went for. (Magdalena Starohorská, Banská Bystrica)

And:

> I send it[the lace] to my son, he knows a lady who sells it.
> *Where does this lady sell the lace?*
> She goes outside of the country too.
> *You don't know what countries she goes to?*
> No, no.
> *And then your son comes with the money, or what?*
> Like that, well he leaves it at his place. Sometimes he gives me some. For example, I just had the floor redone, 30,000 that cost me. I couldn't pay these things from the old age pension. (Mária Červená, Špania Dolina)

There was a strikingly consistent use of lace making money for the purchase of a new home or the refurbishment of an existing household. Vivien Zelizer (1997) has described how the money is incorporated into personalized webs of friendship and families through the process which she calls 'earmarking', which assigns different meanings to particular monies by regulating their use, and also allocates 'appropriate sources of money for specified uses' (Zelizer 1997: 29). Interestingly, I found that not only were the monies for major investments in the household often procured by pulling on the resources of network contacts, but the restricted budget of the majority of my acquaintances meant that the building and refurbishment of the home, as well as the purchase of home appliances and electrical equipment, were done 'by acquaintance' (*po znamosti*) if the opportunity arose. Although my informants were aware that many, if not most, of these purchases 'by acquaintance' were done on a semi-legal (or illegal) premise, they were not shy about admitting that this was how they intended to get hold of what they needed. In fact, my informants explained that they would never be able to afford the item without the discount they gained through their contact. Thus, getting something by pulling on a network of personal contacts was associated with saving money.

Thrift, as Daniel Miller has pointed out, is not value free. Rather, it carries 'connotations of restraint, sobriety and respectability. Thrift comes from the same stock of manners as modesty and an aversion to excess' (Miller 1998: 56). Hence, just as the use of network contacts turns commercial activity into the fulfillment of needs, discounts are turned into savings that in turn reflect positively upon those who managed to obtain them. In his study of shopping, Miller makes the (perhaps surprising) observation that there is no correlation between spending less and the experience of thrift. Shoppers develop manifold strategies for justifying the purchase of almost any good as an act of saving rather than an act of expenditure. Thrift, it seems, is enacted through consumption. Lehtonen and Pantzar (2002) have highlighted how precisely this connection between saving and 'reasoned choice' was promoted by the postwar Finnish government in order to promote consumption. In the case at hand, however, expenditure is not simply made into savings through 'considered choice' consumption, but a direct connection seems to be made between the production of lace and the act of saving via 'earmarking' and the use of networks. In other words, pulling on contacts is not only about thrifty behaviour which is positively valued, but an effort to keep both production and consumption 'close to home', as it were. The use of networks thus seems to be connected to an abstracted notion of self-sufficiency.

Stephen Gudeman and Alberto Rivera (1990; see also Löfgren and Frykman 1987) identify precisely self-sufficiency and thrift as core values in the 'house economy' of the peasant household. Unlike the corporation that generates profits through engaging in market exchange, 'the project of the house is to be self-supporting' (Gudeman and Rivera 1990: 44) and this is achieved through 'making savings', i.e. through thrift. In the view of the valuation of thrift and self-sufficiency, lace makers can be seen to be operating according to a 'house economy' model, in that the household retains a central role as the site of production, as well as the referent and ultimate beneficiary of any profits rendered.[7] In the light of the continued importance of the household as a site of production (of lace, but also foodstuffs, clothing and furnishings) throughout the socialist era, it is hardly surprising that the household continues to act as a framework for the construction of social and material value. Indeed, anthropological studies of Central and Eastern Europe before 1989 and thereafter have repeatedly stressed the importance of the household and household land not only as a resource for economic survival, but as a point of identification and a mechanism for the creation and maintenance of kinship networks (Hann 1995; Humphrey 1995; Pine 1998, 1999, 2002, 2003; Buchli 1999; Haukanes 2001; Crowley 2002; Czegledy 2002; Kaneff 2002).

Networking can be seen as a form of value transformation that converted lace into income and consumer goods, turned expenditure on household goods into savings, and reformulated lace makers' commercial sales into the satisfaction of customers' needs, thereby securing the moral integrity of the individual lace maker. However, even when it was undertaken with reference to the home and could be shown to benefit the household and its members, this practice carried with it its own moral pitfalls. The problem lay not with the pursuit of income or consumer goods per se, but rather in the negotiation of the personal relationships through which they were channeled: just as a moral evaluation lay implicitly in the aesthetic judgement lace makers made of their colleagues' products, the way in which individuals procured goods and services was subject to moral scrutiny by others. In the following examination of wider networking practices, I throw further light on these evaluations. As networks were formed and maintained through the exchange of gifts and favours, I turned to considering the significance of lace as a gift.

The Materiality of the Gift

Well, I give away a lot [of lace] as gifts, someone does something for me, you know, so I do give a lot away. Also if I go somewhere or my son does, we leave some [as gifts].

So when someone does something for you …

I pay like that. Because they don't take money, so I do it like that. (Magdalena Starohorská, Banská Bystrica)

In Central Slovakia, lace was given as appreciation for favours rendered by kin, neighbours and friends, ranging from physical manual labour (such as the hauling of firewood or tiling of balconies) to help getting around administrative hurdles. However, gifts of lace were also common when my respondents were dealing with the local authorities, low-level administration and the educational system. Furniture covers and small pictures were gifted for doctors during or after satisfactory treatment and the homes of teachers were particularly rife with lace artifacts that were presented to them at the end of the school year or a period of important exams.[8]

A gift of lace, I was told, was far superior to that of a bottle of liqueur, a box of chocolates or a bunch of flowers. Ledeneva (1998) notes that in Soviet-era blat transactions the cost of gifts for network contacts was not important; rather what counted was that the gift could not be bought, either because it was difficult to obtain or because it was 'self-made'. My respondents in contemporary Slovakia shared the same opinion: as the lace maker Paulina told me, a gift should be the 'work of one's own hands'. Even if the gift was purchased, it was important that it was not obviously commercial, mass-produced or perishable. This was not primarily because lace was more costly than a bottle of liquor, but rather that my respondents believed lace would lend material permanence to a moment in time or the memory of a person (usually the donor) in a way that perishable items could not. In other words, my informants believe that lace articles could be made to embody memory and that their materiality would ensure the continuation of this memory. Men and women spoke of gifts of lace furniture covers and pictures using the word *pamiatka* (keepsake or souvenir), thus directly linking memory, materiality and the inalienable nature of the gift:

> This I got. Neither my mother-in-law nor I made this. I did some or other service for someone, so they gave it to me as a present. These are nice presents, because they are a reminder of the person who gave it to me. (Zuzana Kollarová, Banská Bystrica)

If the materiality of lace is intimately connected to its symbolism as gift, the question becomes what this materiality itself entails. As I described in an earlier section, lace makers spoke of lace using certain descriptive, relative terms such as 'loose', 'dense' or 'wide-meshed' to describe the quality of the weave. What gives lace its particular material resonance, then, is the manner in which it plays and manipulates with the notion of surface, always begging the question whether it is the weave or the spaces in between which constitute the design. Indeed, the play between the weave and that which lies beneath is necessary in order for the decorative effect to take place; lace is always partially concealing and partially revealing the surfaces it edges and covers. This aesthetic effect was manipulated by women who used lace tablecloths and furniture covers in order to create an interplay between the wooden surface of their furnishings and the textile covers:

> 'When we make lace *dečkas* lately there has been a tendency to … furniture – the beauty of the wood – should not be covered. Covering the complete surface of the table with the tablecloth and the [lace] insert, so you can't see the wood, that isn't done anymore. Rather, [it is] like a detail put into the middle of the table, so that the beauty of the wood comes through. (Jana Horvathová, Banská Bystrica)

Furniture covers, such as the one Jana describes above, were an obligatory component of the representative areas of the home: the entrance and hallway, and especially in the living room. Here they entered into what can only be called a symbiotic relationship with the jumble of plants, decorative objects and mementoes that inhabited the shelves of bookcases and glass-fronted display cabinets that held the family's fine china and glass. Apart from books, common decorative objects were vases (filled with plastic flowers), folk ceramics and special mentions for work received during socialist times. Draped across the coffee tables, television sets and potted plants, small lace doilies were also often placed under these decorative objects on the shelves of living-room furniture, thus framing them.

Lace furniture covers reflect the enclosure and retention identified by Daniel Miller as the materialization of 'thrift as aesthetics' (Miller 1998: 103). Wrapping themselves around the furniture of the home, lace covers and doilies were explicitly identified as having a protective, as well as aesthetic, function by my informants: they maintained that the cover afforded protection, preventing an object from scratching or staining the polished surface of the furniture. Women maintained that lace covers added 'warmth' to the home, representing the care and nurture that the woman of the house invests in her home and family.[9] Indeed, a home without decorative textiles and furniture covers was said to have an 'empty' aesthetic. Yet, in light of the fact that many of these artifacts were gifts from others or purchased using personal contacts, their use cannot simply be seen as the result of the personal expression of those contributing to the decoration of the home. As gifts, these items represent the agency of others and thus constitute a material sedimentation of the social relations of family members within the decor of the family home. More importantly, lace artifacts operate within an aesthetic convention that links beauty and quality with the normative values of thrift, self-sufficiency and egalitarianism. When lace is employed as a gift, the conventions of this moral aesthetic are evoked and set into play in the relation between giver and receiver, leaving the actions of both persons open to the judgements of others.

Much has been made of the discrepancies between the functional practice of barter in 'economies of favour' and the rhetoric of friendship and mutual assistance used by the participants to describe it, as well as the underlying moral issues concerning the selective pilfering, bribes and nepotism which followed in its wake (Pawlik 1992; Bruno 1997; Ledeneva 1998). I found that gifting lace, especially to officials, was a sensitive subject among my respondents. Despite the fact that one or two, such as the woman above, mentioned the gift of lace as a 'repayment', most never used such blunt language. Rather, they took pains to explain that these gifts were 'signs of appreciation' rather than bribes or 'payment':

> You know, we were taught that when you go somewhere you don't go with an empty hand ... It wasn't a bribe. It was just 'like that'. Not a bribe. Not favouritism ... You must give something. Not money, the work of one's own hands. I needed to give something in order that we got something back. (Paulina Oravská, Banská Bystrica)

My informants underlined the fact they were not bribing or buying themselves something they were not entitled to. Rather, these particular gifts were said to be given out of appreciation for the efforts expended by these professionals, who are often said to have done 'something extra' for the patient or pupil. Pierre Bourdieu (1990) maintains that the exchange of gifts happens on the premise of the social misrecognition of the social rules that govern reciprocation. According to Bourdieu, this misrecognition is part of 'habitus'.[10] Thus an individual does not follow social conventions unreflectively, nor can the exchange of gifts simply be the result of intentional action. However, despite the insistence that these tokens were given voluntarily or, as Paulina suggested, given out of custom, there were frequent laments that if one didn't present a gift, this 'something extra' would not be invested in the service rendered. In other words, the men and women I spoke to felt somewhat pressured into producing and handing out these gifts. Indeed, as most of the quotations above reveal, lace makers and their clients are perfectly aware of how their gifts of lace create and expose ties of reciprocity by generating ever stronger bonds of moral obligation between giver and receiver. Networking – that is, the creation and maintenance of social relations and contacts through practices of gifting – can thus be seen as a regulatory mechanism for moral control.

This becomes particularly evident when the rules of social engagement change and individuals may find that their learned practice no longer achieves its social objectives or may even expose them to criticism from others. One afternoon Jana and Paulina were discussing the salaries of teachers that they felt were far too low. They agreed that the collective gift which teachers commonly got from their class at the end of the school year was partly determined by the fact that their efforts were so poorly rewarded. Interestingly, Jana pointed out that this 'tradition' was in fact only three or four decades old: in their own school days in the 1950s and early 1960s such gifts had been uncommon. However, by the time their children attended school in the 1970s, gifts had become obligatory. Jana, a teacher herself, went on to recount how the attitudes seemed to be changing yet again:

> It was one of my last classes. They [the parents] asked me what I wanted, so I said a ring – because had just left my husband. And I missed a ring to wear … it was sort of strange, nothing on my hand. So they bought me a nice gold ring. But then a colleague saw it and said 'Who gave you that?' I told her. And she said, 'You'd better take it off. Someone could report you, you know'. Well, I was shocked. They asked me what I wanted – I didn't ask for it! (Jana Horvathová, Banská Bystrica)

The difficulties encountered by Jana when she received the ring from the parents of her graduating class reveal the complexity of networking practices and related forms of gift exchange as they are reproduced under altered socioeconomic circumstances. While networks seem to have retained a more or less continuous form over time – that is to say, they are composed by the same classes of people (kin, friends, colleagues, neighbours)[11] – they are now increasingly used to navigate the market rather than the bureaucracy. Yet, as postsocialist privatization and liberalization has turned services into commodities and access to them is determined by purchasing power rather than by a system of rights and privileges, 'gifts of appreciation' now look uncomfortably like bribes. What Jana found most hurtful about her colleague's comment was the suggestion that she could be seen as using her position as teacher vis-à-vis the children's parents in order to extract valuables from them.

The significance of gifts exchanged between network contacts must be seen as being produced socially, rather than being absolute (Patico 2002). The presentation of gifts to network contacts can, according to Ledeneva, be seen as 'redundant transactions used for the construction of small social worlds' (Ledeneva 1998: 153). Gifts of lace in today's Central Slovakia do indeed 'construct small social worlds' by keeping people present in the minds of others, yet, in light of the fact that it is through such transactions persons are subject to moral policing by others – as seen in the case of Jana and the ring she received from her graduating class – they appear to be anything but redundant. One effect of such a gift is to 'naturalize' a relation which otherwise may spring purely out of a structural position between two people, one having access to a resource the other is in need of. As Marilyn Strathern comments, in Euro-American society gifts are seen as an 'extension of the self insofar as they carry the expression of sentiments ... Sentiment is supposed to have positive connotations in the same way as near relations are supposed to be benign, and presents carry positive overtones of sociability and affection' (Strathern 1997: 302). In this case, I would argue, gifts are given less out of a recognition of the donor's indebtedness, and more in an attempt to claim a new level of social intimacy. In other words, gifts are meant to transform a relationship from one understood as resting upon structural difference to one conceived as based on personal choice. Strathern notes that gifts are understood as 'transactions within a moral economy, which make possible the extended reproduction of social relations' (ibid.: 294). These moral economies 'consist of small worlds of personal relationships that are the emotional core of every individual's social experiences' (ibid.: 295). In this way, when pulling friends and acquaintances into the 'economy of favours', one is also pulling them into a moral economy. Consequently, persons find that actions they would normally carry out as part of their official function – or would normally be carried out by another – become a personal responsibility (and, possibly, a personal liability).

Small, portable and discreet, lace artifacts can engage with the wooden furniture and decorative objects of any home, forming the particular aesthetic of 'warmth' which most housewives strive to achieve in Central Slovakia. This aesthetics, however, has an undeniable moral aspect. Just as Ana Paliãková in Španía Dolina called the lace of overtly commercially oriented lace makers 'strings', so the lace artifacts within the home derive their aesthetic value just as much by virtue of their representation of inherently morally positive values of network relations as from any conventions on aesthetic form. Gifts of lace used and displayed within the home are quite simply the symbolic and material 'rewards' for actions that are undertaken in the spirit of 'mutual help', and figure as visible markers of a home constructed and maintained – both materially and spiritually – through honest work, and the practices of gifting and saving.

Conclusion

This study has sought to throw some light on the moral conundrum of lace making as small-scale entrepreneurial activity in contemporary Banská Bystrica, Španía Dolina and Staré Hory. Craftswomen found sales of lace morally questionable and often connected transactions with a profound sense of shame. The problem lay not in the fact that women earned an income, but in the methods they employed to achieve this aim. Two issues, in particular, preoccupied lace makers. Within the small village communities of Staré Hory and especially in Špania Dolina, clients and prospective income from lace making were understood as a limited good. This meant that the efforts of individual craftswomen to gain an income from their craftwork was in constant tension with notions of communality. Secondly, and more generally, lace makers were concerned with balancing social relations against economic and material interest. Lace makers attempted to strike this balance by channelling commercial activities through networks of family, friends and acquaintances. This was part of a strategy of figured disinterest in commercial matters, through which craftswomen attempted to show how their sales were a matter of coincidence or luck, and were undertaken to satisfy the needs of others.

Yet, while lace makers in Central Slovakia struggled to unite their role as producers for a commercial market with a moral economy where the social and material (re)production of the home through practices of thrift and self-sufficiency is the normative ideal, there was nevertheless a tightly knit relationship between domestic production, market activity and participation in consumer society. The networks employed by lace makers to sell their products, as well as everyday interactions with friends, acquaintances and low-ranking officials, facilitated this relationship. Networks can be seen as dispersed, loosely connected communities of individuals who experienced themselves as governed by ties of mutual trust and obligation, which provided a 'buffer zone' between the household and the sphere of consumption – two areas of life conceived of as governed by opposing logics. For lace makers seeking to benefit financially from their craftwork and participate in a consumer society, yet adhere to normative values centered around ideals of thrift and self-sufficiency, these networks constitute an expansion of the ideally closed relation between domestic production and domestic consumption beyond the physical boundaries of the household. Networks, in other words, are the household in a socially 'extended' form. Thus, while it remains spoken about as an ideally self-sufficient unit, the lived reality of the household can be seen to have become the informal networks of exchange that accommodate both commercial practices and projects of consumption.

Notes

1. At the time of my fieldwork Dagmar took 20 Slovak crowns for each furniture cover (regardless of size). This corresponded to the price of a litre of milk. Dagmar has a full-time job, so her work making up the furniture covers can be seen as yet another manner in which to gain a second income.
2. 'Kroj' (literally 'folk costume') was one of several folk art collectives in which lace makers in Špania Dolina were organized during socialism.

3. The majority of the respondents were female lace makers between the ages of thirty-five and seventy, the youngest being in her mid-twenties and the eldest nearly ninety. While many had learned how to make lace as children, most women did not start to engage with the craft until after puberty. Often their interest in lace and lace making coincided with marriage and the establishment of their first home.

4. Research showed that small-scale production was not confined solely to craft activity, but was an integral part of life for families and individuals living under the conditions of the shortage economy. The most salient example of the way in which small-scale domestic production was an integrated part of the socialist economy is the vegetable plot, a central feature of many socialist and postsocialist countries (see for example Hann 1995, Verdery 1996, Kaneff 2002). In Central Slovakia this plot was a ubiquitous feature of family life for both urbanites and rural inhabitants. All my informants – whether they engaged in craft activity or not – have or have had a plot where they cultivated vegetables and kept a few domestic animals.

   However, domestic production was only partly about plugging the holes of the planned economy. Fieldwork undertaken by Hann (1995) in Hungary in the 1970s, for example, showed that domestic production could be coupled with full-time employment in order to earn extra income for luxury commodities feeding, ongoing status competition among villagers. My informants recalled using domestic production as a way to mark difference, although in a more modest way. Speaking of the sewing and needlecraft projects, I was repeatedly told by women that during socialism creating one's own garments was the only way to have something 'different' or something 'nice'. The mass-produced clothes which were available were described by my informants as 'ugly' or 'boring' and 'all the same'. To be well dressed and have a well-dressed family, a woman had to create garments herself. These projects also demonstrated their own agency in changing the dull and standardized produce which they were offered by the regime.

5. I found little evidence that younger respondents had markedly different attitudes to lace making as a commercial activity, nor that they employed different tactics for selling their lace. However, due to the fact that my sample of women who had had no adult experience of socialism was very small, it is difficult to draw any firm conclusion as to whether a significant generational difference in fact exists and whether it is conditioned by past experience in socialist society (or lack thereof).

6. Lynne McCallister and Claude Fischer define ego-based networks as 'composed of actors linked to egos and of the relations involved in those links' (1983: 76).

7. The importance of the domestic sphere as the site of production as well as consumption was stressed continually by my informants as necessary for the reproduction of healthy family relations (especially gendered relations). The home is to be built and maintained by the productive labour of both sexes and, ideally, this labour should be materially visible (for example in the form of DIY activities, pickled and preserved produce and in the interior decor). Urban households were frequently berated for being an unhealthy environment caused by a prefabricated environment and a lack of plots for growing foodstuffs.

8. Comparing strategies that populations across Central and Eastern Europe have adopted in dealing with officials, Grødeland, Koshechkina and Miller (1998) conclude that while bribing is common in countries such as the Ukraine and Bulgaria, the gifting of small gifts after the event is overwhelmingly used in the Czech and Slovak Republics. Like my own informants, their interviewees spoke of these gifts as 'tokens', 'rewards' and 'expressions of thanks'.

9. In Slovakia wood is seen as the ideal expressive medium for a man, while textiles take that role for women. Fieldwork showed that the use of these materials – wood and textiles –was important in the negotiation of gender roles through practice. In a context where each of these materials carries gendered connotations, the placing of textiles on the wooden surfaces of domestic furniture in a very general way represents the coming together of the labour, care and expression of the sexes within the home.

10. Defined as 'systems of transportable and durable dispositions, structured structures predisposed to function as structuring structures, that is, as principles which generate and organize practices and representations that can be objectively adapted to their outcomes without presupposing a conscious aiming at ends or an express mastery of the operations necessary in order to obtain them' (Bourdieu 1990: 53).

11. It is probable that even though contacts today may come from the same stock of social relations as before, the contacts themselves may not be the same individuals as before. However, if one takes on board Ledeneva's (1998) observation that contacts are created partly according to which resources, skills or information are needed in a given situation, such changes are not necessarily characteristic of the postsocialist period.

References

Appadurai, A. (ed.). 1986. *The Social Life of Things: Commodities in Cultural Perspective*. Cambridge: Cambridge University Press.

Bloch, M. and J. Parry. 1989. *Money and the Morality of Exchange*. Cambridge: Cambridge University Press.

Bourdieu, P. 1990. *The Logic of Practice*. Cambridge: Polity Press.

Bruno, M. 1997. 'Women and the Culture of Entrepreneurship', in M. Buckley (ed.), *Post-Soviet Women: from the Baltic to Central Asia*. Cambridge: Cambridge University Press.

Buchli, V. 1999. *An Archaeology of Socialism*. Oxford: Berg Publishers.

Crowley, D. 2002. 'Warsaw Interiors: The Public Life of Private Spaces, 1949–65', in D. Crowley and S. Reid (eds), *Socialist Spaces: Sites of Everyday Life in the Eastern Bloc*. Oxford: Berg Publishers.

Czegledy, A. 2002. 'Urban Peasants in a Postsocialist World: Small–Scale Agriculturalists in Hungary', in P. Leonard and K. Kaneff (eds), *Post–Socialist Peasant? Rural and Urban. Constructions of Identity in Eastern Europe, East Asia and the Former Soviet Union*. London: Palgrave MacMillan.

Féhervary, K. 2002. 'American Kitchens, Luxury Bathroom, and the Search for a "Normal" Life in Postsocialist Hungary', *Ethnos* 67(3): 369–400.

Grabher, G. and D. Stark (eds). 1997. *Restructuring Networks in Post-socialism: Legacies, Linkages, and Localities*. Oxford: Oxford University Press.

Graeber, D. 2004. *Fragments of an Anarchist Anhtropology*. Chicago: Prickly Paradigm Press.

Grødeland, Å., T.Y. Koshechkina and W.L. Miller. 1998. '"Foolish to Give and Yet more Foolish Not to Take". In-Depth Interviews with Post-Communist Citizens on Their Everyday Use of Bribes and Contacts', *Europe–Asia Studies* 50(4): 651–77.

Gudeman, S. 1992. 'Remodeling the House of Economies: Culture and Innovation', *American Ethnologist* 19(1): 141–54.

Gudeman, S. and A. Rivera. 1990. *Conversations in Colombia: The Domestic Economy in Life and Text*. Cambridge: Cambridge University Press.

Gudeman, S. 1996. 'Sketches, Qalms, and Other Thoughts on Intellectural Property Rights', in S. Brush and D. Stabinsky (eds.), *Valuing Local Knowledge. Indigenous People and Intellectual Property Rights*. Washington: Island Press.

Hann, C.M. 1995. *The Skeleton at the Feast: Contributions to East European Anthropology*, CSAC Monographs 9. Centre for Social Anthropology and Computing, University of Kent at Canterbury.

Haukanes, H. 2001. 'Women as Nurturers: Food and Ideology of Care in the Czech Republic', in *Women after Communism: Ideal Images and Real Lives*. Bergen: University of Bergen Press.

Humphrey, C. 1995. 'Creating a Culture of Disillusionment: Consumers in Moscow', in D. Miller (ed.), *Worlds Apart*. London: Routledge.

Humphrey, C. and R. Mandel (eds). 2002. *Markets and Moralities: Ethnographies of Postsocialism*. Oxford: Berg Publishers.

Kaneff, D. 2002. 'The Shame and Pride of Market Activity: Morality, Identity and Trading in Postsocialist Rural Bulgaria', in R. Mandell and C. Humphrey (eds), *Markets and Moralities: Ethnographies of Postsocialism*. Oxford: Berg.

Ledeneva, A. 1998. *Russia's Economy of Favours: Blat, Networking and Informal Exchange*. Cambridge: Cambridge University Press.

———. 2000. 'Shadow Barter: Economic Necessity or Economic Crime?', in P. Seabright (ed.), *The Vanishing Rouble: Barter Networks and Non-monetary Transactions in Post-Soviet Societies*. Cambridge: Cambridge University Press.

———. 2001. 'Networks in Russia: Global and Local Implications', in K. Segbers (ed.), *Explaining Postsocialist Patchworks: Pathways from the Past to the Global*. Aldershot: Ashgate Publishing.

Lehtonen, T.K. and M. Pantzar. 2002. 'The Ethos of Thrift: The Promotion of Banks Saving in Finland During the 1950s', *Journal of Material Culture* 7(2):211–31.

Löfgren, O. and J. Frykman. 1987. *Culture Builders: A Historical Anthropology of Middle-Class Life*. New Brunswick: Rutgers University Press.

McCallister, L. and C. Fischer. 1983. 'A Procedure for Surveying Personal Networks', in R. Burt and J. Minor (eds.), *Applied Network Analysis*. Sage Publications.

Miller, D. 1998. *A Theory of Shopping*. Cambridge: Polity Press.

Markova, E. 1962. *Slovenské äipky* (Slovak Lace). Bratislava: SVKL.

Patico, J. 2002. 'Chocolate and Cognac: Gifts and the Recognition of Social Worlds in Post-Soviet Russia', *Ethnos* 67:3.

124 | *Nicolette Makovicky*

Patico, J and M. Caldwell. 2002. 'Consumers Exiting Socialism: Ethnographic Perspectives on Daily Life in Post-Communist Europe', *Ethnos* 67(3): 285–94.

Pawlik, W. 1992. 'Intimate Commerce', in J.R. Wedel (ed.), *The Unplanned Society: Poland During and After Communism*. New York: Columbia University Press.

Pine, F. 1998. 'Dealing with Fragmentation: The Consequences of Privatization for Rural Women in Central and Southern Poland', in S. Bridger and F. Pine (eds), *Surviving Post-Socialism: Local Strategies and Regional Responses in Eastern Europe and the Former Soviet Union*. London: Routledge.

———. 1999. 'Incorporation and Exclusion in the Podhale', in S. Day, E. Papataxiarchis and M. Stewart (eds), *Lilies of the Field: Marginal people Who Live for the Moment*. Boulder: Westview Press.

———. 2002. 'Retreat to the Household: Gendered Domains in Postsocialist Poland', in C.M. Hann (ed.), *Postsocialism: Ideologies and Practices in Eurasia*. London: Routledge.

———. 2003. 'Reproducing the House: Kinship, Inheritance, and Property Relations in Highland Poland', in H. Grandits and P. Heady (eds), *Distinct Inheritances: Property, Family and Community in a Changing Europe*. Münster: Lit Verlag.

Schneider, J. 1989. '*Rumpelstiltskin's Bargain: Folklore and the Merchant Capitalist Intensification of Linen manufacture in Early Modern Europe*', in A.B. Weiner and J Schneider (eds.), *Cloth and Human Experience*. Washington: Smithsonian Institution Press.

Seabright, P. (ed.). 2000. *The Vanishing Rouble: Barter Networks and Non-monetary Transactions in Postsocialist Societies*. Cambridge: Cambridge University Press.

Segbers, K. (ed.). 2001. *Explaining Postsocialist Patchworks: Pathways from the Past to the Global*. Aldershot: Ashgate Publishing.

Strathern, M. 1997. 'Partners and Consumers: Making Relations Visible', in A.D. Schrift (ed.), *The Logic of the Gift: Toward an Ethic of Generosity*. London: Routledge.

Taussig, M. 1980. *The Devil and Commodity Fetishism in South America*. Capital Hill: University of North Carolina Press.

Veenis, M. 1999. 'Consumption in East Germany: The Seduction and Betrayal of Things', *Journal of Material Culture* 4(1): 79–112.

Verdery, K. 1996. *What Was Socialism, and What Comes Next?* Princeton: Princeton University Press.

Zelizer, V. 1997. *The Social Meaning of Money*. Princeton: Princeton University Press.

CHAPTER 5

Vietnamese Narratives of Tradition, Exchange and Friendship in the Worlds of the Global Socialist Ecumene

Susan Bayly

Introduction: The Socialist Ecumene

Building on recent fieldwork in Vietnam and official accounts of the country's move to 'market socialism', this chapter explores the ways in which Vietnamese officials, technical specialists and other socialist moderns reflect on the country's longstanding participation in the life of what I am calling the international socialist ecumene. My key concern is with both official and personal understandings of that ecumene's distinctive forms of long-distance exchange and 'friendship'.

In the case of Vietnam, these relations and interactions have involved the large-scale provision of aid and development expertise to a wide variety of labour- and skill-hungry countries both before and since marketization (known as *doi moi* or 'renovation' in Vietnam).[1] Drawing on both individual and public narratives of these experiences, I focus on the distinctions between giving and receiving made by those who have taken part in the great, ramifying 'friendship' relations of the socialist world system. I deal in particular with the profound differences which have been perceived in Vietnam between being a mere suppliant and taker of expertise and material aid, and being in the superior situation of a socialist giver, someone who imparts and thus exemplifies the empowering tokens of socialist modernity.

My use of the term 'socialist ecumene' is intended to sum up the many claims made by past and current believers in the notion of a worldwide fraternal community forged by both states and individuals on the basis of enduring revolutionary solidarities and socialist 'friendships' (*quan he huu nghi*). In present-day Vietnam, this sensitive issue of who gives to whom in socialist exchange relations has generated a striking body of publicly articulated ideas about matters of enduring socialist tradition or neotradition.

Like Cuba, China and North Korea, Vietnam is emphatically not a 'postsocialist' country. Nevertheless, both its officials and the academics and other professional people I have worked with are acutely aware of the challenges the country is facing as it embraces the Vietnamese version of market socialism. It is in this regard that a language of both socialist and presocialist national heritage has been much employed by those seeking to explain and validate the marketization process.

The legacy and continuing life of the socialist ecumene is currently much invoked in Vietnamese government statements about both the present and the premarketization past. The statements I have in mind are those exalting and legitimating Vietnam's present-day quest for export markets in a diverse array of external sites and settings. These include both China – whose own embrace of the market has been both a challenge and a stimulus to Vietnam's 'renovation' initiatives – and a variety of capitalist states, notably Malaysia and Thailand. Having become a full ASEAN member in 1995 – the first socialist state to do so – it is to these ASEAN neighbours that Vietnam has been directing much of its all-important labour and commodity export drives in recent years.[2]

Africa is yet another key arena in Vietnam's current search for markets and investment partners. The countries involved include many of those in which vast numbers of Cubans, East Germans and Chinese once toiled in the days of the great Cold War aid projects through which the Eastern and Western blocs vied for prestige and influence in the Third World. What is less well known is that Vietnam was also an active participant in such initiatives. Cooperation pacts signed during the grim years of privation that followed the 1961–73 US-Vietnam war and the two costly wars with Cambodia and China in 1978–79 sent thousands of Vietnamese technical specialists to a host of north and sub-Saharan African states. These agreements persisted well into the 1990s, and are still hailed in Vietnam as proud achievements of socialist humanitarianism.[3] But they have also been sources of much-needed remittances, both for the state, and for the individuals taking part in these schemes. My recent fieldwork has focused on the experiences of the many Hanoi intellectuals whose lives and family relations were profoundly affected by these often-protracted overseas work sojourns.

Today, most of the African states which received Vietnamese and other socialist countries' experts in the Cold War years have been moving from centralized planning systems towards economic liberalization. This includes former French and Portuguese colonies such as Algeria, Congo, Benin, Angola, Senegal, Chad and Madagascar, which had avowedly leftist or socialist governments until well into the 1980s or 1990s, and have long professed themselves to be ardent friends and admirers of Vietnam and its revolution. It also includes countries to which Vietnam is a comparative newcomer, such as Egypt, Morocco, Tanzania and South Africa.

Vietnamese government spokesmen now routinely hail the cultivation of economic relations with these African 'friends' in terms which bear directly on issues of continuity or neotradition in both 'late' and postsocialist contexts. One of the key terms in these official accounts of Vietnam's role as a provider of overseas aid and expertise is the word 'tradition' *(truyen thong)*. There is also a whole array of words and references which come from the language of gift giving and beneficent mutuality, with a strong emphasis on qualities of affect, that is, on the power of emotions, sentiments and truthful feeling *(long:* deep feeling; *chan tinh:* heartfelt sentiment). It is these qualities of 'heart' and affect which are widely said to differentiate bilateral relations of benevolence and mutuality from those involving 'profit' or 'interest' *(loi ich)*.[4] I say more below about this affective side of the socialist ecumene experience, focusing particularly on the ways in which Vietnam's distinctive experiences of both socialism and colonialism have shaped the perceptions of those who have taken part in these schemes of overseas specialist aid and development work. First, though, there is the issue of what official writings refer to as tradition. 'Tradition' and 'traditional' *(truyen thong)* are the terms routinely used in public representations of Vietnam's officially acclaimed goal of achieving 'progress' and 'development' in the forging of favourable trade relations with 'undeveloped' countries.

This can certainly be seen as the use of an idiom of shared socialist neotradition, built on a specific historic heritage. Its moral underpinnings are represented as distinctively Vietnamese, being rooted in specific native character traits of sincerity and emotional truth. But official statements and writings also present this heritage in terms of universals, these being the ideals of twentieth-century global anti-imperialism and socialist moral economy. This body of ideals and achievements is defined in a variety of official accounts as a long-term story of 'traditional friendships' *(quan he huu nghi truyen thong)* forged by Vietnam with the wider world.

At the time when socialist Vietnam (the DRV) was still closely tied to its two superpower allies, that is during the long years of war against the French (1946–54) and then the USA and its southern client state the RVN (1961–73), the country's relations with its Chinese and Soviet suppliers and backers were critically important.[5] These bonds – ostensibly fraternal, but often deeply fraught – were central to the life of outreach and dynamic interaction that was appropriate and necessary for a twentieth-century socialist state and its citizens.

It has been especially important for Vietnam to see the world of the socialist ecumene as involving a much wider array of cross-cutting ties and mutualities than those between any individual socialist state, and either or both of the communist superpowers. Thus it was under agreements signed in the name of socialist 'friendship', cooperation and mutuality that the people with whom I have worked were recruited to work abroad as remittance-earning experts (*chuyen gia*) from the late 1980s to the mid-1990s. Thousands of professionally qualified Vietnamese filled such posts in this period. They are not to be confused with the much greater numbers of manual workers who were sent under a different set of pre-1986 cooperation pacts to earn remittances for the national exchequer as factory labourers in East Germany and the other former COMECON states (Hardy 2000).[6]

The sometimes fruitful and sometimes fraught and painful deployment of professionally qualified 'experts' was one of the key unifying factors in the life of the socialist world system. Contemporary accounts of the sending of Vietnamese *chuyen gia* specialists to countries such as Algeria, Mozambique and Madagascar make much of this point about the diversity of the country's socialist friendships. This diversity is stressed particularly in accounts of the massive efforts that Vietnam is now making to strike a new generation of worker export deals in both Africa and capitalist southeast Asia.

My *chuyen gia* informants echo this official language. They speak of their African work sojourns as demanding and often painful, but a worthwhile sacrifice – a gift of the heart made willingly and freely. Of course there was an instrumental and strategic side to these schemes. From the time of the Sino-Soviet split, Vietnam steered a difficult middle course between the two socialist superpowers. The signing of 'friendship' agreements with leftist but noncommunist states secured valuable geopolitical connections that were quite distinct from those involving China and the USSR. A key example of this during the US–Vietnam War were the overtures which bore fruit as helpful backdoor diplomatic contacts with the United States via Algeria.[7]

But these key diplomatic ties of the US–Vietnam war years paved the way for connections which were important in the subtler but more enduring ways that went far beyond the purely instrumental side of these claims about socialist friendship. What was stressed in relation to the overseas 'experts' was not the flow of payments from the African states which paid their salaries. These were remitted directly to Vietnam's Labour Ministry via the Vietnamese embassies in the countries where the experts were employed. As little as 15 per cent was allocated to the experts themselves, with the rest retained by the state. Yet what is consistently emphasized, both in official accounts and the former experts' personal narratives, is the idea of chuyen gia work as an act of disinterested benevolence, a gift of tutelage and enlightenment given freely and without expectation of return to the peoples of 'undeveloped' countries.

I have regularly encountered the use of the words 'backward', 'primitive' and 'undeveloped' in this context, close as this language is to the demeaning terms in which my informants recall Russian technical experts in the 1960s and 1970s speaking of the Vietnamese. This was much resented for making them feel that their homeland was an eternal, unreciprocating taker of the largesse of superior gift givers. Indeed the fact that Vietnam was so badly in need of the employment opportunities which the industrialized COMECON states could provide made it all the more desirable to point with pride to the Vietnamese medics and other qualified professionals doing 'development' work in Africa. This was clearly proof that Vietnam was not itself a 'backward' land, locked into humiliating dependency relations within a narrow circle of richer socialist benefactors. It also explains why it has been so important to insist on the provision of the experts' skills as a matter of disinterested gift giving, rather than transactions involving the sale to other states of knowledge and expertise of which Vietnam itself had urgent need.

The people I have worked with in Hanoi come from intelligentsia families with a history of francophone education during the colonial period. Of those now in their sixties, most received postgraduate education or training in one or more of the ex-COMECON countries. In most cases their parents were officials of the Communist-led Viet Minh movement which spearheaded Vietnam's anti-French liberation war. Most are Russian speakers. Almost all had francophone parents, and they themselves have competence in either French or Portuguese, the compulsory languages for postings as 'experts' in Africa's former French- and Portuguese-ruled colonies. Many also know Polish, German, Chinese, Romanian or Czech. They include both male and female professors of chemistry, agronomists, radiologists, and practitioners of a Vietnamese medical skill they said was warmly received in Africa: electric acupuncture. In the course of my fieldwork I have found it particularly rewarding to travel with some of them to the villages where they had relocated as children during the 1946–54 anti-French liberation war, living with their parents or peasant foster families in the Viet Minh-controlled interzones (*lien khu*).

By the late 1940s, these 'liberated territories' had become the provinces of a nascent revolutionary proto-state, divided by a well-defined but fluid frontier from the French-controlled territories. The 'liberated zones' had an educational system (Bayly 2004). The secondary schools taught French as well as romanized Vietnamese (*quoc ngu*) until 1950, when the language of the colonizer was replaced with Chinese and Russian.

The Morality of Exchange in the Socialist World System

For Vietnamese with this kind of background – self-consciously modern, patriotic, proud of their parents' revolutionary credentials, and of their family traditions of cultivation and educational attainment – the French they had learned from their parents and at school is highly valued. It is perceived in terms that are very unlike what we might expect from the writings of postcolonial theorists like Viswanathan (1989), for whom colonial educators gave only poisoned and demeaning cultural gifts to their empires' intelligentsias. And I have found that like other aspects of their educational experience, knowledge of French and the modern scientific and literary subjects of which it was the medium are spoken of in much the same terms as chuyen gia service, that is, in an idiom of provision and enlightened beneficence. This is something that my informants have explicitly connected with the gifts of modernity which they see themselves as having imparted to Africans through their work as aid givers and development specialists.

The parents or grandparents of my Hanoi friends were among the first generation of Vietnamese to attend colonial lycées and pedagogical colleges in the years immediately following the First World War. These elders are spoken of as revolutionaries who appropriated French as a language of power and modernity, deploying it in the national cause, and then handing it on as a gift of knowledge to their children, the heirs to their epic feats in the liberation war.

Often it is their politically active mothers that these sixty- to seventy-year-olds extol when describing that earlier generation's gifts of care and knowledge. Both men and women take pride in the fact that they come from families whose young women were among the first in Vietnam to earn modern educational qualifications in colonial lycées and colleges during the 1920s and 1930s. (Marr 1981; Kelly 1982) During the anti-French liberation war, many such women held posts as medics, teachers and party cadres in the interzones' nascent revolutionary proto-state. The Hanoi people I know describe their female kin as tireless nurturers of their own educational attainments. Central to the narratives they have shared with me are emotionally charged evocations of this care and nurture. In their accounts, the imparting of both learning and revolutionary examplarship are represented as manifestations of their mothers', aunts' and sisters' devotion and selflessness. As I show below, there are very similar visions of disinterested generosity pervading present-day official writings about Vietnam as a munificent giver of development aid to other lands and peoples.

A number of the men and women who have told me about their lives as chuyen gia experts in African countries – especially Mozambique and Angola – have said that what they saw there gave them a strong sense of contrast with their own homeland's experiences in this matter of cultural giftgiving. They think of the African peoples to whom they provided technical and educational aid as disempowered in ways that they are not. They say that it is sad, even though it was remunerative for them personally, and for Vietnam, that they taught in institutions like Angola's pedagogical and medical colleges in the ex-colonizer's languages. They were sad to see countries without governments like theirs which had ensured that Vietnam had a unifying national language. *Quoc ngu* (romanized Vietnamese) became the medium of modern colonial schooling and popular journalism after the First World War, and has been deployed in Vietnam's schools and universities since independence. It was the key instrument of the great mass literacy campaigns which were brought to fruition by their parents' generation. This modernized version of their mother tongue is thus spoken of as enabling all Vietnamese to unite around a shared national culture, while partaking selectively of the wider world's modern skills and knowledge.[8]

My older friends all know and love the patriotic songs and poetry of the Viet Minh era. Those who studied in the Soviet Union or attended art, music and Russian classes in Hanoi's Soviet-style Children's Culture Palace (established in 1955 and rebuilt with Czech aid in 1973) still read Russian novels, and are keen aficionados of Tchaikovsky and Rachmaninov. Yet those who were at school in the 1940s and early 1950s also say they find it pleasantly nostalgic to recall the Lamartine and Victor Hugo poems that they committed to memory in their interzone classrooms. Their patriotic young Vietnamese teachers extolled these works from the preindependence lycée curriculum as modern in tone and universal in their message, hence suitably inspirational for young patriots.[9] At the same time, the sixty- to seventy-year-olds I know can also still sing the Chinese party anthems which were performed by interzone youth groups at the big night-time assemblies at which visiting Viet Minh officials described their travels to Moscow, Bucharest and Beijing. In their schoolrooms too they heard a great deal about that wider socialist world in which their country's resistance struggle was followed and applauded by admiring comrades in other lands. From these far-away places, they learned, came unstinting aid and moral support imparted by the benevolent providers who inhabited that wider socialist world.

There were other techniques, too, through which the Viet Minh authorities conveyed this message about the resistance war as a cause nourished by the nurturing friendships and solidarities of the socialist ecumene. There were posters and travelling photo-journalism exhibitions presenting images of personal interactions between the nation's leaders and other great figures of the socialist world, often in settings of cordial intimacy. One image from the resistance war years, now displayed in Hanoi's Revolution Museum, is of the Vietnamese revolutionary leader

Ho Chi Minh in battledress, joining hands in a merry impromptu dance with members of a Chinese military delegation.

Gifts and Provisioning in the Moralized Marketplace

Throughout the 1946–54 liberation war, a variety of strategic items were produced within the 'liberated' territories. Some were ingeniously devised from cannibalized foreign consumer items: powdered milk tins turned into storage containers and soldiers' cooking utensils; wine bottles and penicillin ampoules recycled as kerosene-fuelled lamps with coiled-wire wick holders (Dang Phong 2002). Thus it was inevitably through cross-frontier trade with the French-controlled zones that the nascent Viet Minh state met many of its survival needs. Supply and provisioning were essential and highly moral activities of resistance life.

One of the slogans during the anti-French war was 'fight them and trade with them'. The marketplace and the things that came from it – including both home produce and the enemy's industrial commodities – were necessary: to be controlled, corrected of exploitative elements, and bent to the will of the revolution, but not abolished. Even petty traders could be represented as providers living in harmony with the 'people's' needs and mores, rather than immoral exploitaters and 'speculators'. This of course was in sharp contrast to the official thought of other revolutionary states such as China and the USSR.[10] Viet Minh ideology certainly did not stigmatize all market life as parasitical and immoral. The interzone authorities sought to expand or create rural markets, maintained customs posts along the interzones' fluid frontiers, and encouraged small-scale traders to cross back and forth into French-controlled territory so they could obtain and sell both artisanal wares and manufactured products that were essential to the war effort. (Dang Phong 2002)

The Viet Minh's propaganda posters thus made strikingly positive points about the role of small-scale entrepreneurship in revolutionary life. A key theme was the exhortation to consume home products and abstain from costly and corrupting goods such as foreign medicines, sweets and cigarettes. This too was a message which was far from negative about all forms of market activity. Vietnam was by rights a land of trade and healthy productive exchange; it was colonial monopoly and its associated forms of exploitation that were to be expunged, not the market itself. Indeed without money and the market there could be no healthy meeting of human need: home products were to be acquired at a fair price from peasant purveyors or market traders; households were not enjoined to satisfy their needs through barter or subsistence home production.

Among the many didactic posters from the 1946–54 period, one in particular makes this point with notable force: a cycle trader in peasant garb wheels his load of nutritious foodstuffs and other home-produced goods over the body of a top-hatted white man who sprawls in disarray amid his rejected foreign wares (Harrison-Hall 2002: 27, 68). The capitalist foreigner is thus portrayed in precisely the terms one would expect to find in a piece of revolutionary Marxist propaganda. Yet the cycle trader is clearly a virtuous man doing legitimate service by providing those in need with wholesome goods; he is therefore entitled to make a modest profit. Both sellers and consumers were thus to take moral decisions in the marketplace, distinguishing between good and bad forms of commerce under the guidance of a protective revolutionary state.[11]

It is true that imported wares such as brandy and other strong spirits were consistently demonized in revolutionary poster art; the good patriot was to eschew both their sale and consumption. But I have friends who cherish memories of their Viet Minh fathers' love of French wines and other sophisticated consumer products. To them, this was a mark of cultivated knowledge, much like knowing how to play tennis or drive a motor car. These too were marks of one's family's modernity in the 1930s and 1940s, and were therefore distinguished and honourable: such things were thus not indulgences in the colonizer's corrupting luxuries.

Such views were worlds apart from those animating the great Maoist drives against cosmopolitan consumption tastes and other bourgeois corruptions. And they were both like and unlike the ideals of colonial India's early twentieth-century *swadeshi* (home produce) campaigners (Sarkar 1973; for China, compare Gerth 2003). These Indian activists celebrated the wholesomeness of 'native' goods and products and extolled the moral man of commerce as an ideal type of the good, patriotic Indian. But they were often strongly influenced by Gandhian and other revived or neo-Hindu teachings which equated spiritual purity with teetotal vegetarianism, and thus vilified many tastes and pursuits that were considered progressive and modern in Vietnam.[12]

What is most striking about the Viet Minh's home products message is its treatment of the marketplace as a moral arena in which the revolution's new public virtues could be both imparted and absorbed. Within the market, the seller of useful goods was an exemplar of patriotic sociality, setting out his or her wares in a hygienic, well-swept space adorned with patriotic slogans and equipped to provide important modern services like reading rooms and dispensary care. The good trader was of course compliant with the party's demands to renounce the sale of wasteful goods like firecrackers and gold leaf. And out on the road with their cycle loads or shoulder packs, such purveyors were patriots and heroes, doing the work of the revolution by concealing weapons and propaganda leaflets in their bundles and panniers (Malarney 1996; Dang Phong 2002).[13]

Even as a COMECON member state in the collectivization era, Vietnam retained something of this vision. The twenty-year US-led international trade blockade was widely represented as immoral and inhumane, unjustly debarring Vietnam from a world economy in which it could have participated on its own terms, without compromising its commitment to socialist values. Those who were children in the anti-French liberation war have their own narratives of a moralized marketplace, this being a site of marvels from which a long-absent parent would occasionally obtain something rare and wonderful: a sack of St Louis sugar, an American pen called a Warever. Far from being manifestations of capitalism's dehumanizing commodity logic, these things with their bright packaging and evocative brand names were treasures rendered precious and personal, imparted with love by one's revolutionary parents.

Nowadays, it is the challenges of the present that one hears most about, both in official accounts and in personal narratives. Much of what is said about those exalted times of the anti-French war, when dedicated revolutionaries led a superior moral life in a world of patriotic market sociality, is an implicit moralizing commentary on the post-*doi moi* era of 'market socialism'.

In my informants' childhood years, Vietnam did become a net recipient in the great flows of the global socialist gift economy. After Mao's victory in 1949, the Viet Minh received a rapidly increasing inflow of weaponry and other material aid from the Peoples Republic of China. Vietnam's anti-French resistance forces were given staging areas in southern China, where there were also special schools for cadres' children (see Ninh 2002). My informants say that the friendships forged at these schools created networks of mutual support and enduring interaction which were important for their later career moves. And in the grim, post-Reunification austerity years, they were a means of accessing scarce goods and services. These ties thus sound much like the webs of exchange and mutual obligation described in ethnographies of *guanxi* networking in China. And the people I know stress the strength of emotion underpinning these attachments. They see them as potent and 'heartfelt', rather than purely instrumental relationships.[14]

This is much like what both past and present-day official narratives say about the country's life of warm-hearted 'friendships' within the wider socialist ecumene. These official accounts seek to convey that Vietnam has always been as much a giver as a taker, its revolutionary triumphs constituting a gift of exemplarship to the wider world, its war victories emphatically not achieved through dependency on bigger, richer socialist benefactors. Nowadays these transnational solidarities are routinely narrativized in official writings as a forging of lasting affective attachments in circumstances of pre-independence anti-colonialism, as well as more recent 'anti-imperialist' causes like the anti-apartheid movement. The language of affect is widely used in these accounts, with much emphasis on images of feeling and intimacy, for example in evocations of Africa's 'freedom-loving peoples' looking to the Vietnamese as revolutionary role models, and exemplars of anti-imperialist resistance.

In the words of the Vietnamese Foreign Ministry's official newspaper *Quoc Te* ('International Affairs'): 'The image of the Vietnamese nation spearheading the fight for independence has remained deep in the hearts of freedom-loving African people for generations.' This article also maintains that Vietnam's historic bonds with Africa proceed from 'sentiment and tradition', with this 'tradition' being one of loyalty and friendship towards the African people. Elsewhere in this account, an official describing a recent round of diplomatic visits to African countries describes Vietnam's present-day trading ventures in Africa as the fulfillment of a past history of 'tradition', 'obligations' and 'responsibilities'.[15]

The origins of this shared socialist neotradition are said to date back to the preindependence decades when Vietnam's revolutionary leaders forged warm-hearted friendships with African thinkers and activists. They grew stronger in the great days of worldwide acclaim for Vietnam's wars of resistance against both the French and the armed might of the USA and its client, the south Vietnamese RVN. As a result, proclaims *Quoc Te*, 'Viet Nam is viewed with affection and respect everywhere; Viet Nam's wartime [victories] are spoken of as an inspiration by every country.'

The Personalization of Socialist Neotradition

An anecdote exemplifying the power of such friendships, and the enduring webs of affect from which they spring, is a story told by Vietnam's first post-apartheid ambassador to South Africa. The envoy's story is that at the ceremony in 2000 marking the presentation of his credentials to the South African President Thabo Mbeki, Mr Mbeki suddenly tossed aside his prepared text and pointed to one of his teeth: 'broken!', he said, in 1965, by 'the British police' during a demonstration supporting Vietnam against the Americans in his Sussex University student days. According to Mr Dung the Ambassador, those assembled were so moved by this moment of warmth and sentiment that they too broke with protocol, and joined in a spontaneous standing ovation.[16]

Such uses of the idiom of enduring socialist neotradition are often generalized to evoke images of Vietnam as revolutionary hero nation, its technological and material limitations a sign of self-sacrifice and revolutionary austerity, not the poverty of backwardness or 'underdevelopment'. But accounts of these neotraditions are also frequently personalized. When this is done, the language of affect is much deployed, often through evocations of the loving warmth of family elders and siblings. In this context, the moral exemplarship of the revolutionary war leader President Ho Chi Minh regularly comes to the fore as the key source of these affective socialist neotraditions. Often there is particular emphasis on the lapidary phrases in which he expressed these ideals: 'Uncle Ho on Africa: "Love One Another Like Brothers and Sisters"' (*Bac Ho voi chau Phi: Than yeu nhau nhu anh em*), declares one of the *Quoc Te* newspaper's headlines in 2003. The article extols the President's 'boundless, tender love' (*muon van tinh than yeu triu men*) for the colonized African peoples whose plight he had observed at first hand during an undercover tour of French-ruled colonies in 1913.

'[President Ho Chi Minh] cried at the sight of the brutal oppression of the innocent by the colonialists', says *Quoc Te*. The article tells readers that Uncle Ho pledged undying love for his 'African brothers and sisters' (*anh em châu Phi*). His struggle for national independence in Vietnam was thus a mission with a universal moral purpose, to be experienced and enacted in an idiom of inextinguishable feeling and familial intimacy: 'Friends, forgive me if I cannot kiss you before I leave' (*Cac ban tha loi cho toi khong hon cac ban truoc khi di*). *Quoc Te* identifies this as an extract from Ho Chi Minh's 1913 farewell letter to the African comrades he had met on his tour. It offers yet another quotation: 'Our feelings have been fostered since youth' or, more idiomatically: 'My feelings for you date back to the time of my youth.' The word that I translate here as feelings is *long*, which can also be understood as the bodily seat of sensibility and feeling, i.e. the heart, entrails or 'guts'. So this utterance conveys the great depth of attachments made and energized by one's sincere and passionate youthful self. It is identified in *Quoc Te* as a poetic couplet which Ho Chi Minh recited in 1960, forty-seven years after his original African tour, on the occasion of an official visit to Vietnam by the socialist President of Guinée-Conakry. This was one of the French colonies that Ho Chi Minh had visited in 1913. The *Quoc Te* account also attributes to Ho Chi Minh a remark proclaiming his embodied identification with the oppression of his African brothers and sisters: 'The suffering of each individual and family combine to be mine.'

Ho Chi Minh is famously referred to in Vietnam as Bac Ho, usually translated as Uncle Ho. The familial term Bac is one of the many relational terms deployed in everyday family life in addressing or referring to an elder sibling of ego's parents. Normally, then, a Vietnamese speaker would never employ the same relational pronoun that his or her parents would use to address someone: ego's 'Bac' would be 'Anh' (Brother) to ego's father.

In former times one spoke in terms bracketing together all other Vietnamese, regardless of age or standing, only in exceptional circumstances, as when addressing the emperor as the superior of all. In such a case one spoke as 'I your subject', using the impersonal pronoun toi which signals that no other human distinctions are being invoked or alluded to. (Hy Van Luong 1989; Marr 2000). But the appellation Bac Ho signals the seniority of loving family life rather than distant hierarchy (Hy Van Luong 1989; Malarney 2003). At the same time, it is a perception of eldership which is beyond time, overriding the consciousness of age grades and generational difference which is essential to Vietnamese linguistic interactions. So as a loving elder to every member of the Vietnamese national family, both in his own time and in all ages to come, Ho Chi Minh makes the nation a super-family, enduring, indestructible and moral, since it is stamped with the qualities of his own compassionate and bountiful nature. In invoking that compassion in official accounts of the giving of gifts of expertise and exemplarship to African 'friends', what is being suggested is that these cooperative interactions of the socialist ecumene take shape as something akin to the 'empathetic dialogues' which Fennell (2002) says are generated out of the giving of 'illiquid', disinterested gifts between individual exchange partners.

Cosmologies of Socialist Provision and Nurture

Among the many remarkable features of the Ho Chi Minh memorial museum in Hanoi is a display area containing hundreds of gift items presented over many years to President Ho Chi Minh by both socialist and nonsocialist world leaders. Ssorin-Chaikov and Sosnina's innovative work on gift giving to Stalin (2006) has made me recognize the importance of this other giant treasure trove of the humble and the opulent, ranging from crystal glassware to peasant handicrafts. The museum's display turns the world's diplomatic courtesy offerings into a kind of socialist counterpart of the world-ordering tributary homage flows that focused in past centuries on the person of the Sino-Confucian emperor, as described in Marshal Sahlins's celebrated essay 'Cosmologies of Capitalism' (1988). What I am proposing here is a kind of cosmology of socialism, in its own way as world-ordering and universalizing as the regimens of those premodern Chinese statecraft conventions. It too involved an uneven movement of goods, a trafficking in things wanted and appreciated in some places, but not in others: hence cosmology to be seen not as 'structure' but rather as 'traffic', with stops, starts, hesitations and flows.[17]

The profusion of goods and products flowing into Vietnam as gifts to the nation's leader proclaimed Ho Chi Minh's standing as an eternal and cherished elder to all the world, thus the focus of the most moral of enduring, affective ties. These are the ties of pupil to teacher and junior to nurturing elder kin. Both are still regularly given form in Vietnam through the conventions of honorific upward gift giving.[18] These gifts of the socialist ecumene stand in sharp contrast to the 'interested', corrupting practices of the capitalist world, as in capitalist states' giving of development aid to poor countries. For Vietnamese and other socialists, such giving is undertaken merely to gain clients, captive markets and cheap labour: they are not bestowed in token of true 'friendship' and beneficent mutuality.

What this suggests is a clear distinction between the kind of gift giving that has been recognized by ethnographers of *guanxi* – giving that is directed upwards and confers honour on the recipient – and the type which has been more widely portrayed in anthropology. In this second form, gifts flow downwards, pressurizing recipients by demeaning them unless or until they can reciprocate appropriately. Receiving development aid is demeaning in precisely these terms, as it defines the taker as too poor ever to give in reciprocation. Hence the importance of the gifts to Bac Ho which confirm Vietnam's standing as a senior and elder in the socialist ecumene, rather than a junior and 'undeveloped' suppliant. One can thus set aside the shaming image of Vietnam as a country poorer and needier than others by focusing on Ho Chi Minh, the father and exemplar of all, receiving from all lands the respectful gifts of juniors to elders.

In both personal narratives and official representations, the ideals of socialist neotradition are also widely identified with the gifts of self-sacrifice made on behalf of the nation by other heroic exemplars. These include specific classes and types of people: Vietnamese soldiers, workers, women, youth. And they also now include that other key group on whom I focus in this chapter: the thousands of educated Vietnamese who were recruited in the 1980s and 1990s to serve as providers of technical aid and development skills to the wider world.

As I noted above, for the families I know these posts were a source of desperately needed earnings during Vietnam's grim post-Reunification privation years. But these gains came at a high cost. Postings could last for four or five years. Only brief holidays home were allowed, and, unlike the Poles and other Eastern Europeans with whom they worked, few if any Vietnamese were accompanied by their families. Yet it was often married women with young children who took the posts. At home in Hanoi they almost always earned less than their husbands. So it made financial sense for their husbands to stay behind, taking over household responsibilities and working with their older children and other kin to sustain the Hanoi end of the all-important illicit trading operations in which virtually everyone is said to have engaged in those years. The material benefits were thus substantial. But the prolonged separations took their toll, and my friends recall with distress the malicious gossip that often focused on their marital lives.

Even obtaining a *chuyen gia* post was both stressful and costly. Apart from the stringent language exams, amassing the necessary credentials and documents required the giving of 'presents' in cash or kind to a host of official gatekeepers. Particularly for women, this was often a would-be expert's first experience of the upward or tribute-like forms of supplicatory favour and present giving that really do correspond to *guanxi* gifting in China. Such acts are recalled as demeaning and unpleasant, though those involved found these experiences to be a source of useful skills when in post in semi-socialist countries like Algeria, where there was much the same need to supplicate dispensers of ration cards and other essentials. These regimens turned out to be an all too familiar feature of the socialist ecumene wherever they went, but something they could also turn to advantage when the need arose.

All these elements of *chuyen gia* life combined to make the former experts I know feel that those outside their immediate circle have tended to regard them as having done something unseemly, even if they were driven to it by a combination of national need and personal necessity. They find it painful that others clearly thought of them not as givers of aid, skill and uplift, but as takers who made discreditable gains for themselves and their families by making money from their skills and knowledge. Some are deeply resentful about the fact that they are sometimes bracketed with the former factory workers who are widely thought of in Hanoi as profiteers who returned from their sojourns in the COMECON lands with the ill-gotten gains that fuelled the city's notorious local property speculation booms. Thus until recently, chuyen gia work was rarely written about or spoken of in Hanoi. It is therefore very striking to find that the experts are now being officially reinserted into the national narrative of high-minded self-sacrifice in the cause of national and international progress and solidarity.

Imparting Gifts of Friendship in Contemporary Africa

In 2003, Vietnam's Ministry of Foreign Relations launched an initiative entitled 'Vietnam-Africa: Opportunities for Cooperation and Development in the 21st century'. Its aims are explained in the Foreign Ministry newspaper articles quoted above. These texts explicitly invoke and then dismiss the idea of exploitative or demeaning market principles as the basis of Vietnam's current quest for overseas markets for its trade goods and migrant workers. By recalling and extolling the achievements of the *chuyen gia* experts as disinterested gift givers and service providers, they systematically represent the Africa trade initiative in terms which call for a kind of *méconnaissance*, a mental leap of reclassification assigning these involvements with neoliberal market forces to the moral categories of provision and the meeting of need.

Central to this exercise is the use of a highly nuanced language of 'expressive' rather than demeaningly 'instrumental' gift giving. I borrow this terminology from Yunxiang Yan's account of everyday interpersonal gift relations in rural north China (Yan 1996). According to Yan, 'expressive' gift giving arises in situations of longstanding interpersonal relations, notably those that involve enduring and important mutual relationships and emotional ties (1996: 67). 'Instrumental' giving secures favours or other gains. It can of course coexist with expressive gifting, though one form will usually predominate over the other. And while the instrumental form of giving is a necessity of everyday life, it is still dishonourable and demeaning between members of the same community; ordinarily it is a means to a utilitarian end, involving short-term relationships only.

It is not surprising then that what pervades official accounts of Vietnam's current economic life are claims that the country is still a provider, indeed still a giver of 'expressive' rather than 'interested' gifts in a world still recognizably endowed with the superior traditions of the socialist ecumene, a moral order which its own efforts helped to create and perpetuate. So like the gifts of revolutionary exemplarship that Vietnam gave initially to colonized peoples, and then to the latter-day victims of apartheid and global neoimperialism, the sending of the specialist experts to African countries in the 1980s and 1990s is now being described as an enactment of 'traditional friendship', one that is undertaken in the same spirit of generosity to aid needy Africans 'in the fight against hunger and poverty'.

Furthermore, say spokesmen for the 'Vietnam-Africa' trade initiative, Vietnam is still acting in the same spirit, still continuing to meet needs and impart benefits, and doing so in ways that are consistent with the values and traditions of the socialist ecumene. Hence the exaltation of the *chuyen gia* experts of the past: the thousands of Vietnamese remittance earners currently working in countries such as Benin, Senegal and Chad are to be seen as providers of the same kind, contributing skills and knowledge to meet these countries' needs. And even the opening of African markets to Vietnamese rice, textiles, garments and consumer goods is to be understood as generous provision to those who are 'badly in need'.

There is a highly personalized dimension to these accounts, several of which present exemplary anecdotes using a language of affective intimacy to demonstrate the depth and power of these 'traditional' links to Africa. One of these comes in an interview with a Foreign Ministry official extolling the key role played by 'the Vietnamese community in Africa' (*cong dong nguoi Viet o chau Phi*) in fostering friendly cooperation in the form of trade ties between Vietnam and its African friends. The people being referred to here are Vietnamese who would have been unmentionable in official utterances until recently: experts who stayed on in Africa to make money in ways thought discreditable for educated Vietnamese, that is as petty entrepreneurs. Yet far from vilifying them, the official presents an elegiac account of a meeting during his recent travels with a Vietnamese family who were the proud proprietors of a restaurant in the Congo. He said he was delighted by the Vietnamese meal the couple cooked for him. And he emphasized its 'genuineness', the implication being that Africa is not so alien that the delights of the Vietnamese kitchen can not be created there.

The official also says that he was equally delighted by the enterprise the couple were displaying by using their business as a base from which to market Vietnamese export products. It is well known that many Vietnamese have remained in the countries where they went as students, labourers or *chuyen gia* experts in the 1980s and 1990s. Some have prospered. From Lusaka to St Petersburg, these overseas Vietnamese are now running businesses, mostly in the provisioning and grooming trades. Their seed capital often originated in the illicit trading ventures which Vietnamese expatriates pursued in the 1980s and early 1990s, when those working or studying abroad augmented their tiny salaries and maintenance allowances by becoming skilled practitioners in the risky but lucrative arts of suitcase trafficking and shuttle trading (Dang Phong and Beresford 2001; Dang Phong 2002).

Most of the experts went home at the end of their four- or five-year postings. In Russia and Eastern Europe, however, many Vietnamese have stayed on and now live on the fringes of the law like the African shuttle traders described in MacGaffey and Bazenguissa's striking ethnography of *sapeur* (hustler) life in Paris and francophone Africa, *Congo-Paris* (2000). Many of these widely travelled Africans also have an intelligentsia background; they too are heirs to the often painful afterlife of the socialist ecumene. Like the overseas Vietnamese, they too are often targeted by racist thugs and ultranationalist political parties. My Vietnamese friends all know stories about their own and other people's participation in this world of transnational entrepreneurship. Virtually everyone I know has friends or kin who have run a beauty salon or café-restaurant somewhere in Africa or Eastern Europe, or profited from a clandestine marketing operation involving anything from imported pharmaceuticals and blood plasma to costume jewellery and motorbikes.

Almost every conversation I have had with former *chuyen gia* has focused on issues of moral concern involving obligations to both family and homeland. Everyone speaks of their trading profits in relation to the powerful pleasures and duties of provision. The attitudes I have encountered were certainly more varied and nuanced than those identified in many other accounts of the post-1989 period in former or 'late' socialist countries, where it is humiliating to be a former academic or professional reduced to running a market stall. Yet it is still surprising to find official accounts representing 'Vietnam towns' – market traders' enclaves in cities like Lusaka – as a credit to the nation, their residents described approvingly as members of an overseas Vietnamese 'community' (*cong dong*), still strongly connected to the fatherland, and doing virtuous service in the nation's cause.

This message is made all the more explicit in an account of yet another of that same Ministry official's travel encounters. This was in Morocco, an ex–French protectorate where Vietnam has recently been seeking to develop trade ties. This is quite a daring vignette to present because it alludes directly to the highly sensitive issue of intermarriage and interracial liaisons, still a very painful topic in Vietnam.

Even today, to mention Africa and Africans can sometimes lead to uncomfortable exchanges in which older people refer to their war memories of black soldiers in French uniform perpetrating acts of violence against both Viet Minh fighters and civilians. Especially common are stories of rape and its terrible consequences for the women and their families. It is thus very striking that it was a Vietnamese expatriate woman with a Moroccan husband whom the official said he had found an inspiring exemplar of patriotism and 'heartiness' (sincerity, true feeling 'from the heart': *chan tinh*) during his north African visit. This too is a story of an official occasion, transformed into an epiphanic moment by the outflow of profound emotion: a political point being made in the language of affect.

The woman 'touched my heart', says the minister; he would always cherish the memory of her profound and sincere emotion.[19] What is remarkable is that this is a Vietnamese woman who is described as the wife of a man whom readers would visualize as a dark-skinned African.[20] Even more remarkably, the article identifies the man as an ex-soldier, one of the tens of thousands of Africans recruited during the 1946–54 anti-French resistance war to fight under French command against the Viet Minh. Yet far from being a grim tale of a Vietnamese woman defiled and disgraced through her liaison with an enemy soldier and a man of alien race, readers were clearly expected to see this as a positive and uplifting story. The account says that the soldier had changed sides, deserting his regiment to become a decorated Viet Minh war hero. Such cases have been documented and are now cited as yet more evidence of enduring friendship between the Vietnamese nation and other peoples with a heritage of involvement in the anti-colonial resistance cause.

Even more uplifting for readers was the minister's avowal that after many years in Morocco, the woman still retained a 'burning desire' (*long mong moi*: deeply felt, ardent yearning) to see her homeland. He reports as a sign of this keen patriotic devotion the long hours she spent every day watching Vietnam state television's overseas satellite broadcasts.[21] He also recounts that she wept throughout her meeting with him. This depth of feeling is another sign of the moral worth that readers were being called on to recognize in such individuals. This expatriate woman is thus yet another exemplar of their homeland's best qualities. Through her example and that of others in her situation, readers are to grasp that the country's pursuit of overseas commercial and investment activities is in the 'traditional' spirit of Vietnamese patriotism, hence consistent with revolutionary socialist neotradition, and the enduring values of the international socialist ecumene.

Conclusion

What I think the people that I have worked with have wanted me to understand is that they do not see themselves as living in a world of defunct socialist values now dead and discredited by their country's new life of globalized market enterprise. This is true even for elder members of families whose younger kin are beginning to take jobs with multinationals and nongovernmental organizations at salaries far higher than their parents' state service earnings. To the distress of some, this means that their sons and daughters have begun to turn away from the kinds of careers that have long confirmed and perpetuated the proud sense of cultivated family tradition and selfless achievement that are still spoken of as hallmarks of Hanoi intelligentsia life.

I certainly do not mean to paint a simplistic or one-dimensional picture of the views that I have encountered in Vietnam on these sensitive and complex matters. The Hanoi people I know have experienced both gains and losses under market socialism, and are certainly not insulated by family heritage or accrued cultural capital from its dangers and uncertainties. I have been greatly struck by the wide-ranging, international sweep of the sense of living socialist neotradition that is still to be found in Vietnam, hence my emphasis on the extent to which the people I know have felt that they have lived their remarkable national life in a worldwide ecumene, rather than a narrowly regional or postcolonial frame of reference.

I have also been struck by their strongly articulated emotional sense of the things and values that have endured from Vietnam's twentieth-century socialist past, even though their accounts of giving, taking, providing and affective exemplification in the world of the socialist ecumene are often expressed nowadays as a complex moral commentary on the challenges and dilemmas of the country's present-day economic and social transformations.

Acknowledgments

For their valuable comments on earlier drafts of this chapter I warmly thank Caroline Humphrey, Alan Macfarlane, Marilyn Strathern, James Laidlaw, Leo Howe, Nikolai Ssorin-Chaikov, Harri Englund, Magnus Marsden, Jacob Copeman, and the editors of this volume. My research has also benefitted greatly from discussions with Professor Dang Phong, William Smith, Natasha Pairaudeau, Andrew Hardy and Truong Huyen Chi.

Notes

1. The turbulent and far-reaching process of *doi moi* was set in train in the late 1980s. See Dang Phong (1999), Selden and Turley (1993).
2. ASEAN (the Association of Southeast Asian Nations) was founded in 1967 as a basis for regional cooperation between the five founding member states (Indonesia, Malaysia, Singapore, Thailand and the Philippines), all of which considered the repression of internal communist-led insurgencies to be their most pressing political priority.
3. A similar cooperation agreement, which involved the drafting of Vietnamese irrigation experts for specialist work in Iraq in 1990, was aborted at the start of the first Gulf War in January 1991.
4. This term is often employed in ways pointing to the discreditable nature of actions motivated by 'mere' interest (*don thuan*), e.g. 'The bonds between Vietnam and Africa go beyond mere interests' (*Quan he Viet Nam – chau Phi vuot len tren cac moi quan he don thuan dua tren loi ich*).
5. The 1954 partition which followed the formal end of French rule created two states: the US-backed Republic of (South) Vietnam, or RVN, and the socialist DRV or Democratic Republic under Ho Chi Minh's presidency. American withdrawal in 1973 led to the collapse of the RVN, with liberation ('occupation') of the South in 1975, and official reunification in 1976.
6. COMECON (the Council for Mutual Economic Assistance) was founded in 1949 as a Soviet-dominated association of Eastern Europe's communist states. Mongolia became a member in 1962, Cuba in 1972 and Vietnam in 1978; the organization was disbanded in 1991.
7. The online United States Documents Reference System site contains a number of 'sanitized' US intelligence documents indicating that Algeria was among the countries operating as contact points between the USA and the DRV in the 1960s. (e.g. DDRS CK3200147509).
8. The key architect of the 1940s–50s mass literacy campaign was Professor Nguyen Van Huyen, Vietnam's first professionally trained anthropologist; he was a long-serving Minister of Education under Ho Chi Minh, and was one of the many eminent Hanoi intellectuals who relocated to the interzones with his family during the resistance war. On quoc ngu see Marr (1981); and on the literacy campaigns see Ninh (2002); Nguyen Kim Nu Hanh (2003).

9. Compare Hy Van Luong (1992: 68) on the reading of Montesquieu and Rousseau by young revolutionaries in the 1930s.
10. Compare Mandel and Humphrey (2002).
11. Such images were often strongly gendered. Another picture from this period – *Khong mua!* ('[We're] not buying!') – shows two stern male revolutionaries turning their backs on a flashily garbed female shopkeeper who has attempted to beguile them with her stock of American cigarettes and other foreign luxuries (Harrison-Hall 2002: 26, 67).
12. The Indian campaigners, too, viewed small-scale artisanship and craft marketing as fundamental components of a healthy and prosperous national life. So like the francophone Vietnamese revolutionaries who thought of French wine-making as a virtuous craft tradition to be sharply distinguished from the hated colonial distilling monopoly, many Indian *swadeshis* found kindred spirits in the colonial metropole, notably the adherents of Britain's arts and crafts movement.
13. Of course the big capitalist was a true bourgeois class enemy. Indeed, during Vietnam's Maoist-style 1953-56 Land Reform campaign, even traditional healers and other service specialists were demonized as makers of exploitative profits from 'backward' or otherwise antisocial activities. And, in contrast to the patriotic petty trader, the figure of the big merchant was also widely represented as a local non-Vietnamese ally of international capitalist forces. Quintessentially, this meant a member of the ethnic Chinese (Sino-Viet or Hoa) population, which was widely identified as irredeemably un-Vietnamese until well into the postindependence period, hence both immoral in their economic behaviour, and predisposed to subversive political allegiances.
14. On *guanxi* see Smart (1993), Yang (1994) and Kipnis (1996); Gold identifies emotional qualities such as empathy, delicacy and finesse as important components in successful guanxi relations (1985: 660–61).
15. This is from an account of an interview with the Vice Minister of Foreign Affairs, Mr Nguyen Phu Binh, describing his ministerial visits to Africa in the early 2000s: '"Viet Nam is viewed with affection and respect everywhere; Viet Nam's wartime [valour] is mentioned as an inspiration/example by every country [I] visited", he said. The broadest avenue in Angola is named after Ho Chi Minh. Tanzania's senior revolutionary leaders claim to be disciples of President Ho Chi Minh. The Sudanese Government was so enthusiastic that within a day in the country, he was received by as many as six ministers. Even a minister from the opposition UNITA party called the Vietnamese friends "comrades".'
16. This is reproduced in a *Quoc Te* article entitled 'South Africa: Strategic Gateway to the African Market'.
17. I am indebted to James Laidlaw for suggesting the idea of cosmologies as a basis for interpreting socialist gift practices, and to Caroline Humphrey for her insightful thoughts about cosmology as 'traffic'.
18. For China, compare Yan (1996 and 2003). In the Ho Chi Minh museum, items that came originally from capitalist countries would appear to have gained a new, decommodified identity through their incorporation into the moral space of this socialist gift stream.

19. *Ong cung khong bao gio quen su chan tinh cua mot nguoi phu nu ten Lien dang song o Morroco* (He never forgets the heartiness/profound sincerity of a woman named Lien who is living in Morocco).
20. Colour-consciousness is still very pervasive in Vietnam: official declarations of 'friendship' with Africa and Africans coexists uneasily with both tacit and overt attitudes of superiority to dark-skinned peoples, who are still sometimes referred to in official sources as 'primitive' or 'undeveloped'.
21. *Dap lai long mong moi cua ba la duoc tro ve tham que huong, ong da tan tay chuyen ho so, giay to cua ba toi Su quan Viet Nam tai Phap de xem xet cap ho chieu moi cho ba.*

References

Bayly, S. 2004. 'Vietnamese Intellectuals in Revolutionary and Postcolonial Times', *Critique of Anthropology* 24(3): 320–44.
Dang Phong. 1999. 'Itinéraire économique du Vietnam. Evénements et éléments d'orientation', *Etudes Vietnamiennes* 3(133): 91–106.
———. 2002. *Lich Su Kinh Te Viet Nam 1945–2000. Tap 1: 1945–1954* [Economic History of Vietnam 1945–2000. Vol. 1: 1945–1954]. Hanoi: NXB Khoa Hoc Xa Hoi.
Dang Phong and M. Beresford. 2001. *Economic Transition in Vietnam. Trade and Aid in the Demise of a Centrally Planned Economy*. London: Edward Elgar.
Fennell, L.A. 2002. 'Unpacking the Gift. Illiquid Goods and Empathetic Dialogue', in Mark Osteen (ed.), *The Question of the Gift*. London: Routledge.
Gerth, K. 2003. *China Made. Consumer Culture and the Creation of the Nation*. Cambridge, MA and London: Harvard University Press.
Gold, T.B. 1985. 'After Comradeship: Personal Relations in China Since the Cultural Revolution'. *China Quarterly* 104: 657–75.
Hardy, A. 2000. 'L'amitié et ses valeurs: esquisse ethnographique des travailleurs vietnamiens dans les pays socialistes d'Europe de l'Est', *Revue Européenne des Migrations Internationales* 16(1): 235–46.
Harrison-Hall, J. 2002. *Vietnam Behind the Lines. Images from the War, 1965–1975*. London: British Museum Press.
Hy Van Luong. 1989. 'Vietnamese Kinship: Structural Principles and the Socialist Transformation in Northern Vietnam', *The Journal of Asian Studies* 48(4): 741–56.
———. 1992. *Revolution in the Village. Tradition and Transformation in North Vietnam 1925–1988*. Honolulu: University of Hawaii Press.
Kelly, G.P. 1982. *Franco-Vietnamese Schools, 1918–1938. Regional Development and Implications for National Integration*. Madison: Center for Southeast Asian Studies.
Kipnis, A. 1996. 'The language of gifts. Managing *guanxi* in a North China Village', *Modern China* 22(3): 285–14.
MacGaffey, J. and R. Bazenguissa-Ganga. 2000. *Congo-Paris. Transnational Traders on the Margins of the Law*. Oxford: James Currey.

Malarney, S.K. 1996. 'The limits of "state functionalism" and the reconstruction of funerary ritual in contemporary northern Vietnam', *American Ethnologist* 23(3): 540–60.

———. 2003. *Culture, Ritual and Revolution in Vietnam*. Honolulu: University of Hawaii Press.

Mandel, R. and C. Humphrey (eds). 2002. *Markets and Moralities. Ethnographies of Postsocialism*. Oxford and New York: Berg.

Marr, D.G. 1981. *Vietnamese Tradition on Trial, 1920–1945*. Berkeley, Los Angeles and London: University of California Press.

———. 2000. 'Concepts of "Individual" and "Self" in Twentieth-Century Vietnam', Modern Asian Studies 34(4): 769-96.

Nguyen Kim Nu Hanh. 2003. *Tiep Buoc Chan Cha. Hoi Ky Ve Giao Su Nguyen Van Huyen* (Following in our father's footsteps. Nguyen Van Huyen in his children's memory). Hanoi: The Gioi Publishers.

Ninh, Kim N.B. 2002. *A World Transformed. The Politics of Culture in Revolutionary Vietnam, 1945–65*. Ann Arbor: The University of Michigan Press.

Sahlins, Marshall. 1988. 'Cosmologies of Capitalism', in N.B. Dirks, G. Eley and S.B. Ortner (eds.), 1994 *Culture/ Power/ History. A Reader in Contemporary Social Theory*. Princeton: Princeton University Press.

Sarkar, S. 1973. *The Swadeshi Movement in Bengal*. New Delhi: People's Publishing House.

Selden, M. and W.S. Turley (eds.). 1993. *Reinventing Vietnamese Socialism*. Boulder, CO: Westview Press.

Smart, A. 1993. 'Gifts, Bribes and *Guanxi*: A Reconsideration of Bourdieu's Social Capital', *Cultural Anthropology* 8(3): 388–408.

Ssorin-Chaikov, N. and O. Sosnina (eds). 2006. *Gifts to Soviet Leaders*. Moscow: Pinakotheke and the Kremlin Museum.

Viswanathan, G. 1989. *Masks of Conquest: Literary Study and British Rule in India*. New York: Columbia University Press.

Yan, Y. 1996. *The Flow of Gifts. Reciprocity and Social Networks in a Chinese Village*. Stanford: Stanford University Press.

———. 2003. *Private Life Under Socialism. Love, Intimacy, and Family Change in a Chinese Village, 1949–1999*. Stanford: Stanford University Press.

Yang, M.M. 1994. *Gifts, Favors, and Banquets: The Art of Social Relationships in China*. Ithaca: Cornell University Press.

CHAPTER 6

Waste under Socialism and After: A Case Study from Almaty

Catherine Alexander

Introduction

In *Russian Talk*, Nancy Ries (1997) describes the threnody that typified discourse during the period of perestroika in Russia: tales of collapse and decay, of quotidian heroic exploits in the face of overwhelming odds, and the mythic notes that gave structure to accounts. Placed in Almaty, the former capital of Kazakhstan, this chapter also considers disintegration but moves things both forwards and backwards from the period of perestroika.[1] After briefly discussing the socialist urban aesthetic, which is still used as the ideal other against which current decay is implicitly or explicitly positioned, I go on to examine narratives of degeneration that occurred after 1991. These accounts were often presented as being directly consequent upon the 'shock therapy' economic packages that were smartly introduced after independence. The rest of the chapter is concerned with showing that these complaints of confusion and chaos (see for example Nazpary 1999), of pollution, disease and darkness, actually have much deeper roots as one digs back through the late 1980s and perestroika into the period under Brezhnev, if not before. In terms of its effluents and their continuing effects, then, socialism endures indeed. As Marilyn Strathern (1999) observes, pollution is marked by its characteristic of returning at unexpected moments and places, a shadowy, recurrent reminder of what went before. In this sense, waste is extended here to include hidden elements of the socialist period that have resurfaced or at least have forced recognition. As the rest of this chapter discusses, waste itself, whether rhetoric, unwanted by-product or toxic threat, weaves through much of the postsocialist experience.

In common with the other chapters in this volume, then, this traces back an apparently postsocialist moment to its socialist beginnings. Unlike the other chapters, however, which open with triumphal claims of positive social revolution, before brushing back the temporal layers to show continuities with the socialist period, this is more concerned with ongoing tropes of decay. In one sense this is following Nikolai Ssorin-Chaikov's notion of the 'poetics of unfinished construction' (2003: 136–37) where the idea and manifestation of progress is, even from its inception, inscribed with stagnation and failure. But this is more than discourse and something other than straightforward archaeology. Although inescapably the stuff of symbols and rhetoric, the waste I discuss here has both physical substance and tangible effects: it is at once matter, metaphor and material. Even if the consequences are not quite as catastrophic as urban disaster myths would have it, air pollution can be tasted on the tongue, while skin and bronchial complaints have risen, exacerbated by the deterioration of environmental conditions. The archaeology is also not straightforward. Time's arrow may fly in only one direction, but I suggest that the *perception* of time is rather a series of circlings, reframings of different moments, and a continuing conversation between past and present. What we find, therefore, is the distinctly unsettling experience, for ethnographer and informant alike, of past and present being set and understood in opposition to each other – but both being constantly on the move. If current urban troubles are located, by some, in opposition to a sunnier socialist past, then there is a parallel narrative that, disturbingly, points to the past as being a thick broadcloth of lies on the part of the elite: a cover-up of decay.

The temporal placing of waste and/or disorder is manifested in a number of ways, each of which points to a different way of constructing and interpreting the common 'then and now' formulation. First, citizens frequently tied the emergence of various wastes and forms of pollution to the emergence of a market-based system. Here a common illustration was the emergence of unregulated shashlik (kebab) stalls burning foul-smelling fuel which, for many, typified the entrepreneurial, uncontrolled spirit of the free market. Secondly, waste and confusion are, in part, a direct legacy of the socialist period: the toxic soil in Almaty's centre,[2] for example, is directly due to the large number of factories scattered throughout the city which leaked chemicals into the land on which they stood. This, for many, was one of the great shocks of perestroika, glasnost and the early years of independence: the revelation, with the opening up of the media, was not so much the perennial chorus of 'fings ain't wot they used to be' – but that 'fings' never had been what they used to be either.

The inheritance of the disastrous environmental effects of Soviet central planning, with its emphasis on quantity and production (especially in Central Asia), has been well documented (e.g. Peterson 1993; Pryde 1995; Glantz 1999; Weinthal 2004). Though similarly documented, the diverse response to this legacy has been less well analyzed. In some cases, these practices and effects have simply continued (as with the desiccation of the Aral Sea); in other instances the problem has been exacerbated by a new lack of enforceable (or enforced) regulation; and in others still has been modified in answer to international intervention and local protests, the cessation of nuclear testing in the northeast of Kazakhstan being the most well-known example. The degree to which governments are actually addressing such problems, as opposed to drawing up programmes of good intent, is a moot point. There is generally more interest in building anew and starting again, as in Kazakhstan's new capital Astana, than maintaining and mending the old. This tendency is itself, as Peterson (1993) observes, familiar from the Soviet period.

The third instance, with which I conclude this chapter, is where past and present positions evaporate in the face of what seems to be unmanageable disarray. I suggest this is a response neither to socialism nor capitalism per se, but to the apparent dissolution of any recognizable system that frames and permits (re)cognition. In this instance, the source of decay and rot is not to be found in genealogical excavation but in ways of knowing: the logical coherence of any system, whether conceptual, mechanical or organic, relies on the control of excess (whether matter or meaning), and when the system falters in the face of too rapid external change then all that is visible is the uncontainable surplus which was in fact always there but managed out of sight. In defining waste as 'whatever is produced by any system that ... needs to be to be expelled in order that the system continue to function' (1998: 3), Hollander perfectly captures the potentially subversive nature of wastes that threaten to disrupt known and familiar schemes of order.

It is of course worth noting both that many 'socialist' characteristics were themselves reformulations of presocialist modes, and that other capitalist features, often pointed to as consequences of presocialist systems, have been shown, with more careful analysis, to be more akin to socialism. The mechanics of socialism, in other words, are sometimes not so very different from capitalism. James von Geldern's (1993) study of Tsarist and Bolshevik festivals is a nice example of the former, where the licensed irreverence for hierarchy enacted in Tsarist carnivals was curtailed by the distinctly pious stagings of Bolshevik agitprop which drew heavily on church and imperial ritual for its potency and solemnity. The reverse case is neatly presented by Martha Lampland (1995) in her study of Hungarian farms. The relatively easy acceptance of capitalism and a market-based economy here cannot, as commonly supposed, be easily ascribed to a 'return' to a presocialist capitalist mode of production which lay dormant during the latter half of the twentieth century like a folk memory awaiting revival. On the contrary, presocialist agriculture in Hungary was largely feudal. It was the advent of socialism that introduced the idea of regular hours and 'work units', which permitted the commodification of labour.

The means of continuation is thus dependent on each instance, as is the particular understanding, or practice, of socialism in each case. One key to such apparent divergences might simply be that for all the trumpeted difference between socialism and capitalism, both organizational systems in the twentieth century drew heavily on the same assumptions, methods and aspirations. Susan Buck-Morss (2000) calls this the dream of mass utopia – even if the utopias themselves were quite different; something similar is suggested by James Scott (1998) in *Seeing Like a State*, although he is less explicit about comparing regimes. Both, however, are talking about modernism as a reaction, first to the social degradation produced by nineteenth-century industrialization and, secondly, the break-up of the old order signaled by the First World War. With respect to this chapter, the production of wastes in Kazakhstan can be fairly confidently pinpointed to the socialist period simply because it was only then that industry and sizeable conurbations began to appear. The large-scale devastation of lands, previously used for transhumant pasturage, which were turned to intensive agriculture similarly occurred during the socialist regime.[3] It is worth noting, however, that large-scale, intensive production, whether industrial or agricultural, is generally underwritten by a belief in the efficacy of science and technology to maximize efficiency. That belief holds for both capitalist and socialist systems, both of which generate vast amounts of waste, much of which is displaced to peripheral areas of the globe (or, as in the case of Kazakhstan, to the edge of empire). The difference between socialism and capitalism here is the nominal sense of whom the efficiency benefits: shareholders or humanity. How far modernism endures in the twenty-first century through core assumptions and practices is a subtly different question (see Alexander 2004a).

Before embarking on the odyssey of postsocialist waste, however, I sketch out the version of socialist Alma-Ata[4] that dominates most recollections and is supported by fictional and historical accounts, however much the latter were steered by ideological necessity in their Soviet context. This is necessary because it is in such lyrical accounts, gilt with nostalgia, that ideas of the right order – which has been overturned in tales of decay – is glimpsed. There are two points to note. The first is the curious stylistic uniformity of accounts whatever the genre: taped oral history, written autobiography,[5] fiction or history. The second, perhaps in explanation of the first, is that the lyrical mood is intertwined with a notion of the ideal socialist city:[6] the urban aesthetic of natural abundance and greenness which is underwritten by a normative idea of how best to provide the material environment for a model socialist system. The – perhaps inevitable – ultimate failure to create a perfect city resulted instead in a model question.[7]

The Socialist Urban Aesthetic: Harmony, Order and Clarity

The beautiful city of Almaty, nestling in the foothills of the Tien Shan mountain range, was always renowned for its verdure. 'We were the third greenest city in the Soviet Union!' was a tagline to which I rapidly became accustomed when I first arrived in 2000. But the pride was not without reason. Most buildings were only two to four storeys high in deference to the seismic activity in the area and, when the trees were in leaf, the buildings behind them all but disappeared. Alongside the principal roads of the city's large inner grid were pavements with trees planted up to six deep, and small irrigation channels running alongside them. Sometimes these boulevards, up to 25 metres in width, also had wide central stretches planted with roses or trees and set about with benches for the ease of the weary pedestrian.

Older citizens, talking about their city, would acknowledge perhaps that it was still astonishingly green but would rapidly refer to an earlier city that had now been lost, a city that was, in the words of one 72-year-old Kazakh woman, 'a garden city, such a beautiful city, before the 1960s it was perhaps more like a big, green village – but then we began to have wonderful buildings as well and we started to live better.' Strikingly, every account, where the speaker had moved to Alma-Ata from elsewhere, used nearly all these phrases to open their own life history. Contemporary accounts of Soviet Alma-Ata similarly waxed extremely lyrical. Here is one such quoted by the celebrated local historian Iosif Malyar in 1974:

> Huge parks, wide streets, houses drowning in greenery: all of this turns Alma-Ata into a garden city which was build in accordance with social political directions for the creation of healthy conditions for the bright and happy life of human beings.

And everybody, but everybody cites, Yuri Dombrovsky, 1960s author of two novels set in the Alma-Ata of the 1930s:

> The sun was not yet up, but under the acacias the bumble-bees were already humming away and big white butterflies circling around ... Above the acacias were orchards, above the orchards poplars; higher than the poplars there were only the mountains and the forests that covered them. It was the orchards which confused me most of all: how on earth could I find my way about if the whole town was one huge orchard ... (Dombrovsky 197x: xx)

And then, above the poplars, are the mountains:

> ... a spur of the Tien Shan range ... It is as if two great wings had spread themselves round the town, holding it up in the air and keeping it from falling. (Dombrovsky 197x: xx)

Thus, the city manifested the harmonious relationship of nature and the built environment achieved through political and engineering technology; the urban form providing the optimum conditions for healthy and happy lives in a socialist environment. Even if unconsciously, these motifs of urban life and the ideal urban aesthetic directly mirror Moishe Ginzburg, superstar Constructivist architect who, in his 1926 manifesto *Style and Epoch*, wrote of the new spirit abroad in experimental socialist architecture and urban planning: 'these modern plans are open and free, not only to bathe the parts in sunlight and air, but to make the functional elements more readable and to see more easily the organic life unfolding within'.

By the late 1930s, Stalin had firmly stamped on the visionary experiments of the early urban planners (Cooke and Justin 1983, 1991), announcing cities on Soviet soil to be de facto socialist (Alexander and Buchli in press). Quite evidently, however, listening to local architects in Almaty, many of these ideas continued to be taught, even if they were also subject to the constraints of rational economic planning. The key shift in the late 1930s was that rather than disembodying the city, as the 1920s' disurbanists had suggested, into lines of flexible housing and industrial nodes uncoiling across Soviet space along the routes taken by the energy grid, flow and dynamism were to occur *within* the city. Harmony, openness and readability were to be within the city space. It is against this sense of happy concord and clarity within the city and between the city and its natural environment that citizens compared the conditions in Almaty in the period after 1991.

The Anti-urban Aesthetic: After 1991

Kazakhstan seceded from the Soviet Union in December 1991, almost exactly five years after an aborted insurrection against Soviet rule that had taken place in the city centre. With that in mind it was slightly ironic that Kazakhstan was the last republic to leave the Soviet party, almost having to be pushed out. This section is about the massive changes that swung in with independence and how these were understood and spoken about both through images of the city under attack, and through the ill effects on bodies of citizens in the city. In relation to the aesthetic outlined above, many of the images and instances described below harp on obfuscation in the place of clarity, illness in the place of health, dirt, stagnation and shadows in the place of clean, free-flowing openness.

Three common themes appeared which were expressed as related consequences of the mass privatization and restructuring programme which took place in the early 1990s: rural migration to the city, urban unemployment and foreign investment in Kazakhstan. All these themes were articulated through their effects on city and health; they also touch on different scales – body, city, region, international relations – each of which was, in turn, understood through the other scales and domains.

It was decided, by the authorities and their small panel of foreign advisers, that shock therapy, as trialed in Poland in the 1980s, was the way to move the country smartly on to the goal of a free market economy and democracy. Bang in line with most brand medications, the treatment was standardized to home in rather crudely on what was considered to be the principal malfunction of the socialist system: the centralized, command economy. The side-effects, not unnaturally, were localized since the combination of standard treatment and the infinite variety of patients, or actually existing socialisms, produces a corresponding infinite variety of results.

In brief, the shock therapy package proposed mass privatization of housing, urban infrastructure and workplaces along with 'structural adjustments' of remaining services and industries, most of which were sold or auctioned off (Alexander 2004b). The full results took a few years to register fully as factories limped along for a while using up old stock, and the results of minimal maintenance of the city fabric took a while to become obvious. One immediate result of the shift to a private property regime and the cessation of subsidies from Moscow across the country as a whole was the collapse of many collective farms and townships that had been built around one extractive or refining industry far out on the steppe.

With the implosion of these steppe collectives and one-company towns, people suddenly began to pack up and move at an unprecedented level. In other quarters, this movement was exacerbated by the first Constitution that focused on Kazakhs to the exclusion of other national groups, provoking fear of what the future might hold.[8] The problem here was that, in 1991, the titular ethnic group was less than half the entire population. Along with Siberia, Kazakhstan was *the* dumping ground for Soviet political prisoners in their thousands – these areas were the wastelands on the edge of the Soviet Union, to be populated by the people who did not fit into, and were therefore deemed superfluous to, the system (Pohl 1999, 2002). Colonization of Central Asia predated the Soviet period: quite apart from the Russian peasant settlers seeking new lands to farm after Piotr Stolypin's 1861 emancipation of serfs in the Russian Empire, many Germans who had settled in Siberia under Catherine the Great in the eighteenth century moved south into Kazakhstan. German numbers were swelled dramatically by Stalin's deportation of over 400,000 Germans from the Volga region in August 1941, many of whom were sent to Kazakhstan. In the first five years of independence, one and a half million Germans left for Germany, and two million Russians moved to Russia. Overall, Kazakhstan's population dropped from 17 million in 1991 to just under 15 million in 2005. New national borders proved to be leaky in a number of respects.

Internally, thousands came to Almaty in search of work and food. Colloquially, Almaty is known as the Bread City, a soubriquet that had earlier belonged to Tashkent. There are a number of things to observe here. In common with many principal or capital cities in the Soviet Union, Almaty's population size had been carefully controlled. Gaining an official residence permit was extremely difficult, much more so for Kazakhs and other non-Russians. Even once in the city, a distinctly Russian culture dominated in the educational system that produced, whatever their ethnic background, Russian-speaking, Soviet citizens. The people who came to Almaty after 1991 for work or better schooling for their children were frequently Kazakhs from villages for whom Kazakh is their first language. There was huge resentment from longstanding citizens against these incomers. Sometimes this was expressed as more competition for few jobs, but very often a whole raft of anxieties crystallized around these rural migrants. Especially in the peripheral residential districts where the demography changed most sharply, citizens spoke of fear of their children being kidnapped by these new neighbours, of huge steppe farms using the labour of slaves abducted from the city; there were tales of drug gangs, murders and the sale of organs, tales, which as Ries (1997) shows, draw on a long Russian tradition of dramatizing the everyday into a chaotic, absurd world.

There were two ways of talking about this rural-urban shift which were widespread in 2000, becoming less so in the following years. One was the common reference by longer-standing citizens to these reconfigurations in urban demography as a virus entering the city and destroying urban culture. The other, which seems to be connected, came from municipal officials who complained both about the incessant movement, where before there had been containment and stasis, and the fact that most of the swirl of people searching for work were still registered where they had previously lived. They were thus unidentifiable to a bureaucracy that could only *see* through its documentary representations of the population. The object of care, in other words, was becoming invisible. Almaty's chief architect observed[9] that this inability to control movement and *see* was becoming vexatious and that steps were being taken to remedy this problem of free-floating citizens. This was ridiculed by most people I mentioned it to later in Almaty; after all, it suggested a return to the old days of restriction and control. Yet 2004 saw identity cards having a barcode attached detailing the address and personal information of the owner. Without such data, neither voting rights nor welfare were granted.

Thus, one effect of privatization was seen as the unchecked inflow of destructive microscopic elements, a rampaging virus. Expansions of this theme ranged from comments that people from villages spoke too loudly, spoke in Kazakh, looked different, and spat in the streets, to explanations that returned to the theme of obfuscation in the place of clarity, and neglect in the place of care. Rural Kazakhs, it was said, found work through their unbelievably extensive kinship networks that threaded invisibly through the city; there was no more transparency when it came to jobs. Rural Kazakhs, citizens said, were dirty; they dropped litter in the streets and the little canals (*aryk*) that had been so clean and tidy before. Many of the citizens who were saying this were not just from the Russian and non-Kazakh population, but were also Russian-speaking, Russian-educated urban Kazakhs who spoke with some distress of being in their motherland and yet feeling alienated from people with whom they shared a nominal ethnicity. In their turn, rural Kazakhs call urbanized Kazakhs, '*mambet*': this is offensive slang suggesting a person cut off from traditional ways and in the fundamentally alien environment of the city. Neither one thing nor another, a person who is *mambet* is betwixt and between, often materially successful, but at the cost of their place in the world. Such references to rural migrants were thus used to hint at urban ways of living and connecting that existed indiscernibly in the interstices of the recognizable system, and threatened to subvert it. Although the magnitude of migration was new, however, the rapid expansion of Almaty that continued unchecked from the 1920s onwards clearly demonstrates that migration into the city was fairly constant during the twentieth century. The difference after Independence perhaps was that spatial segregation became less marked and the previous understood obscurities in the allocation of work and resources were replaced by a less understood system.

The second immediate effect of restructuring policies in the 1990s was unemployment in its various permutations: lack of work, delays in paying salaries, unpaid leave, being paid in kind and so on. The ensuing poverty produced several results. Inadequate diets and living conditions gave rise to poor physical health, especially coughs, anaemia, bronchial and kidney complaints – problems that continue in the self-built shanty areas around the edge of the city. Lack of money for firewood by owners of the tiny private houses stuffed into every nook and cranny of the more formally planned socialist districts led to burning of tyres, lino and other materials cannibalized from abandoned, decaying houses. The smoke gave off noxious fumes which local doctors and citizens alike said had poisoned the city and caused a rise in bronchial problems.

The poisoning and choking of the city were familiar topics and usually tracked back to privatization and deregulation, or the abnegation of diligence by the authorities over the well-being of the city and its citizens. Adulterated fuel from unlicensed petrol stations belched out black clouds of smoke that hung over the streets. Air pollution from factories had reduced, but that was simply because so many factories had closed. The legacy from factories was soil polluted with heavy metals. The sudden efflorescence of shashlik stalls by petty entrepreneurs was frequently pointed to as a source of bad air: there was no regulation, people said, over what was burned. The parks and trees, the green lungs of the city, were being decimated by the city authorities selling off land, which belonged to the public to businessmen for petrol stations, office buildings, new casinos and leisure centres.

The third effect of privatization again plays into these themes. For the first time, large billboards appeared in the city advertising Western products to the citizens of Almaty, or local products suggesting foreign glamour: sparkling new kitchens, sofas and armchairs ornate with curled varnished wood and plush upholstery. Two of these early advertisements featured respectively a grenadier guard lounging on a sofa, and a woman dressed in a ballgown and tiara in a gleaming kitchen. Obviously more than just furniture was being sold. But alongside these advertisements appeared huge placards and posters for the city, 'our city', for the Kazakh language, or the new Republic, posters which seemed to owe much in terms of genre to Soviet exhortatory messages to the citizenry that still appear blazoned over buildings in other cities. None the less, advertising billboards were generally seen as the work of the Western and Asian firms that poured into Kazakhstan in the 1990s, snapping up the cherries in the privatization free-for-all.

What was said about these large boards straddling streets and squares was that they occluded the city's airflow, choked it. In 2000 municipal officials[10] and citizens alike stressed that foreign companies were asphyxiating the city with big new buildings set across the wind direction, blocking its airways and contributing to the increase in asthma, bronchial problems, allergies and skin complaints that are recorded in the polyclinics if you talk to doctors – but very hard to obtain figures for.

In much the same way, tall buildings (the product of foreign firms, I was told firmly) not only stood in the way of the winds and obstructed the removal of smoke and dirt in the air, but also eradicated the charming individuality of Almaty. Now, as many said, the city had become just another New York, London or Paris. This was not quite the case. In the first place, many of the higher buildings in the centre were built during the Soviet period; the rash of new, private, multi-storey apartment blocks began in 2002. Secondly, many companies supposedly owned by foreign firms turn out, on investigation, to be subsidiaries of a Kazakh-owned holding company, very often owned by the presidential family. 'Kazakhstan has just become a big shop for the President,' a local builder observed bitterly and what most people don't realize is that neither the buyers nor the sellers are real.'

One further scandal was being ground out by the urban rumour mill in 2000 but which disappeared shortly afterwards. This was that that the city authorities had sold off Vodakanal, the company responsible for water and sewerage, to a foreign, probably Belgian, company. This firm had apparently built a huge reservoir outside the city and now, in place of the clean mountain water tumbling down from the spring snowmelt through the little irrigation canals, still, stagnant and, consequently, polluted water was provided to the citizens.

This story, much repeated by medics and by citizens, was in fact not true. There was no such reservoir.[11] But at a time when so much was up in the air, the ephemera of scandal provides some clue to the moral system, or sense of what is right, that is being disturbed by such stories. Here, there is the affronted moral order of the city being taken over by outsiders that is reflected both in the inversion of stillness and movement that runs through many of these stories, and in the litanies of the city's sickness, the puncturing of the safe enclosure and the simultaneous sense of abandonment.

Perestroika: The Beginning of Unrest

Despite the tales of dirt and obscurity that centered round the rapid economic and political changes after 1991, other narratives looked further back to perestroika as the moment of undoing. Again, this occurred on at least two levels: both the unraveling of the socialist system as it was believed to be (through its 'remaking' or rebuilding'), and the revelation (through glasnost) that it never had been entirely what people supposed. This gap between ideal norms and what actually existed was familiar: it was a relatively open secret. The jolt, the scandal of revelations in the late 1980s, was the *extent* of these other urban problems. Far from being a harmonious, ordered place based *on* and conducive *to* healthy bodies and healthy minds – it was an environment of danger and discord. The much-loved functional metaphor didn't work.

The first and most dramatic of these jolts took place on 16 December 1986 as the culmination of three days of protest in Alma-Ata. The riot was prompted by the central authorities' replacement of the Kazakh First Secretary Dinmukhammed Kunaev with a Russian, Gennadii Kolbin. For three days and nights Kazakh students marched slowly round the ring roads of the city before eventually converging on the main square in the centre. Riot police moved in to disperse the crowds. Most were stuffed into buses and driven to a distance about 20 kilometres outside the city where they were dumped and left to walk back through the freezing December night.[12] Some were taken into custody. A few, nobody knows how many, were shot.[13]

The entire event remains shrouded in mystery. It is not known exactly who started it, who participated, nor the fate of those whisked into police cells. Those who will talk about it do so with great reluctance before changing the subject abruptly. 'These were bad times, we don't want to remember them,' was the common refrain. A Russian woman described how she had been told to remain indoors by her husband with their two babies. 'All that time,' she said, 'I didn't move outside once. I could see the streets were empty through the window. And then, every now and then, the tramp, tramp, tramp of marching feet along Furmanova Prospect, right outside my window, day and night. It was very frightening.' Two middle-aged Kazakh men recalled being ordered by their bosses to find big clubs and report to the police if they wanted to keep their jobs.

Echoing many other fragments of memories of this time, a local art historian, in her late fifties, said,

> It was a terrible time. Everybody had been going about their daily lives quite normally, we lived in a normal city, and then suddenly nobody had any idea what was happening. It was as if, out of the blue, we were in a wild west city: no rules, no order. It was frightening. We didn't know what was going to happen.

This was the first demonstration against the Soviet Union. It was firmly quashed, but nevertheless that first moment of realizing that the familiar order of things *could* be overturned had lodged in people's minds. For some, the riot has taken on mythic qualities, the violence and bloodshed heralding transformations and revolutions that Vladimir Propp (1968) points to as a standard feature of folk tales. An old Kazakh woman living on the edge of the city tugged at my sleeve, whispering that thousands and thousands of young Kazakhs had been murdered by the police and dumped in a pit outside the city. It was unlikely, but that was neither the first nor the last time I heard this version. There was another way of remembering this incident: Almaty's main square was always curiously empty, a desolation emphasized by its vastness; in planning it, Kunaev had sought to outdo Red Square before having his wrists slapped by Moscow.[14] Public ceremonies held there after 1991 were usually poorly attended. 'It's a bad place,' people mutter when asked why, 'bad things happened there.'

After that, things subsided, at least in the sense of public protest, though private anxieties continued. The face of the city changed too: some say because of the mismanagement by the city authorities, some say there was just no money coming from Moscow. In any case, trees, usually pollarded within an inch of their lives, were left to straggle and grow unchecked; bushes in the lovely central parks rambled uncontained over previously neat pathways; the fountains were dry, their concrete basins cracked; grass grew to meadow height. All this, together with the sudden cessation of street lighting, transformed these places, formerly the pride of the city, into dark unknowable places, full of threatening shadows. The historian spoke of having been used to wander and dream in these parks when the dreariness of life in the serried rows of apartment blocks ringing the centre became too depressing. But now the parks themselves were oppressive and frightening: you didn't know, she said, who might be lurking in the gloom. There were no more of the evening promenades for which Alma-Ata had been celebrated in the 1970s; squares were left empty. Others remember problems with public transport, not so much the clogged arterial roads that became difficult to move through after the mid-1990s, but a simple lack of fuel and vehicles in good condition. A foundational precept of Soviet urban planning was untrammelled movement between city zones, quite explicitly based on healthy blood circulation (Cooke 1983; Cooke and Justin 1991), but now the flow of workers from the residential districts was sluggish, many opting to walk rather than rely on erratic buses.

Three years later, the Berlin Wall fell, and this unleashed a second wave of protest movements in Kazakhstan. In 1989 it was still illegal to form political parties, so most of these groups were single issue, usually campaigning about environmental problems: pollution, the nuclear polygon in the northeast. For a few years, in the spirit of glasnost, and then the new Republic, newspapers carried reports and discussions about urban crises of overcrowding, health, pollution levels. But as the new presidential family gained control over the media after independence, fewer reports began to surface. Now nearly all these movements have declined or vanished.[15] Then, these campaigns were deeply shocking for people who had not witnessed public protests before in their lifetime. 'They were strange times to be living through,' a government economist said, 'we heard about things that our authorities had done that we did not know about, bad things. We heard about many things from abroad, other ways of doing things, that we had not thought possible.'

Waste before Perestroika

The harmony and beauty for which Alma-Ata was famed was publicly shown to be a mockery, first with the riot and then with the late perestroika newspaper reports of high levels of air and water pollution. To add to these anxieties, Sorbulak, a series of connected lakes approximately 20 kilometres outside the city for the 'natural' treatment of waste water was shown to be heavily polluted (newspaper ref). The sewerage pipes connecting the city to Sorbulak were cracked, leaking untreated waste water from factories and households into the soil and water along the route of the pipes: a long-term problem. Fish riddled with heavy metals from the lakes were suspected of being on sale in the city markets. Poor oversight of the system for urban waste extraction and detoxification might be leading to the poisoning of citizens. But no formal tests were carried out. Rumour flitted along the urban grapevine with the occasional newspaper report as fuel.

Again, in 1989, a green protest movement marshalled local citizens in the outer suburbs of Aynabulak and Dorozhnik[16] to sign a petition against the city's solid waste dump that had emerged in their neighbourhood since the late 1970s. For lack of any other facility to sort and treat waste properly this area, only ever intended as a sorting and transfer station, had developed into a large pit where untreated toxic chemical wastes were tipped alongside household and other municipal wastes. Since the pit was unlined, chemicals leached into the soil and groundwater supply and, once that happened, there was no knowing where and how chemicals might resurface. Evil-smelling clouds of smoke from the occasional explosions on site would drift over the neighbouring suburbs. 'The water tasted strange sometimes,' one ex-resident said, 'sort of metallic, so we tried to boil it first. There were lots of people complaining about bronchial things – not public complaints, but we knew our neighbours' children had the same sorts of illnesses as ours.' Matters were not helped by the fact that these two residential areas, Aynabulak and Dorozhnik, were sandwiched between this official-yet-illegal waste dump and the asphalt factory of Industrial Zone North One: if fumes were not being blown from one direction, they were coming from the other.

Although the demographics of these areas have changed recently,[17] before 1991 they were mainly home to Kazakhs, Uighurs and less well-educated Russians, basically those who were less equal than other citizens. So much for the aspiration to eliminate social inequalities, cited by Nikolai Ladovsky in 1926 as being the fundamental characteristic of the socialist city. So, far from there being social equality in the city, Alma-Ata, in common with other socialist cities, was highly stratified according to ethnicity and party membership, which allowed preferential access to housing, schools, clinics and so forth. Better housing was in the centre and the southern edge of the city that backs up the mountains, the poorer areas were located downwind near the steppe area and the industrial zones. The oft-repeated maxim that a well-planned city must be zoned and so have separate industrial, administrative and residential districts was more often breached than observed simply because the powerful central industrial ministries just rode roughshod over local city councils and their plans that so carefully anatomized the city and planned its growth in the context of the local environment. Although made with an eye to late-twentieth-century Britain, the observation made by Morris

(1995: 18 and passim) on the frequent structural elision between material waste and disadvantaged social groups (see also Stedman Jones 1971: 309, Himmelfarb 1984), as both the metaphorical waste of society and those who live by picking over waste dumps (see also Gay y Blasco 1999), would seem to hold as true for mature socialism[18] (see Baldaeva 2007) as for all stages of capitalism.[19]

The discrepancies between ideals of equality and actual spatial practice in the socialist period were not unknown. Indeed one woman, daughter of an academician and therefore, as she described herself with a nice precision, on the outer edge of the inner circle, explained the multiple geographies of Soviet Alma-Ata: how if you had the right connections you knew that, behind that wall, was your polyclinic, that, down that street, was the school for children of party members and that, behind those identikit façades, lay large and relatively sumptuous apartments.

The blessings of such privileges were mixed. Hospitals for the elite, the nomenklatura, were undoubtedly better equipped than others, but the medical staff were often placed there because they had good connections rather than aptitude. The irony, she said grinning broadly, was that, as a result, the standard of medical care in these gleaming and well-appointed hospitals was often well below that of more run-of-the-mill clinics. The less-commented on inversion is that, in the 1990s, the elite centre actually turned out to be one of the most hazardous places in the whole city, with the worst concentrations of toxic soil from factories, polluted air and unshored-up tunnels for a prestigious but unfinished metro project burrowing under its streets.

The openness and clarity or 'readability', to recall Ginzburg (1982), of the socialist urban aesthetic were thus rarely there in practice. The apparently invisible kin connections of rural migrants which were complained about in the late 1990s were replaying socialist inequities in another form. The differences were, first, that the earlier invisibility was part of a shared fiction that was torn apart when the Soviet Union collapsed, the open secret of social stratification and, secondly, that even the nomenklatura seem to have had little knowledge of the dangers of the elite region where they lived.

More than this, the enchantingly green city of memory and fiction is in fact built on sandy soil in a seismic area. Earthquakes aside,[20] the foothills in which Almaty is located are, in effect, a dip that prevents smog from escaping, while the mountains themselves, evoked in Dombrovsky's tender image, are liable to violent mudslides that in the past have destroyed parts of the city. Harmonious development of town, nature and people was thus always unlikely from the founding of the small Tsarist fortress in 1854 in a pretty, but singularly unfortunate, location.

Conclusion

The Constructivist emphasis on the readability of urban form continued long after Constructivism fell out of fashion in the 1930s, with the same continuing stress of socialist urban planners on openness, and separate functional zones connected by transportation lines. This dynamism within the city depended on the maintenance of the city edges and surfaces. The stories above point to the piercing of those boundaries both by rural migrants and foreign business. So far, the story has strong echoes with nineteenth-century fears that disease would rebound upon the mother city along the very lines of imperial expansion that had moved out, across the city and national borders. As Laura Otis (1999) describes, these metaphors of viral invasion spanned literature, politics and science at the time when miasma theory was becoming supplanted by germ theory that allowed disease to penetrate bodies and so break down the defences of the body (and, by extrapolation, one might suggest, city or nation state). Certainly there were parallel emphases on control and separation in the socialist city – and the contemporary, punctured city was described as a wounded body: poisoned, choked, sluggish. The analogy is limited of course: one would hardly expect socialist city authorities to fear borders being broken down between classes or the unruliness of the mob, although, a social 'map' or indeed a 'health map'[21] of Almaty shows a very clear distinction between classes.

But I would like to take this further. After all, it was not just the viral attack on urban culture that was talked about; people also spoke of the swarming in of foreign firms that led to the ailing city, and to loss of local jobs which led to anomie, depression, poverty, problems with breathing and skin allergies, along with the opacity of the privatization process. If viral infection is microscopic, then the opening up of city and country to global markets equally points to a magnitude beyond immediate human comprehension. Both the very big and the very small are not only invisible to the human eye, and thus unreadable and unknowable, but they also both disturb a sense of what is human and unique or, as was said here, the individuality of the city. From far away people blur into masses.[22] Indeed the macro- and microscopic are frequently conflated metaphorically, as Emily Martin (1994) shows in her accounts of people's descriptions of their immune system which draw on metaphors of outer space to explain the vastness of the infinitely small. Here perhaps it is as much a case of explaining the unintelligible, the abrupt change from the familiar, through analogic metaphors of infinity, beyond comprehension. Both ideas of viral invasion and being taken over by global markets are thus, illegible and like dark matter, known only by their effects on the body of the city and the body in the city.

But I wish to close by proposing another reading of this material. A further constant theme of the postsocialist litanies in Almaty has been the sudden foregrounding of nature, either threatening to burst its bounds (leaking wastes, mudslides, earthquakes) or indeed through unnatural stillness, to become hazardous (stagnant waters), on top of which there are the wastes that are both the legacy of the Soviet period and a result of the sequence of effects unfurling from mass privatization and structural adjustment programmes.

As with any system of logics, both socialism and capitalism are concerned with form, orders that are recognized by their boundedness, but are in fact made by an artificial containment and blanking out of excess. Wastes coexist with such forms. They are more than the returning unwanted by-products of production and consumption that neither system has ever been particularly good at coping with. Wastes are there in the sterility of unused potential, the uncultivated lands,[23] the inability to connect and reproduce social forms. In the material above, this is to be found in the untrimmed trees of city parks that take back their shape if not kept at bay (see Alexander 2000), or the colonial fabrication of empty lands where unwanted people and industrial wastes can be dumped.[24] Waste is also the squandering of wealth and resources, the sheer excess that is frittered away, Thorstein Veblen's (1902) ultimate display luxury. For Georges Bataille (1991), destruction, waste and expenditure characterize the human economy more fundamentally than production; drawing on the anthropological staple of potlatch, amongst other sources, he cites sacrifice as the epitome of this destructive drive (see Baudrillard 1993 for his own replay of symbolic exchange outside a monetary economy). How is this exhibited here? The postsocialist selling-off of Almaty's infrastructure and Kazakhstan's prized enterprises to apparently foreign companies is spoken of by Almaty's citizens as 'selling our future'. Local historians now note that this is only the latest occurrence in a long line of plundering the land's mineral wealth, going back to the extensive extractions of resources during the socialist period, most of which were transported to Russia.

In these more expansive senses, wastes, informal economies and scandals coexist with the formal means of knowing, producing and consuming value and knowledge. Formal and informal thus coexist, as apparent orders and wastes coexist each, by turn, being foregrounded or backgrounded. What was happening in the years when the socialist order was crumbling, and the shadows emerged on the previously well-lit streets, was the revelation of socialism's dark mirror, the wastes that lie in the interstices and surround, the knowable and containable. Before a new system had taken root, if indeed it did, only an ungraspable formlessness seemed to be present, exacerbated by the new speed that overtook the country. Once again it was the uncontainable elements that dominated the scene.

The shock of perestroika and after was thus perhaps the public realization that the normal body, the normal city, had never been normal, that multiple orders live alongside what is recognized as the healthy body, the harmonious city. Or, to borrow from Jeremy Prynne (1971), who celebrates the subversive and creative capacity of waste, the shadowing of language by the accretion of acquired connotations:

Rubbish is
pertinent; essential; the
most intricate presence in
our entire culture; the
ultimate sexual point of the whole place turned
into a model question.

Notes

1. I carried out fieldwork in Almaty, Kazakhstan each year between 2000 and 2005. Even in this short period the changes have been rapid and marked. What I describe later in this chapter as the resentment against privatization and migrants from the countryside and abroad was most marked in 2000. Tropes of confusion, obfuscation and indeed decay which were prevalent then are less noticeable, though still present, now. Levels of air pollution caused by steadily increasing traffic intensity continue to cause complaint. Accounts of what happened during perestroika (and before) have been taken both from life histories gathered between 2000 and 2005 and newspaper archives in Almaty's Academy of Sciences. The current condition of Almaty's environment, including waste management, was gleaned from the city's municipal offices and scientists at the local state university, all of whom remain anonymous – as they requested.
2. The map, and accompanying text, which details Almaty's territory and areas of high toxic concentration are well known to city officials – the map usually being pinned up on office walls of the Ecology Department. It is less well known by citizens.
3. Under Nikita Khrushchev in the 1950s, much of the central steppe of Kazakhstan was ploughed up to create a second grain bowl for the Soviet Union in what was known as the Virgin Lands campaign: *Tselina*. Uzbekistan was turned over to monoculture of cotton, a crop needing intensive irrigation.
4. In common with many Tsarist colonial townships that went through the Soviet period to independence, Almaty has gone through several name changes. Nineteenth-century Verniye became Soviet Alma-Ata before being rechristened Almaty in the early 1990s. The usual reason given is that 'Almaty' is closer to the Kazakh version. This is as possible as other etymologies and other versions.

5. Leon Trotsky's (1975) autobiography, *My Life,* first published in 1930, includes a chapter on Alma-Ata where he spent the first two years of exile. Interspersed with the contempt of the Muscovite intellectual for local flea-ridden, barely human inhabitants (see Buchli in press) are the familiar passages on the scenic beauties of the place.
6. See Alexander and Buchli (in press) for a fuller discussion of changes in ideas about what constituted 'the socialist city'.
7. Note Robert Harbison's (1991) observation that 'model' refers both to the paradigm and to something that is a miniature of itself.
8. Later, revised versions of the Constitution, while still maintaining the primordial right of the Kazakhs to their land, aimed for a more inclusive tone.
9. Interview took place in 2000.
10. It should be noted that some officials were clearly being disingenuous, grinning broadly when the Soviet-era high-rise flats were pointed out. With respect to more recent tall buildings, another department is usually blamed for inadequate attention to regulations.
11. Moreover, only the southern part of the city is supplied with water from the mountains, transported in pipes built by Japanese prisoners of war.
12. Interviews with participants.
13. For more information on the riot see Helsinki report, 1990.
14. Interview with Kuldaibai Montakayev, Chief Architect of Alma-Ata in the 1980s.
15. The movements may have vanished together with public awareness of the issues they advertised – but the problems themselves have far from disappeared. The next section details waste before and during perestroika, but the leaking sewerage pipes and municipal waste dumps continue. The latter has moved location – but nothing is done to treat wastes separately.
16. Both were built in the 1980s.
17. See Alexander (forthcoming).
18. Under Brezhnev, the revised Soviet Constitution of 1977 announced that a stage of mature socialism had been reached.
19. Marx and Engels, in *The Communist Manifesto* (1987: 42), refer to 'the dangerous class, the social scum, that passively rotting mass thrown off by the lowest layers of the old society'.
20. Two earthquakes in 1887 and 1910 both virtually flattened the small Russian town of Verniye.
21. From interviews with head doctors at a range of polyclinics around Almaty.
22. Cf. Raymond Williams' (1990) famous comment: 'there are no masses, there are only ways of seeing people as masses'.
23. Plank 7 of *The Communist Manifesto* exhorts the cultivation of the wastelands.
24. A journalist in 2004 observed in conversation that 'Kazakhstan is like Australia: we are full of other countries' deportees and prisoners.' The northeast of Kazakhstan was used as a nuclear testing ground from the 1950s until a 1990 campaign exposed and halted the programme. In 2001, Kazakhstan's government announced it would take Europe's nuclear waste and use payments to deal with the vast amounts of its own untreated nuclear waste (ref). A huge national outcry prevented this happening.

References

Alexander, C. 2000. 'The Garden as Occasional Domestic Space', *Signs: The Journal of Women Culture and Society.*

———. 2004a. 'Who Owns Native Culture? By Michael Brown', (Review Essay) in *PoLAR (Political and Legal Anthropology Review)* Vol 27(2): 113–29.

———. 2004b. 'Value, Relations and Changing Bodies: Privatization and Property Rights in Kazakhstan', in K. Verdery and C. Humphrey (eds), *Property in Question.* Oxford: Berg.

Alexander, C. and V. Buchli. 2007. 'Introduction', *Reconstructing Urban life in Postsocialist Central Asia.* London: UCL Press.

Alexander, C. forthcoming. *Mercurial City.* Ithaca and London: Cornell University Press.

Baldaeva, I. 2007. 'The Homeless of Ulan-Ude', in C Alexander, V. Buchli and C Humphrey (eds), *Urban Life in Post-Soviet Asia.* London: UCL Press.

Bataille, G. 1991. *The Accursed Share Vol I: An Essay on General Economy: Consumption,* translated by R. Hurley. London: Zone Books.

Baudrillard, J. 1993. *Symbolic Exchange and Death.* London: Sage.

Buchli, V. 2007. 'Astana: Materiality and the City', in *Urban Life in Post-Soviet Asia.* London: UCL Press.

Buck-Morss, S. 2000. *Dreamworld and Catastrophe: The Passing of Mass Utopia.* Cambridge: MIT Press.

Cooke, C. 1983. *Russian Avant-garde: art and architecture.* London: Architectural Design.

———. 1996. *Russian Avante-garde: Theories of Art, Architecture and the City.* London: Academy Editions.

Cooke, C. and A. Justin (eds). 1991. *The Avant-Garde: Russian Architecture in the Twenties.* London: Academy Editions.

Dombrovsky, Y. 1969. *The Keeper of Antiquities,* translated by M. Glenny. New York: McGraw-Hill.

Dombrovsky, Y. 1996. *The Faculty of Useless Knowledge,* translated by A. Myers. London: Harvill Press.

Gay y Blasco, P. 1999. *Gypsies in Madrid: Sex, Gender and the Performance of Identity.* Oxford: Berg.

Ginzburg, M. 1982, [1926]. *Style and Epoch.* Cambridge, MA: MIT Press.

Glantz, M. 1999. *Creeping Environmental Problems and Sustainable Development in the Aral Sea basin.* New York: Cambridge University Press.

Harbison, R. 1991. *The Built, the Unbuilt and the Unbuildable: In Pursuit of Architectural Meaning.* London: Thames and Hudson.

Helsinki Watch. 1990. *Conflict in the Societ Union: the Untold Story of the Clashes in Khazakhstan.* New York: Helsinki Watch.

Himmelfarb, G. 1984. *The Idea of Poverty: England in the Early Industrial Age.* New York: Alfred A. Knopf.

Hollander, J. 1998. 'The Waste Remains and Kills', *Social Research* Vol 65(1).

Lampland, M. 1995. *The Object of Labor: Commodification in Socialist Hungary.* Chicago: University of Chicago Press.

Malyar, I. 1976. *Alma-Ata.* Alma-Ata: Zhalin.

168 | *Catherine Alexander*

Martin, E. 1994. *Flexible Bodies: Tracking Immunity in American Culture from the Days of Polio to the Age of AIDS*. New York: Beacon Press.

Marx, K. and F. Engels. 1987. *The Communist Manifesto*. Harmondsworth: Penguin Books.

Morris, L. 1994. *Dangerous Classes: The Underclass and Social Citizenship*. London: Routledge.

Nazpary, J. 1999. *Violence and Dispossession: Chaos in Kazakhstan*. London: Pluto Press.

Otis, L. 1999. *Membranes: Metaphors of Invasion in Nineteenth-Century Literature, Science, and Politics*. Baltimore: Johns Hopkins University Press.

Peterson, D.J. 1993. *Troubled Lands: the legacy of Soviet environmental destruction*. Boulder, CO: Westview Press.

Pohl, M. 1999. 'The Virgin Lands Between Memory and Forgetting: People and Transformation in the Soviet Union, 1954–1960', Ph.D. thesis, Indiana University.

Pohl, M. 2002. '"It Cannot Be That Our Graves Will Be Here": The Survival of Chechen and Ingush Deportees in Kazakhstan, 1944–1957', *Journal of Genocide Research* 4(3): 401–30.

Propp, V. 1968. *Morphology of the Folk Tale*. London and Austin: University of Texas Press.

Pryde, P. 1995. *Environmental Resources and Constraints in the Former Soviet Republics*. Boulder, CO: Westview Press.

Prynne, J. 1971. *Brass*. London: Bloodaxe.

Ries, N. 1997. *Russian Talk: Culture and Conversation During Perestroika*. Ithaca: Cornell University Press.

Scott, J.C. 1998. *Seeing Like a State: How Certain Schemes to Improve the Human Condition Have Failed*. New Haven: Yale University Press.

Ssorin-Chaikov, N. 2003. *The Social Life of the State in Subarctic Siberia*. Stanford: Stanford University Press.

Stedman Jones, G. 1971. *Outcast London: A Study in the Relationship Between Classes in Victorian Britain*. Oxford: Oxford University Press.

Strathern, M. 1999. *Property, Substance and Effect : Anthropological Essays on Persons and Things*. London: Athlone Press.

Trotsky, L. 1975. *My Life: An Attempt at an Autobiography*. Harmondsworth: Penguin Books Ltd.

Veblen, T. 1902. *The Theory of the Leisure Class: An Economic Study of Institutions*. New York: Macmillan.

Von Geldern. 1993. *Bolshevik Festivals 1917–1920*. Berkeley: University of California.

Weinthal, E. 2004. 'Beyond the State: Transnational Actors, NGOs and Environmental Protection in Central Asia', in P. Jones Luong (ed.), *The Transformation of Central; Asia: States and Societies from Soviet Rule to Independence*. Ithaca and London: Cornell University Press, pp. 246–70.

Williams, R. 1990. *Culture and Society*. London: Hogarth Press.

CHAPTER 7

Corruption and the One-party State in Tanzania: The View from Dar es Salaam, 1964–2000

John R. Campbell

Opinions on the socialist experiment in Tanzania diverge sharply between those who celebrated the politics and policies of *ujamaa* ('socialism'), and its critics. In this paper I am interested in a neglected aspect of the political processes of the period, namely the role played by bureaucratic 'corruption' under socialism and the one-party state. With few exceptions, commentators on Tanzania have had little to say about corruption until the mid-1990s, when donor pressure to implement neoliberal reforms converged with popular perceptions to make corruption a central electoral issue (Heilman and Ndumbaro 2002). In fact, during the 1995 national elections corruption became *the* issue and was subsequently the object of a number of (ineffective) anti-corruption policies and programmes. It is odd that so little has been written on the subject when Tanzanians have been acutely aware of and affected by some form of corruption for decades; perhaps it became such a routine part of state practices that it has attracted little consideration or perhaps the nature of corruption has changed as the economy deteriorated.

I seek to examine corruption as a set of related transactions carried out either by, or with the support, of party officials and civil servants in the city of Dar es Salaam. I intend to argue that, despite official condemnation that corruption is the work of individuals who seek to undermine government policy (i.e. socialism), corrupt practices are better understood as fitting into a continuum of officially condoned activities which provide indirect support for failing party policies. In particular, corruption is directly related to official restrictions/regulations – on trade, ownership of private property, personal incomes etc. – imposed to combat capitalism, which allow the state to redistribute income to *mwanchi* (citizens). Corruption is permitted, if not actually encouraged, to mitigate the worst vicissitudes of socialist policies, e.g. food and commodity shortages. Thus by turning a blind eye to a bureaucrat's misuse of her position, the party condones the redistribution of state resources to middlemen who in turn sell goods on illegally (e.g. for political favours or via the parallel economy) to individuals who would not otherwise obtain them.

I find Mbaku's distinction between 'political' and 'bureaucratic' corruption useful in the context of Tanzania where a one-party state has governed since independence. Mbaku (1996: 2) argues that political corruption involves 'activities such as vote rigging, registration of unqualified, dead, or non-existent voters, purchase and sale of votes, and the falsification of electoral results'. On the other hand, bureaucratic corruption entails 'efforts by civil servants to enrich themselves through illegal means'. While a shift to multiparty politics in 1985 certainly opened up the possibility for the former, here the focus is on bureaucratic corruption operating in an economy of scarcity.

The section that follows sets out the context in which corruption began, that is, the creation of the one-party state and the promulgation of ujamaa in 1967, which initiated a wave of nationalizations of private property and a variety of controls over the economy and society. I focus on bureaucratic 'inefficiency' in the development of Dar es Salaam between 1965 and 1984. The second section focuses on the 'retreat' of the state in the wake of structural adjustment and neoliberal reforms introduced in the early 1980s. This period ushered in deepening poverty, multiparty politics and, in the face of the declining authority of the party/state, an expansion in the level and scale of corruption. A central point here is that by the 1980s corruption became so endemic and deep-rooted that it is now embedded in urban culture. Finally, I conclude with observations about the link between the externally driven economic reform process and corruption.

The Socialist Transition: Corruption in the City

In the early 1960s the Tanganyika African National Union (TANU) – which became Chama Cha Mapinduzi (CCM, the 'Party of Revolution') in 1977 – embarked on a wide range of nation building (*kujenga taifa*) programmes. The socialist state's raison d'etre was to intervene to bring about development. At independence all Tanganyikans nominally stood in the same relation to the state as citizens. Soon afterwards, however, the party began to define a political programme based on a radical new vision of *ujamaa* ('socialism'). Through a one-party state the political elite articulated a project of rule based on a distinction between the party, party members and citizens: the country was to be led by an enlightened party, and citizens would willingly comply with and 'participate' in party institutions and policies.

In 1964, largely in response to the slow pace of development and the aspirations of party members, there occurred a rapid institutionalization of TANU as *the* political institution, and of the civil service as the tool of the party. Local 'ten-cell' (Swahili, *nymba-kumi*) party cells were created which were given responsibility for fund raising, party organization, etc. Ten-cell leaders were also responsible for law and order: they liaised with police and the courts; and were expected to deal with crime and tax collection; to call people to work on development projects; and to ensure 'security' by registering strangers (O'Barr 1971; Levine 1972).

Following a failed coup d'etat in 1965, TANU consolidated its control over the unions, military and police and, shortly afterwards, the cooperative movement and local government (Pratt 1976). The party bureaucracy expanded, particularly at regional and district level, and activists became paid officials exercising authority in ways that overlapped with the civil service (Maguire 1969: 319; Pratt 1976). With the adoption of a one-party Constitution in 1965, the ten-cell system was expected to be 'the eyes and ears of the nation … [to] expose dangerous characters like thieves and other infiltrators who may poison our nation and put its safety at stake' (Levine 1972: 330). Indeed, party officials and Tanzanians saw the creation of a one-party state as a merging of TANU and the government, an impression reinforced by subsequent political reforms.

The party/state pursued a growing range of developmental and domestic issues and, not surprisingly, it exercised considerable power[1] as its reach extended over citizens, allowing it to collect tax, conscript for the military and militia, etc. In short, by the mid-1960s the party had established a 'standard grid' through which it exercised a growing level of control over ordinary citizens (Scott 1998: 2). The party repeatedly changed the constitution to give it greater control over the cabinet, parliament and the civil service, allowing it to pursue a socialist agenda without being accountable for its actions (Kituo cha Katiba. n.d.; Duggan 1976: 56 passim).

A key element of the party's ability to 'embrace' the population derived in part from its secular nationalist political programme. The power to define national identity was at the core of the state's ability to control territory and govern. The idea that Indians should become citizens provoked considerable public debate. Indeed the 'Indian Question' proved to be a useful symbol which the party periodically invoked to focus attention on 'race' and away from issues of governance and the rule of law. Public debates on the rights and obligations of Asian citizens moved in tandem with growing bureaucratic regulations linking definitions of citizenship with popular discourses on race.

As occurred in other socialist societies, an expansion in state 'documentary controls' reflected attempts 'to establish and maintain control over particular territories by constructing enduring identities that permit them [the state] to "lay hold" of their subjects/citizens' (Torpey 1997: 838). It is notable that documentary controls – in the form of passports and passport controls, internal passes, identification documents, censuses, household registration exercises, permits to migrate/travel, birth and marriage records, etc. (Torpey 1998) – proliferated in Tanzania and became the sine qua non of citizenship.

However, the state's need for information on citizens to assist central economic planning (for social services, housing, health care, education, etc.), to conscript, organize communal labour, ensure payment of taxes, control access to food supplies and so on was matched by its use of documentation to monitor and control citizens. Documentary and other controls were increasingly used to define the rights of urban dwellers to education, health services, food and other services.

Additional control was achieved by mapping and registering urban land. Here the intention was to roll back land claims based on customary tenure to pave the way for broader statutory control. At its most basic, government sought to regulate development by allocating rights of occupancy, collecting land rent, and making land available for housing, roads and industry. Large amounts of land were transferred to public ownership but this created a class of urban 'squatters', a new political category viewed with anathema.

As the party expanded its reach it encountered pockets of resistance, in response to which it drew on popular discourse to develop ever finer distinctions between *mwananchi* ('citizens') – defined broadly in terms of approved forms of employment, marriage and implicit loyalty to the party – and a range of other less deserving individuals (Scotton 1965; Brennan 2002). The party distinguished social parasites or *wanyonyagi* ('exploiters') who undermined *ujamaa* ('socialism') and *kujenga na taifa* ('nation building'). Socialist rhetoric identified an increasing number of parasites/enemies such as: the *bwanyenye*, property owners or the 'bourgeoisie'; *kabaila* or feudalists/rural exploiters; *bepari* or (Indian) 'merchants'/'capitalists'; *kibwanyenye* or 'petty capitalists'; and *mhuni* or male 'hooligans' in the cities (complemented by the term *guberi* or 'prostitute' that was extended to young, unmarried urban women). Following the Arusha Declaration the pressure to transform society saw new terms added to this rich political vocabulary in the form of *mfanyakazi* ('workers'), *mkulima* ('peasants'), 'squatters', the urban unemployed/loiterers, and economic saboteurs (*walanguzi*).

Urban policy sought to alleviate a severe housing shortage facing urban Africans by intervening in the urban land and housing market (Campbell 1990). However, these policies failed to assist the poor. Indeed, through nationalization of businesses, housing and land was rationalized as a redistribution of resources from the wealthy to *mwananchi*; poor management and corruption reinforced existing disparities of wealth along class lines. Furthermore, the party's approach to urban squatters was authoritarian and lacking in political vision; attempts to bulldoze squatter settlements led local residents to utilize patronage networks to TANU to bypass an unresponsive state bureaucracy and block urban redevelopment.

The Second Five Year Development Plan (1969–74) heralded *ujamaa vijijini* ('villagization') and called for an abrupt shift in urban policies in accord with the party's commitment to socialism. However the policy environment was riddled with contradictions and despite the proliferation of urban master plans there was virtually no investment in urban infrastructure or housing. At the same time, the urban population, many of whom were fleeing villagization, increased massively with most living in the rapidly expanding squatter areas of the city (squatting increased at 16.6 per cent per annum between 1963 and 1972; Stren 1975).

Fearing the loss of public support, and in the face of unrest in urban factories, in 1972 the cabinet decided that urban development should take the form of a national sites and services programme (Campbell 1988). The World Bank sites and services projects (1974–83) resulted in massive urban changes. The projects were supposed to benefit 475,000 low-income people through the provision of serviced building plots in Dar es Salaam and other up country towns. In addition, squatter areas were to be upgraded to create 18,575 fully serviced building plots. Health clinics, primary schools, piped water, markets, roads and storm drains were also to be provided.

The sites and services programme became a highly centralized scheme run by bureaucrats who created the rules governing it and who were perfectly positioned to manipulate the system (Stren 1982).[2] During this period power over urban development shifted away from the party to a bureaucracy that set in place a quasi-market for urban land and housing.

Rather than establishing an 'enabling' environment to assist the urban poor to secure housing, an increasingly regulatory system was imposed. Bureaucratic processes took on a life of their own, providing ample scope for corruption in which 'applicants' with money could bypass the labyrinth of regulations[3] to acquire a plot. Furthermore, large numbers of low-income beneficiaries lost their serviced plot because inflation squeezed incomes thus preventing them from completing house construction, which resulted in the government revoking unfinished plots (for failing to meet stipulated building covenants). These plots were subsequently 'sold' illegally. By the late 1980s at least 42 per cent of the plots allocated in Dar es Salaam had been illegally transferred to upper-income households in this manner. At the same time a large number of 'new' plots – 17 per cent of the total – were created as a result of 'lax' development controls (Kironde 1991). It has been estimated that, in contradistinction to the programmes stated intentions, 40–70 per cent of serviced plots were acquired by middle- or high-income households. In addition, officials managing the housing credit programme also redefined the eligibility criteria such that 60 per cent of the urban population were disqualified from access to credit (which left considerable scope for official discretion in the allocation of resources).

The sites and services programme in Dar redeveloped 1,500 hectares of prime real estate which fuelled land and housing prices across the city. The project: (1) caused considerable social disruption and dislocation, especially for the poor; (2) imposed high, unsustainable financial costs on government; (3) had a significant amount of work that was not completed or maintained; and (4) primarily benefited the upper and middle classes.

Furthermore, somewhat surprisingly none of the projects involved 'popular participation', which helps to explain why so many were displaced and why residents attempted to work the system to personal advantage. For example, soon after it was announced that an area was to be redeveloped people moved in hoping to obtain compensation. Resistance to the sites and services programme could only be expressed indirectly by beneficiaries, and many refused to pay the 'user charge' which allowed the project to recover costs. By the time the project ended in the early 1980s the city had over 1 million residents; about 50 per cent were squatters and at least 50 per cent earned below the minimum wage.

The 'Retreat of the State' and the Rise of Bureaucratic Corruption, 1980–2000

During the first two decades of independence donor funding allowed the party to pursue a range of social and economic projects. Urban policies resulted in extensive redevelopment and contributed directly to the growth of an illegal market for land and housing which helped to shift the locus of urban power away from party patronage towards emerging forms of economic power by groups that were anathema to the party. This shift in the balance of power to 'the market' gradually eroded the authority of the party and shaped its attempts to control market forces.

In the face of continued economic decline, the party adopted a series of structural adjustment measures in the early 1980s which paralleled the decline in per capita incomes: it introduced a massive currency devaluation and substantially cut public expenditure in health and education (Helleiner 1987). The party sought to maintain its authority by relying increasingly on its regulatory powers through, for example, controlling the allocation and marketing of food. Such a strategy was undermined, however, by massive commodity shortages (there were too few goods to distribute). Instead state controls gave rise to a network of 'clientage' relations based in collusion and corruption involving senior managers and petty officials (Bryceson 1987: 185). When the food supply in Dar sharply deteriorated in 1983 the party responded by establishing a rationing system for registered party members/households (Byrceson 1990: 204). However, rationing failed because many residents were not on the official list and because commodities disappeared into the illegal, parallel market operated by petty traders, itinerant hawkers and licensed stores. Donor pressure in 1984, together with the maladministration of the programme finally forced the party to end its policy of subsidizing food (Bryceson 1990: 202).[4]

Throughout the 1970s and 1980s the party was concerned with the threat posed by the market, which provided scope for individual self-advancement and thus ran counter to socialism. There were five basic challenges to the authority of the party between 1980 and 2002: (1) struggles centering on the livelihoods of the urban self-employed; (2) the growth of the illegal parallel economy; (3) the work of 'fixers' and 'saboteurs'; (4) the role of the police in criminalizing specific social groups; and finally, (5) elite strategies aimed at ensuring a sinecure over public housing.

Despite efforts to prohibit the informal sector, for instance by withholding permits and licences, urban self-employment grew rapidly because it allowed households to supplement wages and it provided a livelihood for many residents. Urban self-employment grew in the face of the party's utter disregard for those not in wage work. Equally important, every urban household came to depend on self-employed individuals directly (e.g. for domestic staff) or indirectly through the services provided by craftsmen, small manufacturers, petty traders, hotel and bar keeping, house rental, urban farming, etc. (Bienefeld 1975; Ndanshau and Mvungi 2001).

Intriguingly, party attempts to control the 'unemployed' show a remarkable similarity with colonial programmes that sought to arrest and repatriate 'undesirables' from the city (Burton 2005). 'Control' campaigns were used intermittently between1961 and 1964, 1967 and 71, in 1976, 1978, 1982/3, and in 1996 to clear the streets of the 'unemployed' and 'criminals' by arresting and transporting unproductive *wahuni/wanyonyagi* to the rural areas where they were supposed to be transformed into productive citizens (*mwananchi*). Remarkably there is no evidence that this policy, which was introduced in 1919, has ever succeeded (Armstrong 1987; Paddison 1988; Kironde 2000: 26–28).

Urban control campaigns follow a typical pattern: residents are first harangued by party leaders, then intimidated, arrested and repatriated (though most deportees eventually return). The 1983 Human Resources

Deployment Act (*Nguvu Kazi* or 'hard work') illustrates how these campaigns work (Armstrong 1987). The Act sought to ensure that all 'able-bodied persons' were in 'productive work'; it was no coincidence that the repatriation campaign occurred at the same time as a crackdown on 'economic sabotage', corruption and smuggling (Shivji 1990: 31–f.; Bryceson 1993: 24–27). Officials rationalized the policy in terms of the evils of 'unemployment' and the value of cooperation; exhortations to be voluntarily repatriated were quickly followed by the registration of unemployed persons (21, 772 were identified in Dar), followed by police raids. Between October and November approximately 7,548 individuals were detained and 976 were ascertained to be 'unemployed'(including individuals arrested for trading without a council licence); by the end of the year 1,500 were repatriated.

The public response to this campaign was negative, in part because the round-up included many self-employed people (not to mention relatives and friends), which reduced the availability of services. In April 1984 the government was forced to amend the act to allow informal sector enterprises provided that individuals obtain a licence.[5] Like earlier repatriation campaigns, Nguvu Kazi failed to achieve its objectives and it antagonized the urban population.

Due to long-term economic decline, the majority of urban residents needed to pursue a variety of livelihoods which inevitably included an 'illegal' *miradi* ('project') of some kind to supplement low wages. However, these livelihoods generated very limited returns whilst putting individuals at risk of having their goods confiscated and/or being arrested. The economy deteriorated so rapidly that by 1987 'the average-sized household of six can feed itself for only four to six days of the month if it relies solely on a formal wage' (Tripp 1988: 4). All told, economic liberalization and the sharp deterioration in social and economic conditions weakened the party's authority. In 1985 Nyerere announced his retirement from politics and the first multiparty elections were held.

There were many attempts to harass the urban 'unemployed' – for example, the attempt to control 'illegal' water sellers in Dar in the late 1960s and the 'war on loiterers' in 1976 (Armstrong 1987: 16–18) – and to control their activities. Thus the 1982 Act of Parliament that reestablished local government required municipalities to undertake urban development, collect tax, provide basic services, license small business and collect a 'development levy' (Kulaba 1989: 229–f.).[6] In the face of limited revenue and rapidly deteriorating services and infrastructure, Council officials and the police sought to 'control'[7] the informal sector by demolishing 'illegal markets' and stalls (Tripp 1997; Kaare 2001; Mhamba and Titus 2001). Many petty traders could not afford the licence, but those who attempted to secure a licence soon found that 'they had to pay bribes three or four times the cost of the license itself' (Tripp 1988: 12).Very slowly the self-employed began to organize and, instead of fleeing from officials, they began to flout[8] or block the law by refusing to pay taxes; some formed associations to lobby and/or take the council to court to obtain services (Kironde 2000).

A second area of political contention arose when the party attempted to control the parallel market. Attempts to ban this sector have been unsuccessful (Bryceson 1987; Tripp 1990) and have been followed by periodic attempts to arrest *walanguzi* (black marketeers), 'loiterers' and various 'unemployed' people involved in the secondary sale of 'controlled' goods and foods. The level of official vituperation reserved for these 'parasites' belies their significance. *Walanguzi*, 'fixers' and petty traders represented a ubiquitous and important urban career which allowed officials to maintain the pretence that their policies worked while at the same time enabling some residents to access public services, housing, serviced plots, controlled commodities, food and foreign exchange.

The range of economic activities deemed by officials to be 'illegal' was endless. At one extreme were individuals accused of being 'economic saboteurs'. Thus in a 1983 crackdown on 'economic saboteurs' and racketeers approximately 4,216 individuals were arrested for hoarding or smuggling goods (profiteering), of whom 2,872 were Asian businessmen and the rest were African civil servants (Nagar 1996: 72). Arraigned under special legislation, the individual's property was confiscated and s/he was imprisoned; however, in 1992 the government acknowledged 'lapses in carrying out the anti-economic sabotage campaign' and made available Sh.700 million to compensate individuals who had been wrongly accused. An example of official corruption occurred in 1993 when an Asian businessman obtained a 3.3 million dollar loan from a Minister of State which was then diverted overseas to a private account (Heilman and Ndumbaro 2002: 4). Invariably the majority of senior officials caught in corrupt practices were not prosecuted.

Less spectacular but no less apparent was the role played by 'friends'. In the mid-1980s expatriates utilized 'friends' in government offices to secure a range of goods and services. For instance, it was necessary for a friend in the bank to intercede to secure a contractual entitlement to remit foreign exchange (officials often failed to remit this money overseas). The same friend might also arrange for the private sale of household goods (fridges, cars, etc.) that were supposed to be handed to a parastatal to be sold at 'controlled' prices. Needless to say, the careers of fixers flourished until the economy was deregulated.

Obtaining access to rent-controlled public housing illustrates another avenue where corruption flourished. Housing was nationalized in the early 1970s in an attempt to transfer it from Asian 'capitalists' into African hands. One by-product of nationalization was the establishment of a number of Asian 'fixers', individuals who used their knowledge of housing still occupied by Asian tenants to fix an illegal transfer of occupancy from the sitting tenant to individuals who could afford the 'key money' (to pay the agent and his bureaucratic counterpart and make a substantial payment in foreign exchange to enable the sitting tenant to move overseas). In an attempt to facilitate access to housing for low-paid civil servants, the rent charged to tenants in public housing was frozen. Low rents and good-quality housing soon led to the illegal transfer of significant levels of public housing (Mwita 1978: 154).

In 1985 the Registrar of Buildings, the corporation that managed public housing, announced a registration exercise to establish whether sitting tenants were legal occupants. The Registrar sought to revise rents upwards to generate capital to construct new housing and maintain existing stock (Kulaba 1981a; Kironde 1992).[9] However, sitting tenants quickly mobilized and argued that rent increases were unfair given the poor condition of their housing and their low incomes. Unlike other groups disadvantaged by economic reform, these individuals had good political connections. The Tenants Association petitioned the Prime Minister,[10] the (Asian) Dar es Salaam Merchants Association appealed to the party Secretary General,[11] tenants in NHC buildings in Ubungo petitioned the Registrar, and tenants at Keko used the University's Legal Aid Committee to file an injunction.[12] The injunction stopped the rent increase and tenants persuaded the party to direct government to withdraw the proposed rents. In the face of party pressure the government backed down.

CCM also controls the judiciary and police, and both have played important roles in implementing party policy. This relationship came about in the mid-1960s when senior police and military officers were co-opted into the party. In this regard the use of the paramilitary Field Force Unit, attached to the National Police, to control situations as diverse as strikes, the compulsory relocation of rural residents to planned villages, the arrest of 'economic saboteurs', and suppression of 'religious fundamentalists' is not surprising (Shivji 1990; chap. 7). However, the role played by the police has expanded in step with party objectives and includes responsibility for upholding the 'law', regulating borders and the port, currency control, development-related work, and exercising oversight of quasi-legal vigilante networks (see below). Its basic organization and principal functions – maintenance of law and order, crime prevention, protection of life and property, traffic control, national security, etc. – are modelled on the colonial police force. Interestingly, after a decade of political liberalization the police remain under party control. This relationship raises important questions concerning in 'whose interests the police act as agents' (Hills 1996: 274), and, indeed, about how to define the boundary between legal and illegal activities.

Given the tendency of the party, police and the courts to blame rising crime on anti-social elements, including unemployed young men, the very nature and definition of 'crime' requires careful scrutiny. This is all the more important given the decline in the number of police.[13] Statistics[14] indicate that crime has grown rapidly, though accurate figures are difficult to find. A 'victimization survey' in Dar suggests that between 1987 and 1991 crimes – i.e., car-related theft, vandalism, burglary, robbery, assault and sex offences – are twice as high as official statistics. Officials only acknowledge the difference between reported and unreported crimes at 7–10 per cent above official statistics. Data from police records suggest that between 1995 and 1997 reported crimes numbered 126,000 cases or 26.9 per cent of nationally reported crimes. A second 'victimization survey' for 1995–2000 suggests that burglaries increased by 43 per cent, muggings by 32 per cent, assaults by 16 per cent etc.; a total of 1,016,865 'crime incidents' were reported (an annual increase of 5.3 per cent). Two further observations are worth making. First, rising public anxiety about crime has resulted in an unknown number of 'thieves' being stoned, beaten or burned ('neck-laced') to death on city streets.[15] Second, there is no data on 'economic' crimes like corruption or 'white collar' crime.

In a context of ineffective policing and the criminalization of a wide swath of the population, a situation arose in the early 1980s where the party used the pretext of rising crime to justify its support for community-based vigilante groups (*sungu sungu* or *wasalama*; Abrahams 1996).[16] In Dar es Salaam every household was encouraged to participate in night patrols in their community. In the first year of operation a substantial drop in the level of crime was reported. However, *sungu sungu* quickly became part of the problem: some members were convicted of violating basic human rights while others failed to cooperate with the police. In 1987 the Courts ruled that *sungu sungu* were operating outside the law, but it was not until 1989 that legislation legalized and defined their role.

Somewhat tellingly, though crime rose rapidly in Dar es Salaam, some local political leaders refused to sanction the reintroduction of *sungu sungu* as part of a new urban crime prevention strategy because the vigilante groups were linked to the party. In 2000, opposition to the reintroduction of *sungu sungu* in fifteen wards led to the development of an alternative 'Block Security System' in which 'community agreements' with 'private security companies' contracted unemployed youth to patrol the streets. The resurrection of urban vigilantes coincided with the suspension of the municipal government by CCM over allegations of corruption. The willingness of the party to use the law – police, courts and vigilantes – to regulate growing areas of social life challenges conventional assumptions about the separation of law and politics and strongly suggests that for some Tanzanians the 'law' may be a symbol of oppression and lawlessness.

This blurring of the boundary between law and criminality provides ample opportunities for well-placed individuals to use their political identity/social position to operate with impunity. This blurring is also observable with regard to the way that different social groups are policed. Thus 'religious fanatics' are subjected to fairly ruthless treatment (Campbell 2005) while the transgressions of the elite and middle class are ignored.

For example, in the early 1980s a relatively small group of 'pirate' transporters challenged the authorities for the right to compete with municipal buses which were the only authorized form of public transport. In the face of state regulation and harassment (which involved paying bribes) they persevered. Even though the public transport system collapsed, it was not until 1996 that the government fully deregulated the sector (Rizzo 2002). Regardless of continued attempts to regulate licensing and allocate transport routes, which still led to extensive bribery, deregulation resulted in a massive increase in private transport and a relatively stable fare system. However, the majority of *dala dala* operators, as the sector is called, fail to comply with licensing requirements and they do not abide by road safety rules. The result is a poorly integrated transport network plagued by poor roads and a poor safety record. Private transporters have exploited the lack of regulation and, in the context of official steps to establish self-regulation, have used their association to create a private rent-seeking institution that operates at the expense of the public.

Political and economic reforms have provided numerous opportunities for the middle class and elite to privatize public property/services with impunity. Thus thousands of households illegally tap into municipal water and electricity supplies; others produce and sell unsafe food, drink and 'medicines' which pose a health risk to consumers; yet others empty pit latrines on public land, etc. Such activities carry a high cost to public health and public finance.

In the context of privatization the Municipal Council has not been able to provide basic services to residents. A small number of local businesses, 'community' associations/NGOs and 'nonprofit' organizations have entered the market to obtain contracts to clean markets and streets, sell water, establish private schools and provide other services. By the late 1990s twenty-eight associations had obtained contracts from the municipality, though most failed to deliver the contracted services (Kironde 2000; Kaare 2001). One reason for this situation is that the associations are led by an 'elite' who are widely seen as acting opportunistically (Kessy 2000). While residents have become increasingly articulate about the failure of this government and the nascent private sector to provide services, nevertheless

Demands are not made on behalf of all residents of the city, and city-wide alliances have not occurred. The overwhelming reaction of people ... to escalating urban problems can be said to be that of performing operations themselves, either individually or collectively. (Kironde 2000: 227)

During the 1980s corruption became so endemic and widespread that, despite universal condemnation, everyone in a position to extract a fee or bribe was involved. It should be clear that only those in the civil service or party were in a position to bestow favours, goods or a service and that peasants, workers and the poor were not directly involved. The poor do not possess any assets with which to demand favours, though such individuals are of use to corrupt officials and middlemen who divert black-market goods to them (invariably it is petty traders etc. who are caught by the police and castigated in the press).

The pervasive nature of corruption is best understood by examining the myriad acts of officials – teachers, civil servants, accountants, planners, doctors, tax officials, police officers – as they provide a client with access to a service or scarce good. The vast majority of those involved in dispensing such services are educated, middle-class individuals drawn from ethnic groups across the country: they simultaneously require a bribe to provide an official service and pay bribes to obtain something they need. In some ways corruption inverts gift giving: the language in which such transactions are clothed is that of gift and counter-gift but in actuality the relation is one of extortion. The ubiquitousness of corruption is captured in local anecdotes:

If you apply for a permit and then go to an office to check on it, the clerk will say, 'The file isn't visible.' Each time that you return, that happens, until you give him *chochote* [slang Swahili for a bribe, literally 'a little something'] saying 'take these, get a soda'. He will go inside and come back a few minutes later: 'the file appeared.' (Lewinson 1999: 138–39)

One reason why corruption is so pervasive is that it has become embedded in popular culture. As Lewinson notes in her study of the urban middle class in Dar, urban life is driven by 'cash hunger': 'More than other Tanzanians, urbanites are fully integrated into a cash-based lifestyle, and Dar es Salaam's residents worry constantly about obtaining enough money for their household and ritual needs' (1999: 110). Economic liberalization has introduced a variety of new consumer goods even as it has been accompanied by a drastic decline in incomes. The result is that 'Competition and frustration increase. Office workers now live in a continual state of cash hunger, where hunger connotes both a lack and a continual desire for more' (ibid.: 111).

A further paradox is that for the middle class the party/state – which provided them with an education, a career, and a 'common belief that the welfare of the nation was linked to the patronage of the state' (Harrington 1999: 215) – represents in abstract a promise of modernity while at the same time it has become a symbol of corruption (Lewinson 1999: 130). It is hardly surprising that the middle class can cite a litany of complaints about corrupt officials who, as gatekeepers, deny them access to services and goods, while at the same time they engage in similar practices themselves. In this regard Lewinson comments that

> ... while office workers felt frustrated with the endemic corruption – especially when it interfered with their lives – they seldom blamed the specific individuals. Instead, they blamed the economic situation. (1999: 139–40)

Njaa (Swa. for 'hunger') and *tamaa* ('the lust for things') in an urban context of competition and hierarchy provide the emic explanation for endemic corruption. In this view neither individual failings nor lapses in morality[17] are responsible, instead the fault lies with society.

Conclusion

Corruption has become an intrinsic part of politics, but it was not always this way. While some level of corruption existed in the early 1960s, socialist nationalization of the economy and the establishment of an unaccountable ruling party and state bureaucracy provided scope for it to flourish. In Dar es Salaam party officials and bureaucrats have created opportunities – through the proliferation of regulatory controls – for personal enrichment which (initially) had the unintended result of creating illegal commodity, land and housing markets.

By the early 1980s bilateral and multilateral aid agencies sought to impose economic/market[18] reforms on Tanzania. Agencies assumed that an isomorphic relation existed between 'the structure of the market and the incidence of corruption', thereby overlooking the fact that '[S]ince rules define market outcomes, greater reliance on markets for the allocation of resources without reforming the existing rules will have little effect on the outcome, including bureaucratic corruption' (Mbaku 1996: 5). However, the party readjusted its political strategy to maintain control through its control of the army, police and vigilante groups, and indirectly via its ability to pressure the state/civil service to secure favours, influence and economic benefits (e.g., food subsidies, distribution of commodities, rent freezes) for the political elite and party supporters.

The party has consistently positioned itself, in part through control over the media and the political process, as the institution that fights for ordinary Tanzanians by resisting the neoliberal/economic reforms imposed on the country.[19] Paradoxically, because it has maintained control over the political system the party/state has exercised responsibility for implementing the reform process – regardless of the impact of the reforms – which has resulted in a rolling but piecemeal and partial deregulation of the economy. Not surprisingly, the results of such reforms have been mixed. Thus the deregulation of transport was a long drawn-out process with complete deregulation occurring twelve years after the first steps were initiated. Implementation of reforms – e.g., land tenure (Coldham 1995), food supply and distribution (Santorum and Tibaijuka 1992), the administration of tax (Bjorvatn, Torsvik and Tungodden 2004) etc. – created space for private enterprise while simultaneously maintaining the power of party officials and 'middlemen'/brokers who offer a way through the red tape.

In apparent contradiction to donor-imposed reforms elsewhere in Africa and to reforms in other 'socialist' countries, in Tanzania the party reorganized its hold on power. Nor is there any evidence to suggest that the social and regulatory power of the state has devolved to non-state/international agencies (i.e., bilateral agencies or NGOs; Ferguson and Gupta 2002). The international community has not provided significant levels of development assistance and the small number of non-state organizations are unable to bypass the state or take over some of its function.[20] The situation is not so much one of 'unbundled' space, in the sense of transnational organizations filling in for the state, as of massive holes in the political fabric, which allows local institutions and the elite to carve out their own domain of influence.

Corruption *is* endemic in Tanzania, but is it a symptom of the criminalization of the state (Bayart, Ellis and Hibou 1999) and does it emanate from a 'moral economy' which has developed in response to 'the demands of a modern economy' (Chabal and Daloz 1999: 101)? Those who write[21] about corruption agree that it is pervasive, that individual acts need to be seen as part of a continuum (dichotomies are unhelpful), that corruption may be clothed in the language of gift giving/reciprocity (which implies the operation of clientage networks) etc., though they disagree about its causes.

Furthermore, it may be the case that in Tanzania, as Bayart et al. (1999) and others have argued for Africa generally, corruption is primarily concerned with immediate consumption ('the politics of the belly') rather than international crime (drugs, smuggling, money laundering). The international dimension may, however, simply be invisible and in any event the politics of the belly and criminal acts are different faces of the same transaction.

What is remarkable is that in Tanzania the same political party that introduced socialism in the mid-1960s, when corruption began to embed itself in political culture, has successfully weathered major political and economic challenges to its authority by astute political manoeuvring vis-à-vis Western aid agencies and by reinventing itself as the people's champion against donor-imposed reform. The party has achieved this at the expense of a collapsing economy and social infrastructure – because the cost of corruption comes at the expense of development – while maintaining a level of social and political stability unseen elsewhere in Africa. This seeming paradox is understandable only if one bears in mind the ideological legacy of socialism and the durability of the institutional power wielded by the political elite who govern via the ruling Chama Cha Mapinduzi political party.

Notes

1. The power which accrued to bureaucrats by the late 1960s quickly led to corruption in cooperatives, the courts and police, government parastatals etc. (see Coulson 1982: 150, 221, 281).
2. World Bank loans for sites and services totalled US$46 million and required Tanzania to meet all other costs. The project was one of three Bank projects, none of which was repaid on schedule.
3. Seibolds and Steinberg (1982: 119–ff) argue that official procedures to obtain a plot required at least six months and that the fees required to obtain a THB loan for a Sh. 15,000 house amounted to Sh. 2,290. Low-income households could not afford either the time or the money.
4. Tellingly, the maize subsidy had primarily benefited the well-off (Horton 1985: 20).
5. See: Government Notice 47, published on 20/4/1984.
6. In 1996 the government abolished the Municipal Council of Dar es Salaam due to allegations of corruption (Lerise and Ngware 2000: 124).
7. There were thirty-two illegal markets in 1982 (*Daily News* 21/2/1982), and fifty-two in the late 1990s (Kironde 2000: 38).
8. E.g. 'Crackdown on pirate taxis underway', *Daily News* 24/7/85; 'City told to control (unlicensed) bars', *Daily News* 21/1/1982.
9. See: 'NHC resumes building projects', *Daily News* 6/2/1984; 'NHC to repair its houses', *Daily News* 20/2/1985'; 'The fairness of NHC rent rises', *Sunday News* 3/10/85.
10. 'TTA seeks PMO's help', *Daily News* 17/5/1985.
11. 'Dar merchants want rent suspended', *Daily News* 1/6/1985.
12. 'Government asked to intervene', *Daily News* 26/2/1985; 'Suit on NHC rent in court today', *Daily News* 01/3/1985; 'High Court blocks NHC rent rises', *Daily News* 14/3/1985.
13. The figure most often cited is a total of 23,000 police officers, or one officer per 1,000 persons.
14. Data on 'crime' is taken from: Tanzania (2000); USAID (2002); Masanche (1993), Safari (1993), and Kironde (2000). Interpol data suggests that crime has rapidly escalated (Winslow. n.d.). Between 1996 and 2000: murder increased by 4.5%; rape by 516%; robbery by 29.1%; aggravated assault by 767%;

burglary by 4.2%; larceny by 180% etc. resulting in an overall increase of 59.9%.

15. Many residents have witnessed such events (see: 'Police bullets injure 5 as mob kills "thief"', *Daily News* 9 May 1985).
16. See Paciotti and Mulder (2004). For an official view see Tanzania (2000).
17. Despite such protestations, such practices may carry a high price for the public. Thus during the liberalization of the health services in the 1990s, doctors and nurses were known to take bribes for access to medical treatment and drugs (medical treatment was supposedly a right, and the drugs were paid for by the public taxes). Increasing reliance on self-regulation has not adequately protected the public from such abuses, including abandoning a patient in a public institution in order to attend patients at a private hospital or clinic (Harrington 1999: 231–32).
18. In contrast, the same donors were attempting to impose legal reforms on Kenya in an attempt to curb bureaucratic and political corruption in there.
19. Regardless of the fact that Party policy and practices have directly contributed to economic collapse.
20. NGOs have a poor record of local accountability to constituents/members and the absence of funds has restricted them to urban areas (cf. Campbell 2001).
21. See: Scott (1969), Olivier de Sardan (1999), Szeftel (2000). I necessarily exclude the large body of writing concerned with managing anti-corruption reform but for a review of this literature see Fjeldstad (2003).

References

Abrahams, R. 1996. 'Vigilantism. Order and Disorder on the Frontiers of the State', in O. Harris, *Inside and Outside the Law*. London: Routledge, pp. 41–55.

Armstrong, A. 1987. 'Urban Control Campaigns in the Third World: the Case of Tanzania', *Occas. Paper Series* no. 19. Department of Geography, University of Glasgow.

Bayart, J.F., S. Ellis and B. Hibou. 1999. *The Criminalization of the State in Africa*. Oxford and London: J. Currey and IAI.

Bienefeld, M. 1975. 'The Informal Sector and Peripheral Capitalism: The Case of Tanzania', *IDS Bulletin* (Sussex) 6(3): 53–73.

Bjorvatn, K., G. Torsvik and B. Tungodden. 2004. 'How Middle-men Can Undermine Anti-corruption Reforms', *Discussion Paper 20/2004*. Norwegian School of Economics and Business Administration. Bergen.

Brenna, J. 2002. *Nation, Race and Urbanization in Dar es Salaam, Tanzania. 1916–76*. Department of History, Northwestern University. Unpublished Ph.D.

Bryceson, D. 1987. 'A Century of Food Supply in Dar es Salaam. From Sumptuous Suppers for the Sultan to Maize Meal for a Million', in J. Guyer (ed.), *Feeding African Cities*. Studies in Regional Social History. Manchester: Manchester University Press, pp. 155–202.

———. 1990. *Food Insecurity and the Social Division of Labour in Tanzania, 1919–85*. London: MacMillan.

———. 1993. *Liberalizing Tanzania's Food Trade*. Oxford: J. Currey.

Burton, A. 2005. *African Underclass. Urbanisation, Crime and Colonial Order in Dar es Salaam*. Oxford: J. Currey.

Campbell, J. 1988. 'Tanzania and the World Bank's Urban Shelter Project: Ideology and International Finance', *Review of African Political Economy* 42: 5–18.

———. 1990. 'The State, Urban Development and Housing', in N. O'Neill and K. Mustafa (eds), *Capitalism, Socialism and the Development Crisis in Tanzania*. Avebury: Aldershot. pp. 152–76.

———. 2001. 'Autonomy and Governance in Ethiopia: The State, Civil Society and NGO's', in O. Barrow and M. Jennings (eds), *Faith, Hope and Charity. Relief, Development and NGO's in North East Africa*. London: J. Currey. pp. 149–66.

———. 2005. 'The Politics of Dissent: "Fundamentalists" and the State in Dar es Salaam', paper given to the First European Conference of African Studies (AEGIS). London: SOAS. June.

Chabal, P. and J.P. Daloz. 1999. *Africa Works. Disorder as Political Instrument*. Oxford: J. Currey.

Coldham, S. 1995. 'Land Tenure Reform in Tanzania: Legal Problems and Perspectives', *The Journal of Modern African Studies* 33(2): 27–42.

Coulson, A. 1982. *Tanzania. A Political Economy*. Oxford: Clarendon Press.

Duggan, W. 1976. 'Tanzania and Nyerere', in W. Duggan and J. Civille, *Tanzania and Nyerere*. Maryknoll, NY: Orbis.

Ferguson, J. and A. Gupta. 2002. 'Spatializing States: Toward an Ethnography of Neo-liberal Governmentality', *American Ethnologist* 29(4): 981–1002.

Fjelstadt, O. 2003. *Dencentralization and Corruption. A Review of the Literature*. Bergen: Christian Mikelsen Institute.

Harrington, J. 1999. 'Between the State and Civil Society: Medical Discipline in Tanzania', *Journal of Modern African Studies* 37(2): 20–39.

Heilman, B. and L. Ndumbao. 2002. 'Corruption, Politics, and Societal Values in Tanzania: An Evaluation of the Mkapa Administration's Anti-corruption Efforts', *African Journal of Political Science* 7(1): 1–19.

Helleiner, G. 1987. 'Stabilization, Adjustment, and the Poor', *World Development* 15(12): 1499–1513.

Hills, A. 1996. 'Towards a Critique of Policing and National Development in Africa', *The Journal of Modern African Studies* 34(2): 271–91.

Horton, S. 1985. 'Food Subsidies and the Poor: A Case Study of Tanzania', *Working Paper no. B10*. Department of Economics, University of Toronto.

Kaare, S. 2001. 'Contracting Out of Provision of Social Services in Tanzania: The Case of Contracting Out of Refuse Collection by the Dar es Salaam City Commission'. Paper Given at the 6th REPOA Research Workshop. White Sands Hotel, Dar es Salaam.

Kessy, J. 2000. 'Promoting Good Governance at Community Level: The Case of Tabata', in S. Ngware and J. Kironde (eds), *Urbanising Tanzania*. Dar es Salaam: University Press.

Kironde, J. 1991. 'Sites and Services in Tanzania: The Case of Sinza, Kitjitnyama and Mikocheni Areas in Dar es Salaam', *Habitat Int. Natl.* 15(1–2): 27–38.

———. 1992. 'Rent Control Legislation and the National Housing Corporation in Tanzania, 1985–90', *Canadian Journal of African Studies* 26(2): 306–27.

————. 2000. 'Rapid Urbanisation in Tanzania: The Government's Coping Strategies', in Kironde, J. and S. Ngware (eds), *Urbanising Tanzania*. Dar es Salaam: Dar es Salaam University Press, pp 21–58.

Kituo cha Katiba. nd. 'Tanzania: Key Historical and Constitutional Developments'. Makerere University, Faculty of Law. see: http://:kitcuochakatiba.co.ug/tz%20const.htm

Kulaba, S. 1981. 'Housing, Socialism and National Development in Tanzania'. *Occasional Paper no. 1*. Centre for Housing Studies, Ardhi Institute, Dar es Salaam.

————. 1989. 'Local Government and the Management of Urban Services in Tanzania', in R. Stren and R. White (eds), *African Cities in Crisis, Managing Rapid Urban Growth*. San Francisco and London: Westview Press, pp. 203–45.

Lerise, F. and S. Ngware. 2000. 'Managing Urban Development in Tanzania', in S. Ngware and J.K. Kironde (eds), *Urbanising Tanzania*. Dar es Salaam: Dar es Salaam University Press, pp. 117–32.

Levine, K. 1972. 'The TANU Ten-house Cell System', in L. Cliffe and J. Saul (eds), *Socialism in Tanzania*. Vol. 2. East African Publishing House: Nairobi, pp. 320–37.

Lewinson, A. 1999. 'Going with the Times: Transforming Visions of Urbanism and Modernity Among Professionals in Dar es Salaam, Tanzania'. Unpublished Ph.D thesis, Department of Anthropology, University of Wisconsin-Madison.

Maguire, A. 1969. *Toward 'Uhuru' in Tanzania*. Cambridge: Cambridge University Press.

Masanche, J. 1993. 'Crime Prevention and Control in Tanzania', in A. Alvazzi del Frate, U. Zvekic and J. van Dijk (eds), *Understanding Experiences of Crime and Crime Control. Acts of the International Conference*. Rome (November 1992). Ministry of Justice The Netherlands and Ministry of the Interior, Italy, pp. 357–9. Downloaded at: http://www.unicri.it/rcvs/publications/pdf_files/understanding-files/

Mbaku, J. 1996. 'Bureaucratic Corruption in Africa: the Futility of Cleanups', *CATO Journal* (Spring/Summer) 16(1): 1–10.

Mhamba, R. and C. Titus. 2001. 'Reactions to Deteriorating Provision of Public Services in Dar es Salaam', in A. Tostensen, I. Tuedten and M. Vaa (eds), *Associational Life in African Cities*. Uppsala: Nordiska African Institute.

Mwita, D. 1978. 'Urban Landlordism and the Acquisition of Buildings Act'. LLM thesis, Faculty of Law, University of Dar es Salaam.

Nagar, R. 1996. 'The South Asian Diaspora in Tanzania: A History Retold', *Comparative Studies of South Asian, African and the Middle East* 16(2) 62–80.

Ndanshau, M. and A. Mvungi. 2001. 'The Kongo St. Culture: Making of Wealth or Creation of Employment from Petty-trade Businesses for Poverty Alleviation'. Paper given at the 6th REPOA Research Workshop. Whites Sands Hotel, Dar es Salaam.

O'Barr, J. 1971. 'The Role of the Ten-house Cell Leader in Rural Tanzania', *Geneve-Afrique* 10(2): 70–85.

Olivier de Sardan, J.P. 1999. 'A Moral Economy of Corruption in Africa?', *The Journal of Modern African Studies* 37(1): 25–52.

Paciotti, B. and M. Mulder. 2004. 'Sungusungu: the Role of Pre-existing and Evolving Social Institutions Among Tanzanian Vigilante Organizations', *Human Organization* 63(1): 112–24.

Paddison, R. 1988. 'Ideology and Urban Primacy in Tanzania.' *CURR Discussion Paper no. 35*. Centre for Urban and Regional Research, University of Glasgow.

Pratt, C. 1976. *The Critical Phase in Tanzania, 1945–68*. Cambridge: Cambridge University Press.

Rizzo, M. 2002. 'Being Taken for a Ride: Privatization of the Dar es Salaam Transport System, 1983–98', *Journal of Modern African Studies* 40(1): 133–57.

Safari, J. 1993. 'Dar es Salaam (Tanzania)', in A. Alvazzi del Frate, U. Zvekic and J. van Dijk (eds), *Understanding Crime Experiences of Crime and Crime Control. Acts of the International Conference*. Rome (November 1992). Ministry of Justice The Netherlands and Ministry of the Interior, Italy. pp. 501–5. See: http://www.unicri.it/rcvs/publications/pdf_files/understanding-files/

Santorum, A. and A. Tibaijuka. 1992. 'Trading Responses to Food Market Liberalization in Tanzania', *Food Policy* (December): 431–42.

Scott, J.C. 1969. 'The Analysis of Corruption in Developing Nations', *Comparative Studies in Society & History* 11(3): 315–41

———. 1969. *Seeing Like A State*. New Haven: Yale University Press.

Scotton, C. 1965. 'Some Swahili Political Words', *The Journal of Modern African Studies* 3(4): 527–41.

Seibolds, P. and F. Steinberg. 1982. 'Tanzania: Sites and Services', *Habitat International*. 6(1–2): 109–30.

Shivji, I. 1990. *State Coercion and Freedom in Tanzania*. Human & Peoples Rights Monograph Series no. 8. Institute of Southern African Studies, National University of Lesotho. Roma.

Stren, R. 1975. *Urban Inequality and Housing Policy in Tanzania*. Institute of International Studies, University of California, Berkeley.

———. 1982. 'Under-development, Urban Squatting and the State Bureaucracy: A Case of Tanzania', *Canadian Journal of African Studies* 16(1): 67–91.

Szeftel, M. 2000. 'Clientelism, Corruption & Catastrophe', *Review of African Political Economy* 85: 427–41.

Tanzania. 2000. 'Crime and Policing Issues in Dar es Salaam Tanzania, focusing on Community Neighbourhood Watch Groups – "Sungu Sungu"'. Paper presented at the First Sub-Saharan Executive Policing Conference International Association of Chiefs of Police (IACP). Durban. South Africa. (August). Downloaded from: http://www.nclay.com/reference/country/backgrounds.html

Torpey, J. 1997. 'Revolutions and Freedom of Movement: An Analysis of Passport Controls in the French, Russian and Chinese Revolutions', *Theory & Society* 26: 837–68.

———. 1998. 'Coming and Going: On the State Monopolization of the Legitimate Means of Movement', *Sociological Theory* 16(3): 239–59.

Tripp, A.M. 1988. 'Defending the Right to Subsist: The State vs the Urban Informal Economy in Tanzania'. Paper presented at the 31st Annual Meeting of the African Studies Association, Chicago, October.

———. 1990. 'The informal economy and state in Tanzania', in M.E. Smith (ed.), *Perspectives on the Informal Economy*. Monographs in Economic Anthropology, no. 8. University Press of America. pp. 49–71.

————. 1997. *Changing the Rules. The politics of Liberalization and the Urban Informal Economy in Tanzania*. Berkeley: University of California.

USAID (United States Agency for International Development). 2002. 'Dar es Salaam, Tanzania'. *Making Cities Work. Urban Profile*.

Winslow, R. nd. 'Tanzania – Comparative Criminology'. San Diego State University. Downloaded from: http://www-rohan.sdsu.edu/faculty/rwinslow/africa/tanzania.html

CHAPTER 8

Media and the Limits of Cynicism in Postsocialist China

Kevin Latham

Introduction

In socialist China, media and communications have always been closely related to social change. The Maoist project aimed to transform the country and its people in order to create a communist utopia out of the weary, divided and war-stricken country that the Chinese Communist party (CCP) claimed victory over in 1949. This project and this transformation were to be realized in no small part through communicative processes (see for example Chu 1979; Blecher 1983; Cell 1983). The media – in those days principally radio, newspapers, posters, street banners, political meetings and lectures – played a crucial role in the implementation of mass mobilization campaigns that constituted the building blocks of socialist transformation.[1]

However, following the disasters of the Great Leap Forward in the late 1950s and the Cultural Revolution in the late 1960s, Chinese people became increasingly sceptical about the value of party messages and about exhortations to participate in campaigns for the public good. By the late Mao period and early reform period we find scholarly attention increasingly asking what the effect of public cynicism towards the party, the state and in interpersonal relations was on the standing of the party and the effectiveness of government and mass campaigns (e.g. Bennett 1977; Dittmer 1981; Falkenheim 1982: 238). Mass campaigns, it was noted, trod a fine line between persuasion and coercion (Cell 1983). By the late 1970s and early 1980s we find even the official Chinese press talking about the problem of a 'crisis of faith' (*xinyang weiji*)[2] in the official ideology (Dittmer 1981; Falkenheim 1982; Gold 1991: 603), particularly among the younger generations (Liu 1984; Rosen 1990; Gold 1991; Kwong 1994).

These issues painted an important part of the backdrop against which the emerging post-Mao period was judged. Writing in 1978, at what we now know was the start of China's period of momentous economic reform, veteran China scholar Lucien Pye suggested that in relation to communications and social change in China, the most pertinent question to be answered was whether the Chinese people would 'respond to the new appeals of their current rulers: (a) in the same conformist manner as in the past, (b) with cynicism and apathy, or (c) with the reflective evaluations and sceptical judgements expected of mature people?' (Pye 1978: 920).³

Nearly thirty years after Mao's death, we may be in a good position to reflect upon the progress of reform and the degree or nature of cynicism that may remain in China. In this paper I offer a preliminary investigation of these issues, concentrating in particular on media cynicism.⁴ I will suggest that although the issue of cynicism has been decentred from within China studies in recent years, it is still commonplace in contemporary China and represents one kind of continuity between so-called socialist and postsocialist China. However, I argue that the social, political and economic contexts of contemporary China are entirely different from those of thirty years ago and these differences have to figure in our understandings of contemporary China and Chinese media cynicism. I argue that in the past, cynicism drew the attention of China watchers because it was considered subversive and as an indicator of dwindling party legitimacy and authority – a legitimacy presumed to be maintained by tight ideological control. Now, by contrast, since the legitimacy of the party is attributed, in addition to the continual threat of state violence, to mechanisms other than ideological control, such as consumerism (e.g. Tang 1998; Ci 1999), the 'rhetorics of transition' (Latham 2002) or the revival of Confucianism (e.g. Yang 1996; Croll 2006), the whole issue of 'faith' – and hence cynicism – in the party and its ideology has been substituted by a range of alternative discourses. However, I suggest that a closer analysis of contemporary cynicism reveals ways in which it is not only still an important feature of the Chinese political and social landscape but, in relation to media at least, plays a fundamental role in maintaining the party's authority.

Drawing partly on Peter Sloterdijk's (1987) formulation of cynicism in contemporary Western societies, I contend that we need to consider different kinds and understandings of cynicism in order to differentiate also the kinds of changes that cynical practices have undergone over this period. Overall I will argue that although media consumers are no less critical in their reading of media output, the significance of their cynicism, where it occurs, is nonetheless diluted by the radically changed context of

China's new information economy. However, at the same time, I suggest that other cynical practices of journalists, editors and television producers play a key role in perpetuating party hegemony. Although mass campaigns are no longer the principal vehicles for social change, the media, journalism and journalists still play a central role in maintaining relations of power and the conceptual space of social transformation.

This paper therefore offers a slightly twisted perspective on enduring socialisms compared to others in this volume. A common theme in several other chapters is how despite claims to or aiming at revolutionary change, we often find underlying continuities in practice that at least change our perspective on the revolution and possibly lead us to see it as undermined in some way. In this paper, however, I am dealing with a slightly different formula.

There was indeed a 'revolutionary' change in China that came with economic reform vociferously promoted and driven by the Chinese authorities from the early 1980s onwards. However, although Chinese media have been obliged to become commercially viable, if not profitable, the official definition of the media's role in society and politics is remarkably unchanged from the Mao period. The media are still regarded as the 'mouthpiece' (literally 'throat and tongue' – *houshe* 喉舌) of the Chinese Communist party. Their officially declared, and often pronounced, principal function and purpose is to support and promote government policy. This means assisting as required in the project of national modernization and development through their propaganda role and not contradicting, undermining or criticizing party policy (see for example Zhao 1998). Thus, there has been an economic or commercial revolution in Chinese media but, in theory at least, no political one.[5] Hence, rather than arguing that a revolutionary change has been undermined by continuities in actual practice, I argue that the whole question of continuity and change needs to be carefully considered.

This paper engages with at least two realms of continuity and change: on the one hand, scholarly interest in China and on the other hand, practices of media production and consumption in China. The paper deals with a shift of interest in China scholarship from issues of 'belief', ideology and political control in the late 1970s and early 1980s to other themes such as consumer satisfaction, hegemony and religion in more contemporary scholarship. This shift of interest is mapped by the keen interest in a 'crisis of faith' and cynicism twenty-five years ago compared with its seeming insignificance, revealed by a lack of scholarly interest, in the present. However, this paper will argue (a) that cynicism is still of fundamental importance in understanding the political economy of Chinese media but (b) that although one can still identify cynical attitudes towards propaganda among media consumers, the context of that cynicism has changed to such a degree that it is less politically important than the cynical practices of media producers, which were largely neglected by scholars in the past. Consequently, even when we are dealing with continuities – such as cynicism in this case – these continuities are intricately intertwined with series of changes that require us constantly to reevaluate our expectations and understandings of 'enduring socialisms'. Continuity and change are not necessarily polar opposites; in many cases they accompany each other on a rather more complexly defined historical trajectory.

The 'Crisis of Faith' in Early Reform Period China

At the end of the Mao period and in the early reform period there was an officially recognized 'crisis of faith' (*xinyang weiji*) that marked the ideological transition that the country was starting to undergo. The crisis was seen to be largely concentrated among younger people, including the so-called 'lost generation' of the Cultural Revolution period, but was also associated with a broader cynicism afoot in the country at large (Dittmer 1981: 31–32; Falkenheim 1982).[6]

This crisis of faith was associated with 'eroding popular moral and regime credibility' and the 'decline of "socialist norms of behaviour and moral standards"... "indifference to state interests," "unwillingness to undertake social labor," and on the part of "many people" the lack of even "rudimentary concepts of law, discipline and morality"... and an unwillingness to "consciously subordinate individual interests to those of the collective"' (Falkenheim 1982: 238). In short, it was seen as the unwillingness of an increasing proportion of the population to accept at face value the principles, messages and exhortations that had supported the theory and practice of the CCP since 1949 and before.

The cynicism of this period was the result of a combination of factors. Lowell Dittmer (1981) summarizes them in terms of three different sets of structural criteria associated respectively with the reemergence of 'deeply-rooted tendencies' from the pre-Cultural Revolution period, patterns of behaviour associated with the Cultural Revolution itself and new problems arising from the difficulty of adjusting to economic reform. Pre-Cultural Revolution problems included various aspects of the working of the Chinese bureaucracy, characterized increasingly by forms of cadre privilege, corruption and gerontocracy (1981: 45–46). Problems from the Cultural Revolution period included the continuation of factionalism through informal loyalty groups within the bureaucracy and the rise of criminal gangs in society more broadly, while the tensions of the post-Mao period often come down to the contradictions between a newfound enthusiasm for consumer-based materialism and the reversal of political constructions of the Maoist past. Although these served the purposes of legitimating Deng Xiaoping's position as new paramount leader and saviour of the country, they nonetheless undermined the established legitimacy and coherence of the party and its position (Dittmer 1981: 47–50).

All of these features can to some degree be summed up in terms of what has been called a 'credibility gap' (Falkenheim 1982: 240) that had emerged due to the widely perceived differences between the ideals espoused by the party and its representatives on the one hand and the realities of people's everyday lives on the other (see also Gold 1991: 603; Wang 2002: 3). This 'crisis of faith' has also been put down to a loss of public confidence in party-led modernization (Falkenheim 1982: 240) and scepticism about the state's ability to act as an arbiter of moral values (Baum 1992: 500). In short, there was a rise in cynicism characterized by doubt about the party's honesty or sincerity on the one hand and its ability to deliver its promises on the other. This was accompanied by cynicism regarding interpersonal relations that had become coloured by fear, suspicion, caution and uncertainty in the late Mao period.[7]

The close relationship between the party, policy implementation and mass communication in China means that this cynicism and 'crisis of faith' has to be seen as extending to the realm of the media. Particularly in the late 1970s and early 1980s, the Chinese media were little more than the vehicle by means of which the party sought to convey its messages to the general population. Cynicism towards the party could not but mean some (if not an equal) degree of cynicism towards the media.

Provisional Thoughts on Cynicism in Postsocialist China

Further into the post-Mao period the issue of cynicism did not disappear entirely. Indeed, in 1989 we saw many of the grievances associated with the earlier 'crisis of faith' being aired more openly for the first time with the protests and demonstrations of May and June that year. Although the demonstrations are often described as being a 'democracy' movement, for instance, the protests and demands being made by students and other demonstrators were against the corruption of government officials and party cadres as much as they were calling for greater freedom of speech or some kind of often rather naively formulated notion of democracy.

However, the violent end to the protests of 1989 in the short term at least gave China's cynics even more reason to be cynical. The immediate military crackdown was followed by a massive and unrelenting propaganda campaign over the following months that clearly established the official line that the protests had been a 'counter-revolutionary criminal conspiracy'. More importantly, the 1989 crackdown clearly demonstrated that certain lines could not be crossed, that the state and the

Party were still willing, if pushed to it, to defend and reassert their position through the use of force. Cynics were therefore clearly reminded of the potential costs of voicing their cynicism in inappropriate ways or contexts. Indeed, many Chinese people's reaction to the events of June 1989 were 'passive resignation, dismissiveness and withdrawal', or what Richard Baum calls 'the hallmarks of an atomized, politically inarticulate populace'(1992: 493).[8]

This much said, it is nonetheless important to question how widespread and how deep any feeling of cynicism was at this stage of reform. At the end of the 1980s many people would complain about rising crime and other social problems arising during the reform period as well as the withdrawal of welfare support and public services. They might also privately complain about corruption and bureaucracy. However, apart from a degree of nostalgia on the part of some older citizens for the times when one could leave one's door unlocked without fear of being burgled, very few ordinary people would have said that the reform process was misguided.

Nonetheless, the events of May and June 1989 did mark an important turning point in the whole trajectory of the reform period. They were followed by a stern crackdown and manhunt for the leaders of the protests around the country; the manifest use of state violence reestablished the authority of the Party and drove cynicism either back into the private realm or into the areas of minority political dissidence and intellectual alienation.

The following decade and a half, however, was a period of continued social, economic and technological change. There was a 'surprising political restabilization' (Baum 1992: 491) in the years immediately following 1989, helped by the reinvigoration of the economy following Deng Xiaoping's 'Southern Tour' of 1992. In the early 1990s people in the large cities and the wealthier eastern coastal provinces increasingly found themselves with tens of cable television channels to choose from. They increasingly had pagers and access to telephones and later on also either mobile or fixed-line phones of their own. In the mid-1990s came satellite television, widening access to and use of the internet and ever more opportunities to travel both within China and overseas. Many urban and rural landscapes changed with the construction of roads, bridges, high-rise luxury flats and office buildings as well as symbolic structures like the Shanghai Oriental Television Tower. At the same time sports, leisure, entertainment and consumer opportunities continued to proliferate and disposable incomes for many in the cities continued to rise.

In short, this was a decade and a half in which many Chinese people saw their lifestyles and their social and physical environments changing all around them. This does not mean that cynicism disappeared in China. Indeed, I have argued elsewhere (Latham 2002) that the link between

China's consumer revolution and political stability is often oversimplified. However, reflecting upon the issues associated with the 'crisis of faith' in the early reform period is instructive.

It is, for instance, undeniable that the CCP has delivered some kind of modernization that has touched the lives of the majority of Chinese citizens in one way or another. Hence, even if one may dislike some of the symptoms or characteristics of that modernization process, it is difficult to see how the regime can be questioned on its ability to modernize the country. At the same time, the contradictions between the party ideology and emerging market-oriented practices of the early post-Mao period are no longer such a glaring concern in many people's eyes. They still exist and Chinese people still see them but twenty-five years into economic reform, few people seriously consider the legitimacy of the CCP's policies to be founded upon the principles of Marxism-Leninism and Mao Zedong thought. There is still distaste for corruption but the mobilization of guanxi networks, the more individualistic nature of Chinese social and interpersonal relations, the pursuit of materialist ends and the logic of market forces are generally taken-for-granted features of reform period China (see e.g. Gold 1985; Yang 1994; Davis et al. 1995; Davis 2000). These aspects of contemporary Chinese society no longer have the novelty, moral shock-value or air of contradiction in relation to state ideology that they once had.

In 2005, it is therefore far more difficult to point to a 'credibility gap' that might threaten the Party's authority in the way that it appeared to do in the early 1980s. Indeed, with the CCP's emphasis on pragmatism rather than ideology and the decentring of communism and socialism in the practice of government, it would be difficult to define precisely what Chinese people should be 'losing faith' in at the beginning of the twenty-first century.

It is therefore perhaps not entirely surprising that more recent scholarly literature on China also makes far less reference to issues of cynicism, reflecting the shifting interests of authors as much as changes in Chinese society. Hence, the issues of political 'control', mass mobilization, faith in Party ideology and the degree of fear or coercion involved in Chinese policy implementation – issues that were key features of China scholarship twenty to thirty years ago – are now replaced by attention to, among other things, consumerism, social division, fragmentation of the national polity, privatization, state enterprise reform, migration, the emergence of civil society, labour discontent and globalization (see for example. Chao and Dickson 2001). In relation to Chinese media, there is also a general consensus among China scholars and media practitioners alike, that even if party control does still exist and it can still be strictly, even brutally enforced, there is no doubt that the Chinese media enjoy degrees and kinds of 'freedom' unimaginable in the past (see Zhao 1998,

2000; Huang 2000; Latham 2000, 2001; Lee 2000; Hemelryk and Keane 2002; Rawnsley and Rawnsley 2003; Yin and Li 2004; Yu 2004).

However, this does not mean that cynicism has disappeared from the Chinese social, cultural and political landscapes. For one thing, there have been many critiques of the shortcomings of economic reform from Chinese artists and intellectuals in recent years, ranging from the 'hooligan' literature of Wang Shuo to the sixth-generation films of directors such as Zhang Yuan (*Beijing Bastards, East Palace West Palace*), Wang Xiaoshuai (*Frozen, Xiaowu, Beijing Bicycle*), Jia Zhangke (*The Platform*) or Li Yang (*Blind Shaft*). At the same time, it is not difficult to find individual instances of cynicism exhibited by Chinese people in their everyday lives (see for example Latham 2000: 648). People skip over what they see as party propaganda in the newspaper, they critically assess CCTV and other sources of government information bearing in mind its propaganda intent, or they resign themselves to instances of familism and corruption that they may encounter or hear about in their daily lives. Chinese media consumers still exhibit a range of cynical practices that suggest both their sense of ultimate powerlessness when confronted with mediated relations of political power, and also their efforts to side-step and minimize the effects of Party-driven media representations (Latham 2000).

Hence, considering that, on the one hand, we still have cynicism, and on the other, it does not seem to constitute the same kind of threat to the regime as it once appeared to, we require a different perspective to that of the late 1970s and early 1980s for understanding cynicism in contemporary China. Identification of cynicism no longer logically means that we have to question the Party's legitimacy or authority.

It is at this point, therefore, that we need to move from the general to the specific and to focus upon particular examples from specified areas of social practice. In this case my interest is in practices of media production.

Playing the Game in Newspaper Journalism

In the course of fieldwork based in Guangzhou in the summer of 2001, I spent some time following journalists at a newspaper in Guangzhou where I had also previously conducted research and for which I had written a number of articles in the past. The newspaper was a non-Party organ newspaper and subsidiary of a local newspaper group headed by a much older and better nationally recognized newspaper title. The newspaper where I was working had been opened as a commercially oriented project in the late 1990s and had offices in the same buildings in Guangzhou as the main newspaper of the group. Although the two papers had their own separate journalistic and editorial staff and they operated as quite independent entities, there was nonetheless considerable sharing of resources and occasionally personnel between them.

On one occasion in 2001, I accompanied a fairly senior reporter, Mr Li, on a trip to an outlying county in Guangdong Province about two hours drive from Guangzhou. I had known Li for several years and having accompanied him on previous occasions and talked at some length in the past, I felt we had a fairly open working friendship. We (Li, the staff driver from the newspaper and myself) set out at about 8.00 a.m. from the newspaper offices and arrived in the county seat mid-morning. The journalist was working on a story about the experiences of migrant workers from other provinces who came to Guangdong because of the higher wages and greater work opportunities. The piece was due on the editor's desk the following day.

Our first port of call was to find the propaganda officials at the local government. This was common practice – indeed it was the expected etiquette and procedure – for journalists working on stories outside of Guangzhou. On occasions, particularly if they were working on a story that might prove critical of the local government, journalists would not contact local officials immediately, but on all the occasions that I accompanied reporters on such trips we visited the local propaganda officials.

On this occasion we were warmly greeted by Mr Zhang and Mr Sun, who were both well-known to the journalist, the driver and the newspaper as journalists regularly visited the county on business. Mr Zhang was a former journalist in his fifties who had worked at the local radio station. Mr Sun was a former newspaper journalist who had worked on a local paper for whom he still occasionally provided articles. In their roles as propaganda officials for the local government both were responsible for writing copy that would appear in the local media, particularly on government-related stories but also more general stories of social, cultural or business interests.

Zhang and Sun both knew already what the mission was about and had provisionally arranged a number of visits for the afternoon at Li's request. However, first we spent about an hour at Zhang and Sun's office drinking tea while Li explained once again the kind of story he was hoping to write. He wanted to cover the human interest aspects of migrant workers' lives: how they felt about being so far from home, whether they felt welcome in Guangdong and generally how they felt about what they were doing. Zhang and Sun made some suggestions to Li for visits they could make and they discussed the various options before Li decided which he would like to do. Mr Zhang made a series of calls on his mobile, some of them to finalize the arrangements for the visits in the afternoon, and then we went to lunch.

Thinking of an exposé story that had been run by the main newspaper in Guangzhou a couple of years earlier, which I had discussed at some length with the journalists who covered it, I asked Zhang and Sun over lunch whether there had been problems of mistreatment of migrant workers in the county. The story I had in mind had exposed what was effectively a prison camp-style factory in another part of Guangdong where workers from Sichuan were locked in on-site, given basic food and accommodation but were not paid for months. Following the publication of the newspaper article the local government had come under some stern pressure to investigate the issue and identify those responsible.

The answer was predictable. Mr Sun explained that there had been no major problems in the county, that workers did of course get homesick and they could feel out of place in Guangdong where the language, food and other customs could be quite different from what they were used to at home. When I mentioned the story of the prison factory, both Sun and Zhang nodded and said that they knew of the case and occasionally such things did happen, but fortunately very rarely and not in their area.

After lunch we headed out on the interviews. Zhang and Sun had their own car and driver, while Li and I went with our driver in our car. I asked Li what he thought about their answer to my question and he smiled. 'There was a case here last year when a factory was closed down and the owner prosecuted' he said 'it was embarrassing for the local government.' I suggested that they probably wouldn't want to mention it in front of me. 'It's their job' Li replied.

In the afternoon we visited a local shoe factory and spoke first with the manager. We made a quick tour of the factory and then Li asked if he could spend some time with the workers. At this point Li disappeared with Sun back onto the shop floor of the factory while Zhang accompanied me back to the manager's office where we drank tea and chatted. They explained that it would be better if I were not present while Li interviewed people as the workers might not feel happy talking in front of a foreigner. Li confirmed this opinion later in the car.

Li returned about an hour later looking fairly pleased. We made another factory visit and one more to a workers' dormitory that afternoon before setting off on the trip back to Guangzhou. We bad farewell to Zhang and Sun as we left the dormitory and they headed back to their office before going home.

The journey provided me with a good opportunity to discuss with Li how his interviews had gone. He explained that he had some good materials on homesickness and how the workers felt that they were worked too hard and that they were really exploited. Local people, they said, would never do the work that they did for the same money, even if compared to home the wages were good. The workers at the first factory hated Cantonese food, Li told me. They were mainly from Hunan and liked their food hot and spicy. For them Cantonese food didn't taste of anything, he laughed.

Then Li turned to me and said smiling, 'There's something else that will interest you – I'll give you a present!' He went on to explain that some of the workers had told him about another factory in the town where there had been protests among the workers about working conditions and some tension between workers from Sichuan and others from Hunan. There had been some minor violence at the factory and production had stopped for three days while the dispute was sorted out but it all seemed to be calming down now. In the end the managers had had to separate the two groups in both working and living areas. There was some talk of the local government getting involved in negotiating a swap of one group of workers with another state-owned factory in the county but Li didn't know whether that would really happen. He said he thought it would be too complicated. 'Now that would make a good story, don't you think?' he laughed.

The following day Li's article about food, homesickness and feelings of exploitation was published and praised by the editors of the paper. It included mention of county government policies aimed at ensuring good treatment of migrant workers. There was no mention of the dispute. The next time I saw Li I asked him about it. 'You didn't feel like mentioning the dispute?' I asked. 'I couldn't', he said, 'there was a short deadline for the article so there was no chance to go to the factory and investigate. You can't go saying such things just on secondhand reports and if you are going to cause someone problems you need to be doubly sure of everything. Besides,' he said, 'I have to go back there next week for a more important story and I don't want to upset Mr Zhang and Mr Sun.' Li's last point was a practical one. For journalists, it was generally a good idea to maintain good relations with local propaganda officials as they helped reporters get stories easily, quickly and with little fuss.

Indeed, I was reminded of what the journalist who had worked on the exposé story two years previously had told me. They had followed up the story following a tip-off from a local journalist, and friend, who had managed to speak with a worker who had escaped from the factory. The local journalist could not run the story because his newspaper was under the authority of the local government, which was criticized in the exposé. The Guangzhou journalists had gone down to the county in question and investigated without at first telling the local authorities. They told me that once the story broke, relations between the newspaper and both propaganda officials and other local government officials had been very frosty for quite some time and seriously affected the reception that journalists from the paper received and the ease with which they could operate when they visited the county.

I talked about this story with other journalists – anonymizing Li – on various subsequent occasions and another theme that came out on several times was that such a story would also have been politically sensitive. It was different from the straightforward case of the 'prison factory' which could be easily reported as a case of those responsible for exploitative and illegal labour practices being brought to justice. Li's case, by contrast, included a strong element of 'ethnic' conflict and tensions between groups from different parts of the country. Most of the journalists I spoke to said that this would certainly have made the story unreportable. Even if it could be presented as the local authorities successfully finding an amicable solution to the conflict, they thought that it would still be unacceptable as a story for fear of stirring up other ethnic tensions.

Rethinking Cynicism

At this point it is useful to reflect upon the notion of cynicism. There is a general meaning of cynicism referring to what the *Oxford English Dictionary* describes as a disposition to disbelieve in human sincerity or goodness (*OED2*, CD-ROM version, 1994). In terms of the literature on China this often extends, or refers more specifically, to the disposition to disblieve the sincerity or goodness of the CCP or the government and its representatives. This is the kind of cynicism discussed earlier in relation to sceptical attitudes towards television broadcasts or official propaganda news – forms of cynicism that mark some of the continuities between the Maoist and post-Mao periods.

However, German philosopher Peter Sloterdijk's account (1987) of the age of cynical reason offers an alternative way of thinking about cynicism that is useful here. Sloterdijk presents a comprehensive philosophical analysis of what he sees as the intellectual malaise of contemporary Western society. He identifies cynicism 'as the dominant operating mode in contemporary culture' (Huyssen 1987: xi) and analyses the 'pervasive sense of political disillusionment in the wake of the 1960s and the pained feeling of a lack of political and social alternatives in Western society today' (1987: xi).[9]

However, one of the dominant features of contemporary cynical practices identified by Sloterdijk, and one that introduces an important twist to our understanding of cynicism, is the sense of resignation and acceptance of relationships of power even if they may be analysed as undesirable. Sloterdijk refers to this cynicism with the formulation of 'enlightened false consciousness' (1987: 5–6). That is, the way that in contemporary society the course of enlightenment, including the lessons from Marx on ideology, have been both successful but also in vain. People are aware of the power and implications of ideology but live with it all the same.

In relation to media cynicism in particular, Sloterdijk focuses on the way that media saturation in contemporary life requires us to overlook the connections between the thousands of items that make up our everyday media landscapes. Reading a newspaper or a magazine, for Sloterdijk, inevitably becomes a cynical process in what is almost a reversal of Saussure's structuralism:

> We now regard it as normal that in magazines we find, almost like in an Old World theater, all regions close to one another: reports on mass starvation in the Third World next to advertisements for champagne, articles on environmental catastrophes beside a discussion of the most recent automobile production. Our minds are trained to scan and comprehend an encylopedically broad scale of irrelevancies – in which the irrelevance of the single items comes not so much from itself but from its being arranged in the flood of information from the media. (1987: 308)

Slavoj Žižek comes to a neat formulation of Sloterdijk's analysis by reconfiguring Marx's famous axiom about the working of ideology through false consciousness: *'they do not know it, but they are doing it'*. Following Sloterdijk, Žižek writes: 'The cynical subject is quite aware of the distance between the ideological mask and the social reality, but he none the less still insists upon the mask. The formula, as proposed by Sloterdijk, would then be: "they know very well what they are doing, but still they are doing it"' (1989: 29).

However, Žižek pushes Sloterdijk's logic a step further. For Žižek, the problem with Sloterdijk's formulation is that it suggests that we may live in a postideological society, that the force of ideology must be undermined by the fact that we know the artifice through which it tries to work. Sloterdijk leaves the emphasis on the knowing rather than the doing (see also Myers 2003: 65–67) in ideology whereas Žižek suggests that we have to shift the balance towards the doing:

> Cynical reason, with all its ironic detachment, leaves untouched the fundamental level of ideological fantasy, the level on which ideology structures the social reality itself (1989: 30)

That is to say, it is in our actions, in daily practices and behaviour, that we maintain the working of power. In Sloterdijk's formulation the agency of the cynical subject is removed such that enlightened false consciousness: 'Knows itself to be without illusions and yet to have been dragged down by the "power of things"' (1987: 6). By contrast, Žižek is arguing that it is in practice, in the things that people do, that ideology works its 'illusion' – an '"illusion" which structures our effective, real social relations' (1989: 45).

Sloterdijk's notion of cynicism has a resounding pertinence in China, even though the historical circumstances that have brought it about are rather different. In China cynicism does not arise as the disillusionment of an intellectual idealism so much as a direct practical reaction to the past mobilization of social violence through political leadership at all levels.

Tom Gold, who describes one of his informants talking about social encounters in the 1960s, neatly exemplifies this:

> When he passed the leading cadre in his unit, the safest ploy was to recite the latest slogan. 'I knew I didn't believe what I said,' the man informed me, 'and the cadre knew I didn't believe it either, and I knew he knew that I didn't believe it, but as long as I said it, it was sufficient to get me through the interaction.' (Gold 1985: 668)

Encounters like this one are generally a thing of the past in contemporary China.[10] However, that does not mean that such cynical practices do not persist. A broader review of examples is beyond the scope of this paper. However, I suggest that their identification in relation to media practices – in particular journalism – is crucial for understanding the operation of the media in contemporary China.

Journalistic Cynicism in Postsocialist China

Sloterdijk and Žižek's accounts of cynicism offer us a framework for understanding my trip with reporter Li, where I suggest that we have a clear example of just such cynicism in practice. When Li pointed out that Zhang and Sun were just doing their job he was casually accepting the fact that they presented an account of things which everyone present, except myself at the moment of utterance, knew was not true. Yet all of them understood, and accepted, why the statement was made.

Li also passed up the opportunity of what would really have been a 'good story' – that of the migrant worker dispute – in part because it was not practically feasible (although if he had wanted to and had his editor's approval, he most certainly could have followed it up subsequently) but also because he did not want to upset Zhang and Sun as he needed their help on another story. He knew that reporting the migrant conflict story would have caused problems of one kind or another for Zhang and Sun.

Although Li did not himself make the point, my discussion with other journalists – including editors at the paper – also made it clear that this was a case of self-censorship in line with what counted as acceptable and unacceptable criticism. Li was a senior, experienced journalist and was undoubtedly aware of these issues.

In this one example, therefore, we can identify a range of cynical practices, understood in Sloterdijk and Žižek's sense. An important issue to note here, however, is that the smooth operation of journalism did not only *involve* these kinds of practices but rather *presupposed* them. Li, Zhang and Sun were all working in ways that depended upon their mutual understanding of the rules of the game, of what was acceptable and what not and at the same time of what the others were doing.

However, it is important also to note that this was not an isolated or exceptional incident. Certainly my presence affected the dynamics of the situation to some degree, but the 'cynicism' that we can identify in this situation, I suggest, lies at the heart of the operation of journalism in China. Brief consideration of two more examples may help establish the point.

On another occasion in 1999, I was travelling around Guangdong province with my partner, a journalist and a driver from the same newspaper. The situation was broadly similar to that of the trip with Li, only that in this case I was the principal 'journalist' of the group and we were on the road for ten days. I had been asked to write a series of articles on topics of my choice for publication in the newspaper. For one of these articles I decided to write about state enterprise reform, which had been drawing a great deal of attention in the press and on broadcast media because of the social problems – such as unemployment, withdrawal of welfare services and so on – that were associated with it.

I therefore found myself making two visits over two days to two different factories undergoing reform. One was a textile factory employing about 5,000 people and one a large steel plant, which employed around 20,000 people and was effectively a small town in its own right. The two factories had been selected, I was told, on the grounds that they offered distinct experiences of reform. The key problems associated with state enterprise reform – how to make large inefficient enterprises profitable without sacking thousands of workers and massively reducing the welfare burden that they carried – were widely known and discussed in the Chinese media. In my role as honorary journalist I therefore asked questions around these issues. How many people were likely to be laid off? How were the factories seeking to reduce their welfare bills? What kind of support was offered to the unemployed?

However, in both cases, the interviews rapidly turned into farce. Fortunately, in both cases, I was told, there were likely to be very few or no redundacies. Fortunately, both factories were enjoying some commercial success and improvement in economic fortunes which enabled them to carry the welfare burden relatively well. Fortunately, there were no real issues of contention among different sectors of the workforce or between management and workers. If these factories, as presented to me, were representative of state enterprise reform in China, then there was really nothing to worry about.

There were several factors at play here. Most importantly was my status as a foreigner and a stranger, which virtually ruled out any kind of frank, open discussion of the issues. This was partly tempered by the fact that I was travelling under the flag of one of the most highly respected and prestigious newspapers in the province, and indeed the country. I was therefore treated with a degree of caution and respect as a 'journalist' because in the end everyone knew that I would write articles for publication in the newspaper. For my Chinese interlocuters, both propaganda officials and interviewees, this situation undoubtedly presented a problem of unpredictability, even if there was always the safety net of editorial control at the newspaper.

At the first – textile – factory, I tried earnestly – and one might say rather naively – to make the interviews work, to find ways of skirting around the obvious responses, while also trying to develop a rapport of trust with the factory managers. However, at the second factory it became apparent within five minutes of starting the interview how it was going to proceed. At that point, I was also drawn into the game of pretence. I could not terminate the interview on the grounds that it was a waste of time, as to do so would have meant to lose face myself and also not to give face to my hosts. I had also been insistent with the local propaganda officials that I wanted to make this visit, despite their efforts to persuade me not to. At the same time, I had to write the article for the newspaper and it would not say much for my tenacity as a would-be journalist to have left the interview after only five minutes. I therefore at least had to go through the motions of attempting a semi-serious interview. However, the outcome was a situation in which we all knew what was going on, we all knew that little if anything more than banalities would be gleaned from the interview and that at the end of it we could all leave having fulfilled our respective duties.

My final example relates to a television journalist who worked on a weekly documentary programme for one of the Guangzhou-based television stations. I became acquainted with the producer, Ms Wang, through one of the local universities where she was studying part-time for an MA. She invited me to follow her and some of her colleagues in the making of several of their programmes for the weekly series. Like many journalists, in private, Wang was a highly articulate critic of the Chinese media system. In conversations with myself, teachers at the university, other journalists or colleagues at the television station, I regularly heard her voice criticisms of, for example, the propaganda role of media or the inability to conduct truly investigative television journalism. However, there was a striking contrast between what she and her colleagues would say and the programme that they produced.

The programme was locally focused and consisted of twenty-minute films about various human interest, economic and social stories. For example, one programme reported from a hospital in Guangzhou that had recently won a prize for excellence and earned an international reputation for certain kinds of surgery for which paying private patients travelled to the hospital from all over Asia. Another programme reported on plans recently approved to re-landscape and reorganize the traffic around a well-known traffic jam blackspot in the city. Another programme reported on the high level of pollution in the city and measures being taken to deal with it.

All of Wang's programmes that I either saw or followed in the making (twelve in all) fitted a standard presentational format for Chinese news documentary films. They were often positive in outlook, reporting local economic, scientific or commercial success stories – such as the hospital story, for instance. They were occasionally on a 'negative' theme – such as the pollution programme – but adopted the standard practice of turning the programme into a combination of educational instruction (how to help reduce pollution) and positive reporting of action taken (outlining government anti-pollution initiatives being implemented) (see Xu 2000).

When it came to making programmes, several factors had a key influence role on the production. One was time – the one-week turnaround for researching, investigating, writing and shooting the story meant that time was always rather tight on the programme. This undoubtedly made conformity and formulaic production practical and attractive. Another related factor was the relatively small team (basically three or four people) responsible for all aspects of the programme. Once again, this made practicality a high priority.

At the same time, Wang was a busy person outside of work. She was studying for her MA, she had a young daughter and childcare responsibilities as well as looking after her ageing mother; she enjoyed a busy social life and she also had an active interest in music. She was also leading an active, relatively exciting life with a high status and well-paid job as well as having family responsibilities and people depending upon her. This was important for the programme for two reasons. Firstly, it tightened further the production schedule each week. Secondly, Wang was politically aware and critically minded, but she was no dissident and had no wish to upset the delicate balances that made her lifestyle possible. From a personal perspective, the last thing she either needed or wanted was to take risks in her programme making.

Conclusion

In this paper, I have argued that even if scholarly attention in recent years has been drawn away from questions of ideology, faith and cynicism, we can nonetheless trace remnants of past cynicism in contemporary China. However, the context of that cynicism has fundamentally changed since the Mao period and in contemporary China we will not generally find cynicism by looking for disillusioned people distrusting of the government, lacking commitment to socially oriented movements and activities and despondent about the inability of China to modernize under the leadership of the CCP. The Chinese economic, political and social context has changed so much in the last two decades that most aspects of this 1970s formulation of cynicism are no longer appropriate as frames of reference. To use a phrase from Sloterdijk, the 'charmingly mediated alienation' that we are looking for 'envelopes itself in discretion' (1987: 7).

Recent literature on Chinese media and journalism has often focused upon how commercial pressures in particular have led journalists to push the limits of Party control, to experiment with popular journalism and to introduce new forms of critical reporting into Chinese media production (see for example Liu 1998; Zhao 1998; Xu 2000; Latham 2000, 2002). However, in this paper I suggest that it is important to focus on what is changing and how in Chinese media, but also on some of the practices of continuity. Any instance of Chinese journalists testing the limits of Party restrictions is balanced by tens, if not hundreds or thousands, of instances of conformism of the kind discussed in this paper. Although the changes and transformations that Chinese media have undergone in recent decades are vital for an understanding of Chinese media production, it is, nonetheless, conformist, cynical practices that make the system work.

If we reflect upon the issue of cynicism viewed both from the present and from the beginning of the reform period, we can certainly identify continuities and remnants of the past in the present. However, the context of cynical practices has been completely transformed. Considering a general notion of media-related cynicism as a tendency to treat Party and government propaganda with a greater or lesser degree of caution and scepticism, then we can say that it is a common feature of most Chinese people's general approach to media and politics in China – as it was in the past. It would nonetheless be wrong to suggest that people do not believe CCTV, Xinhua or other official news organizations as a matter of routine. I would suggest quite the opposite.

However, another important issue to consider in comparing cynicism at these two times is that the broader context of the information economy has changed dramatically. In 1979, if you did not trust official news sources you had few if any alternative sources to check them against. By contrast in 2007, although there are still important media restrictions in place, in addition to a much broader range of 'official' media sources (including newspapers, television and radio, for instance) Chinese people – particularly in large urban centres and the more economically developed parts of the country – often have access to the internet, the use of fixed-line and mobile telephones, some experience of foreign media, the possibility of travelling both within and outside China, greater interaction with foreign tourists, students and businesspeople and generally much greater access to information than could ever have been imagined in the early post-Mao period. All of this radically affects the potential significance of any media cynicism among readers, viewers and listeners directed towards official sources.

However, this paper has also shown that it is important to differentiate between different kinds and contexts of cynicism. Media cynicism is not only about readers, viewers and listeners, but also pertains – in different ways – to the realm of media producers, in this case journalists. It might be contested that the cynicism of media consumers and that of producers is simply not the same thing, given that the former sceptically distrust what they are told while the latter cynically participate in its construction. However, I argue that you have to see all of these practices – media consumers and journalists – as related and similar.

Sloterdijk makes distinctions between different kinds of cynicism and we need to acknowledge that we are dealing with different kinds or manifestations of different cynical practices. However, importantly, they are all cynical practices nonetheless. As Huyssen put it: 'the reproach, often leveled against him, that he constructs a merely binary opposition between cynicism and kynicism simply misses the mark ... rather ... Sloterdijk postulates the split within the cynical phenomenon itself' (1987: xvii). In other words, the cynical phenomenon is made up of a range of diverse cynical practices. If we take scepticism to refer to someone who maintains a doubting attitude with reference to some particular question or statement or who is habitually inclined to doubt rather than to believe apparent facts presented to them, then both consumers and journalists in the Chinese context are sceptical. Confronted with a dominant system of political authority that configures media production in particular ways, consumers are sceptical and adjust accordingly. Journalists are also sceptical and adjust in their own ways as necessary in order to fulfil their duties and get on with their lives. Viewed in this way, the apparent distinction between consumers' and journalists' cynicism blurs into the distinction between consumers and journalists.

However, as this paper has argued, cynicism need not be thought of simply in terms of disbelief and, in relation to media production at least, if we rethink cynicism in terms of practices of 'enlightened false consciousness' we can identify many other instances of continuity and conformity. In this case, the significance of such practices has not diminished over recent decades. Indeed, I have argued that the smooth operation of China's media is utterly dependent upon these forms of cynical practices. Taking Žižek's line on ideology and cynicism we also therefore need to see these practices as deeply implicated in the structuring of social realities. In more concrete terms, given the intimate relationship between the Party, the government and the media in China, these practices also play a crucial role in maintaining the authority and legitimacy of the regime and its hegemonic rhetorics of transition.

The examples discussed in this paper have therefore shown that media producers' cynical practices, as outlined here, are core elements of China's constantly shifting party hegemony. Journalists in this sense are utterly complicit in these hegemonic practices, as much for the things that they do not do as for what they do. Yet, importantly, in the Chinese context such complicity should not be seen as a condemnation. On the one hand it is pragmatic survival and on the other hand it also represents the only way in which changes to the system, however slow and frustrating, can be initiated. In this respect the everyday cynical practices of journalists are also what make possible the occasional transgressions, the testing of limits, attempts at media popularization, commercialization and critical journalism. It is in the end the 'faith' that the Chinese Communist Party and the country's political leadership has in its journalists to toe the line, not to rock the boat and not to promote dissidence, that gives those same journalists the limited freedoms that they have to push the system in new directions. That 'faith' is ultimately the product of the cynical practices of journalists.

Returning briefly to Pye's question quoted earlier about how the Chinese people might respond to their rulers' changing appeals at the beginning of the reform period, we can see that it is not a matter of choosing one or other of Pye's three options. Rather, we can see that a full response to the question requires identifying how conformism and cynicism – which are not necessarily opposites, but can be seen as two sides of the same coin – exist alongside, are interrelated with and mutually inform reflective evaluation and sceptical judgement, both among media consumers and producers.

Notes

1. Some also argue that mass mobilization campaigns played a key role in maintaining social control (see e.g. Bennett 1977; Greenblatt 1977).
2. See references in Falkenheim (1982).
3. There are problems with Pye's formulation of the question. Most notably it suggests a rather simplistic choice between the given options when conceivably the answer might entail some configuration of all three. At the same time, it suggests that the past was simply characterized by conformism – a view that many present China scholars would seek to complicate. Furthermore, we need to question the assumption that 'maturity' may only apply in one of these cases. Nonetheless, Pye's question does offer a useful introduction to the key issues relating to communication at the end of the Mao period.
4. It is beyond the scope of one paper to deal with cynicism across all groups in Chinese society and across all kinds of social practices. Indeed, even to discuss the relatively focused issue of media cynicism in this context we

inevitably have to make some generalizations and approximations about social attitudes and behaviour.

5. This does not mean there has been no change in the actual political role and functioning of Chinese media. For instance, there has been a boom in critical investigative journalism (see e.g. Xu 2000), there is now much greater interactivity and reader or audience involvement in media production (see e.g. Erwin 2000; Latham 2007); and Chinese media executives regularly question the political definition of the media in industry publications (see e.g. Yin and Li 2004; Yu 2004). The key point is that these changes are only possible within clearly understood, if not always explicitly stated, rules of practice (see below).

6. Falkenheim's account outlines how the Chinese authorities, although openly identifying the problem and discussing it, nonetheless maintained that these crises were confined to relatively small numbers of people. Falkenheim (1982: 240–44) offers complementary data suggesting that the problem could have been more widespread than the authorities were willing to concede publicly, although he himself concluded that there was no real way of settling the issue one way or the other.

7. However, we might also add here that the focus upon faith and cynicism at this time resulted also from the way in which China scholarship characterized China and the Chinese polity. It is at least in part due to the fact that scholarly attention was centred around questions regarding the force, nature and effectiveness of Communist Party ideology in society that it became necessary to focus upon the degree to which people believed in or succumbed to these ideological pressures.

8. Perhaps at this stage we can see the answer to Lucien Pye's question in terms of a regression from his response (b) to response (a), or at least a combination of the two.

9. Sloterdijk actually makes much of the distinction between cynicism in general, which 'does not glaringly draw attention to itself' (1987: 7) and 'kynicism', a particular form of cynicism reminiscent of the vulgar plebeian humour of Diogenes (1987: 101–3). Kynicism comes to represent the base ridicule of power, a mocking raspberry blown in the direction of authority. There are examples of 'kynical' humour in contemporary media consumption, particularly on the internet and in mobile phone culture, where symbols of the revered Maoist past, for instance, are regularly digitally defaced or annotated for comic effect. However, this chapter is concerned with more mainstream manifestations of media cynicism, rather than kynicism, on the part of media producers and consumers.

10. One exception might be the compulsory attendance of senior party cadres at political education meetings. In my experience, these were often viewed by participants as rather a waste of time and events at which one went through the motions of political sloganeering because one was required to.

References

Baum, R. 1992. 'Political Stability in Post-Deng China: Problems and Prospects', *Asian Survey* 32(6) (June).

Bennett, G. 1977. 'China's Mass Campaigns and Social Control', in A.A. Wilson, S.L. Greenblatt and R. Wilson (eds), *Deviance and Social Control in Chinese Society*. New York: Praeger.

Blecher, M. 1983. 'The Mass Line and Leader-mass Relations and Communication in Basic-level Rural Communities', in Godwin, C. Chu and Francis Hsu (eds), *China's New Social Fabric*. Kegan Paul International.

Cell, C.P. 1983. 'Communication in China's Mass Mobilization Campaigns', in Godwin, C. Chu and Francis Hsu (eds), *China's New Social Fabric*. Kegan Paul International.

Chao, C.M. and B.J. Dickson (eds). 2001. *Remaking the Chinese State: Strategies, Society, and Security*. London: Routledge.

Chu, G.C. 1979. 'The Current Structure and Functions of China's Mass Media', in G.C. Chu and F.L.K. Hsu (eds), *Moving a Mountain: Cultural Change in China*. Honolulu: University Press of Hawaii.

Ci, Jiwei. 1999. *Dialectic of the Chinese Revolution: From Utopianism to Hedonism*. Stanford, CA: Stanford University Press.

Croll, E.J. forthcoming. 'Conjuring Goods, Identities and Cultures', in K. Latham, S. Thompson and J. Klein (eds), *Consuming China: Approaches to Cultural Change in Contemporary China*. London: RouteldgeCurzon.

Davis, D.S. (ed.). 2000. *The Consumer Revolution in Urban China*. Berkeley: University of California Press.

Davis, D.S., R. Kraus, B. Naughton and E.J. Perry. 1995. *Urban Spaces in Contemporary China: The Potential for Autonomy and Community in Post-Mao China*. Woodrow Wilson Center Series. Cambridge: Cambridge University Press.

Davis, D. and E. Vogel (eds.). 1990. *Chinese Society on the Eve of Tiananmen: The Impact of Reform*. Cambridge, MA: Harvard.

Dittmer, L. 1981. 'China in 1980: Modernization and its Discontents', *Asian Survey* 21(1), A Survey of Asia in 1980: Part I (Jan. 1981).

Erwin, K. 2000. 'Heart-to-Heart, Phone-to-Phone: Family Values, Sexuality, and the Politics of Shanghai's Advice Hotlines', in D.S. Davis (ed.), *The Consumer Revolution in Urban China*. Berkeley: University of California Press.

Falkenheim, V.C. 1982. 'Popular Values and Political Reform: the "Crisis of Faith" in Contemporary China', in S.L. Greenblatt, R.W. Wilson and A. Auerbac Wilson (eds), *Social Interaction in Chinese Society*. New York: Praeger Publishers.

Gold, T. 1985. 'After Comradeship: Personal Relations in China Since the Cultural Revolution', *China Quarterly* 104: 657–75.

———. 1991. 'Youth and the State', *The China Quarterly* 127, Special Issue: The Individual and the State in China (Sept. 1991).

Greenblatt, S.L. 1977. 'Campaigns and the Manufacture of Deviance', in A.A. Wilson, S.L. Greenblatt and R. Wilson (eds), *Deviance and Social Control in Chinese Society*. New York: Praeger.

Hemelryk Donald, S. and M. Keane. 2002. 'Responses to Crisis: Convergence, Content Industries and Media Governance', in S. Hemelryk Donald, M. Keane and H. Liu (eds), *Media in China: Consumption, Content and Crisis.* London: RoutledgeCurzon.

Huang, C. 2000. 'The Development of a Semi-Independent Press in Post-Mao China: An overview and a case study of Chengdu Business News', *Journalism Studies* 1(4).

Huyssen, A. 1987. 'Foreword', in P. Sloterdijk, *Critique of Cynical Reason.* Minneapolis: University of Minnesota Press.

Kwong, J. 1994. 'Ideological Crisis among China's Youths: Values and Official Ideology', *The British Journal of Sociology* 45(2) (June).

Latham, K. 2000. 'Nothing But the Truth: Media, Power and Hegemony in South China', *China Quarterly* 163 (September) 2000.

———. 2001. 'Between Markets and Mandarins: Journalists and the Rhetorics of Transition in Southern China', in Brian Moeran (ed.), *Asian Media Worlds.* Richmond: Curzon Press.

———. 2002. 'Rethinking Chinese Consumption: Social Palliatives and the Rhetorics of Transition in Postsocialist China', in C.M. Hann (ed.), *Postsocialism: Ideals, Ideologies and Practices in Eurasia.* London: Routledge.

———. 2007. 'Sms, Communication, and Citizenship in China's Information Society', *Critical Asian Studies* 39(2): 295.

Lee, C.C. (ed.). 2000. *Power, Money, and Media: Communication Patterns and Bureaucratic Control in Cultural China.* Evanston: Northwestern University Press.

Liu, A.L.P. 1984. 'Opinions and Attitudes of Youth in the People's Republic of China', *Asian Survey* 24(9) (September).

Liu, H. 1998. 'Profit or Ideology? The Chinese Press Between Party and Market', *Media, Culture & Society* 20(1).

Myers, T. 2003. *Slavoj Žižek.* London: Routledge.

OED, 1994. (*Oxford English Dictionary*) CD-ROM, version 1.13. Oxford: Oxford University Press.

Pye, L. 1978. 'Review of "Radical Change through Communication in Mao's China"', by Godwin C. Chu, *The China Quarterly* 76 (September).

Rawnsley, G.D. and M.Y.T. Rawnsley. 2003. *Political Communications in Greater China: The Construction and Reflection of Identity.* London: RoutledgeCurzon.

Rosen, S. 1990. 'The Impact of Reform on the Attitudes and Behavior of Chinese Youth – Some Evidence from Survey Research', in *Political Implications of Economic Reform in Communist Systems –Communist Dialectic.* New York: New York University Press.

Sloterdijk, P. 1987. *Critique of Cynical Reason.* Minneapolis: University of Minnesota Press.

Tang, X. 1996. 'New Urban Culture and the Anxiety of Everyday Life in Contemporary China', in Tang Xiaobing and S. Snyder (eds), *In Pursuit of Contemporary East Asian Culture.* Boulder: Westview Press.

Wang, Xiaoying. 2002. 'The Post-Communist Personality: the Spectre of China's Capitalist Market Reforms', *The China Journal* 47 (January).

Xu, Hua, 2000. 'Morality Discourse in the Marketplace: Narratives in the Chinese Television News Magazine Oriental Horizon', *Journalism Studies* 1(4).

Yang, M. 1994. *Gifts, Favors and Banquets: The Art of Social Relationships in China.* Ithaca: Cornell University Press.

———. 1996. 'Travelling Theory and Modernity in China', in H.L. Moore (ed.), *The Future of Anthropological Knowledge.* London: Routledge.

Yin, H. and D.G. Li. 2004. '2003: Zhongguo dianshi chanye beiwang' (2003: reflections on China's television industry), *South China Television Journal* 1(45): 32–37.

Yu G.M. 2004. '2004 zhongguo chuanmeiye fazhan dashi tuixiang.' (2004: Thoughts on the general situation of development in China's broadcasting industries), *South China Television Journal* 1(45): 28–31.

Zhao, Y. 1998. *Media, Market, and Democracy in China: Between the Party Line and the Bottom Line.* Urbana and Chicago: University of Illinois Press.

———. 2000. 'From Commercialization to Conglomeration: The Transformation of the Chinese Press', *Journal of Communication*, Spring 2000, 50(2).

Žižek, S. 1989. *The Sublime Object of Ideology.* London: Verso.

CHAPTER 9

The Rooted Anthropologies of East-Central Europe

Chris Hann

Introduction

A good deal of the anthropological literature on postsocialist societies has been concerned with highlighting continuity in change, in other words with modifying the notion of sharp break or rupture that is implicit in the notion of postsocialism. For example, reliance upon kinship networks and traditional patterns of informal cooperation can help people to cope with the problems created by the collapse of socialist rural institutions (Ventsel 2005; see also Hann et al. 2003, Hann 2005). Of course even the most traditional features of the 'moral economy' (Thompson 1991) may also undergo changes as the institutional environment evolves. The disintegration of the Soviet bloc provided anthropologists with an opportunity, unique not only in terms of its scale, to investigate rapid social change and to theorize its complexities.[1] Clearly some aspects of society and culture can be modified much faster than others and the speed of change is experienced differently in different social groups. Kristina Sliavaite (2005) has shown in her study of a model socialist community in Lithuania how processes of postsocialist transformation can be deliberately slowed. However, the challenge to formulate a general theory of these different temporalities and the links between them has not been met. Fifteen years into 'the transition', I see only plenty of 'weasel words' (Ellen 1994).

According to Roy Ellen a minimal requirement for such a theory would be the specification of different levels and dimensions of analysis, including a distinction between the social and the cultural. He sees no alternative to applying some version of systems analysis (1994). This also entails drawing distinctions between domains: a focus on rural studies alone cannot possibly be sufficient for a general theory of postsocialist transformation. In this chapter I discuss a sector that I have not written about previously. Like most fieldworkers who tread conventional paths in the countryside, I have over the years built up a lot of experience of capital cities and had ample opportunity for close-up observation of the institutional dynamics of research colleagues. Recently I combined forces with Mihály Sárkány and Peter Skalník to organize a workshop and edit a volume of papers exploring the history of anthropology in East-Central Europe (*Ostmitteleuropa*) – Poland, Hungary, Czechoslovakia, and the German Democratic Republic (GDR) – in the socialist era (Hann, Sárkány and Skalník 2005). In this chapter I follow this story into the postsocialist years. I adhere to the same broad definition of the field that we followed in that volume, to include strands that are very different from the social anthropology in which I was trained in Britain. While some have called for radical change, I shall show that the anthropology of the socialist era has persisted vigorously, not only in the memories of its practitioners but in institutions, methods, theories and the very definition of the field.

It is difficult to generalize about the anthropologists of the 'second world'. There were vast differences between, say, cultural philosophers in the former Yugoslavia who participated from the start in Western debates about postmodernism and the evolutionist Marxists who dominated the anthropological establishment in the former Soviet Union. It is nonetheless possible to identify some common features in the 'struggles for sociocultural anthropology' (Skalnik 2002), at least in East-Central Europe. The most important feature is the prominence of what George Stocking termed the nation building function of anthropology, in contrast to the empire-oriented anthropologies of countries such as Britain and France (Stocking 1982). Germany, where many of the most important foundations of modern anthropology were laid in the eighteenth century, forms an intermediate case, very strong in both branches of anthropology at the beginning of the twentieth century. *Volkskunde* was the study of one's own people, typically focused upon preindustrial rural groups as the embodiment of the national spirit. *Völkerkunde* was the comparative study of 'savage' peoples – in principle worldwide, in practice with a bias to regions where the newly united German state had acquired colonies. In the other countries of East-Central Europe the nation building orientation dominated. Those who studied other peoples were a small minority and, unlike Germany, they were not separately institutionalized.

Following the collapse of the Habsburg Empire and its replacement by several new sovereign states the links to the nation and to nationalism intensified during the interwar decades. In the German case some scholars slid into racism, with the consequence that after 1945 Völkerkunde and Volkskunde had to be reestablished on new foundations. In the Soviet sector, which in 1949 became the German Democratic Republic, Volkskunde and Völkerkunde were brought together in a unified Marxist *Ethnographie*; this was modelled closely on Soviet Etnografiya, though the GDR scholars soon developed their own distinctive profile (Noack and Krause 2005). Elsewhere in East-Central Europe the continuities with the presocialist years were greater, as I shall show.

In 1968 Tamás Hofer published an essay in *Current Anthropology* in which he juxtaposed the 'native ethnographers' of Hungary with American cultural anthropologists (Hofer 2005; see also Fél and Hofer 1969). Ignoring political and ideological factors, Hofer's basic contrast corresponded to the dichotomy drawn by Stocking (cf. Boskovic forthcoming). The historically-oriented, nation focused discipline, known in Hungary as *néprajz*, had little in common with the goals of a generalizing comparative social science. Whereas the Hungarian *néprajzos* was deeply immersed in the history of the Hungarian people, the typical US cultural anthropologist carried out a synchronic study of one small community, while remaining oblivious to the details of its spatial and temporal embeddedness. In Hofer's balanced and witty account of the two 'tribes', each type of enquiry had its own rationale and 'professional personality'. Hofer himself has always been a mediator between the two. He has supported the expansion of teaching and research in sociocultural anthropology, while holding that néprajz should retain its own distinct identity and not be swallowed up in a comparative science with global pretensions; he continues to adhere to this position in the postsocialist years (Hofer 2005).

Let me illustrate the gulf between the two types of anthropology with reference to my own work in late socialist Hungary (Hann 1980). After just a year of preparation based in the capital, I spent ten months in a village and wrote a dissertation that was dominated by economic analysis of the small-scale farming I observed. I argued that the unusually loose form of cooperative in the village of Tázlár exemplified the pragmatic flexibility of Hungary's post-1968 'market socialism', and drew more on the works of Hungarian sociologists and rural economists than on those of my colleagues in anthropology. During my fieldwork the Budapest Professor István Tálasi, a specialist in material culture and one of the leading figures in the néprajz of that era, published a wide-ranging introduction to the history and traditional folk culture of the wider region in which Tázlár was located (Tálasi 1977). I felt obliged to include the work in my bibliography but it was of little relevance for my interests in the contemporary economic anthropology of Tázlár. It is a similar story in the postsocialist era. Whereas I have concentrated on the recent economic transformation (Hann 2006), the Szeged néprajzos Antal Juhász has conducted meticulous research into the settlement processes of the region between the Danube and the Tisza, beginning in the eighteenth century (for example Juhasz 1997). He has taken no professional interest in postsocialist changes.

Whereas I prefer to recognize anthropology on both sides of this divide, many in Hungary distinguish between *néprajz* and *antropológia*. Not all are satisfied with Tamás Hofer's calls for fruitful coexistence on the basis of complementarity. The very title of Peter Skalnik's recent collection (2002) draws attention to his purpose: to transform the anthropological landscape in East-Central Europe by replacing the theories and methods of the local, 'people science' strand with those of the contemporary Anglophone world. When the barriers of the Cold War finally collapsed, this goal was attractive to many, especially younger scholars with good English who saw this kind of anthropology as a logical concomitant of a new, westwards-looking internationalism. For obvious reasons it was a goal viewed with the greatest suspicion by others, particularly older scholars, independently of their political stance. Similar tensions could be observed in other social sciences, but I shall argue that the case of anthropology is especially instructive. We must be wary of assuming that developments in anthropology are typical of what has taken place elsewhere, even in closely related academic fields.

I shall focus my discussion on Hungary because this is the country I know best. I think it provides a good illustration of postsocialist continuities, but also of contested new initiatives. I stress that even for this country my data are far from systematic. The only other country to which I shall make repeated reference is the former GDR, which I see as the epitome of discontinuity. The fate of GDR anthropologists was different from the fate of anthropologists elsewhere in East-Central Europe because this socialist state ceased to exist in 1990. The Academy of Sciences was disbanded and the unified discipline of Ethnographie abolished. West Germans were appointed to head up new departments which, in effect if not in name, reaffirmed the traditional distinction between Völkerkunde and Volkskunde. The Max-Planck-Institut für ethnologische Forschung can be viewed as one of the successor institutions on the Völkerkunde landscape in the former GDR, a fact which provides me with an additional motivation for coming to grips with the complexities of recent disciplinary history in this part of the world.

The Struggle for Anthropology in Postsocialist Hungary

The great majority of Hungarian anthropologists are and always have been specialists in Hungarian folk society (*a magyar népi társadalom*). The discipline played an important role in the national movement from its beginnings in the nineteenth century, a role which peaked in the 1930s (Kósa 2001). Unlike the German case, the Hungarian equivalents of the

Völkerkundler (sometimes labelled *etnológusok*) were too few in number to warrant separate institutions. This remained the case throughout the socialist period when, in spite of political alliances to numerous Third World countries, it was generally very difficult to conduct fieldwork outside one's own country. The outcome, then, was a rather extreme version of the dilemma that has been commented upon by countless anthropologists in the past: Hungarian néprajz was professionalized and rather generously funded to conduct research into a rural folk culture which, a result of socialist industrialization, was rapidly disappearing. In any case it was, for political reasons, impossible in the early socialist decades to conduct research into contemporary transformations. Before the 1970s, even field enquiries had therefore to be directed to an increasingly distant idealized past. As Klára Kuti has shown, the concern to document the essence of a timeless traditional folk culture meant in practice setting aside conventional chronological historicity (Kuti 2005).

By a curious coincidence, the first postsocialist government in Hungary in 1990 resembled the first socialist government of four decades earlier by appointing a professor of anthropology (néprajz) as the Minister for Education (Sárkány 2005). In 1949 Gyula Ortutay had summoned his colleagues in the Hungarian Ethnographical Society to embrace sweeping reforms, based on Marxist-Leninist materialism. One might have expected Bertalan Andásfalvy, Minister of Education and Culture in the conservative government formed by József Antall in 1990, to seize the moment in a similar way and proclaim a new agenda for his discipline. In fact Andrásfalvy did nothing of the sort – and this was not only because he himself, recently appointed to a chair at the small department in provincial Pécs, did not compare to Ortutay in terms of political clout (though his professional standing was high). Hungary experienced dramatic changes in some fields in the early 1990s, but the rupture could hardly be compared to the disruption of the early 1950s. The continuities in higher education were strong, as they were in almost all other sectors of public life. Existing staff and structures were left in place.[2] Under Antall's right-of-centre government a discipline that was so strongly associated with the nation did not need to have a representative in high office to face the future with confidence.

Yet pressure for change had been building up in some quarters. During the last decade of socialism Tamás Hofer was a leading figure in the adaptation of new, Western styles of historical anthropology and a pioneer of the study of national symbols. Among his students and colleagues, Péter Niedermüller was the most radical, calling into question the entire national focus of the discipline (1989) and urging the adoption of antropológia in its place. Niedermüller moved in 1996 to take up a professorial appointment at the newly established department of Europäische Ethnologie at Berlin's Humboldt University. Despite his departure, in 1990 the Latin Americanist

Lajos Boglár and a few colleagues secured funding from George Soros to launch a new teaching programme in *kulturális antropológia*. In 1993 this was formally incorporated at the main humanities university in Budapest (Eötvös Loránd Tudományos Egyetem, hereafter ELTE), independently of the existing departments of néprajz and *folklor*. The term 'antropológia' was very fashionable, not only with students but also with scholars in several adjacent disciplines who felt that more qualitative, culturalist approaches had something to contribute to their own fields. But, given the dearth of potential teachers, what kind of anthropology could it be?

A decade and a half later the situation is very complex. The ELTE department still exists today (2005) but it remains very small (only two full-time staff members) and it lacks effective leadership. Kulturális antropológia has nonetheless been extremely popular with students, recruiting more strongly than the long-established néprajz department. The latter has recently introduced a graduate programme which includes kulturális antropológia in its title; but, as in many other departments throughout East-Central Europe where the same nominal change has been approved, the traditional profile and nation-centered paradigm has not been significantly modified.

In provincial universities the situation is similarly complicated. A new programme in cultural anthropology, linked tightly to visual anthropology, was established by Ernö Kunt in Miskolc. It has managed to survive Kunt's premature death in 1994.[3] While the department of néprajz in Debrecen has changed little, that in Szeged has added kulturális antropológia to its title. The department specializes in the study of folk religion, but here as in other branches the focus is restricted to Hungary. Meanwhile anthropology teaching has also been launched in the department of media studies. A similar pattern can be observed at the University of Pécs, where anthropology was introduced around 1990 in two quite distinct forms. On the one hand there was a department of néprajz, headed by Andrásfalvy until he was appointed Minister, but including significant components of etnológia, taught primarily by the Southeast Asia specialist Gábor Vargyas. On the other hand, another strand of anthropology was established by Péter Niedermüller in the media studies department. Students here were familiarized with culturalist approaches to discourses and symbols but received little instruction in the history of social and cultural anthropology, or in any theoretical ideas from the era preceding postmodernism.

One further institution should be mentioned in this brief survey of university developments. The Central European University, founded and generously endowed by George Soros, and teaching internationally recruited students at graduate level only, epitomizes the winds of change. Under its third Rector Yehuda Elkana, a joint Department of Sociology and Anthropology was created in 2002.[4] The influence of this department on Hungarian anthropology has, however, been negligible to date. The staff have been recruited internationally, and all teaching takes place in English.

Hungarian anthropology today, then, is a highly contested field. Those who are most familiar with the history and theory of Western anthropology find themselves torn between, on the one hand, their (former) colleagues in departments of néprajz, who focus almost exclusively on rural Hungary and, on the other, those promoting the newer styles of research associated with scholars such as James Clifford, Michael Fischer and George Marcus. All of those who identify with any form of antropológia complain about the fact that decisions on their research grant applications and on the accreditation of their degrees are taken by committees controlled by néprajzosok, who dominate. Moreover, néprajz has always been assigned to the Faculty of Humanities, but the new antropológia is classified as a social science. At ELTE (but not in Pécs) a separate Faculty of Social Sciences has been created, with the result that the two departments of anthropology are in different faculties and students wishing to attend both must be prepared to pay additional fees.

Perhaps eventually neoliberal university management regimes will seek to rationalize this chaos, and the number of student enrolments will determine which departments survive. But that day seems to be still some way off.[5] Under socialism the number of students was carefully restricted, since a degree in anthropology was supposed to be a qualification to work in the field for the rest of one's life. In postsocialist conditions the number of students, especially females, has soared; some older professors deplore the fact that only a tiny proportion of those who graduate are likely to pursue their career in this field.[6] At the same time, teaching patterns and examination structures have hardly changed at all so far. The introduction of the 'Bologna process' is likely to change this in the near future (see Sárkány 2002).

In Hungary (as in Poland, Slovakia and the Czech Republic) museums and research institutes of the Academies of Sciences have remained major components of the anthropological landscape. The Néprajzi Kutatóintézet is still housed in the same prestigious building on Budapest's Castle Hill that I first visited as an exchange scholar in 1975 when Gyula Ortutay was still Director.[7] It employs almost as many full-time staff as all university-sector néprajz and antropológia staff combined. Some of the routines still follow the patterns to which I became accustomed then (the foreigner is always spoiled by a hospitable secretary who offers to make a strong espresso coffee!). Most staff work at home and the rooms are largely deserted except on the official Institute days, currently Tuesday and Thursday. One innovation of the postsocialist years was that staff were able to influence the appointment of their Director. When the post fell vacant a few years ago two senior colleagues allowed their names to go forward. The scholar who seemed less likely to rock the boat by introducing structural changes emerged victorious.[8]

A new central research council (OTKA) administers the distribution of research funding via a competitive grants system (*pályázati rendszer*). This seems to be working well. My impression is that many scholars have become more productive, at least in terms of the quantity of publications. Research patterns have not varied much: fieldwork generally consists of short trips, and two weeks is considered a very lengthy sojourn (see Vidacs 2005). The great majority of Hungarian néprajzos continue to work on Hungarian-speaking groups, for the most part inside Hungary but also in neighbouring countries, especially in Romania, where archaic survivals appear to be thicker on the ground. I am not aware of any néprajzos who continue such innovations of the socialist period as 'ethnography of the working classes'. As for work on documenting memories of socialism, this seems to be much more common among historians and sociologists. The anthropologists have retained their bias towards the rural and the national. However, interest in topics such as the material culture of the traditional peasantry, long viewed as central to néprajz, has dwindled in favour of an increase in the number of studies focused on postsocialist transformation of the countryside (Szilágyi 2002; Schwarcz, Szarvas and Szilágyi 2005). There is an overlap in these 'post-peasant' studies with the investigations of a large and well-developed rural sociology. Mihály Sárkány has initiated a restudy of the North Hungarian village of Varsány, first investigated by an Academy team in the 1970s, and this promises to be the most comprehensive anthropological analysis of rural Hungary's second 'great transformation' (Hann and Sárkány 2003).

Let me close this brief outline of postsocialist anthropology in Hungary by selecting two scholars to illustrate the contemporary spectrum of opinion. Péter Niedermüller, the *enfant terrible* of the 1980s, has recently moved back from the department of Europäische Ethnologie in Berlin to resume teaching in media studies at the University of Pécs. His empirical work over the last decade has continued to focus on symbols and nationalist discourses, but he is better known in Hungary as a purveyor of the latest North American theoretical debates about textuality, cultural flows and multi-sited ethnography. From sociologists such as Ulrich Beck and Anthony Giddens he has picked up concepts such as that of 'late modernity' and from the philosopher Charles Taylor that of 'social imaginary'. A recent article (Niedermüller 2005) goes beyond his earlier calls to replace néprajz with sociocultural anthropology. Emphasizing the changes which have affected not just anthropology but the humanities and social sciences worldwide over the last two decades, and endorsing the conclusions of the Gulbenkian Commission (1996, translated into Hungarian in 2002), Niedermüller concludes that the anthropology of the future can only be 'transdisciplinary'. My own work in a postsocialist rural community would not, I fear, meet his standards; it would be classified together with that of colleagues working as néprajzos. I would classify Niedermüller's bricolage as radical cultural studies and I note that he continues to have an almost charismatic appeal for many younger scholars.[9]

Turning to the other end of the spectrum, the first edition of Academician László Kósa's history of Hungarian néprajz was published in 1989. The second, published in 2001, includes new materials in which the author is critical of his colleagues for not doing more to investigate contemporary social life after it had become possible to do so in the 1970s. Kósa distinguishes three possible future scenarios for his discipline. If it simply continues to do more of the same, he is sure that it will not survive for long. The second possibility is a process of fragmentation: historical anthropologists will affiliate to departments of history, those interested in contemporary transformations to sociology, and subgroups such as folklorists may declare independence. The third scenario is the hardest but it is the one favoured by this author: a process of renewal, which will conserve the accumulated knowledge of the last two centuries while specifying selected topics for further investigation. The deficit in the area of synchronic studies must now be made good, he argues. Using established historical methods it should also be possible for the néprajzos to make good the dearth of knowledge concerning the 1950s and 1960s, when the old peasantry was so cruelly destroyed. Additional fields to which the discipline might be expected to contribute are the expansion of ethnic and national sentiments and local responses to globalization. Kósa notes the arrival of new ethnic and religious groups in postsocialist Hungary, but suggests that these should be the object of research by sociologists. The Hungarian néprajzos should remain primarily concerned with the Hungarians. Kósa rejects the charge of nationalism in any period of the discipline's history: rather, the discipline is respected and accepted by Hungarian society because of its 'values'. He dismisses the criticisms of those who favour the introduction of a generalizing comparative antropológia that would subsume néprajz as an 'unfriendly' assault on academic freedoms.

While Niedermüller's iconoclastic cosmopolitanism has many admirers, especially among younger intellectuals, it seems to me that the sentiments expressed by Academician László Kósa also command a wide measure of support in the contemporary intelligentsia. Certainly the néprajz programmes continue to attract plenty of applicants and their new BA programmes have all been approved by the accreditation committee. Cultural anthropology, in contrast, remains fragmented. In Budapest the ELTE department has recently decided that it is not able to offer a BA programme at all. At the Pázmány (Roman Catholic)

University, proposals to launch a programme in cultural anthropology were recently rejected by the accreditation committee. To understand these developments and the continued vitality of néprajz we need to look more carefully not only at the socialist *ancien régime* but at complex legacies dating back to the presocialist era.

Complex Legacies

The first reason for the continuities that have characterized Hungary's academic life in general in the postsocialist era is the successful liberalization that took place in the later decades of socialism. The criteria governing scientific appointments were basically scientific, so that even in the most sensitive of political fields, very few academics lost their positions after 1990. Although the senior figures in néprajz were almost all members of the Communist Party, they were not rigid doctrinally and allowed quite different, non-Marxist styles of enquiry to flourish in the institutes they headed. In the GDR, there was more pressure from above to engage with the theories of Marxism-Leninism. It affected the Völkerkundler wing of the unified discipline more strongly than the Volkskundler (e.g. long-running debates over primitive communism and later modes of production: see Noack and Krause 2005). This made it easier for the post-1990 West German evaluators to justify dismissing staff who had been Party members, even though the individuals concerned might argue that their motives were no different from those of their counterparts in Hungary.

But how was socialist era anthropology in Hungary able to maintain its traditions and avoid becoming embroiled in the sort of debates which dominated the scene in the USSR and the GDR? Implementation of the programme announced in 1949 by Gyula Ortutay was inconsistent and at best half-hearted. The anthropologists of East-Central Europe were expected to work within a Marxist-Leninist framework and to supply data which would confirm the doctrines of historical materialism, but only in the 1950s was there real pressure to follow the Soviet model and to cite dogmatic texts. It proved impossible to bring anthropology, as formed and practised in this part of the world, into line with the dictates of the ideology. The key concepts of 'culture' and 'peoples' (later 'ethnic groups') had no place in Marxist-Leninist analysis of class-divided societies, the mainspring of which lay in the forces and relations of production. This entire intellectual apparatus left little room for studying domains of 'superstructure' as interesting objects of research in their own right. Ortutay himself barely tried: he was best known for his work on folk tales, with particular regard to the relationship between narrator (performer) and audience. Even studies of the new working classes were carefully grafted on to older styles of enquiry and emphasized transitional forms (Katona 2000; Paládi-Kovács 2000).

Whereas theory and ideology were by and large rejected, the Soviet system of scientific organization was emulated, above all through the creation of new research institutes within the framework of the Academy of Sciences. Hungarian néprajz received such institutionalization in 1967, substantially later than most neighbouring countries, and it turned out to be highly productive in all the branches it covered. University departments also flourished. The bulk of these scholars worked in well-established fields such as material culture and folk beliefs (Sárkány 2005; Vidacs 2005; see also Hoppál and Csonka-Takács 2001 for detail on specific insitutions). They paid no more than lip service to the prevailing ideology.

The Hungarian anthropological community under socialism was not a narrow 'church', either in the service of or opposed to socialism. Rather, as it expanded it became more diverse. There were a few scholars who took Marxism seriously and some of their work was highly original. Sárkány (2005) singles out Tamás Hoffmann's application of historical-materialism to the history of the Hungarian peasantry and Ferenc TŒkei's studies of the Asiatic Mode of Production. In addition, a minority continued to cultivate wider interests in what was traditionally termed etnológia, that is, in empirical studies outside Hungary. Such enquiries had a stronger tradition in Hungary than in neighbouring countries, for reasons which may be traced back to the late Habsburg period, when Hungary was a partner in the imperial system and, like Germany, complicated the dichotomy drawn by George Stocking. Some of the scholars of this era concentrated on peoples related (or thought to be related) to the Magyars, such as the Voguls, whose folklore was the object of intensive investigations, but others organized successful expeditions to East Africa and New Guinea.[10] Important *etnológusok* of the socialist era included Vilmos Diószegi, one of the pioneer investigators of Siberian shamanism, and the above-mentioned Lajos Boglár, who specialized in the Indian communities of South America. Mihály Sárkány (Head of the Academy Institute's department of non-European studies since 1988) carried out fieldwork in East Africa and Gábor Vargyas in the Central Highlands of Vietnam. Tibor Bodrogi was not primarily a fieldworker (only one brief stint in Oceania) but a polymath who wrote extensively on a great range of topics, including Hungarian kinship terminology, tribal art, and the evolutionism of Lewis Henry Morgan. As Ortutay's successor as director of the research institute of the Academy of Sciences, he encouraged the introduction of new theories and methods into néprajz. The subdiscipline of *társadalomnéprajz*, literally 'society ethnography', applied perspectives from social and cultural anthropology in studies of contemporary rural transformation within Hungary. The major example was the teamwork carried out in Varsány in the 1970s (Bodrogi 1978).[11]

Sárkány (2005) suggests that these innovative tendencies peaked in the 1970s and that the last decade of socialism was less creative. Nonetheless the legacy left by the mainstream national ethnographers to the postsocialist generation is immense, both in the form of individual studies and in the mammoth dictionaries and atlases which are now available for use by their successors. This was a living tradition, scarcely tainted by the minimal accommodations it had been obliged to make to socialist ideology. Kósa's account of the discipline's history, emphasizing continuities over more than two centuries, is justified. In the GDR, by contrast, where the presocialist Volkskunde was the most discredited, the socialist era ended as it had begun, with an emphatic rupture. However, here it is interesting to note that, even when the official goal was a unified Ethnographie, the pursuit of anthropology at home remained largely separate from 'universal', comparative anthropology. Throughout East-Central Europe, the Volkskundler received more attention and resources in the socialist era than did the Völkerkundler.[12] This is surely a puzzle that demands an explanation.

Conclusion

There can be no *tabula rasa* in the specialized communities of the academic world, any more than there can be in the life of a village or any other human community. Most studies of postsocialism reinforce this basic point, which in essence is the same point that emerges from careful examinations of the impact of Stalinism. The complex legacies of the socialist period have contributed to the controversies over the future of the discipline in the postsocialist years; to understand these legacies it is also necessary to explore the anthropology of the presocialist era. By extending the temporal frame, I have suggested in this chapter that Hungarian néprajz is a case of persisting national ethnography rather than a case of persisting socialism.

In the terms of Roy Ellen's systemic approach to social change, it does not seem possible to generalize about a conservative 'academic domain'. Although the Hungarian case demonstrates great continuity of personnel in most subject areas, in disciplines such as political science and economics the changes have gone much further than they have in néprajz. The GDR case shows us, however, that even this branch of study can be subjected to major upheaval: political factors dictated a radical transformation of this field in Germany on two occasions within half a century.

I suggest that the case of the GDR is the exception that proves the rule concerning the continuity of 'national ethnography' in Ostmitteleuropa. The most plausible explanation for this continuity is that the regimes of this region saw the study and cultivation of national traditions as an element in their own legitimation strategies. Even in the GDR case there is some evidence that the regime sought to instrumentalize Volkskunde research in order to strengthen feelings of *Heimat* and cement a new socialist patriotism (Mohrmann 2005). This branch of anthropology might have been a suspect 'bourgeois' science, but socialists never became sufficiently cosmopolitan to dispense with local, regional and national rootedness. The nation-oriented branch of anthropology proved itself highly resilient through all the vicissitudes of twentieth-century history. The backwards-looking focus on the pure folk culture provided a helpful antidote to future-oriented ideologies of modernity. In terms of Ellen's systems theory it could be modelled as a countercurrent. Perhaps it was more than a minor sweetener: we should consider the possibility that the support given to this strand of anthropology reveals something more fundamental about the nature of socialism, belying its cosmopolitan, modernist pretensions. Adapting Stalin's famous slogan, one might say that the discipline of anthropology underwent significant changes of *form* under socialism, particularly through the founding of the Academy Institutes, an institutional innovation of enormous long-term significance (except in Germany, where for political reasons it had to be eliminated); but in terms of *content*, anthropology never became a Marxist science and the nation-centered legacy was always dominant.

Some scholars who, in the past, were highly critical of socialism and of the lip-service that sometimes had to be paid to Marxist-Leninist ideology, now see the period in a quite different light. The discipline of néprajz gained in numerical strength and in both social and academic prestige in this period, being identified with the national culture rather than with the ideology of Marxist-Leninism. At the same time it remained small enough to preserve traditions of collegiality. This serendipitous combination was bound to come under pressure after 1990, but the reasons for the continued vitality of néprajz are not hard to seek. To some, today's imperialist threat from the neoliberal West looks more insidiously threatening to the moral economy of this part of the academy than the former threat from the East. There are some who wish to engage with this world, making use of the latest buzzwords of postmodernism, transnationalism etc., and to do so under the name antropológia. But others will identify themselves in opposition to these trends, and for the time being the future of néprajz can probably be best secured if its practitioners continue to play the cards that connect them intimately to their nation. As in the socialist era, the 'values' of the discipline are the key to its survival: popular sympathy for culture-blind or culture-obliterating neoliberal globalization is no greater than for the ideologies of the past.

Unfortunately, this does not help those who would prefer, on intellectual grounds, to promote not just a modus vivendi but a genuinely productive integration of the two strands of anthropology which Tamás Hofer contrasted in the 1960s. The danger in the present situation, in Hungary and elsewhere in the region, is that *both* of these will wither. Instead of witnessing a gradualist process of continuity in change, it is possible that we shall witness rupture in this corner of the academic world. The name 'antropológia' may still survive, but only as a curiosity within departments of cultural studies and media studies, whose students will be taught that they can afford to ignore the prehistory of the term (everything down to about 1985).

Acknowledgements

I am grateful to Mihály Sárkány, Gábor Vargyas and Bea Vidacs for information and for saving me from numerous errors, though they cannot be held responsible for those which remain. Thanks also to Tamás Régi for sending information from Budapest, and to the editors of this volume for their helpful comments on the first draft.

Notes

1. The only adequate comparison is with the original impact of industrial capitalism, for which the classic model remains that of Karl Polanyi (1944). Later historians and anthropologists have recognized that the concept of a 'great transformation' is overstated; our models of postsocialism need similar critique and refinement.
2. Some scholars were obliged to have their degrees revalidated as a result of the transfer of authority away from the Academy and back to the universities but I am not aware of any néprajz cases in which this proved to be problematic. It is said that Andrásfalvy personally favoured a more thoroughgoing reappraisal of senior academic staff in both sectors, with evaluations based strictly on scholarly criteria; this was vetoed by Prime Minister József Antall, since it would have contradicted the general tenor of continuity to which his government was committed.
3. László Kürti, probably Hungary's best-known anthropologist as a result of his role as Secretary of the European Association of Social Anthropologists, teaches in Miskolc, but is affiliated to political science rather than to anthropology. For his own assessment of recent developments in the discipline in Hungary see Kürti (2002).
4. Even before this, summer schools were organized in the discipline; and there was a significant anthropology component in other courses offered at the institution, including the Nationalism programme originally launched by Ernest Gellner shortly before his death in 1995.

5. It may not be so far away. At the Babes-Bolyai University of Cluj (Romania), where the politics of anthropology are perhaps even more complicated than elsewhere as a result of the dual ethnic constitution of the university, academic salaries depend heavily upon the number of students in their department.

6. As in the past, it is possible for Academy researchers to negotiate part-time contracts after retirement. This has limited the number of new appointments and increased the sense of frustration experienced by graduates with no prospects of employment in their chosen field.

7. Although 'néprajz' remains the key term in the title of the institute, the official English name is 'Institute of Ethnology'. This emerged as a compromise between the traditional translation of néprajz, ethnography, and the term 'anthropology', which was unacceptable to the majority of senior staff.

8. The internal vote had of course to be confirmed at higher levels. Recently the system has been altered again: the nominating initiative has been taken away from the scholarly community, but the proposal of a new Director from above must still be ratified by the staff (if more than 50 per cent object, the proposal must be referred back).

9. For example the editors of the new journal *Anthropolis*, the first issue of which contained a substantial article by Niedermüller (2004).

10. I thank Mihály Sárkány for emphasizing the relevance of this early history.

11. Similar team research was undertaken a little later in the southern village of Zsombó, near Szeged. I was fortunate to be able to join these researchers for a week in the field in early 1976; few of the data collected in this project have been analysed in publications, but see Szabó (2000).

12. It was much easier for the Volkskundler to undertake fieldwork, and in some cases their adaptations of Marxism reflect this. Thus the GDR Volkskundler were able to develop the concept of 'demos' in the course of developing new approaches in social and cultural history – approaches which have stood the test of time rather well. In other words, here too it was the 'home ethnography' branch of the discipline which seems to have adapted more successfully, at any rate from the vantage point of the literature that is still read nowadays.

References

Bodrogi, T. (ed.). 1978. *Varsány: tanulmányok egy észak-magyarországi falu társadalomnáprajzához*. Budapest: Akadámiai Kiadó.

Boskovic, A. forthcoming. 'Anthropology in Unlikely Places: Yugoslav Ethnology Between the Past and the Future', in A. Boskovic (ed.), *Other People's Anthropologies*. Oxford: Berghahn.

Ellen, R.E. 1994 'Rates of Change: Weasel Words and the Indispensable in Anthropological Analysis', in C.M. Hann (ed.), *When History Accelerates; Essays on Rapid Social Change, Complexity and Creativity*. London: Athlone, pp. 54–74.

Fél, E. and T. Hofer. 1969. *Proper Peasants: Traditional Life in a Hungarian Village*. Chicago: Aldine.

Hann, C. 1980. *Tázlár: a Village in Hungary.* Cambridge: CUP.

Hann, C. (ed.). 2005. *Property Relations; the Halle Focus Group, 2000–2005.* Halle: Max Planck Institute for Social Anthropology.

Hann, C. 2006. *Not the Horse We Wanted! Postsocialism, Neoliberalism and Eurasia.* Münster: LIT.

Hann, C. and the 'Property Relations' Group. 2003. *The Postsocialist Agrarian Question: property relations and the rural condition.* Münster: LIT.

Hann, C. and M. Sárkány. 2003. 'The Great Transformation in Rural Hungary; Property, Life Strategies and Living Standards', in Chris Hann and the 'Property Relations' group, *The Postsocialist Agrarian Question: Property Relations and the Rural Condition.* Münster: LIT, pp. 117–42.

Hann, C., M. Sárkány and P. Skalník. 2005. 'Introduction: Collisions and Continuities in an Essentially Contested Field', in C. Hann, M. Sárkány and P. Skalnik (eds), *Socialist Era Anthropology in East-Central Europe.* Münster: LIT, pp. 1–20.

Hofer, T. 2005 (1968). 'Comparative Notes on the Professional Personalities of Two Disciplines', In C. Hann, M. Sárkány and P. Skalnik (eds), *Socialist Era Anthropology in East-Central Europe.* Münster: LIT, pp. 343–61.

Hoppál, M. and E. Csonka-Takács (eds). 2001. *Ethnology in Hungary: Institutional Background.* Budapest: European Folklore Institute.

Juhász, A. 1997. 'Tázlár puszta benépesedése', in A. Juhász (ed.), *Migráció és település a Duna–Tisza közén 2,* Szeged, pp. 37–69 (*Táj és Népi Kultúra 1*).

Katona, Imre. 2000. 'Átmeneti rétegek az agrártársadalom peremén', in A. Paládi-Kovács et al. (eds), *Magyar Néprajz 8 (Társadalom)*Budapest: Akadémiai, pp. 173–238.

Kósa, L. 2001. *A magyar néprajz tudománytörténete.* Budapest: Osiris.

Kürti, L. 2002. 'Hungarian Ethnography and Anthropology: Some Questions and Some Answers About Disciplines and Identities', in P. Skalnik (ed.), *A Post-Communist Millennium: The Struggles for Sociocultural Anthropology in Central and Eastern Europe.* Prague: Set Out, pp. 75–86.

Kuti, K. 2005. 'Historicity in Hungarian anthropology', in C. Hann, M. Sárkány and P. Skalnik (eds), *Socialist Era Anthropology in East-Central Europe.* Münster: LIT, pp. 273–84.

Mohrmann, U. 2005. 'Volkskunde in the German Democratic Republic on the Eve of its Dissolution', in C. Hann, M. Sárkány and P. Skalnik (eds), *Socialist Era Anthropology in East-Central Europe.* Münster: LIT, pp. 195–209.

Niedermüller, P. 1989. 'A néprajztudomány válaszútjai avagy a kultúrakutatás elméleti dilemmái' *BUKSZ* 1: 79–84.

———. 2004. 'Ten Years Later'– avagy mi történt a kultúrakutatás dielemmáival?' *Antropolis* 1(1): 8–19.

———. 2005. 'Az antropológia metamorfózisai: perspektívák a (késŒ) modern társadalom kutatásában', *Tabula* 8(1): 3–18.

Noack, K. and M. Krause. 2005. 'Ethnographie as a Unified Anthropological Science in the German Democratic Republic', in C. Hann, M. Sárkány and P. Skalnik (eds), *Socialist Era Anthropology in East-Central Europe.* Münster: LIT, pp. 25–53.

Paládi-Kovács, A. 2000. 'Az ipari munkásság', in A. Paládi-Kovács et al. (eds), *Magyar Néprajz 8 (Társadalom).*Budapest: Akadémiai, pp. 239–308.

Polanyi, K. 1944. *The Great Transformation*. Boston: Beacon Press.

Sárkány, M. 2002. 'Cultural and Social Anthropology in Central and Eastern Europe', in M. Kaase, V. Sparschuch, and A. Wenninger (eds), *Three Social Science Disciplines in Central and Eastern Europe: Handbook on Economics, Political Science and Sociology (1989–2001)*. Berlin and Budapest: Social Science Information Centre (IZ) and Collegium Budapest, pp. 558–66.

———. 2005. 'Hungarian Anthropology in the Socialist Era: Theories, Methodologies and Undercurrents', in C. Hann, M. Sárkány and P. Skalnik (eds), *Socialist Era Anthropology in East-Central Europe*. Münster: LIT, pp. 87–108.

Schwarcz, Gy., Zs. Szarvas and M. Szilágyi (eds). 2005. *Utóparaszti hagyományok és modernizációs törekvések a magyar vidéken*. Budapest: MTA Néprajzi Kutatóintézet/MTA Társadalomkutatóintézet.

Skalník, P. (ed.). 2002. *A Post-Communist Millennium: The Struggles for Sociocultural Anthropology in Central and Eastern Europe*. Prague: Set Out.

Sliavaite, K. 2005. *From Pioneers to Target Group: Social Change, Ethnicity and Memory in a Lithuanian Nuclear Power Plant Community*, Lund Monographs in Social Anthropology, 16. Lund: Department of Sociology.

Stocking, G.W. 1982. 'Afterword: A View from the Center', *Ethnos* 47 (1–2): 172–86.

Szabó, P. 2000. 'Zsombó. Egy Szeged vidéki tanyás település', in A. Paládi-Kovács et al. (eds), *Magyar Néprajz 8 (Társadalom)*. Budapest: Akadémiai, pp. 929–34.

Szilágyi, M. (ed.). 2002. *Utak és útvestŒk a kisüzemi agrárgazdaságban 1990–1999*. Budapest: MTA Néprajzi Kutatóintézet/MTA Társadalomkutatóintézet.

Tálasi, I. 1977. *Kiskunság*. Budapest: Gondolat.

Thompson, E.P. 1991. *Customs in Common*. New York: New Press.

Ventsel, A. 2005. *Reindeer, Rodina and Reciprocity; Property Relations in a Siberian Village*. Münster: LIT.

Vidacs, B. 2005. 'An Anthropological Education: a Comparative Perspective', in C. Hann, M. Sárkány and P. Skalnik (eds), *Socialist Era Anthropology in East-Central Europe*. Münster: LIT, pp. 331–42.

CHAPTER 10

Historical Analogies and the Commune: The Case of Putin/Stolypin

Caroline Humphrey

The theme of 'enduring socialism' asks us to consider the equivocal relation of socialist thought to the past. This chapter will address the representational practices through which continuities and transformations of rural Russia are being conceived. I suggest that there are strains of socialist thought abroad in Russia that take their inspiration from pre revolutionary Russian social forms. And I shall argue that an important rhetorical nexus in which we can discover this undertow of inveterate socialism is historical analogy. In fact, as a popular way of thinking about history, analogy has swamped and taken over from conventional Marxism – to the extent that the main political leaders often use it as a form of legitimation of their policies. Historical analogies are used by people across the political spectrum, on both the 'right' and the 'left', and this means that representations of the past have become arenas of fierce debate. To put this another way, people are now seeking to comprehend their present circumstances by looking for precedents in another, seemingly understandable, time – a displacement in which the present is taken to be somehow 'the same as' some feature in history.

These arguments about history are taking place in a situation of extraordinary uncertainty, for the transformation of agriculture that was expected with the end of the Soviet Union has not taken place. Despite the efforts of the Yeltsin and Putin governments, collective forms of farming have not been replaced to any significant degree by capitalist-type small farms. In 2003 individual farms had declined in number from the mid-1990s, holding only around 5 per cent of the land and producing 2.5 per cent of agricultural output (Lindner 2004: 18 quoting state statistics). Rural life is dominated by large collective enterprises. Many of them even retain the old status of collective farm (*kolkhoz*) or state farm (*sovkhoz*), while around 47 per cent have become closed shareholding firms owned by the members of the former collective.[1] In practice, these collective enterprises are enormously varied, ranging from large market-oriented firms dominated by one or a few powerful shareholders to more egalitarian farms with collective decision making. In all of them a number of the villagers are somehow left out of the membership, and in vast swathes of depressed regions the collectives have become little more than carapaces to support the mostly elderly villagers left eking a living from the tiny 'subsidiary plots' they had held from Soviet times (Fadeeva 2002: 165; Humphrey 2002: 160). What had been expected – that reformed collectives would be productive, would pay workers regularly for their labour or that they would continue to support the community by providing kindergartens, culture clubs, and so forth – often does not happen. In fact, almost everywhere the familiar rural community has become unfamiliar, even to its own members, as its inner workings and character changed. Yet for people working in agriculture the private individual farm is too risky, isolated and underfinanced to provide a solution – and while in the 1990s it was seen a 'threat' (Van Atta 1993) to communal resources, now it is more like an irrelevance. For the reformist policy makers the widespread resistance to private farming was a surprise and disappointment. Yet they have not given up the attempt to find new, more productive and market-oriented forms. Thus at many different sites in society it has been a puzzle how to conceptualize (or what even to call) the emergent hybrid types of farm. In these circumstances there is a general casting around for models to make sense of the unfamiliar, and from a variety of different stances people have recourse to the repertoire of what they 'know' – stereotypes and images from the past.

Within the torrent of opinions there are strains that we might call socialist. Rather strangely perhaps, given the modernizing, statist and industrial emphasis of Soviet socialism, the new forms of socialism often harken back insistently to the pre revolutionary village commune. They do not, however, make up an ideology in the sense of a structured intellectual system. Rather, the 'conservative' Marxist class-struggle theoreticians are in combat not only with one another (Macey 1993) but also with the interactive and ongoing activity of probing, wondering and trying out ideas for their fit with actual circumstances. So I am not arguing that that Russian socialists today are 'transmitters' of a system that has coherence separate from political contingencies or their own idiosyncratic interpretations, still less that there is some path-dependent scheme of 'socialism' that has survived through history from the commune to the present day (for discussion see Lindner and Nikulin 2004: 32–33). The present collectives are not necessarily the locus of socialism. Rather, in various sites throughout society we find people who for one reason or another are attached to the values of social equality, 'honest labour' and corporate mutual support. These values may, or may not, be linked with admiration for a strong state or nationalism. Russian socialists therefore do not form a coherent social movement and are not confined to a political party. As this chapter will suggest, they can be seen as forming two types, however: those publicists, journalists, academics, etc. who advocate socialism (for society as a whole) and those ordinary people who simply think they are themselves living socialism. I attempt here to sketch a broad sweep, providing examples of how people are imagining socialism, from politicians to the farmers themselves. What exists across the board is a repertoire of images of the past imbibed through the universal education system, as well as films, novels, the media, and so forth, and this provides 'counters' to think with and argue about. Mostly such images enable people to come up with what we might call an interpretative framework, but sometimes, as this chapter will attempt to show, they have the force of reality-shaping discourse-as-action. I shall suggest later that in the former case we have to do with analogy, while sometimes in the latter a more 'substantive' identity with the past is imagined, one that we could call homology.

Why is the peasant commune, the *obshchina* or *mir*, evoked today in capitalist Russia? What the commune stands for has been a matter of dispute ever since the mid-nineteenth century. It was always seen as quintessentially 'Russian', as opposed to 'European', but the issue was whether it was to be understood as a backward brake on progress or a cornerstone of the future society (Kelly 2002: 499). For many early socialists, who turned their eyes firmly away from its reality, the commune represented a glowing utopian vision of egalitarian society. The crucial thing about the commune is that it stood against private property in agricultural land. It allocated strips of land to each household on an egalitarian basis, for example according to the number of male workers in the family, and the land would be returnable when the number changed. Periodically, all the village plots were reallocated, to make equal access to good land fairer. The communal aspect of this way of life was underpinned by the institution of *krugovaya poruka* (literally 'circular helping hand'), whereby the commune as a whole was responsible for the taxes, debts, crimes and misfortunes of each single household. This meant that in principle the dues of weak households were paid for by the wealthier and more efficient. And it was the village as a self-governing whole, not individuals, that confronted the exigencies of heavy state taxation on the one hand, and the ever present spectre of famine on the other. I will discuss later exactly which situations in contemporary life are held up as 'like' this ideal of grass-roots socialism, but first let me sketch how the contemporary socialist argument goes.

First, 'socialism' has been detached from its earlier prescriptive identity with the Soviet system. Socialist-inclined journalists and publicists, whose interests lie in appealing to supposedly popular values, now propose that the Soviet structure distorted and mangled the ur-socialist wellspring of the commune, partly because of its reliance on the mistaken Marxist theory of class struggle, partly because of its 'foreign' atheism, and further, because it gave way in its later stages to acquisitive, incipiently 'capitalist' urges. The pure and self-denying communal way of life, in this discourse, only just survived the USSR and now is again virtually overwhelmed (but not quite) by the new capitalism. What we should note about these arguments is that 'socialism' ceases to be a theory about humanity in general but is identified with the specifically Russian institution of the peasant commune. Forget the Marxist proposition that peasant agriculture is a universal precapitalist stage found all across Europe and elsewhere and destined to be dissolved away through class war. Instead, reconceptualize the village commune as an original, noncapitalist, morally superior and enduring form of existence, indeed the foundation of a whole distinctive Russian civilization (Kara-Murza 2002: 8).

Now, theoretical definitions of socialism, as a historical stage and a type of political economy, are neither here nor there as far as these journalists are concerned. Rather, what interests them is analogies between historical personalities, who have come to stand for whole political economic processes. This is what gives the edge to the Putin–Stolypin analogy I shall discuss in this chapter.

Petr Stolypin was both the Prime Minister of the last Tsarist government and the head of the secret police. He was renowned as a strong, authoritarian advocate of the modernization of Imperial Russian government and agriculture along Western European lines. What historical analogy does is to draw a parallel between Stolypin's attempt to get more independent-minded peasants to leave their communes and set up as private farmers and Yeltsin's and Putin's policies of disbanding collective farms and promoting '*fermery*' today. Stolypin, in a famous phrase, said that Russia must now 'place a wager on the strong'. In brief, since both Stolypin and Putin attempted to impose private individual ownership of agricultural land, what they both represent is *the destruction of the commune*. And what is at issue is whether this is to be seen as an entirely beneficent and long overdue reform of Russia's 'backward' social organization, or (as the socialists claim) as a malign, deeply mistaken, annihilation of all that is best and most distinctive in Russia's contribution to the world.

Historical analogy has become an extraordinarily popular pastime in Russia and President Putin has been likened by his friends or enemies to other figures, such as Peter the Great and Stalin. We know that Putin himself cast around for a suitable historical precedent for his presidential role from an anecdote recounted by Simon Sebag Montefiore. In the early 1990s Sebag Montefiore was writing a biography of the great eighteenth-century general Potemkin, the lover of Catherine the Great who conquered and ruled huge tracts of the Empire and attained the title 'Serenissimus'. 'During the first months of Vladimir Putin's presidency,' Sebag Montefiore writes, 'I was secretly approached by a top Kremlin official who met me in a London hotel and told me that a most elevated personage, who could not be named, was casting about for historical models for the Russian state and wondered if I thought Potemkin, with his mixture of humanitarianism and authoritarianism, might be a useful basis for a 21st century Russian president. He asked me to write a memorandum on the subject, which I did. I heard nothing further' (Sebag Montefiore 2005: 33). Presumably the memorandum was unconvincing. In the event it is the analogy with Stolypin that has come to the fore. Numerous books, articles, web pages, as well as conversations among ordinary citizens, have alluded to the theme. Putin himself has frequently referred to Stolypin's ideas in his public speeches.

Historical analogy carries great possibilities for irony, of course. It can be 'taken too far', so the rhetorical effect may bizarrely undercut a literal reading. No more so than in the Stolypin-Putin case, we should note, for Stolypin managed to make an enemy of practically everyone, survived several assassination attempts, and indeed was in the end murdered in 1911.

Most of the current debate, however, is devoid of irony. As far as the general public goes, the main grounds for the likeness are that both men were strong proponents of centralized state power, both were in charge of the secret police, and both pushed through, against fierce opposition, a series of reforms introducing private property in agricultural land in Russia. The goal in both cases was to transform Russian agriculture into a modern market-oriented European type made up of enterprising farmers, loyal to the state, and who would supply products to the cities. These parallels are so striking that a number of serious historical studies have attempted to analyze their import (Macey 1993; Pallot 1999; Lohr 2000; Danilov 2002; Skyner 2001, 2003; Klimin 2002). This paper is concerned, however, with a different issue: the way that historical analogies are used in contemporary public debate about essential values. The stakes are high. The 'socialists', the defenders of collective farming and the commune ideal, are pitted against the entire 'reformist' trend of postsocialist policy, against, that is, the admirers of Stolypin/Putin.[2]

One set of arguments concerns whether Stolypin's reforms in fact worked or not – it being rather difficult to judge, as they were cut short by the First World War and the Revolution. Some present-day polemicists

argue that Stolypin's reforms were successful and constituted the best
hope for a modernized and Europeanized Russia (Fedorov 2002). Another
popular version sees Stolypin as the proponent of a 'third' Russian way,
providing a patriotic and 'Great State' alternative to Western free-market
capitalism and Soviet-style communism. Others insist that his reforms
were bound to fail because they contradicted the deeply rooted peasant
culture of the Russian people – indeed, Stolypin's heavy-handed
measures incited peasant anger and were a prime cause of the Bolshevik
revolution (Kara-Murza 2002). Another series of passionately held
disagreements is over the moral import of the reforms. Stolypin's own
concern with increased productivity is not the issue here. What matters is
whether private property in land is morally right or not and whether a
just society could ever be created on that basis.

Private property in agricultural land has never been 'naturalized' in
Russia as the bedrock or default position. Indeed, one could argue that
Russia has never really had such private property, since even the nobles'
estates could be confiscated by the Tsar. In the Soviet Union land relations
were founded on the legal prohibition of private property. The state in the
name of the people was the sole formal owner of land until the passage of
the RSFSR law of November 1990 'On land reform' (Skyner 2003: 891–92).
Even after this law, as in Stolypin's time, private property still has to be
explicitly legislated for. And in Russia the existence of legislation does not
mean that people on the ground are able to use it. Even today, local political
permission has to be given for any particular parcel of land to be extracted
from a collective type of ownership. The debate over private land thus
engages historians, sociologists and journalists, but the protagonists take
part too – the politicians, administrators and famers who have to take
decisions one way or another. Not only have Putin's presidential decrees
been held back by foot-dragging in the Duma, but regional administrators
usually give decisions in favour of public/collective as opposed to
individual ownership (Skyner 2001). For the deep assumption lurking in
the background is that landed private property is the cornerstone of
capitalism, and with this the debate is instantaneously rendered in black
and white terms. Capitalism, it is widely assumed, is the deathly enemy of
a socialist way of life.

I hope I have said enough in this introductory sketch to indicate
something of what is at stake in the Putin–Stolypin parallel. But before
moving on to discuss its ethnographic actuality in present-day Russia, let
me examine in more detail the kinds of reasoning involved in making
such historical analogies. It has to be admitted that no precise terminology
exists for defining different kinds of sameness across time. There is a
range of possible types of relation, which may be described as follows.
Historical analogy proper is perhaps the weakest of these links, for it
states only that X today is in some respects like Y in the past. A second

kind of historical relation, proposing not just likeness but a connection of an actively productive kind, is the idea of the historical exemplar (for example, the notion that a current leader like Putin would be inspired to take some decision by the example of Peter the Great). Historical homologies are stronger than either of these, in that they claim X today is structurally the same as, or descends from, Y in the past.[3] Thus we frequently find reification in the language of these debates, the notion of continuous ongoing identity. One form of this is when a current social phenomenon is given a 'displaced' backward existence, as though it were actually present in the past. For instance, Petr Stolypin, who died in 1911, is said to have 'fought all his life against the communists' (Fedorov 2002: 1), when 'the communists' as a party and even as a single political category did not exist in his lifetime. Forward displacements are even more commonly used. Contemporary successful farmers may be attacked as 'kulaks', for example, as if they 'are' in some sense the richer peasants of the early twentieth century. Note that in the disunited and verbally promiscuous ambience of post-communist discourse, the word *kulak* could imply either a noxious insult or even be considered a compliment. Finally, in what is probably an incomplete list, writers sometimes refer to fateful historical parallels, the linking of destinies. An example of this is the 'mystical connection' that Fedorov finds between the fates of Stolypin and the Emperor Alexander II. Both were great reformers and both were assassinated; indeed Stolypin was killed on the occasion of a festive commemoration of Alexander's freeing of the peasants from serfdom fifty years before (Fedorov 2002: 7).

Such time-annihilating ways of thinking about history are incompatible with Soviet Marxism. It is not that Soviet historians did not tie together events and processes from disparate times and places. But this was done in order to argue that diverse phenomena were examples of one and the same unrepeatable historical category or evolutionary stage. What could not be argued by Soviet historians was that the present, in the country that was building socialism, was objectively 'the same as', or even simply 'like', a past social formation. The idea of the revolutionary break was essential.

Stalin, in his conversation with H.G. Wells, put the official position bluntly. Wells had been trying to persuade Stalin that Roosevelt's New Deal amounted to adopting the principle of planned economy. State control of banks and regulation of industry and so forth would bring about a better, more equal and more scientific, organization of society. 'In my opinion,' said Wells, 'they are socialist ideas.' He even boldly hinted at a likeness between Stalin and Roosevelt. 'You and Roosevelt begin from two different starting points. But is there not a relation in ideas, a kinship of ideas and needs, between Washington and Moscow?' But this was completely impossible for Stalin to stomach. He responded heavily that

American capitalism might not have quite disappeared, but it belonged to a different historical category from socialism. 'Subjectively perhaps, these Americans think they are reorganizing society; objectively, however, they are preserving the present basis of [capitalist] society.' It was not possible, he said, to realize the principles of planned economy while preserving the economic basis of capitalism – an economic system that must inevitably lead to anarchy in production and eventually collapse (A Conversation, 1934: 601).

Now this conversation was held in 1934 and it is well known that later, after the 1937–38 purges and during the Second World War, an analogy was drawn between Stalin and Ivan the Terrible – an analogy whose force Stalin himself realized. I would argue, however, that his tacit acknowledgement of such an analogy was a reaction to popular ways of thinking about history, and that it was always at odds with orthodox Marxism. What is significant is that analogies between personalities concede to the fascination with individual motivation in a way that the class struggle or stages of development cannot. So Stalin intervened in the editing of Eisenstein's film about Ivan the Terrible, for example, in order to portray the monarch not as a crazed tyrant but as a determined victor, in order to demonstrate that Ivan's defeat of foreign foes justified his ruthless treatment of his 'internal enemies'. Scenes depicting Ivan's agonized repenting for his cruelty were cut on Stalin's orders, as he thought they indicated the Tsar's weakness (Perrie 2001: 87). Clearly, Stalin recognized the force of the popular tendency to see history in terms of personalities and allegories. But the Marxist type of explanation of Ivan of the professional historians, in terms of abstract class struggle, was never entirely abandoned during the war. It is documented that Stalin himself never inclined to the personalized kind of history (Van Ree 1997: 23; Perrie 2001: 196). What he was doing was manipulating the swirling forces of a kind of popular history that he himself never espoused. It was as a political leader in need of broad support that Stalin – like Putin after him – stepped into the analogy game.

In seeing that the analogy between Ivan and Stalin essentially came from below –if only from certain historians who were anxious to curry favour and from the Soviet propaganda institutions casting about for means to enthuse the public for war –we can understand that historical analogies have an existence in society broadly considered. My second point, therefore, is to reiterate that historical analogy is rarely a tidy matter, a simple legitimation of a leader's current position by reference to a positive image from the past. As Kevin Platt has argued (2004: 134–35), all such analogies have to deal with what he calls 'historical inertia', the process of re-interpreting heroes that accumulates layer on layer of meanings. In the case of Ivan the Terrible the Soviet public had long been accustomed to the crazed mediaeval despot interpretation. So strong was this image that when making cuts to Eisenstein's film was being debated in Stalin's presence, no one dared say the film was a direct reference to Great Leader. 'What's the problem?' Eisenstein impudently asked. And a memoir of the occasion recalls, 'But in Eisenstein's boldness, in the gleam in his eyes, in his defiant sceptical smile, we felt that he was acting consciously, that he had decided to go for broke. This was awful' (quoted in Perrie 2001: 177). The dangers of the presence of a many-layered popular consciousness – which the film could quite possibly evoke – were ever present. Platt has rightly pointed out that for historical analogies to work as intended, previously popular histories have to be 'forgotten' or eliminated (2004: 142).

So, to return to the case of Putin and Stolypin, the present positive view of Stolypin as an enlightened reformer, the one that is taught in post-Soviet schools, has to be understood in the light of the previous Soviet image, which was highly negative. For decades Stolypin was interpreted as the pitiless agent of late Tsarist repression, who put down justified peasant revolts with force and shipped recalcitrant offenders off to Siberia in the famous railway trucks that are still today known as 'Stolypin's cars'. Such images have not in fact been 'forgotten', so among the general public, as distinct from the battling ideologues, irony in the analogy with Putin cannot at all be ruled out. And the circumstances of Stolypin's assassination offer yet further ironic possibilities. The murder has long had an existence in historical popularizations as a 'mystery' (Fedorov 2002, vol. 2: 7–41). For Stolypin was shot by a member of his own security guard, a man called Bogrov, who furthermore was a double agent. Bogrov was Jewish and was a member of a revolutionary group, which he apparently betrayed to the secret police. At the same time, as an agent of the security force he could have been induced to kill Stolypin, according to rumours, by the Tsar himself, who is known to have resented his Prime Minister's power. This tangle provoked endless speculation about the 'mystery' of what Bogrov's motivation really was. The explanation in fact seems relatively straightforward, as can be seen from Zenkovsky's positive biography of Stolypin (which could not be published in Russia during Soviet times). During his interrogation before his execution, Bogrov was asked whether he had not planned to kill the Tsar. He denied this, saying that he had been afraid, being a Jew, that assassinating the holy sovereign would give rise to a pogrom. His motive for killing Stolypin was to vindicate himself before the revolutionary comrades he had betrayed. Bogrov explained his reasoning: Stolypin was the state leader whose reforms, by improving conditions for the peasants and workers, would alienate their sympathies from the revolutionaries and thus prevent them from seizing power (Zenkovsky 1986: 97–98). Now my reason for mentioning all this is that the whole personalized tangle (the rigid Stolypin, the jealous Tsar, the corrupt secret police, the double-dealing revolutionary) is reminiscent of the environment of secret police 'provocations' that also surround Putin (Kara-Murza 2002: 202–7). It is another layer of meaning hovering around the historical analogy – one, like the assassination itself, of course, that the present Russian executive would have to eliminate from public consciousness if the analogy is to work in a positive way for the leader. And perhaps it is because this has not happened that the Stolypin–Putin analogy has died away in the last few years.

For anthropologists, it is the unruly presence of popular fascinations with 'mysteries', and the whole heterogeneous variety of layered assumptions about the values that political leaders stand for, that is interesting. Historians ignore the social life of such phenomena when they write about analogies in terms of a linear history of thought. And attempts seriously to compare situations that are structurally similar but separated in time likewise have a different goal from mine, for in that case the analogy is drawn by the historian not the living subjects. From an anthropological point of view what is interesting are the questions of from whom these analogies and homologies emerge and why, and to find out what purchase they have among the people who are supposedly their subject, in this case, the farming people of Russia.

So let me return now to the subject of socialism and the commune. Whether we see Stolypin's reforms as successful or not, they did not last very long and were overtaken by the Revolution. After 1917, peasants went back into communes, which came to completely dominate the rural scene, holding around 90 per cent of agricultural land by 1930, after which they were replaced by collective and state farms. I am not now going to analyze the communes themselves, but want to draw out the aspects that are extolled by the socialists who try to influence opinion today. The commune, they say, is something that arose from the nature of Russian agriculture itself, its habits of work, and above all its fragility. Russian peasants were desperately poor – hunger was a reality. In the face of poverty and heavy taxation, the peasants' mutual support for one another, along with levelling institutions, were not just cultural traditions, they were objectively necessary. Polemicists writing about this today leave it to be understood by readers that poverty is again a reality in Russia (see Visser 2003). And furthermore, village institutions arose from a particular sensibility, it is pointed out, a cosmological closeness between the peasant and the land, a sacral attitude to working the soil enshrined in the phrase 'to plough is to pray' (Kara-Murza 2002: 219). Finally, the commune is the source of social solidarity, rooted in joint activity. People outside Russia sometimes think that collective production was imposed from on top by the Soviet system but in fact Russian peasants always had performed certain crucial farming tasks together as a body.

As for the politics of the commune, an early English observer described peasants as speaking their minds openly, with only women relegated to the sidelines, and he called this 'thoroughly democratic' (Wallace 1877: 193). But for present-day Russian socialists the word 'democracy' has only the negative connotations of the capitalist West, and they choose to emphasize something rather different – the 'freedom' (*svoboda*) of the peasant to say what he thinks openly, secure in his little world, in fear of no-one (Kara-Murza 2002: 102). The jewel of Russian civilization has two forms: firstly, the long-suffering patience of the peasant, who sees the landlord as a spoilt child, and secondly, his pride and decisiveness at the moment when it becomes clear that something must be done. This responsibility for everyone, including even the sinful landlord, is the peasant's virtue (ibid. 2002: 244). What all this leads up to is a moral for today. Kara-Murza is trying to persuade people to see the world differently, and he provides a little parable of 'peasant freedom' when he describes its present incarnation in the raggle-taggle of hired workers on his own dacha, their natural gestures, their laughter, their way of bearing themselves as though restraint was an unknown concept (Kara-Murza 2001: 249).

Those who are trying to persuade the public of the benefits of agrarian reform paint a completely different picture. These people, again a mixture of journalists and polemicists, follow all those commentators from Chekhov, Bunin and Gorky onwards (Figes 1996: 88) who portrayed the commune as a sink of apathy, drunkenness and hard brutality. It was not a haven of harmony, but a place of quarrels and manipulation by the richer patriarchs. It turned people into spongers, sentimentalists and sadists (Globachev 2005). Carried forward to today the same features are seen in the doddering and corrupt collective farms. In the reformists' view, there can be no freedom here. In the old peasant commune it was impossible to leave and set up a private farm, even under Stolypin's reform, without the agreement of a majority of the assembly,[4] just as today one cannot leave the collective farm without unanimous agreement of all the members.[5] Such permission is only given to a tiny number of people, those with external political clout. Meanwhile, the little personal allotments of remaining members depend crucially on inputs from the collective. As a result, the remaining peasants cling to the collectives and now only 6 per cent of them even want to leave. Their enslavement (*zakabalen'ye*) is complete (Manzanova 2004: 9).

In these diametrically opposed epithets – the socialist vision of 'freedom' and the reformist one of 'enslavement' – we have to do, it seems to me, not with analogies but with homologies. The noble bodily stance of the hired man *is* the freedom of the timeless Russian peasant; the depressed inertia of today's collective farmer descends from, somehow is 'the same thing as', the enslaved condition that Stolypin tried to change.[6]

Something similar has happened with the idea of *krugovaya poruka*, the system of collective responsibility that Geoffrey Hosking sees as 'the basic concept' underlying the village commune (2004: 51). In 1903 krugovaya poruka was legally abolished, as it was no longer effective in gathering taxes – peasants were using it as a shield, whereby they all allowed one another to fall into tax debt to the extent that the total could never be recovered. Although legally ended, the practice did not disappear, however. During Soviet times, krugovaya poruka morphed into a negative concept, denoting the cosy and corrupt circles of self-protection that were established to manipulate and bypass official rules (Ledenova 2004: 97–104). Thus in the present day, citizens usually locate krugovaya poruka in the Mafia world.

However, krugovaya poruka is not just an image borrowed from peasant history, it can also be a consciously applied model for current practice. An example is the organization of a large urban working-class family, the Semenovs, described in a newspaper article. The mother had won a 'Mother Heroine' medal and the purpose of the article was to hold her up as an exemplar to other struggling women with the maxim 'the disintegration of the family – is the disintegration of the state'. The mother, Aleksandra Dmitrievna, was asked how she had managed to bring up ten children while both she and her husband were working. 'I taught the children to survive,' she replied. 'I gave them rules like don't go to school before the floors have been cleaned and the beds made. They had *krugovaya poruka*. Serezha answered for Natasha, Natasha for Alyosha, Alyosha for Kolya, Kolya for Larisa, Larisa for Shurik, Shurik for Tanya, Tanya for Slava, and Slava for Katya. Lena was the youngest, and I answered for her myself.' 'What did that mean, the children "answered for one another"?' asked the journalist. Aleksandra Dmitrievna replied, 'Well, if Natasha got a bad mark at school I punished Serezha … and so on. After that Serezha wouldn't allow her to go out playing instead of doing her homework. This *krugovaya poruka* was good for them, it was their shield!' (Gorokhova 2005).

If these cases can be seen as historical homologies, the use of analogies is far more widespread. One has to ask – why are people likening what is happening today with *the past*? An answer could be that the past furnishes a series of models that have implications in time. Since they belong to the past something is known of their tendency – in brief, of what happened next. This may provide a tool for the imagination of those people today who are bewildered about what kind of social institution they are experiencing and where it is going. There are many examples from contemporary rural life, but let me cite just one.

In 1999–2000, the sociologist Aleksandr Nikulin carried out some fieldwork in the Kuban, one of the richest regions of Russia. Here, though many collectives were in debt, some of them had evolved into what Nikulin calls by the English word 'holdings'. The former chairman of a collective farm had managed to acquire the majority of the members' shares and now ran the place like his personal fiefdom. Most of the members were now effectively his hired workers. Nevertheless, the chairman, Kravchenko, held back from taking all of the shares, as he knew what resentment this would cause. Kravchenko, as one of the rare success stories in Russian agriculture, had gone abroad on delegations and tried to introduce Western technologies into his farm. One day he asked Nikulin, 'Well, it's true isn't it, here in my place, it's like in the West?' Nikulin replied that, well, the Kuban wasn't quite like the West and that Kravchenko's rule reminded him more of the Tsarist enterprising landowner (*pomeshchik-samorodka*), who was introducing original technologies. The one thing that is valued in the West, the freedom of the independent producer, was absent on his farm. And Nikulin then told the chairman about Lenin's book depicting two types of development of capitalism in agriculture – the Prussian and the American. If the American type was based on independent farmers in a democratic society, the Prussian involved large landowners maintaining top-down control over rural communities in a conservative society. 'You,' Nikulin said, 'seem to be taking the Prussian path.' At this, the chairman was silent, thought for a bit, and changed the subject. Soon it was the month of July, the month of the traditional harvest festival. The members of the farm, which was called 'Rule' ('*Upravleniye*'), by the way, gathered in a remote gully and, headed by Kravchenko, drank to their harvest of 50 tsentners per hectare. The feast was in full swing, when the chairman suddenly turned to his workers and made a speech. 'O! Have you all heard about the latest discoveries in agrarian sociology? Do you know that there are two paths of development in agriculture? Well the American one goes with democracy, freedom, and independent farmers. But what's the good of that for you? You don't need freedom! Yeltsyn gave you freedom, I gave you freedom, but you don't take it! So you won't have the American way, it'll be the Prussian way here. And do you know what the Prussian way is? Ha! Again, you have no idea. Well, it is very simple. I will be your *pomeshchik* [Tsarist landowner] and you will be my *khlopy* [working lads].' Apparently, this tirade was received with polite, understanding smiles, without comment (Nikulin 2002: 366).

Here we can perhaps see the chairman genuinely struggling to understand the nature of the enterprise he himself is creating. The analogy with Lenin's historical types and the archaic language is not so much a self-justification as a means of conceptual clarification for 'agrarian capitalists' in a genuinely new economic-political situation. This can be compared with people who see themselves as living socialism, where we find the stronger form of the manifested homology, along the lines of the Semenov family's krugovaya poruka. There are people who say they are 'creating communism' in Russia today. What can they possibly mean by this? One such example is a private farmer who separated from his state farm in 1991 and now runs a successful business with thirty-five cows, thirty or so pigs and 35 hectares of arable land. He has eight full-time workers on the farm, all of them relatives. This is what the farmer said:

> The people round here have no work, and so there's terrible thieving. They sell the wood from the forest and take any light metal they can find. But that will be used up soon. And they also thieve from the fields. It's not too bad for me because I have a lot of land, but it's a real blow to people with only a small plot. There is only one road to my farm. We don't keep any security except the dogs. We don't have guns. Here we have communism. Yes, we are building communism. We six-seven men, we are not afraid of anything. The main thing is, we don't depend on the government nor on the surrounding people (Klyamkin and Timofeev 2000: 337–38).

Another example is provided by the director of a state-owned chicken farm in Novgorod Oblast. His farm is much reduced in size and now has only 160 workers. This is what he said:

> I sacked practically no-one. Just a few left quietly by themselves. I gave jobs to all my chicken workers, you see we worked together for many years, some of them had only a couple of years to go before their pensions, so how could I sack them? [...] Among us in the *kollektiv* relations are fine. It's an old *kollektiv*, there are not many changes among the people. They work here permanently, right up to their pension and even beyond. All the specialists prepare successors for when they leave. The people have not changed in our enterprise. We work in a communist regime. (Klyamkin and Timofeev 2000: 350–51)

What 'communism' seems to mean in these examples is certainly not a matter of the whole political-economy, nor even does it depend on a particular legal form of ownership (since the first example is a 'private' farmer and the second the inheritor of a state collective). Rather, 'communism' is a way of being – enclosed, self-reliant, independent of the state, and mutually supporting. Not so different from the ideal peasant commune, in fact.

Conclusion

Western writers on a Putin/Stolypin theme often adopt a monitory tone. Putin should 'learn the lessons' of Stolypin in order to adapt his policies to Russian realities (Lohr 2000). Such an omniscient attitude to historical analogies is only rarely taken in Russia. There, rather, one seems to find a widespread noncognizance of our own time, a difficulty in giving it its own contemporary name. The historical analogy in such circumstances is more like an act of recognition, of an institution of personality in the past. It is the pursuit – through such recognition – of identity and it thus becomes an imaginative trying-out of models – possibly to be rapidly discarded when the ironic or parodic layers of meaning implied by the analogy come to the surface.

This is perhaps the point where I should differentiate what I am arguing from Nietzsche and Foucault's strictures about historical analogy. In discussing how genealogy (history) should be done, Foucault wrote that the historian offers the confused and anonymous European, who no longer knows himself or what name he should adopt, the possibility of alternative identities, more individualized and real than his own. 'But the man with historical sense,' he continues, 'will see that this substitution is simply a disguise.' Such identities are 'ephemeral props, whose unreality points to our own. The good historian will know what to make of this masquerade. He will not be too serious to enjoy it; on the contrary he will push the masquerade to its limit and prepare the great carnival of time where masks are constantly re-appearing. No longer the identification of our faint individuality with the solid realities of the past, but our 'unrealization' through the excessive choice of identities.' But making up these masks, creating a kind of history 'totally devoted to veneration', bars access, Foucault writes following Nietzsche, to the actual intensities and creations of life (Foucault 1998: 385–86). This tirade has some validity if we see historical analogy as a practice of historians. But I have tried to show in this paper that creating and performing analogies has a life in society and in particular historical situations. In this case, the historical analogy has to be rethought, not as a 'masquerade', but as a situated practice of recognition, bearing with it the undertow of previous meanings, and thus containing within itself its own possibilities of irony and parody.

In present-day Russia there are two kinds of actors who use analogies most actively: the polemicists, who are trying to push a particular policy or set of values (analogy suggested for others), and the ordinary people trying to conceptualize their worlds (analogy created for oneself). Both have to eliminate irony for their images to 'work'. But it is another matter with the general public observing the heated debates through the media. Here there is nothing to prevent detached amusement and the resurrection of incongruities.

In this regard, it is relevant that censorship (or self-censorship) is increasingly present in Russia. Since his advent to power in 2000 Putin has progressively blotted out dissenting voices in the media, and one effect of this – my Russian friends tell me – is that there is now a general silence about Putin himself. Thus books and articles about Stolypin may or may not contain a section called something like 'contemporary agriculture in the light of Stolypin's reforms', but they increasingly decline to mention Putin by name. Whatever metaphors and analogies remain in the public arena tend to be safe ones, such as playful fantasies where 'our President' is likened to the hero of a folk story set in 'traditional' times. In one such picture book, *Skazki pro Nashego Prezidenta* (Fairy Stories about Our President),[7] an ordinary lad, who is a great athlete, likes skiing and loves nature, and who looks just like Putin, comes to be president through the advice given to him by a magical bird whom he had befriended. Politics and current issues are studiously avoided. The president pays a visit to the English Queen in Buckingham Palace, and the story revolves around whether he can prove himself a 'real gentleman' by arriving on time despite being set upon by London bandits and criminals. Needless to say, he magically defeats the bandits and arrives to the second, and the Queen has to admit that he is a gentleman.

This kind of analogy with the folk hero is interesting in itself, nevertheless. What the book does, even if it is 'not meant to be taken seriously', is to resurrect the whole patriarchal Tsarist idiom of government. Thus the president is called '*prezident-batyushka*' (president patriarch), he succeeds in outwitting 'cunning' bureaucrats and, above all, he rules by edict (*Ukaz*). For example, part of the delay in getting to his appointment with the Queen of England is caused by him issuing edicts that polar bears must not be hunted and boggy areas with frogs must be preserved for cranes to live on (2004: 47). The good president, with his beneficent edicts, has the whole cosmos of his realm in his thoughts, is the message. Why do I mention this? The adult reader is inevitably reminded that Putin does in fact rule by edict. In fact, the very laws that have legislated for private ownership of land are presidential edicts. What has been happening is that presidential decrees have been faced with consistent opposition from the parliament to attempts to introduce land reform (Skyner 2001: 984). There is a contradiction at the heart of Russian politics that is not resolved: thus in 2001 it was still possible for regional parliamentary delegates to argue that presidential decrees about land ownership should be suspended until a federal code is accepted (Skyner 2001: 989) and, as I have mentioned, even after the passing of a Federal Land Code, local practices still make it impossible for individuals to acquire absolute private land rights.

The spectre whose threat causes such widespread opposition derives from a lingering socialism – the 'enshrined historical fear', as Skyner puts it, that if the free sale of land is allowed, it will be bought up by wealthy urban and foreign interests, leaving the majority of the population landless and impoverished (2001: 994). The evidence suggests that despite the confusion in the law the situation on the ground does seem to be moving in this direction. There are a few successful large commercial farms, there are ramshackle collectives, and there are regions where dire subsistence poverty on tiny plots is all that remains. I have pointed to some features of how this situation is being conceptualized. Firstly, by the widespread popular use of historical analogies, that is, a backward focus rather than an attempt to coin a new vocabulary. And second, in contrast to Soviet argument in terms of 'classes' and reified categories like 'the state', here we observe a fascination with personalities. In the new Russia, it is the political personality that is subject to a process of objectivization and reification, such that it comes to stand for wider policies, economic processes and technologies of government. In turn, this reification sets in train habits of caution and self-censorship. Analogical thinking is patchy, temporary, taken up and cast aside, and it does not reach the status of a meta-narrative (see Lindner and Nikulin 2004: 32). But it is a currency of popular historical thinking that deserves attention (Platt 2004). Socialism appears somehow in the interstices of all this, not embodied in a particular representative personality, but manifest in stubborn practices. These could be described from the outside as referring to 'the past' and employing historical vocabularies, but from inside they seem to have another nature. I have called these practices homologies rather than analogies. One way to put this would be to say that Putin/Stolypin, or Stalin/Ivan the Terrible, constitute relations of metaphor or analogy, while the relation between the peasant commune and contemporary self-declared living communism is metonymical (that is, the two parts are attached and somehow part of one another). But actually I think that literary tropes give out here. With contemporary socialism in Russia we find a perspective that is not concerned with implementing progress towards an ideal in the future but rather with manifesting what is *felt* to be a timeless ever-presence. From the actor's point of view there is a socialism that is not in the future, nor in the past – it is here.

Notes

1. Only small numbers of other kinds of farm exist: open shareholding firms (1%), cooperatives (8%) and associations of private farmers (4%) (Lindner 2004: 19).
2. This is a generalization; for a more nuanced view of the various assessments of Stolypin among Russian historians, see Macey (1993).
3. Butler and Saidel (2000: 846–53) discuss the problems with the term 'homology' as used in psychology and biology and suggest that a new vocabulary is necessary. To distinguish similar structures that result from the same generative pathways from those that result from different origins, they suggest the terms 'syngeny' and 'allogeny' respectively.
4. The Stolypin Agrarian Reform, Ukaz of 9 November 1906. http://www.dur.uk/-dml0www/stolypin.html

5. This is in the statutes (*ustav*) of Buryat collective farms, 2002, a document which has a local rather than federal legal standing.
6. 'From the time of Stolypin's reforms, as the experience of agricultural reform in Russia has shown, after each breakthrough forwards to economic independence of the peasant and his liberation from the kolkhoz or commune, there necessarily follows a recoil backwards, as a result of which even greater administrative and economic dependency of the peasants always follow' (Manzanova 2004: 9). See also Globachev (2005).
7. Subtitled 'Stories written from the words of the people in various towns, villages, trains and airplanes being within Russian state boundaries', the book is, as it were, a collection of tales written down by various people and illustrated by a number of named children. However, the illustrations are all evidently by the same hand, and perhaps authorship of the book should be credited to the person mentioned as having come up with the idea, Yevgenii Myachin (*Skazki* 2004).

References

'A Conversation between Stalin and Wells'. 1934. *News Statesman and Nation,* 27 October: 601–5.

Danilov, V.P. 2005. 'Agrarnyye reformy I krast'yanstvo v Rossii (1861–9995 gg.)', priv-agr@fadr.msu.ru

Fadeeva, O. 2002. 'Sposoby adaptatsii sel'skikh semei k izmeneniyam ekonomicheckoi sredy,' in T. Shanin, A. Nikulin and V. Danilov (eds), *Refleksivnoe krest'yanovedenie Shanin,: desyatiletie issledovanii sel'sloi Rossii.* Moscow: MVShSEN ROSSPEN.

Fedorov, B.G. 2002. *Petr Stolypin: 'ya veryu v Rossiyu',* 2 vols. St.Petersburg: Limbus Press.

Figes, O. 1996. *A People's Tragedy: the Russian Revolution 1891–1924.* London: Jonathon Cape.

Focault, M. 1998. *The Essential Works of Foucault Vol II: Aesthetics, Method, Espitemology.* New York: The New Press.

Globachev, M. 2005. 'The Law of Negative Selection', *New Times,* January 2005 p. 3.

Gorokhova, T. 2005. 'Horosho, chto nas mnogo', *Argumenty I Fakty* (http://www.aif.ru), 20 December 2003.

Hosking, G. 2004. 'Forms of Social Solidarity in Russia and the Soviet Union', *Proc. Brit Ac.* 123: 47–62.

Humphrey, C. 2002. *The Unmaking of Soviet Life: Everyday Economies After Socialism.* Ithaca and London: University of Cornell Press.

Kara-Murza, S. 2001. *Sovetskaya Tsivilizatsiya.* 2 vols. Moscow: Algoritm.

Kara-Murza, S. 2002. *Stolypin: Otets Russkoi Revolyutsii.* Moscow: Algoritm.

Kelly, A. 2002. 'Historical Diffidence: a New Look at an Old Russian Debate', *Common Knowledge* 8(3): pp 496–515.

Klimin, I.I. 2003. *Stolypinskaya agraranaya reforma I stanovleniye kreas'yan-sobstvennikov v Rossii.* St. Petersburg: Tsentr Istoricheskikh I gumanitarnykh issledovanii 'Klio'.

Klyamkin, I. and L. Timofeev. 2000. *Tenevaya Rossiya: ekonomichesko-sotsiologicheskoye issledovaniye*. Moscow: Rossiickii Gosudarstevnnyi Gumanitarnyi Universitet.
Ledenova, A. 2004. 'The Genealogy of *krugovaya poruka*: Forced Trust as a Feature of Russian Political Culture', in *Proc. Brit Ac.* 123: 85–108.
Lindner, P. 2004. 'The Kolkhoz Archipelago: Localising Privatization, Disconnecting Locales', Unpublished Manuscript.
Lindner, P. and A. Nikulin. 2004. '"Everything around here belongs to the kolkhoz, everything around here belongs to me": Collectivism and Egalitarianism: a Red Thread Through Russian History?', *Europa Regional* 12(1): 32–41.
Lohr, E. 2000. 'Firm Ground for Putin's Reforms', *Russia Watch* 3(Oct–Nov): 10–11.
Macey, D.A.J. 1993. 'Stolypin Is Risen! The Ideology of Agrarian Reform in Contemporary Russia', in D. Van Atta (ed.), *The 'Farmer Threat': the Political Economy of Agrarian Reform in Post-Soviet Russia*. Boulder: Westview Press.
Manzanova, G.M. 2004. 'Traditsii I novatsii v agrarnom sektore Rossii v usloviykh insttitutsional'nykh reform (na primere natsional'nogo regiona)'. Unpublished manuscript.
Nikulin, A. 2002. 'Kubanskii kolkhoz mezh kholdingom i as'yendoi: paradoksy postsovetskoi modernizatsii yuzhnorusskogo sel'skogo soobshchestva', in T. Shanin, A. Nikulin and V. Danilov (eds), *Refleksivnoye krest'yanovedeniye: desyatiletiye issledovanii sel'skoi Rossii*. Moscow: MVShSEN and ROSSPEN, pp. 343–72.
Pallot, J. 1999. *Land Reform in Russia, 1906–1977*. Oxford: Oxford University Press.
Pierre, M. 2001. *The Cult of Ivan the Terrible in Stalin's Russia*. London: CREES/Palgrave.
Platt, K. 2004. 'History, Inertia, and the Unexpected: Re-cycling Russia's Despots', *Common Knowledge* 10(1): 130–50.
Shanin, T., A. Nikulin and V. Danilov (eds). 2002. *Refleksivnoe krest'yanovedenie,: desyatiletie issledovanii sel'koi Rossii*. Moscow: MVShSEN ROSSPEN.
Sebag Montefiore, S. 2005. 'An Affair to Remember', *New York Review of Books* 52(3) 24, February: 30–33.
Skazki pro nashego prezidenta. 2004. Moscow: Izdatel'stvo 'Russkaya Sem'ya.
Skyner, L. 2001. 'Political Conflict and Legal Uncertainty: the Privatization of Land Ownership in Russia', *Europe-Asia Studies* 53(7): 981–99.
———. 2003. 'Property as Rhetoric: Land Ownership and Private Law in Pre-Soviet and Post-Soviet Russia', *Europe-Asia Studies* 55(6): 889–905.
Van Ree, E. 1997. 'Stalin and Marxism: a Research Note', *Studies in East European Thought* 49(1): 23–33.
Visser, O. 2003. 'Property and Postsocialist Poverty', *Focaal – European Journal of Anthropology* 41: 197–201.
Wallace, D.M. 1877. *Russia*. London, Paris and New York: Cassell, Petter and Galpin.
Zenkovsky, A.V. 1986. *Stolypin: Russia's Last Great Reformer*, translated by Margaret Patoski. Princeton, NJ: The Kingston Press.

CHAPTER 11

Signifying Something: Che Guevara and Neoliberal Alienation in London

Parvathi Raman

Matilde Zimmermann has suggested that any discussion on Che Guevara is really a discussion on the Cuban revolution (Zimmermann 1999). But such discussions can also be seen as an ongoing debate on the nature of socialism in general at certain moments over the last fifty years. The things that Che and his image have come to represent, to both left and right, reveal wider thoughts on the current thinking, and representation, of socialism. Taken from this perspective, the man and his myth can be used as a starting point from which to explore aspects of the idea of socialism under the current orthodoxy of neoliberalism. What constitutes the socialist imagination in the present moment? Do older forms of socialist thinking merely 'endure', or have they been irrevocably transformed? Or has neoliberalism, in constituting a complex new nexus of international power, succeeded in reducing socialism to a 'relic of the past'? If so, is socialism's redundancy in part illustrated by the way that Che has been so ruthlessly commercialized, supposedly emptying him of content? Has socialism come to nothing, and Che come to 'signify nothing'?

This chapter is a part of a wider study that sets out to compare the 'Che phenomenon' amongst youth in London and Havana, tracing its history and contemporary significance. This is the first part of that journey, where I look at emergent forms of political subjectivity amongst young people in Britain, and explore aspects of their political imagination, whilst interrogating certain dominant left and right perspectives on contemporary politics. For example, Slavoj Žižek has argued that in the world today we live under a common condition of post-politics in an era of postsocialism. According to Žižek, we are, as never before, implicated in the programme of capitalist expansion. He argues that the discourse of capitalism increasingly promotes a certain kind of subjectivity that corresponds to a depoliticization of the economy, and an ethics of desire that relies on levels of collective fantasy in order to reinvent itself. Taken from this perspective, collective fantasy sets out to mask that it is we ourselves, not 'terrorists', who are the greatest threat to democracy, in our failure to challenge the political horizon. This has supposedly produced an ideological closure, an inability to think beyond the current political system, which is a result of both the collapse of the socialist states, and the fragmentation of a politics of opposition. According to Perry Anderson, 'three decades of nearly unbroken political defeats for every force that once fought against the established order [has meant, intellectually and imaginatively] a remorseless closure of space' (Anderson 2004: 71). Neoliberalism has apparently naturalized itself to such an extent that Fredrick Jameson has even suggested that 'people find it easier today to imagine the end of the world than the end of capitalism' (ibid. 74–75). Given this rather bleak landscape, where do older left tropes of liberation, utopia and authenticity lie?

Meanwhile, according to the right, neoliberal 'regimes of value' have triumphed and rendered socialism obsolete. The commercialization of Che is but one of the myriad illustrations of that fact, where, from his heady status as a militant revolutionary martyr, Che has been reduced to a fashionable 'pop icon' (see 'Che Chic' in *Newsweek*, 1997). The implication then, from both left and right is that any alternative to the current system is presently 'unthinkable'.

Moreover, some suggest that in Britain any discontent that prevails plays itself out passively. Distrust of the government and voter apathy is growing amongst a considerable percentage of the general populace, leading to a cynical detachment. But it is the 'youth of today' who are deemed to be the most cynical, disillusioned and distanced from politics. In the 2001 election in Britain, only just over 50 per cent of under-25-year-olds voted, dropping from around 60 per cent in 1997. Eighty per cent of youth claimed that they were uninterested in news on the general election, and at least 20 per cent were not even registered to vote. There is, apparently, an overwhelming indifference amongst them and a withdrawal from political participation (Fahmy 2003). Feelings of powerlessness and disenfranchisement are also supposedly widespread. In the run-up to the 2005 election, this was presented as a moment of crisis for liberal democratic governance in Britain. One indication of this was the decision of the *Sun* newspaper to start a campaign encouraging young people to vote, and there were also several television programmes, such as a question and answer session with British Prime Minister Tony Blair hosted by youth presenter June Sarpong on Channel Four, which were squarely aimed at the same constituency.

It is, of course, amongst the young that the image of Che primarily continues to flourish. But in the popular imagination the Che T-shirt-wearing youth has come to represent a set of rather negative messages: at worst the rule of 'cool', a triumph of commercialism, and the subsequent emptying of any inherent socialist message, rendered meaningless through its commodification; at best an immature romanticism, naïve to the true meaning of Che. They evidently barely know who he is, beyond an incoherent notion that he expresses a rebellious individualism.[1] The historian Robert Conquest once claimed that 'cults' like that of Che amongst the young are based on 'one of the unfortunate afflictions to which the human mind is prone ... adolescent revolutionary romanticism' (Conquest quoted in O'Hogan 2004). The student wearing a Che t-shirt has become one of the most common-place clichés of our time:

Thirty seven years after his execution in the Bolivian jungle, Che Guevara lives on, immortalised on more T-shirts than ever ... But the image is weirdly denuded of its associations: it is depoliticised and dehistoricised. Now Che is pure image, pure icon. Even Jimi Hendrix has more content (Bradshaw 2004).

It is an irony of cultural history that the politically apathetic youth of today appear to have chosen Ernesto 'Che' Guevara de la Serna as their cult hero. The anti-capitalist, Argentinean idealist (who died in 1967) would no doubt be horrified if he knew how much revenue his image earns T-shirt and poster companies today ... Guevara's image indicates nothing except the pure idea of cool itself (Richardson 2004).

The Che T-shirt can thus be read as evidence of the triumph of the market. Youth, combined with this particular image, articulates into a particular kind of politics that needn't be taken seriously; it represents a passing fad, an immature impulse that the young will grow out of, in some ways almost a necessary rite of passage resulting from the freedoms afforded by liberal democracy.

But *if* Che has been denuded of political significance in the West, he has also long provided a text for the construction of a new politics of being in Cuba, where children have been urged to 'be like Che' and his features adorn banknotes and hoardings across the land. More recently, Che has become 'the unofficial logo' for socialist Cuba (Margolin 1999: 84). Rather than this fading with the encroaching market in the Cuban economy, there has been a large increase in Che memorabilia, in part for the expanding tourist industry, but Che merchandise is also finding popularity amongst sections of Cuban youth. However, there seems to be an ongoing struggle over what Che means in the present moment. For some, Che's image still strives to represent socialist values. But he is also packaged in ways that symbolize Cuba's attempt to 'walk the thin line between maintaining the values and services of the revolution, and creating a market sector to attract foreign capital' (ibid.). And for young people, he appears to offer a critique of 'socialism gone wrong', where he represents the possibility of a 'truly' socialist society in opposition to the Cuban government's 'repressive regime' and current compromise with capital. In the West this 'political Che' is most often trivialized. Cuba is generally perceived to be on its last legs before it succumbs to the rationale of the neoliberal market, and Che's 'commodification' read as yet one more sign of this inevitability. He has also long provided an agenda for oppositional movements throughout South America and his image can be found daubed on walls from Palestine to South Africa. Whereas the politics of the South American left are portrayed as a relic of a bygone age, the pursuit of which has led to needless violence and death (Castenada 1997: 192), the Palestinian struggle has come to represent one of the faces of twentieth-century terrorism, a role that Che himself once filled.

As yet, little has been done to add to our understanding of what Che might mean in the West beyond 'empty signifier', and no serious work has yet been undertaken to explore why Che merchandise has emerged in Cuba amongst youth,[2] or indeed how 'Che texts' are themselves informed by the contexts within which they arise (McLaren 1999a: 303). Is the Che T-shirt wearing youth as politically vacuous as dominant narratives suggest? Here, I endeavour to disrupt the false dichotomy between a failed socialist past and a rational neoliberal present, where Che has become mere commodified ephemera. Instead, I look to the emergence of more complex articulations of political and cultural subjectivity that are grounded in context, but are also subject to transformation, through a continuing transnational dialogue of socialist ethics which sets out to challenge neoliberalism's 'delusions of grandeur'. These 'socialist ethics' have most often been revived in unintentional ways, where revolutionary intent has given rise to commercial possibility, and mass commodification, far from silencing the socialist message, has helped generate new meanings which critique neoliberal ambition. As Žižek also argues, the market feeds on desire, but the very nature of capitalism requires that this desire remains unfulfilled, thus fuelling our consumption. This need for the market to endlessly expand leaves space for the appearance of 'ironic' critiques of the system itself, giving rise to an articulation of political sentiments that go beyond socialist politics, expressing a disposition that challenges perceived oppression and injustice – a disposition which predates socialism, but also animated the socialist project, and perhaps will frame socialist opposition again. By giving voice to those usually dismissed as naïve, this chapter examines the enduring but changing significance of Che in the contemporary political climate, indicating an instance of the enduring but changing significance of aspects of socialism itself as 'critical discourse'.

On Che

Che Guevara is 'the favourite son of the unfinished, [if unrealisable,] revolution' (Widener 1999: 222). In the last thirty years, a mammoth amount of material has been released on Che, analyzing his life, death and legacy. Shortly after his death, a number of books were published which were, in the main, either hagiographies, or rather unsophisticated right-wing propaganda portraying Che as a murderous tyrant.

Hollywood also had its first go at a Guevara biography in 1969, with the film *Che!*, which starred Omar Sharif, playing to Jack Palance's Castro. There were relatively few published texts until 1997, the thirtieth anniversary of his assassination, when a new wave of literature emerged, pouring over his political ideas, attempting to reveal Che the man, and debating his establishment as martyr, icon and perennial image. Three major biographies were published that year, which included previously unseen material, adding new dimensions to Che's historical legacy (Widener 1999: 217–29). Large-scale commemorations also took place in Havana, which were perhaps also stating to the world that, against all odds, socialist Cuba still survived. Che's remains were recovered from under a Bolivian airstrip as the celebrations drew nearer, adding an extra poignancy to the encroaching anniversary. When they buried Che's remains in Havana, thousands upon thousands flocked to file past his coffin and pay their respects.

The thirtieth anniversary of Che's death took on a multidimensional significance. Whilst Che's life was reappraised, 1997 also provided a point in time that was sufficiently removed from the 'collapse of communism' where a new world order could not only be naturalized, but also allowed a vantage point from which to review the socialisms of a supposedly bygone era, as well as its heroes and villains. He made the cover of *Newsweek* that year, and the accompanying article claimed that his continuing appeal was due to the fact that his revolutionary ideals no longer posed a threat in a post-Cold War world; 'Thirty years have tamed the anti-imperialist and turned him into the "Rebel Without Claws"' (*Newsweek*, 21 July 1997). He also began to draw popular commentary on his commercialization. Despite this, Che was awarded heroic status in many quarters and in particular he also found a new liberal constituency, nostalgic for a time of radical possibility. The success of the film The Motorcycle Diaries, released in 2004, bears testament to his continuing popularity and another biographical film, starring Benecio del Torro, is due for release in 2008. Yet another with Antonio Banderas might be on the cards.

The left also continue to debate his relevance, whilst simultaneously mourning his commercialization at the hands of consumer capitalism. Some members of the South African Communist Party have even suggested banning the Che memorabilia that the party sells, claiming it has been robbed of political content. However, Che refuses to remain in the domain of the left. In North America and Europe, certain right-wing tropes have emerged through numerous other texts, certain ways of understanding what Che has come to stand for, and means to us. Dominant amongst these is that Che's life remains trapped in a modernist narrative of failed revolution, now made obsolete by the triumph of neoliberal capitalism. Instead of looking to the past, we are urged to think in the present.

Although his image remains all around us, it is argued that it has been reduced to mere commodity, 'signifying nothing'. The same *Newsweek* article also suggested that 'he is now no more than a cuddly pop culture icon'. Che lives, but he lives in postmodern hyperspace, an open-ended site of desire, conveying cultural rather than ideological or political messages (Zimmermann 1999: 201). His image, now emptied of real political content, can do little more than invoke nostalgia for a history that might have been otherwise, whilst pointing to the apolitical present that we now inhabit. Although Che was the 'face' of the 1968 Paris uprisings, and the hero of 1970s campus radicalism, when Che came to stand for the anti-Vietnam protests that shook the States, he is now supposedly encased in a predominantly posterized commercialism, and been appropriated by a radical chic consumer culture. Posters bearing the image of Che made famous by the Cuban photographer Albert Korda have also moved out of student bedrooms and can now be purchased in Habitat, ready to adorn the walls of the Western middle classes, those beneficiaries of capitalism whom Che would presumably have despised. Che thus lies inscribed in a neutered space, a romantic, but doomed, martyr from a bygone era, reduced in the present to a 'structured absence' (McLaren 1999b).

These views are embedded in certain presuppositions, where pedagogical interpretations have been naturalized through the culture of commerce and the dominance of neoliberal political understanding, conjoined with a postmodern cultural sensibility, which, although it points to the open-ended and nonhierarchical, reorganizes our conceptual understandings within new (or not so new and not so innocent) hierarchies (McLaren 1999b: 287–88). Hence, Che's relevance as a political figure is reduced to anachronism, and 'disaffected youth' to inarticulate fashion victims.

'History Decays into Images, not Stories'

The details of Che's life are now well documented, but the reiteration of certain key aspects and moments in numerous biographies, and now also on many sites on the internet, have been crucial in building the 'myth' of Che, charting his transition from mere mortal to 'new socialist man'. Amongst these, some suggest his asthma-ridden childhood in Argentina supposedly equipped him with an inner strength, whilst his training as a doctor is read as an early indication of his altruism and self-sacrifice. Che's youthful travels around Latin America and his stay, and exploits, in Mexico and Guatemala in 1954 and 1955 revealed his transformation into a socially conscious young adventurer, combining an intoxicating mixture of sexual discovery and social awareness, and paving the way for his burgeoning anti-imperialism. Most significant is his personal conversion into New Man through meeting Castro and becoming a part of the Cuban revolution, where he became an agent of both self and socialist transformation, a redemptive figure and a new moral being, who is 'the new man ... glimpsed on the horizon' (Guevara 2005: 14–17). These biographical fragments also point to Che's authenticity, a politics of the self whose core is an original condition of the open and incomplete, which seems to stand in stark contrast to the 'economic man' of liberal orthodoxy. Che also seemed to become 'new man' in a sense beyond Eurocentric prescriptions of Marxism, through his developing internationalism, his aborted mission in the Congo in 1965, and his discovery of the writings of Franz Fanon. His famous 'Message to the Tricontinental' helped generate a transnational sense of socialist possibility which could not be contained by American capitalist ambition.

This was heady stuff. But the mythic retelling of Che has been made immeasurably more potent by the proliferation of photographic images of his life, to the point where, paraphrasing Walter Benjamin, history has decayed into 'images, not stories', and the myth has been retold through a rich photographic record, lending us the impression that we 'know' Che.[3] It also suggests Benjamin's sense of history in the way that these 'fragments' of Che throw light on current moments of crisis, throwing them into stark relief. The photojournalist Albert Korda shot the now most famous picture of him on 5 March 1960, at a memorial service for 136 Cubans who had been killed when the Belgian ship *La Coubre* exploded in Havana harbour. Right-wing sabotage was suspected, and occasioned a major demonstration of left solidarity, which included the presence of such luminaries as Simone de Beavoir and Jean-Paul Sartre. Che stepped forward briefly into the light, and Korda captured the image. According to the story, the picture wasn't used, as it was slightly out of focus, but Korda later gave a copy to the famous Italian communist Giangiacomo Feltrinelli, who used it on the jacket of Che's Bolivian Diary, and then made it into the hundreds of posters that took such prominence in the student uprisings in Paris in May 1968. Che rapidly seemed to link numerous struggles across the world: his sudden accessibility to a mass audience conveyed a message that was inherently political, and transnational:

> From Paris to Prague, ... Che linked these struggles, ultimately producing a critique of lasting force that eroded the legitimacy of domination across a variety of social spectrums. Che forced the issue of possibility, which is to say he opened a space for the posing of new questions. (Widener 1999: 277)

It was Che's assassination in Bolivia in October 1967 that lent an even greater potency to the events of 1968, rendering him not only a tragic hero, but an unfinished product of the revolution. His death was made into an international spectacle, where Che's corpse was used as a message that there was no redemption from the 'real' of the present, and that there was no possibility of his chosen course providing a path to socialist redemption. His bedraggled body was displayed to the world, whilst his severed hands were preserved in formaldehyde as proof of his mortality. The irony of this is well known. As Che's image was transmitted internationally in the guise of a ruthless terrorist brought to justice, he was simultaneously being transformed into a Christlike figure across South America, and taken up by the left as a martyr of the revolution. In the famous pictures of his body that were released worldwide, Che's eyes were still open, and this image, along with Korda's photograph, where Che seems to be gazing ahead into the distance, at once combined an impression of the possibility of what might have been, with the injustice of the system that brought him down. Even as the images became mass produced, they still seemed to bear the trace of a life lived hard for the cause, conveying an aura of revolutionary potential itself. The struggle over the significance of Che's death, and life, continues to be waged to this day, suggesting that, far from 'empty signification', the 'meaning' of Che is a part of a wider struggle over the status of conflicting political philosophies.[4]

Marketing Che

Despite the socialist experiments that were soon to sweep large parts of the African continent after Che's death, the revolutionary fervour that gripped parts of the West in the late 1960s and 70s gave way to a growing cynicism towards both left and right politics. Che soon began to spread beyond the domain of left wing politics and inhabit capitalist consumer culture as well, and was employed in ways that illustrated, for some who had been on the left, an ironic and cynical gaze back to their younger, naïve selves. As capital realigned and neoliberal forms of governance took hold, what could be more fitting than to use one of the foremost icons of revolution to fuel our endless desire to consume? As the Berlin Wall came down, and the Soviet Union collapsed, the message seemed complete: the socialist experiment had failed, capitalist rationale had won out, and Che, now urging us to buy anything from beer to aftershave, had become a part of the apparatus of our own oppression. This use of Che's image was, of course, only possible because Korda had not taken out copyright on his original photograph, but this had not been the result of a fit of absent-mindedness. Fidel Castro famously considered that copyright was 'imperialist bullshit', and lack of copyright was seen as a revolutionary act that allowed the free flow of information to 'the masses', communal ownership standing in ideological opposition to private property rights. Ironically, this 'revolutionary act' is precisely what has enabled the image to be used so pervasively commercially, and his widespread use in fashion and advertising is precisely what has given rise to the postmodern sensibility of Che as 'empty signifier'. However, Che's ubiquitous presence also gave rise to oppositional voices alerting us to what he 'really' stood for. As early as 1969, possibly inspired by the commercial opportunities provided by his sudden worldwide popularity, Hollywood released a biography of Guevara, publicized with the tag line: 'With a dream of justice, he created a nightmare of violence!'[5] According to one review of the time:

> The film portrays the July 26th movement as an inept band of unwashed desperados who want to take over Cuba, but with only sheer luck, and government ineptitude, helping them to ultimately win through. The film truly dies when Guevara leaves Cuba for Bolivia, with Shariff becoming

more asthmatic and psychotic by the minute, until his ultimate capture in the mountains and his eventual murder in the backroom of La Higueras village schoolhouse. (Ebert 1969)

In the film, Castro is depicted as a bumbling fool who can barely string a sentence together (perhaps a case of wishful thinking, given that Castro has proved more than capable of stringing several thousand sentences together on numerous occasions!), and the overall message is quite clear: whilst Che's intentions might have been good at the start, almost inevitably he 'turned bad'. The film highlights the violence at the heart of the Che project, and asks us to question framing him as a hero or messenger of hope. *Che!* projects a nightmare of the self, expressed both through Sharif's increasingly unkempt body and his crumbling mind. Its central theme is that violence corrupts even the noblest of intentions, and it comes across as a crude political tract of its time. However, critiques of Che which highlight the violence of the socialist vision have been a persistent theme over the ensuing years.

Writing in The Observer in July 2004, sparked off by the imminent release of *The Motorcycle Diaries*, the journalist Sean O'Hagan remarks:

Osborne[6] sees Che's iconographic status as being maintained in part by 'the absence of questioning voices addressing the darker side of the man and his ideology'. In Guevara's political writing he detects a 'puritanical zeal and pure and undisguised hatred' that, in places, becomes almost pathological. 'This was a guy who preached hatred, who wrote speeches that were almost proto-fascist,' he says, quoting a speech that ends, 'Relentless hatred of the enemy impels us over and over, and transforms us into effective and selective violent cold killing machines ...'[7] 'In his trenchant short study, Che Guevara, the British historian Andrew Sinclair concludes that, during the guerrilla war, Che 'discovered a cold ruthlessness in his nature. Spilling blood was necessary for the cause. Within two years, he would order the death of several hundred Batista partisans at La Cabana, one of the mass killings of the Cuban Revolution.' Later too, after the botched Bay of Pigs invasion by anti-Communist Cuban exiles, all the survivors were summarily shot. (O'Hagan 2004)

O'Hagan's quotes suggest that the methods of socialist politics are a relic of the past, which at its heart has implications that hint of 'the primitive' and 'savage other'. Guevara, far from being the freedom fighter of left politics, is rather a ruthless terrorist of an outdated project. His methods stand in stark opposition to 'war done properly' in the contemporary world, where violence has supposedly been all but eliminated. Many of the young people I spoke to, as I discuss below, saw these characterizations of Che as blatant hypocrisy, given America's history of overseas interventions in the last fifty years.

O'Hagan also turns to Che's branding:

> In 1967, the same year that Che died, the radical French activist Guy Debord wrote *The Society of the Spectacle* which, among other things, predicted our current obsession with celebrity and event. Nowhere is this dictum more starkly illustrated than in the case of Che, who, in the four decades since his death, has been used to sell everything from china mugs to denim jeans, herbal tea to canned beer. There was, maybe still is, a brand of soap powder bearing his name, along with the slogan 'Che washes whiter'. Today, Che lives! all right, but not in the way he or his fellow revolutionaries could ever have imagined in their worst nightmares. He has become a global brand. (O'Hagan 2004)

He is equally damning in his depiction of the current trades union movement in Britain:

> Almost 40 years on, the wave of romantic revolutionary idealism Che helped ignite seems as unreal as Alice's wonderland, and the Communist ideology that inspired it dated and anachronistic. Che's defiant image may still hang in the offices of Andy Gilchrist, leader of the Fire Brigades' Union, and Bob Crow of the Rail, Maritime and Transport Union but, politically at least, it is a relic of a bygone era, as arcane in its way as those old ornate union banners. Internationally, too, Guevara's ideological legacy is in tatters, his memory kept alive only by the few remaining leftist guerrilla movements such as the Zapatistas in Mexico, or the recently established People's Democratic Republic of the Congo, whose guerrilla leader Che trained back in the Sixties ... (O'Hagan 2004)

Political Subjectivity in Britain

If Che is so dead, why does O'Hagan need to keep killing him? Quite a tongue lashing for a washedup old terrorist! To answer this, I turn to T-shirt-wearing youths in Britain, for whom he lives, and ask how. But first I must contextualize them historically. O'Hagan himself provides a good starting point: his characterization of the trades union movement in terms of 'old ornate union banners', is indicative of a wider shift in the relationship between capital and labour in Britain, a shift which allows for its depiction as a 'relic of a bygone age' and, more generally, suggests the dissolution of a coherent left wing that is able to challenge capital.

The dominant expression of socialism in Britain has remained within the boundaries of social democracy, and the growth of a strong communist movement has been severely curtailed by the nature of the working-class movement there. Historically, the British labour movement has been highly successful at negotiating with the capitalist class, resembling not so much the classic Marxist vision of workers as the emancipators of humanity from the strictures of class power, but Zygmunt Bauman's analysis of the emergence of an industrial class which was capable of gaining entry to the 'unequal banquet within'. A militant workers' movement has predominantly aimed to win concessions, protect skilled workers and build alliances with the parliamentary Labour Party in order to secure its interests, an instance of Žižek's 'implicated subject'. The Keynsian economics employed by the Labour Party after the Second World War furnished the structures of the welfare state, and political and social conduct was predominantly shaped under the umbrella of mutual provision, membership of the nation state (albeit one in painful transition from its position as a dominant imperial power), and the ability to participate in a burgeoning consumer culture. Militant action thus also allowed workers to be 'good citizens', as the restructuring of domestic manufacture and an entrenched neocolonial economic policy gave scope for financial rewards to workers. But by the 1960s there was already the emergence of conflicting interests between London-based finance capital operating on the international market, and Britain's domestic market and manufacturing interests. The negotiated contracts between capital and labour through which resources and finances were distributed had become highly restrictive to capital accumulation by the 1970s, something that was greatly exacerbated by the economic stagnation that characterized that decade.

By 1974, when the Labour Party returned to power, it could no longer afford its previous relationship with the unions, and from 1975, partly as a result of pressure from the International Monetary Fund, cuts to the welfare state and confrontation with the unions changed the Labour Party's position as an instrument of working-class power. With the coming to power of Margaret Thatcher's Conservative government in 1979, a neoliberal agenda increasingly shaped domestic and international policy, aiming to reduce the labour movement's bargaining power and open Britain up to foreign competition and investment through deregulation of the economy. The Conservatives were, however, unable to successfully dismantle the welfare state, which was largely kept intact. Welfarism remained deeply embedded within the political psyche of many parts of the nation even as individualism was promoted and the unions demonized. The victimization of unions, which were deemed responsible for Britain's inability to compete successfully in international markets, resonated with the British public, however. The historic defeat of the miners in 1984/5 has come to stand for the wider 'taming of labour', the spread of middle-class values, and the rise of a consumer culture made possible by a 'debt economy'. By the time Labour returned to power in 1997, Britain's labour movement was a shadow of its former self, able only to mimic its latter-day strategies and negotiate relatively small gains, whilst the Labour government was tied into a wider web of financial and political relations and class alliances, which has given shape to a new vision of political subjectivity and 'good citizenship'.

The rearticulation of the morally responsible citizen has tried to negotiate a tension between a sense of individual ambition and responsibility, and a tradition of collective provision, and this has been produced, where necessary, through state intervention. In Britain, neoliberal governance has taken shape under a complex array of circumstances where the encouragement of individual enterprise and responsibility is tempered with attempts to discipline citizens through interventions on smoking, diet, exercise and civil liberties, to name but a few. These interventions are deemed necessary if collective provision is to continue, and collective provision has thus become dependent on engagement in a set of mutual obligations which will allow the continuation of welfarism, albeit a welfarism modulated by neoliberal doctrine and practice. Enforced obligations are thus justified through the promotion of a global necessity of enhancing economic freedoms, and a morality which increasingly promotes freedom through coercion. The paradox of neoliberal government in Britain (and elsewhere) lies in a moral philosophy that adheres to a belief in limited government, but requires state intervention in pursuit of its overall aims. Within this nexus, the production of political subjectivity is more than ever a subject of 'collusion' as Žižek understands it, even as collusion is produced by increasingly diffuse methods, and relies on new 'collective fantasies' to mask the machinations of capital.

In earlier times, if the labour movement in Britain thrived through its collusions with capital, its collective fantasy was nevertheless its intention to challenge capital. By the late 1960s and early 1970s, a new politics of opposition emerged which was sceptical of the politics of class and the system of parliamentary democracy, but seemed to lack a specific target. A new cynicism towards 'traditional' politics appeared amongst youth movements in particular, and issues of freedom of expression and identity challenged the old politics of the left. Che found a space in these new movements in Britain and came to represent not so much the old communist message of class war but rather a 'fight against oppression'. Che died at the cusp of revolutionary possibility, where older forms of left struggle were being questioned for their methods and outcomes. The manner and perceived injustice of Che's death gave scope for him to be adopted by those seeking new horizons, not least because he himself, as one person I spoke to stated, 'never got old and fat'.

But some of the concerns championed by these 'new social movements' fared well under the programme of neoliberal reform, feeding the notion that government was increasingly capable of absorbing dissent, and not to be trusted. Other sectors struggled to articulate a wider political vision, despite a growing lack of trust in the system and a decline in symbolic faith. In addition, as the radicalism of the 1970s and 1980s (partly in response to neoliberal reform) in Britain failed to challenge government authority, and oppositional politics increasingly focused on issues of 'rights', by the 1990s and beyond dissent seemed to some to have been reduced to a meaningless act. As 'critical event', the anti-war march in 2003, the largest protest ever seen in the country, was viewed as a watershed, both in the decision of private individuals as to whether to protest or not, but also as a final indication that the state won't listen, that dissent has been reduced to a neutralized safety valve, a demoralizing action against a government that does not truly represent its people. Rather than acting to protect its citizens, government seemed to become increasingly at war with them. However, despite this political climate, sales of Che T-shirts continued to be healthy.

For a time, it seemed that the only large-scale radical opposition in Britain was restricted to 'hunts people'.[8] In other spaces, racism against the Muslim 'other', nationalist warring, and 'perceptions of the omnipresent threats posed by hooligans, immigrants, paedophiles etc dominate the pages of the media and infect public debate' (Glynos 2001: 82); in Žižek's terms, 'collective fantasies' which deflect attention from new forms of capitalist exploitation. In this climate, cynicism, voter apathy, mob hysteria in response to perceived threats to children, and the love of conspiracy theories seem to be the order of the day. The politics of opposition is said to have splintered to the point of disintegration and, as a result, left in this 'political vacuum', a cynical and dissatisfied youth are deemed to be shaped more by the desire to consume than to revolt, whilst nevertheless wanting to make apparent their disillusionment and distance from the 'system'. Some would argue that this provides the perfect grounding for the mass production of Che iconography. They suggest that producers can appeal to youthful 'disgust' with the system, combining desire and fantasy in ways that imply opposition, whilst oiling the capitalist machine. If, as Žižek argues, fantasy is a narrative that covers over the necessary dissatisfaction of the subject (Žižek 1999: 346), the commodification and marketing of revolutionary iconography can be viewed as a part of a 'collective' fantasy masking the dissatisfaction of modern political subjectivity, cynical of the existing system, yet unable to protest, and incapable of moving beyond it. The fantasy supposedly serves to mask a nothingness. and gives the impression of a detached, individualized protest, perfectly suited to the neoliberal world we now inhabit. It also obscures the process of collusion. It is 'speech in a dead language', ripped away from its revolutionary roots and history. This post-left, postmodern analysis coincides comfortably with the neoliberal notion that wearing Che's image is now no more than a 'hip consumerism'.

The Fieldwork in London

With these dominant views of Che in mind, I set out to ask young people why they wore Che iconography. In this climate of youthful alienation, does the Che T-shirt merely provide an open-ended site of desire that helps maintain the capitalist subject? Or can it represent some attempt to 'cross the fantasy' and think otherwise? What did Che signify to them? When I told friends and colleagues about my research, I was greeted with sceptical amusement. 'They don't even know who he is' was the most common response that I got. However, many of them proceeded to tell me tales of images of Che they had come across in various places, and expand on what these might or might not mean. From Spanish football fans who wore him on their T-shirts as a sign of their opposition to fascist supporters, to a 'blackened Che' daubed on a wall in New York, to his image in the bar of the Groucho, or his distorted face spread over a gigantic map of South America in a Portuguese market, to a giant painting on a wall in Ramallah, nearly everyone seemed to have some sort of Che story. I also acquired a number of Che postcards, badges, key rings, etc., being told 'I saw this and thought of you', and I began to see Che T-shirts everywhere. In addition to the stories, many friends and colleagues also had strong opinions as to what Che might or might not mean in the current political landscape. Whatever else, Che seemed to readily generate debate amongst the people I knew. It was 'others', they suggested, who were ignorant of who he was and what he meant, the mindless fashion victims of neoliberal and left discourse, and I duly set out to find some of these numerous dupes of the system, sporting Che's image in such a careless fashion. I approached people I saw wearing Che T-shirts and asked if I could interview them. I was struck by their willingness to talk. I was then contacted by friends who had also come across people wearing T-shirts, and had asked them if they'd mind speaking to me. Another friend's son also put me in touch with one or two others who he knew owned Che clothing. I was even woken up at 1 a.m. by my daughter and told to speak to someone sporting a Che T-shirt in a club in Glasgow. This could have gone on indefinitely, so I settled on a random sample of twenty people, who were, interestingly, predominantly male, and aged between 18 and 25. They could not speak for every T-shirt wearing individual, needless to say, but I was hoping some common themes might emerge.

Some of the people I first approached were foreign students studying in London, and I was curious to discover if their views would differ significantly from English youth. They were mainly South American or South African, and unambiguous in their attitude to Che and why they wore his image. For them, Che represented a fight against oppression. Rodriguez, echoing others, said he wore Che's T-shirt 'because I love and respect what he stood for, and continues to stand for, years after his cowardice [sic] assassination'. He was quick to add that he respected 'what he really stood for' and not youthful appropriations of his image which connoted a mere rebelliousness, and an ignorance about his life 'beyond the Motorcycle Diaries'. N'Kosi, from South Africa, declared that Che had his respect because 'he was willing to fight for others' and expressed a selflessness not found in modern politicians. Enrico, like others, seemed bemused as to why his image generated such scepticism in the West, concluding that it was indicative of the 'pathetic understanding of politics' here, and 'people's disinterest in changing the system'. This group of people was keen to discuss what was happening internationally, and in particular kept expressing anger towards America. 'Che opposed American imperialism', Aleksi told me, and wearing Che seemed to represent an opposition to American politics in the current moment. There was also much antagonism to the thought of Che being misappropriated. One young man went so far as to say that he challenged some people he saw wearing his image, in case they were showing 'disrespect'.

In fact, a young Englishman I talked with had been stopped by an Argentinian and challenged as to why he was wearing a Che T-shirt where Che's face was depicted as a monkey from *Planet of the Apes*. The Argentinian duly accused Michael of 'disrespect', and asked him what he knew about Che. Michael admitted with embarrassment that he did not know much beyond '*The Motorcycle Diaries*', but, stung by the encounter, he was later prompted to 'find out more', and concluded that 'Che, like, provided inspiration in the way that he lived his life, so different to the politicians we have in Britain'. This was another recurring theme, where Che seemed to project an aura of authenticity which acted as a mirror to the 'lying politicians' in parliament, who were seen as 'fake'. For another respondent, David, who was still at school at the time of the interview, Che's importance lay in the fact that he was involved in a revolution that succeeded, and was determined 'to achieve the revolution for the world … He was devoted to his cause, and died fighting for the revolution', depicting a sense that he 'lived authentically … fought hard, stood by his beliefs and died at the hands of his opponents' (McCormick 1997: 78).

In many of the interviews Che's legacy was seen as bound up with the current predicament of Cuba, a country which was seen as 'standing up to American bullying'. David also related how his 'discovery' of Che was part of a wider discovery of an alternative history, which was unknown to him. Describing how he was 'bored by the history at school', when he was younger, he told me how he found an old atlas at home depicting 'West Germany'. 'I thought to myself, what's West Germany? Does that mean there's an East Germany?' Research on the internet revealed a different world to him, one that he says opened up the idea that there were other forms of politics, and other types of education than those he received at school. Again, this drove him to comment on the impoverished political climate in contemporary Britain, and that finding out about Che had been a way of filling what he saw as a political vacuum with meaning. When asked why he wore a Che T-shirt, David (who also had Ho Chi Min and Assata Shakur T-shirts) claimed that he wanted to provoke debate, that he wanted people to ask who Che was in order to start a political discussion, which would otherwise be lacking. As with Michael above, Che initiated or was a part of a wider questioning of politics which involved a search for alternatives. 'When I see someone wearing a Che T-shirt', he commented, 'it makes me smile. There might be someone else who thinks like me. No-one at school seems interested in politics, they all just want to get off their heads and have a good time.' He was quick to add, though, that he thought many people who wore the T-shirts didn't know who he was.

David claimed that on one day when he was wearing a Che jacket (the item of choice amongst school kids during the period I was conducting interviews), he was challenged aggressively by one boy who accused him of sporting the image of a 'violent git who murdered people'. An 'animated discussion' on political violence ensued, with David holding American 'imperialist aggression' responsible for people having to resort to arms. 'They're hypocrites', he claimed, referring to the American administration, 'look at the invasion of Afghanistan and Iraq … people have no alternative but to defend themselves.'

When I asked questions about the image of Che itself, Simon remarked that 'it was a beautiful picture, I like it because he kind of looks hopeful?' When pushed to say in what way, Simon continued that he saw no one to vote for in parliament, because 'they're all the same', something echoed many times. 'I want to make a difference, you know, but I just don't feel that the politicians in parliament would really do anything, they just look after themselves and their cronies. And the way that we're involved with America, it's disgusting. I wear my Che T-shirt as you might wear a piece of art, to get a reaction and express my disgust with what America is doing right now.' These young men all knew anecdotes about Che that they used to illustrate their points. Some had read biographies, but most of their information came from the internet. They seemed to be using 'fragments' of Che to make sense of and give meaning to their world.

In response to enquiring if any of them considered themselves to be socialists, the foreign students were the most unequivocal. The only young woman I interviewed, Shanti, who was from India, declared that Che was an inspiration to her and had convinced her of the need for a socialist alternative to the current system, especially in places such as India. The young people from Britain were not so forthright. They all voiced the desire for some alternative, and the need to 'defend Cuba', but were unsure of what to call themselves: 'I don't like labels', one remarked. After coming across Che's image, most of them had gone and found out more about him, but were already asking political questions. Above all, Che seemed to offer integrity in opposition to 'greedy self-seeking politicians', convey an anti-American message, spark a sense of internationalism *and* come in a package that was attractive and accessible. He allowed them to make some sense of their place in the world. They didn't deny that they thought he was 'cool', but he was 'cool' because of his politics. He was also 'cool' because of the way Korda had captured his image, forever young, seemingly looking hopefully towards a better future. The photograph here is a relic of the past, but bears the traces of that past, spurring these young people to excavate fragments of that history. Korda, with his out-of-focus shot, accidentally captured an 'aura' of Che that has had an extraordinarily enduring appeal, which is why it has been so marketable. And the continued presence of Che's image in the public domain through marketing is an important part of how he has acquired a 'living context'. Just as the revolutionary act of lack of copyright enabled his mass commercialization, his mass commercialization has enabled Che to carry on 'signifying something', a possibility of a politics beyond capitalism. As for the 'inarticulate fashion victim', I'm still waiting to meet him!

New Utopias?

However, it didn't seem to me that the people I spoke to were about to follow Che's path, to take up arms and pursue revolutionary war. Rather, they were expressing a desire for an alterity which 'interrogates the self, a presence that addresses, appeals to and contests the ego, and has the ability to challenge a partial truth which is being totalised', and in some sense, 'demands a justification of the self'(Mickunas 1978: 5). Che comes to be a challenge, to oneself and others, through an alterity: 'The self experiences an alterity which brings an awareness of the arbitrary, limited, and egocentric views attained by an uncriticized freedom' (ibid.). But Che was also a product of 1960s and the utopian projects of that time. What kind of utopia do people imagine now? Utopia is a site of alternative possibility, but the nature of utopia changes, the idea undergoes transformations. The concept of utopia is about the capacity to assert truths and universals against the existing social order; it offers a critique of the present through the imagination of future possibility. But now, it seems, we need to imagine utopia in the absence of radical challenge, a reconciliation to capitalism by left-wing intellectuals, and the abandonment of an idea of an alternative social order.

Žižek locates us in the moment of ideological closure, but leaves us there. Jameson takes us slightly further, and suggests that the seeming unchangability of the present 'opens up a moment of ideational and utopian free-play in the mind itself or in the political imagination' (Jameson 2004: 45). However, this Utopia is somehow negative, is 'most authentic when we cannot imagine it. Its function lies not in helping us to imagine a better future, but demonstrating our utter incapacity to imagine such a future – our imprisonment in a non-utopian present without historicity or futurity – so as to reveal the ideological closure in which we are somehow trapped and confined' (ibid.: 46). The ideological closure is thus revealed to us.

Adorno, perhaps, offers us a more far-reaching trajectory when he talks about art and how it can present an image of freedom. It enables us to see Korda's image as 'social critique'. However, Adorno's ideas need to be 'radically historicised', and untied from his idea of 'high art' and his dismissal of non-European forms of representation, instead locating them in the commonplace, the everyday and the transnational. Adorno does not suggest that art should be a form of propaganda directing people towards political activity, rather that it works as radical critique, it can make us 'vividly aware of the shortcomings of our society and its utter inability to justify itself even on its own terms' (Geuss 2000: 304). This 'negative utopia' works as a form of radical social criticism, and is negative in two ways. Firstly, it points the 'evil' of the present moment, but it also works as a projected vision of a society which can ideally be good, but without the ability to imagine a specific content, beyond the fact that it would be 'radically different' to the one we now inhabit (ibid.: 306). This goes beyond Jameson, and I felt it was closest to what this group of young people were telling me. In this context, the Che T-shirt gives us 'internal critique' in its sharpest sense, coming as it does from the mass commodification of an image, from the universal commodification characteristic of modern capitalist society itself. From that which is least able to speak radically, which supposedly shapes our oppression, comes a critique of the system itself. It also represents a 'negative utopia' in that in Korda's picture, Che is looking to the future, but we are unable see what he is looking at – his 'future vision' is lost to us.

Internal criticism is coupled here with an appeal 'to the other', in the sense of the non-European 'other' as alterity, which has helped produce transnational, empathetic circuits of socialist understanding. Che has come to mean many things in many places, and has entered a cosmology of socialism and socialist neotradition. One person I spoke to talked of how the world would change, but not from our position in the West, and not from some arising in the former socialist states, but from those other places in the world where the sharpest contradictions of the system are felt. Perhaps it is this 'other' who will write the transcript of how utopia is to be imagined, if we are currently unable to do so.

As the Che story is retold in the current moment 'his myth hovers over neoliberalism's delusions of grandeur' (Taibo 1997: 587). These fragments of a socialist cosmology endure in the ordinary and everyday, even as their meaning is transformed. In 1968, a slogan on a wall in Paris declared: 'I have something to say, but I don't know what it is.' Like the students of 1968, the young people I spoke to are not naïve, but nor are they explicitly socialist. Instead they lie somewhere in between, not fully satisfied with the system but not fully oppositional to it. It is opposition that is evoked – much as it was for Che himself in *The Motorcycle Diaries* – and that endures. For the British youth I spoke to, Che does not so much serve as a vehicle for socialism to endure in the neoliberal age, but rather provokes a wider oppositional spirit that once animated the socialist project, but also animated presocialist forms of opposition to oppression and injustice. Now, Che has come to ignite a wider set of concerns with contemporary governance, concerns that were once expressed in an explicitly socialist language, and perhaps will be again.

Notes

1. During my fieldwork I haven't as yet met anyone who does not know who Che is is, but everyone claims that no one else knows who he is.
2. I discovered this during the European Social Forum in London in 2005.
3. Che himself was a press photographer when he met Castro in Mexico.
4. The concept of 'empty signification' is extremely problematic, a translation of Marx's extended section in *Capital* on alienation and fetishism that is both reductionist and constricting. More fruitfully, Marx writes on how commodities contain multiple meanings, but suggests that these transform in certain contexts, and still retain traces of their past. In other words, commodities have a history, borne of their social circumstances. Jean Comaroff (1985) has instead talked of how we can see commodities as 'saturated signs', or social hieroglyphs. But the contest to hegemonize their inherent ambiguities is not to be confused with a simple proliferation or emptying of meaning. Žižek comments that 'signification can never be neutral. It is produced with a specific political economy within which the mode of production of truth is operative'. There will always be a dominant discourse that will try to control and delimit meaning, but this will be open to contestation. 'The struggle for this content is the political struggle.' Che's commodification can thus be read as a 'hegemonic struggle' over the meaning of the relationship between socialism and capitalism in the contemporary world.
5. Remarkably, this rather poor film had an explosive effect on potential audiences. It was considered so offensive in Chile and Argentina that Molotov cocktails were reportedly thrown at the screen in some cinemas. Ironically, in the States, the right wing also mobilized against *Che!* without having seeing it. A theatre in New York was bombed, and a Chicago letter-writing campaign urged reviewers to denounce this film 'glorifying' Guevara. The film was scheduled to open on 'Memorial Day', but local vigilantes prevented that with threats of picketing: it was claimed that the opening would be an insult to every veteran of the Vietnam War.

6. Lawrence Osborne is an American liberal writer.
7. Sean O'Hagan (2004). The quote, taken rather out of context, is taken from Guevara's 'Message to the Tricontinental'.
8. In Britain, 'hunts people' go hunting foxes on horseback with packs of dogs. The Labour Party has attempted to ban the sport with limited success, spawning instead the Countryside Alliance, a conservation coalition representing rural interests.

References

Anderson, P. 2004. 'The River of Time', *New Left Review* 26, March–April.
Bradshaw, P. 2004. 'Review of the Motorcycle Diaries', *The Guardian* August 27.
Castenada, J. 1997. *Compañero: The Life and Death of Che Guevara*. New York: Alfred Knopf.
Comaroff, J. 1985. *Body of Power, Spirit of Resistance*. Chicago, London: University of Chicago Press.
Ebert, R. 1969. *Chicago Post*, 10 June.
Fahmy, E. 2003. 'Young People's Political Participation – results from a 1996 MORI Omnibus survey', *Centre for the Study of Social Exclusion and Social Justice*.
Guess, R. 2000. 'Art and Criticism in Adorno's Aesthetics', *European Journal of Philosophy* no. 6(3): 297–317.
Glynos, J. 2001. 'There is No Other of the Other: Symptoms of a Decline in Symbolic Faith, or Žižek's Anti-capitalism', *Paragraph* 24(2): 78–110.
Guevara, E. 2005. *The Che Reader*. Melbourne: Ocean Press.
Jameson, F. 2004. 'The Politics of Utopia', *New Left Review* 25 (January–February).
Margolin, V. 1999. 'Che and Nike in Havana', *Print* (January–February): 84–90.
McLaren, P. 1999a. 'Rejoinder-Postmodernism and the Eclipse of Political Agency: A Response to Spencer Maxcy', *International Journal of Leadership in Education* 2(3): 301–05.
———. 1999b. 'Revolutionary Leadership and Pedagogical Praxis: Revisiting the Legacy of Che Guevara', *International Journal of Leadership in Education* 2(3): 269–92.
McCormick, G.H. 1997. 'Che Guevara: The Legacy of a Revolutionary Man', *Reconsiderations* (December).
Mickunas, A. 1978. 'Two Philosophers of Lithuanian Origin: Emanuel Levinas and Alphonso Lingis', *Lithuanian Quarterly Journal of Arts and Science* 23(1) (Spring).
Newsweek. 1997. 'Che Chic', *Newsweek* 21 July.
O'Hagan, S. 2004. 'Just a Pretty Face?', *The Observer* 11 July.
Richardson, M. 2004. 'Review of The Motorcycle Diaries', *The Film Journal*.
Taibo, P.I. 1997. *Guevara, Also Known as Che*. New York: St. Martin' Press.
Widener, D.L. 1999. 'Buscando el Comandante: Recent Writings on the Life and Times of Che Guevara', *Radical History Review* 74: 217–30.
Zimmermann, M. 1999. 'Che Guevara and the Cuban Revolution', *Latin American Research Review* 34(3): 197–208.
Žižek, S. 1999. *The Ticklish Subject*. London: Verso.

Index